Contending Voices

Biographical Explorations of the American Past

Volume II: Since 1865

FOURTH EDITION

JOHN HOLLITZ
College of Southern Nevada

CENGAGE
Learning·

Australia • Brazil • Mexico • Singapore • United Kingdom • United States

CENGAGE
Learning®

Contending Voices: Biographical Explorations of the American Past, Volume II: Since 1865, Fourth Edition
John Hollitz

Product Director: Paul Banks

Product Manager: Clint Attebery

Content Developer: Cara Swan

Product Assistant: Andrew Newton

Marketing Manager: Kyle Zimmerman

IP Analyst: Alexandra Ricciardi

IP Project Manager: Betsy Hathaway

Manufacturing Planner: Sandee Milewski

Art and Design Direction, Production Management, and Composition: Lumina Datamatics, Inc.

Cover Image:
© Bettmann/CORBIS

For product information and technology assistance, contact us at
Cengage Learning Customer & Sales Support, 1-800-354-9706

For permission to use material from this text or product, submit all requests online at **www.cengage.com/permissions**. Further permissions questions can be emailed to **permissionrequest@cengage.com**.

Library of Congress Control Number: 2015948750

Student Edition:
ISBN: 978-1-305-65594-2

Cengage Learning
20 Channel Center Street
Boston, MA 02210
USA

Cengage Learning is a leading provider of customized learning solutions with employees residing in nearly 40 different countries and sales in more than 125 countries around the world. Find your local representative at **www.cengage.com**.

Cengage Learning products are represented in Canada by Nelson Education, Ltd.

To learn more about Cengage Learning Solutions, visit **www.cengage.com**.

Purchase any of our products at your local college store or at our preferred online store **www.cengagebrain.com**.

Printed in the United States of America
Print Number: 01   Print Year: 2015

Contents

PREFACE   viii

1   Race and Redemption in the Reconstructed South: Robert Smalls and Wade Hampton   1

SOURCE 1: Zion Presbyterian Church, *"Memorial to the Senate and House of Representatives"* (1865)   13

SOURCE 2: *Wade Hampton Protests to the President* (1866)   14

SOURCE 3: *A Northerner Assesses Southern Attitudes* (1866)   16

SOURCE 4: *Wade Hampton Testifies Before a Congressional Committee* (1871)   18

SOURCE 5: *Representative Robert Smalls Protests the Withdrawal of Federal Troops* (1876)   22

SOURCE 6: *Instructions to Red Shirts* (1876)   24

2   Culture and Conflict on the Late Nineteenth-Century Plains: Sitting Bull and Richard Henry Pratt   27

SOURCE 1: *Scenes from Sitting Bull's Pictorial Autobiography* (1882)   40

SOURCE 2: *Richard Henry Pratt Discusses the Fate of Blacks and Indians* (ca. 1923)   41

SOURCE 3: *Sitting Bull Testifies Before a Senate Committee* (1883)   42

SOURCE 4: *Luther Standing Bear Recalls Carlisle* (1933)   43

SOURCE 5: *Richard Henry Pratt on the Indian and Indian Education* (1892)   45

SOURCE 6: *Taking a Crow Child to Carlisle* (1891)   46

3   Organizing Labor in the Age of Industry: Terence Powderly and Samuel Gompers   49

SOURCE 1: *Terence Powderly, Preamble to the Constitution of the Knights of Labor* (1878)   60

SOURCE 2: *Terence Powderly Calls for Cooperatives* (1880)   61

SOURCE 3: *Samuel Gompers on Trade Unions* (1898)   62

SOURCE 4: *Samuel Gompers on Female Workers* (1906)   64

SOURCE 5: *An Investigator Reports on Steel Workers* (1910)   66

4   Monopoly, Money, and Power in Progressive America: John D. Rockefeller and Ida Tarbell   70

SOURCE 1: *Rockefeller Discusses Consolidation and Rebates* (1909)   83

SOURCE 2: *Ida Tarbell Reflects on the Oil War* (1939)   85

SOURCE 3: Ida M. Tarbell, *The History of the Standard Oil Company* (1904)   87

SOURCE 4: Ida M. Tarbell, "John D. Rockefeller: A Character Study" (1905)   89

SOURCE 5: *Rockefeller Discusses Large-Scale Enterprise* (1909)   91

SOURCE 6: *Standard Oil as an Octopus* (1904)   92

5   Progressives at War: Randolph Bourne and George Creel   94

SOURCE 1: Bachelor of Atrocities   105

SOURCE 2: *Committee on Public Information Army Recruitment Poster* (1917)   106

SOURCE 3: *An Advertisement for Publications of the Committee on Public Information* (1918)   106

SOURCE 4: Randolph Bourne, *"The War and the Intellectuals"* (1917)   108

SOURCE 5: Randolph Bourne, *"The State"* (1919)   108

SOURCE 6: *George Creel on the Committee on Public Information* (1920)   109

6   Science, Religion, and "Culture Wars" in the 1920s: William Jennings Bryan and Clarence Darrow   112

SOURCE 1: *An "Imperial Wizard" Explains the Ku Klux Klan's Appeal* (1926)   123

SOURCE 2: *A Preacher Defends Tennessee from Attack* (1925)   124

SOURCE 3: *Clarence Darrow Attacks the Antievolution Law as Unconstitutional* (1925)   125

SOURCE 4: *William Jennings Bryan Argues Against Expert Testimony* (1925)   126

SOURCE 5: *Clarence Darrow Questions William Jennings Bryan on the Bible* (1925)   127

SOURCE 6: *A Black Intellectual Comments on the Scopes Trial* (1925)   129

7   Politics and the Big Screen in the Great Depression: Upton Sinclair and Louis B. Mayer   132

SOURCE 1: Upton Sinclair, *"EPIC Answers"* (1934)   143

SOURCE 2: *Anti-Sinclair Leaflet* (1934)   145

SOURCE 3: *"California, Here We Come"* (1934)   146

SOURCE 4: *"Hollywood Masses the Full Power of Her Resources to Fight Sinclair"* (1934)   147

SOURCE 5: *Upton Sinclair Assesses His Loss* (1934)   148

8   Racism and Relocation During World War II: Harry Ueno and Dillon Myer   152

SOURCE 1: Dillon Myer, *"Constitutional Principles Involved in the Relocation Program"* (1943)   163

SOURCE 2: *"Rifles Cow Manzanar Japs After Fatal Riots"* (1942)   164

SOURCE 3: *Censored Letters of Harry Ueno* (1943)   165

SOURCE 4: *Dillon Myer on Japanese Resettlement* (1943)   166

SOURCE 5: *War Relocation Authority Questions for Resettlement Applicants* (1943)   167

9   Confrontation and Compromise in the Cold War: James Byrnes and Henry A. Wallace   169

SOURCE 1: George F. Kennan, *"The Long Telegram"* (1946)   180

SOURCE 2: *James Byrnes Restates American Policy Toward Germany* (1946)   181

SOURCE 3: Henry A. Wallace, *"The Way to Peace"* (1946)   182

SOURCE 4: Harry S. Truman, *The Truman Doctrine* (1947)   184

SOURCE 5: Henry A. Wallace, *"The Path to Peace with Russia"* (1946)   185

10   Politics and Principle in the Second Red Scare: Joseph McCarthy and Margaret Chase Smith   188

SOURCE 1: *McCarthy Assaults the State Department* (1950)   200

SOURCE 2: *HUAC Investigates Subversion in Hollywood* (1947)   202

SOURCE 3: Margaret Chase Smith, *"Declaration of Conscience"* (1950)   203

SOURCE 4: *Margaret Chase Smith Feels McCarthy's Sting* (1952)   204

SOURCE 5: *McCarthy Investigates Overseas Libraries* (1953)   205

SOURCE 6: *Edward R. Murrow Attacks McCarthy* (1954)   207

11 From Black Protest to Black Power: Roy Wilkins and Fannie Lou Hamer   209

SOURCE 1: *Testimony of Fannie Lou Hamer Before the Credentials Committee of the Democratic National Convention* (1964)   220

SOURCE 2: Stokely Carmichael, *"What We Want"* (1966)   221

SOURCE 3: *Fannie Lou Hamer on the Lessons of the Democratic National Convention* (1967)   222

SOURCE 4: *Poverty Rates, by Race and Family Relationship, 1959-1999*   223

SOURCE 5: Roy Wilkins, *"Sail Our N.A.A.C.P. Ship 'Steady as She Goes'"* (1966)   224

12 The Battles of Vietnam: Robert McNamara and Jan Barry   226

SOURCE 1: *Robert McNamara Assesses the Situation in Vietnam* (1964)   238

SOURCE 2: *Jan Barry Assesses the Situation in Vietnam* (1997)   240

SOURCE 3: *McNamara Offers a Bleak Assessment* (1967)   241

SOURCE 4: *A Marine Describes a Technological War of Attrition* (1977)   242

SOURCE 5: *A Black Soldier Sees Another Enemy* (1984)   242

13 From Mystique to Militance: Betty Friedan and Gloria Steinem   247

SOURCE 1: Betty Friedan, *The Feminine Mystique* (1963)   258

SOURCE 2: *NOW's Statement of Purpose* (1966)   259

SOURCE 3: *Ms. Cover* (1972)   260

SOURCE 4: Gloria Steinem, *"Sisterhood"* (1972)   261

SOURCE 5: Betty Friedan, *"Beyond Women's Liberation"* (1972)   262

SOURCE 6: Phyllis Schlafly, *"What's Wrong with 'Equal Rights' for Women"* (1972)   263

14 Individualism and the Environment in the 1980s: Edward Abbey and James Watt 266

SOURCE 1: Edward Abbey, *The Monkey Wrench Gang* (1975) 276

SOURCE 2: *Map of Federal Lands* (1978) 278

SOURCE 3: *James Watt Outlines His Program* (1981) 279

SOURCE 4: James Watt, *"It's the People's Land"* (1983) 280

15 Fighting a "War on Terror": Richard Clarke and John Yoo 282

SOURCE 1: *Memorandum to John Yoo* (2001) 292

SOURCE 2: *Memorandum to Alberto Gonzales* (2002) 293

SOURCE 3: *Richard Clarke on George Bush's War on Terror* (2004) 295

SOURCE 4: Richard A. Clarke, *"Land of Sweet Liberties"* (2008) 298

SOURCE 5: *John Yoo Defends Warrantless Wiretaps* (2007) 300

SOURCE 6: *Edward Snowden Discusses NSA Spying* (2014) 301

Preface

The encouraging reception from students and instructors to the previous editions of *Contending Voices: Biographical Explorations of the American Past* has led me to create a fourth edition. As before, this book uses paired biographies to bring alive the debates and disagreements that have shaped American history. It is based on the assumption that students find history more engaging when they realize that it is full of conflict. Through biography, individual men and women emerge from the tangle of events, dates, and facts that often make history so challenging for students.

Following the organization of most survey texts, each chapter examines two individuals who stood on different sides of an important issue. Their stories, combined with a small set of primary sources in each chapter, show students how individuals—from the pre-English settlement of the New World to the present—influenced their times and were influenced by them. At the same time, the book's biographical approach naturally incorporates political, social, economic, cultural, religious, and diplomatic histories while underscoring the diversity of those who shaped the past. This biographical approach highlights competing perspectives, prompting students to think about issues from multiple viewpoints. The biographical essays that introduce the Sources were written with these pedagogical goals in mind.

Although students will encounter familiar names in these pages, many of the thirty individuals in each of *Contending Voices'* two volumes rarely appear in survey texts. All of them, however, addressed significant events and issues of their times. In Volume I, sixteenth-century *conquistador* Hernán Cortés and Dominican priest Bartolomé de Las Casas contest the fate of Native Americans. In the seventeenth century, the pitched battles between Governor William Berkeley and rebel Nathaniel Bacon reveal forces shaping early Virginia. Other chapters illuminate the American Revolution, the ratification of the Constitution, and political conflict between Federalists and Republicans in the 1790s. Later, the life-and-death conflict between William Henry Harrison and Tecumseh reflects the larger struggle between whites and Indians sparked by westward expansion in the early nineteenth century. In the same period, chapters pairing union organizer Sarah Bagley with industrialist Nathan Appleton and Governor Juan Bautista Alvarado of Mexican California with merchant Thomas Larkin focus on the rise of the factory system and Manifest Destiny. At mid-century, George Fitzhugh and Hinton Rowan Helper debate slavery's impact on the South and reveal deep fears at the heart of a growing sectional conflict. Still later, antiwar Democrat Clement Vallandigham and radical Republican Benjamin Wade demonstrate the limits of dissent during the Civil War.

New biographies in Volume I include New England minister Jonathan Edwards and Benjamin Franklin, who highlight the conflict between faith and reason in the eighteenth-century colonies.

Volume II offers a similar diversity of individuals and topics. The new biographies in Volume II feature the Sioux chief Sitting Bull and Indian education advocate Richard Henry Pratt, who battled in the late nineteenth century to define the place of Native Americans in American society, and John D. Rockefeller and Ida Tarbell, who clashed in the early twentieth century over the power exercised by Rockefeller's Standard Oil trust.

In the early twentieth century, antiwar critic Randolph Bourne and war propagandist George Creel further illuminate aspects of progressive reform as well as the new power of advertising and the effects of World War I on American society. Japanese-American internee Harry Ueno and internment director Dillon Myer illustrate the experience of Japanese relocation during World War II. Later battles are brought to life in chapters pairing civil rights activist Fannie Lou Hamer with black leader Roy Wilkins; women's rights champion Betty Friedan with feminist Gloria Steinem; and Interior Secretary James Watt with novelist Edward Abbey. They illustrate the challenges confronting the civil rights, women's, and environmental movements and the conflicts dividing them. Finally, Richard Clarke and John Yoo, two officials in the administration of George W. Bush, illuminate the sharp and ongoing differences arising out of the "war on terror" after the September 11, 2001, attacks on the United States.

While permitting easy access to often unfamiliar topics, *Contending Voices* is also designed to build students' critical thinking skills. Each chapter begins with a brief essay providing an introduction to the lives and ideas of the two individuals who held conflicting views on an important issue. The essay does not offer a complete accounting of subjects' lives—an impossible task—but focuses instead on aspects that illuminate the chapter's main topic. Each essay begins with a short vignette designed to capture the reader's attention and includes a running glossary, which defines terms that may be unfamiliar to many survey students. A set of four to seven primary sources illustrating and amplifying the chapter's central themes follows each essay. These sources demonstrate the variety of sources historians use to understand the past and reflect another premise behind this book—that the best way for students to learn history is to explore it themselves. Their explorations are assisted by a brief set of Questions to Consider following the primary sources. In addition, references to each primary source appear in the essays, helping to integrate the primary and secondary material. A brief introduction to each primary source also aids student analysis. Finally, a brief Further Reading section contains both biographical and general works that will help interested students explore each chapter topic further.

Many people made valuable contributions to these volumes. At the College of Southern Nevada (CSN), Charles Okeke offered welcome encouragement, while administrative assistants Alaina Priscu and Terresa Waters provided technical assistance. CSN Interlibrary Loan librarian Marion Martin and library assistant Jessica Caseman cheerfully and efficiently tracked down the needed material. At Cengage Learning, Clint Attebery and Tonya Lobato oversaw the revision process, and Cara Swan brought a keen eye to the manuscript and offered numerous helpful suggestions throughout the revision process. Margaret Bridges carefully guided the manuscript through the production phase.

Numerous colleagues around the country reviewed these chapters and offered many useful ideas, suggestions, and criticisms. These volumes benefited greatly from their efforts. They include Ginette Aley, University of Southern Indiana; Daniel Ashyk, Cleveland State University; Matthew Bloom, Bowling Green State University; Michelle Brattain, Georgia State University; John Bullion, University of Missouri-Columbia; Larissa Fergeson, Longwood University; James Paradis, Arcadia University; Stephen Shwiff, University of Texas-San Antonio; and Timothy Thurber, Virginia Commonwealth University.

As always, my biggest debt is to Patty. Once again, this book is dedicated to her.

—J.H.

1

Race and Redemption in the Reconstructed South: Robert Smalls and Wade Hampton

In the predawn hours of May 13, 1862, the small Confederate ship *Planter* made its way out of Charleston Harbor. As it steamed toward the ships blockading the South Carolina port, Union lookouts strained their eyes, then prepared to sound the alarm to open fire on the small vessel. Suddenly, one lookout spotted a white flag flying on the boat, and the Union ships held their fire. As the *Planter* came alongside, Union naval officers were shocked. No whites were on board. Instead, they saw only black men, women, and children, who were dancing, singing, and shouting for joy. When a Union officer boarded, a well-dressed black man stepped forward to address him. "Good morning, sir! I've brought you some of the old United States guns, sir!" Indeed he had. An armed Confederate vessel, the *Planter* contained a cargo of unmounted cannon and sixteen slaves who had captured the boat and escaped to freedom. The man who had organized the capture was the ship's pilot, a twenty-three-year-old slave named Robert Smalls.

The very next month in the Battle of Seven Pines, a forty-four-year-old Confederate brigadier general named Wade Hampton led his brigade into an entrenched Union force near the Chickahominy River, east of Richmond, Virginia. Hampton and his men confronted a hail of Union fire. Half of his brigade fell dead or wounded. Hit in the foot, Hampton remained on his horse and under fire while a Confederate army surgeon extracted the bullet. After the battle, Confederate General Robert E. Lee, the new commander of the Army of Northern Virginia, cited Hampton in his official report. "General Hampton," Lee wrote, "… was remarkable for his coolness, promptness, and decided practical ability as a leader of men in difficult and dangerous circumstances. In these high characteristics … he has few equals and perhaps no superior." In fact, Wade

Robert Smalls

Wade Hampton

Hampton would go on by the end of the Civil War to establish a reputation on the battlefield that few commanders, Union or Confederate, could match.

Robert Smalls and Wade Hampton served bravely in the Civil War. Both men called South Carolina home and came to be involved in politics there in the period after the war known as Reconstruction. As political leaders, both would find themselves deeply embroiled in a struggle to determine the political fate of their state. And, as in the Civil War, they would fight for very different causes. A Republican representative from South Carolina, Smalls would support his party's efforts to reconstruct the South and guarantee political equality for the freedmen. A prominent planter and governor of the state, Hampton could never accept racial equality and in time would lead Democrats in overthrowing the Republican regime in South Carolina. Hampton and Smalls were only two of the millions of Americans who contributed to the Union and Confederate war efforts. Like so many other Americans, they did not agree about what should occur in the South when the war was over. For that reason, the stories of these two Civil War heroes may help us understand what many in South Carolina and beyond saw at stake in the fight over Reconstruction and why that battle ultimately turned out as it did.

"THE SMARTEST *CULLUD* MAN"

Little in Robert Smalls's background could have foretold his rise in life. In fact, he would rise from utter obscurity. He was born in 1839 in Beaufort, South Carolina, to a slave woman who worked as a domestic servant. His father was an unknown white man, although many believed that he was John McKee, his mother's master. John McKee died when Robert was six, and his son Henry sent Smalls to live with relatives in Charleston when he was twelve. He lived in the home of his master's sister-in-law, working as a waiter, a lamplighter, and a stevedore. Smalls was "hired out," meaning that he worked for wages. He kept some of his pay for himself and sent the rest to his master. This situation gave the young slave relative autonomy. He may even have had enough freedom to pursue an education during his years in the city. Smalls apparently taught himself to read and possibly attended for a few months a school run by one of Charleston's many black societies. Formed in violation of the South Carolina law that prohibited more than four slaves from assembling at one time, such societies often provided education and other services to the African American community.

In 1858, Smalls married Hannah Jones, a hotel maid who was also a slave. He was nineteen; she was thirty-one. Smalls said he married Hannah because he wanted "to have a wife to prevent me from running around—to have somebody to do for me and to keep me." Slaves, of course, were not allowed to marry legally, but Smalls made a deal with his master. He would pay McKee $15 a month so that he could marry Hannah. Smalls made a similar deal with Hannah's master, paying him $15 a month. This allowed the two slaves to keep enough money to support themselves and even have children. Smalls later agreed to purchase his wife and daughter for $800. When he fled the city in 1862, he had $700, having never paid any of the agreed-upon amount to his wife's owner. How he accumulated this sum and managed to keep his household running is difficult to imagine. His own wages as a deck hand in 1861 amounted to only $16 a month, and Hannah probably made no more than $10 a month as a maid, assuming that she continued to work after their marriage.

Somehow the little family managed to make it, probably due to Smalls's abilities as a trader. His position as a deck hand on the *Planter* allowed him even greater autonomy than his job on the docks. Traveling on the river and coastal steamer, Smalls was able to make regular visits to friends and associates in a wider area. He traded goods within the slave community and probably with whites as well. As a sailor, Smalls acquired valuable skills. He learned to handle the ship and eventually became a wheelman. (Actually, he was a pilot, a title white Southerners refused to give blacks.) When the Civil War offered him the opportunity to escape bondage, his skills, education, and position served him well. Smalls carefully planned the escape of his family and friends. One night when the ship's three white officers were on shore, he pulled off his plan in a dramatic fashion.

The theft of the *Planter* brought not only freedom but also an economic windfall. The northern press jumped on the story of Smalls's heroic action. *Harper's Weekly*, for instance, ran a picture of Smalls and an article on the "plucky Africans." One New York newspaper commented that few events during the Civil War "produced a heartier chuckle of satisfaction" than the theft of the *Planter*. The "fellow" behind the feat, it observed, "is no Small man." Given such favorable reaction, Smalls and his fellow hijackers were awarded a bounty by Congress for liberating the *Planter*. As leader of the party, Smalls got the largest share, $1500. He continued to work as a pilot on the *Planter*, which was now operating as a troop transport for the Union. The ship shuttled men and supplies between the Sea Islands* off South Carolina and mainland areas occupied by Union

---

Sea Islands: Low-lying islands off the coast of South Carolina and Georgia. Occupied early in the war by Union forces, the islands were home to a large number of blacks who worked on the rice plantations there.

forces. In addition, he piloted other ships, including some engaged in unsuccessful attacks on Charleston.

At the same time, Smalls worked to improve the condition of fellow blacks. In Union-occupied Beaufort, he engaged in fund-raising to assist freedmen with education and employment. He also traveled to New York during the war to raise awareness of the condition of the growing ranks of free blacks in the South. He had been sent north by freedmen in Beaufort County who were eager to help themselves rather than wait for charity or government assistance. Such efforts were widespread throughout the postwar South, but African Americans in Beaufort County became organized—and politicized—several years before those in most other areas. A highly concentrated black population, early occupation by Union forces, and a large number of black soldiers and white teachers and missionaries contributed to their efforts. Already in 1864, blacks in the area had expressed their political preferences by organizing a delegation to the Republican convention in Baltimore. Although the delegates could not secure official representation at the convention, they made it clear that they were ready to "fight for the Union [and] die for it" and that they also wanted the right to "vote for it."

Unfortunately, that right was not immediately forthcoming, even when the Civil War ended. When Andrew Johnson became president after Lincoln's assassination in April 1865, he promoted a Reconstruction plan that excluded blacks from politics. Committed to white rule in the South, Johnson wanted a policy that would bring the rebellious states back into the Union without a fundamental restructuring of southern society. Under his Reconstruction plan, white Southerners—often former Confederates—quickly reorganized state governments. By early 1866, southern state legislatures elected under the president's plan had passed Black Codes. These laws severely limited the rights of African Americans to own property, assemble, move about freely, and vote. Often they prevented interracial marriage and upheld labor contracts that favored white landowners. The Black Codes in South Carolina legalized harsh labor practices regarding blacks and placed severe restrictions on freedmen. At a convention in late 1865, South Carolina blacks protested the new laws. In an address to the state's whites, the convention demanded that blacks "be governed by the same laws that control other men." **[See Source 1.]**

For several years after the war, Smalls was more concerned with improving his own position than with getting involved in politics. Even before the war ended, he returned to Beaufort and opened a store. He did well enough to purchase his former master's house by paying the back taxes on it. In 1867, he purchased an eight-room building at a government tax sale and deeded it "to the Colored children" of Beaufort as a school. These actions are a measure of his status in the community. One observer, capturing the dialect of Sea Island blacks, noted that Smalls was "regarded by all the other negroes as immensely rich, and decidedly 'the smartest *cullud* man in South Carolina.'" Widely known, well-off, obviously intelligent, and self-possessed, Smalls was a natural leader in his community. His emergence as a prominent black politician during Reconstruction was almost inevitable.

"A HORDE OF BARBARIANS"

If nothing in Robert Smalls's background seemed to prepare him for fame and political fortune, virtually everything in Wade Hampton's marked him for both. Hampton was the oldest son of Wade Hampton II, a South Carolina planter and businessman and one the South's richest men. Though only one generation removed from his southern frontier roots, Wade Hampton II had established himself as a leader in the southern planter aristocracy. The Hampton seat was a sprawling plantation near Columbia, but the family owned other plantations in South Carolina, Mississippi, and Louisiana. A generation earlier, Wade Hampton I had settled in the back country, made a fortune, and went on to serve in the House of Representatives. By the late 1820s, he owned more than two thousand slaves, and his annual income from his Louisiana plantations alone was $100,000—a princely sum at the time. Wade Hampton III was born in 1818 into this world of wealth and privilege—made possible, of course, by the South's slave system.

Hampton's upbringing reflected the family's circumstances. He attended a private academy, where he received a classical education, then enrolled at South Carolina College (now the University of South Carolina) at the age of fourteen. Graduating in 1836, he went on to study law. At the age of twenty, he married Margaret Preston, the daughter of a prominent Virginia family. Meanwhile, he had also gained a valuable education elsewhere. As a young man, Hampton learned something about plantation management on the family's vast holdings in South Carolina and Mississippi. He also took to the outdoors. Both his father and grandfather were skilled sportsmen, and at an early age, he became an accomplished horseman and experienced hunter. It was later said that Hampton had killed as many as eighty bears on his hunting expeditions, sometimes with nothing more than a knife. Maturing into a powerfully built six-footer, he had learned skills that would help win him a reputation on the battlefield and in time make him in the minds of many South Carolinians a natural leader of a white supremacist counterassault on the state's Reconstruction government.

Befitting a man of his station, Hampton would also gain political experience. In 1852, he took a seat in the South Carolina assembly and six years later moved to the state senate. By then South Carolina was a hotbed of growing secessionist sentiment. Whites in the Palmetto State were literally surrounded and outnumbered by their black slaves. Naturally insecure, they had long been hypersensitive to any action they perceived as harmful to their interests or that weakened their "peculiar institution." In 1832, South Carolina had sparked the Nullification Crisis when it declared a new federal tariff of 1832 null and void. As the sectional crisis of the 1850s intensified, Robert Barnwell Rhett and other "fire eaters" easily stoked secessionist sentiment in the state. Wade Hampton was not one of them. A generation earlier, Hampton's father had fallen into the Whig camp, as had many business-minded Southerners who valued the bonds (and commercial ties) of Union. Hampton inherited this Whig orientation—and views that were moderate for his time and place. In fact, he spent late 1860 at his Mississippi plantations, which had just produced a generous cotton crop. Removed from his home state's fervor, Hampton greeted the news of its secession with no enthusiasm.

Hampton's loyalties, though, lay with South Carolina. When the Civil War began with the firing on Fort Sumter, he resigned his seat in the senate and enlisted as a private in the state militia. Despite his lack of military experience, the governor immediately commissioned him as a colonel. Then Hampton formed and partially financed "Hampton's Legion," a unit more than one thousand strong made up of infantry, cavalry, and artillery. Reassigned that summer to the Confederate army, Hampton's unit saw combat at the First Battle of Bull Run, where he was wounded the first of five times during the war. As the war progressed, Hampton's bravery and skill as a horseman earned him increasing respect and additional promotions. At the Battle of Fredericksburg in 1862, he led cavalry raids behind Union lines, capturing both prisoners and supplies. At the Battle of Gettysburg the next year, he led a cavalry attack against Union forces, received multiple wounds, and was taken back to Virginia in an ambulance. After returning to action and receiving command of the Cavalry Corps, he went on to defeat Union general Philip Sheridan's cavalry in 1864 during the Overland Campaign in Virginia and never suffered a defeat during the remainder of the war. He ended the war as a lieutenant general in the Confederate cavalry service—a rank shared only with future Ku Klux Klan founder Nathan Bedford Forrest.

Hampton was a hero by war's end. His unwavering commitment to the Confederate cause, however, had exacted a high price. Among his losses, Hampton counted one of his two sons. Much of his wealth was gone, consumed by war or used to supply his soldiers. While laying waste to large swaths of Confederate territory, General William T. Sherman's forces destroyed Millwood, Hampton's childhood home near Columbia, which had also been reduced, according to one Northern journalist, to "a wilderness of ruins." Finally, of course, Hampton's slaves—one of his biggest assets and the very foundation of the family's wealth, power, and social position—had been freed. As a female acquaintance told the South Carolinian diarist Mary Boykin Chesnut, "General Hampton is home again. He looks crushed."

Hampton's attitude reflected the feelings of many former Confederates. For a brief time at war's end he had contemplated guerrilla action against the victorious Union forces. He even toyed with the idea of leaving the country for Mexico or Brazil. Hampton decided to stay and rebuild his fortunes. Like many former Confederates, though, he was unable to accept fully the implications of the Union's victory. In fact, he believed that Andrew Johnson had no constitutional authority to remake the state governments of the defeated South. In a speech to a mixed audience of whites and blacks in late 1865, he declared that slavery had been destroyed "by a single despotic stroke of the pen." And, of course, Hampton shared the racial views of most whites as well. He would warn his black listeners not to "think, because you are free as the white people, that you are their equal, because you are not."

Hampton would have no direct role in the government that emerged under Andrew Johnson's plan for Reconstruction. That plan excluded former Confederate political and military leaders from participation in the political reconstruction of the former Confederate states without an individual pardon, which Hampton likely did not earn until 1872. Yet he was a natural political leader in the minds of many white South Carolinians. Thus, when the Johnson-appointed provisional governor called a convention to reorganize the state government, Hampton was elected as a delegate. Later that year, many voters again defied the prohibition against participation by former Confederates when they nearly elected him governor over his own protests. Such defiance did not bode well for the smooth reconstruction of South Carolina.

In fact, the Johnson plan had laid down minimal conditions for the political reconstruction of former Confederate states. Aside from excluding from politics former Confederate leaders without a presidential pardon, it required states to ratify the Thirteenth Amendment prohibiting slavery, invalidate Confederate debt, and repudiate secession. Black voting, of course, played no role under the Johnson plan, and the new governments that arose in South Carolina and other former Confederate states virtually ignored the political and economic aspirations of the freedmen. In South Carolina, the new legislature enacted a Black Code that severely restricted the freedom of blacks, forcing the federal military commander in the state to invalidate it. In the end, Johnson's terms proved quite acceptable to Hampton and most other whites in the South. At the same time, the results of Johnson's plan created ample cause for alarm elsewhere. Fearing that former Confederates sought to overturn the results of the war, Congress refused to seat representatives and senators elected under the president's plan and thereby acknowledge the new governments' legitimacy.

In the face of growing Republican outrage over presidential Reconstruction, Hampton stepped forward to express support for a beleaguered Johnson. Speaking for the white leadership in late 1865, he advised South Carolinians to overlook Johnson's lack of constitutional authority to remake the state's government and accept the terms laid down by the president, including an end to slave labor. South Carolinians, he declared, should support Johnson "so long as he manifests a disposition to restore all our rights as a sovereign state." In a public letter to the president the next year, Hampton declared gratitude that Johnson had prevented "life itself" from being "utterly crushed out of our unfortunate country." He also pointed to evidence of the "bitterest and most vindictive hatred" harbored by northern Republicans against the South: the creation of the "hydra-head monster" known as the Freedmen's Bureau* and the decision to send black troops into the state, "pouring into our whole country a horde of barbarians." **[See Source 2.]** Speaking to Confederate veterans in the fall of 1866, Hampton chastised the North for failing to live up to its word by refusing to seat the delegates elected to Congress under Johnson's plan. Responding to his speech, the *New York Times* declared that "complaints of a breach of faith are utterly without foundation." Going further, one northern journalist who traveled through the South after the war singled out Hampton as an "exemplar" of white Southerners' "proud and domineering spirit." **[See Source 3.]**

Such accounts fed growing northern alarm about the southern state governments set up under Johnson's plan. They also helped rally the Radical Republicans* to action. In 1866, Congress passed the Fourteenth Amendment and submitted it to the states for ratification. The amendment extended citizenship to African Americans, barred former Confederates from holding office, and penalized states that did not allow blacks to vote by reducing their representation in Congress. All but one of the former Confederate states rejected the amendment (although it was ratified in 1868). James Orr, then governor of South Carolina, expressed the sentiment of many southern whites when he declared that blacks were "steeped in ignorance, crime, and vice" and should not be allowed to vote. This resistance to the wishes of Congress further angered many northerners, who now believed that Johnson and the southern politicians were overturning the Union's victory in the war. In late 1866, therefore, Republicans made big gains in the congressional elections, and the Radicals in Congress seized the initiative. Early the next year, they passed the first of the Reconstruction Acts,* which overturned the governments established under Johnson's plan and imposed military rule on most of the former Confederate states. Under the watchful eyes of the military, the freedmen would be registered to vote, new state constitutions drafted, and new elections held. In South Carolina and across the South, Republicans were swept into power.

As these events unfolded in South Carolina, Hampton emerged as a leading spokesman for the state's alarmed whites. At the same time, he began to take a more conciliatory approach, conceding that *some* blacks should be allowed to vote. "We can control

---

Freedmen's Bureau: A temporary bureau established by Congress in 1865 to provide assistance to the freedmen and oversee abandoned lands in the South.

Radical Republicans: Those Republicans who wanted the abolition of slavery, an extension of citizenship to former slaves, and punishment of Confederate leaders. After the war, the Radicals believed that Reconstruction could not be achieved without a restructuring of southern society.

Reconstruction Acts: Acts passed by Congress in 1867 and 1868 that divided former Confederate states into five military districts, subjected them to martial law, and gave military commanders the power to register voters and oversee elections.

and direct the negroes [sic] if we act discreetly," he wrote to a white associate in 1867, "and in my judgment the highest duty of every Southern man is to secure the good will and confidence of the negro [sic]. Our future depends on this." Any attempt by white South Carolinians to appeal to black voters, however, was destined to fail. The overwhelming majority of freedmen were in no mood to be led by the state's traditional white leaders, especially when Hampton and other prominent Democrats repeatedly endorsed white supremacy.

In fact, as the career of Robert Smalls illustrates, the overturning of South Carolina's Johnson government finally gave the freedmen an opportunity to assert themselves politically. After helping form the Beaufort Republican Club in 1867, Smalls received its nomination as a delegate to the state's constitutional convention. Meeting early in 1868, the convention brought together 124 delegates, 78 of whom were black. Although one South Carolina newspaper charged that the black delegates were "misguided as to their true welfare," South Carolina's new constitution was revolutionary for the South and reflected the concerns of the state's black majority. It called, for instance, for state assistance to help people in "their homeless and landless condition." It declared that "no person shall be deprived of the right of suffrage for non-payment of the poll tax."[*] It abolished segregation. The delegates also recognized that the maintenance of a government "faithful to the interests and liberties of the people" depended "in great measure on the intelligence of the people themselves." Thus, following a resolution offered by Smalls, the constitution provided for free elementary schooling for all children.

Submitted to South Carolina's now largely black electorate, the new constitution was overwhelmingly approved. Shortly after that, new elections brought Republicans to power. Responding to these events, the state Democratic Party's executive committee, chaired by Hampton, issued *The Respectful Remonstrance on Behalf of the White People of South Carolina*. It contained a litany of objections to Republican rule in the state, including the enfranchisement of all black males and the disenfranchisement of former Confederate office holders. "The superior race," it declared, "has been made subservient to the inferior." Protest, though, is all that Hampton could do by the end of 1868. His political rights were still not fully restored and Republicans were in control. Like many other white Democratic leaders across the South, he retreated from politics. For a number of years, Hampton focused on repairing his tattered finances. His labor force needed to be reestablished under new terms. He was badly in debt, crops were poor, and he had lost some of his Mississippi property. As he had earlier written in despair to a Virginia relative, "The war was full or sorrows and griefs to me, but peace has been worse."

"MASSACRED IN COLD BLOOD"

While Hampton withdrew, Robert Smalls's career continued to embody the hopes that many freedmen placed in Reconstruction. In 1868, Smalls won a seat in the lower house of the legislature—the only one in the reconstructed South made up of a majority of black legislators. In fact, the majority of the state's legislators were ex-slaves. Smalls and the other freedmen often deferred to whites and the better-educated freeborn blacks, but Smalls continued to fight for issues that affected his black constituents. He served on a commission "to establish and maintain a system of free common schools" and sponsored

---

[*]*Poll tax:* A tax established in many southern states as a requirement for voting in order to discourage blacks from casting ballots.

a bill to enforce the Civil Rights Act of 1866, which granted the same civil rights to all persons born in the United States. He also served on a panel that investigated the intimidation, even murder, of Republican voters in the state during the 1868 election.

Smalls devoted much of his energy in the legislature to mundane issues that benefited his constituents in Beaufort County. He championed the construction of roads, railroads, government buildings, and docks in his district. He mobilized voters with brass bands and torchlight parades, and he knew how to arouse them with passionate rhetoric. He called on black voters to "bury the democratic party so deep that there will not be seen even a bubble coming from the spot where the burial took place," and he vowed to "pour hot shot into the ranks of traitors." At the same time, his financial support of the widow and family of his former master built up the goodwill of many whites in the county. All these efforts paid off, as Smalls built a political machine* based on the loyalty of his constituents. As one observer put it, "The men, women and children seem to regard him with a feeling akin to worship." Although Smalls was not highly educated, another noted, he was "a thoroughly representative man among the people" and had "their unlimited confidence." That confidence was evident in 1870, when he handily won election to the upper house of the state legislature. Smalls sat in the state senate for four years and then in 1874 won election to the U.S. House of Representatives. Mobilizing his Beaufort County machine, he swamped his opponent by a margin of more than four to one.

Taking his seat in Congress in 1875, Smalls continued to mind the needs of his South Carolina constituents—white and black. In 1876, for example, Smalls fought a minor battle over federal control of the Citadel, the military school in Charleston that had been seized by the national government during the war. The takeover of the school had upset many white South Carolinians, and Smalls demanded that the secretary of war at least pay rent to the city of Charleston for use of the grounds. As in the state legislature, however, much of his energy was devoted to the passage of bills concerning such mundane matters as appropriating funds for the maintenance of harbors. Although such work was not glamorous, Smalls recognized its importance for his district's well-being.

At the same time, Smalls worked to protect black workers. Labor disputes were a frequent source of friction between the freedmen and white landowners, especially in South Carolina's rice producing low country. In 1876, laborers on Combahee River plantations walked off their jobs, demanding higher pay and cash wages. The strike eventually produced a confrontation between armed whites and the strikers that likely would have led to bloodshed but for Smalls's intervention. After failing to receive the support of Republican authorities, the planters eventually gave in to laborers' demands—an outcome that no doubt reinforced their desire for a change in government.

Smalls was at the height of his power, but troubling developments beyond his own district had already begun to undermine Reconstruction. The bastion of anti-Reconstruction whites, the Democratic Party had made a remarkable comeback elsewhere in the South by the early 1870s. In fact, by the time Smalls first took his seat in Congress in 1876, the Democrats had a majority in the House of Representatives for the first time. About two-thirds of the Democrats in the House were southerners, and eighty of them were veterans of the Confederate military. Calling themselves Redeemers,* these

---

Political machine: A type of political organization that often dominated city and state politics in the late nineteenth century. The bosses who ran these machines often built up support by dispensing favors to constituents.

Redeemers: Conservative white Democrats who vowed to save, or redeem, the South from Republican rule.

southern Democrats launched a violent assault against Republican rule. As white terrorist organizations such as the Ku Klux Klan and the Red Shirts used violence and even murder to intimidate Republican voters, the Democrats began to regain political control in one state after another.

South Carolina was a particularly fertile field for the growth of vigilante groups. Although whites were able to join the state militia there, it had become an all-black force. White South Carolinians responded by flocking into the Ku Klux Klan and numerous "rifle clubs." Often founded by former Confederate officers, these clubs were usually nothing more than armed bands of night riders. The inevitable result was a rising tide of violence, mostly committed by whites against blacks. In 1870 and 1871, Congress passed the so-called Ku Klux Klan Acts,* which gave the president the power to suspend the writ of habeas corpus* in areas of armed insurrection. After federal agents arrested more than five hundred white South Carolinians across nine counties, a congressional committee investigated the bloodshed in 1872. One of its witnesses was Wade Hampton, who had spent much of his time out of South Carolina but remained visible enough in the state to still be one of its "natural" leaders. Hampton suggested that blacks had intimidated other blacks who wanted to vote for Democrats, but denied any knowledge that Democrats in the state were using violence to suppress black voting. **[See Source 4.]**

Smalls, on other hand, knew that without the protection of federal troops white vigilante groups would be free to terrorize black voters and eventually overthrow Republican control of the state. His fears were well-founded. By 1876, whites in South Carolina had organized about three hundred rifle clubs, with twenty-four in mostly black Beaufort County alone. In one particularly gruesome incident that summer in Hamburg (now North Augusta), South Carolina, a mob of about a thousand armed whites surrounded a black militia unit and murdered a number of militiamen after they surrendered. As one newspaper put it, they "were shot down like rabbits." In the face of such assaults, Smalls fought to save what was left of Reconstruction. Shortly after the massacre, he unsuccessfully attempted to amend a force reduction bill, arguing that no military forces should be withdrawn from South Carolina "so long as the militia of that State … are assaulted, disarmed, and taken prisoners, and then massacred in cold blood by lawless band of men." **[See Source 5.]**

South Carolina Democrats, meanwhile, did not rely solely on violence to battle Republicans. They had also launched a vocal propaganda campaign against the alleged corruption and mismanagement of the Republican-controlled state government. As with the Reconstruction governments in other states, South Carolina's legislature had made large expenditures to help rebuild the war-torn South. Increased spending on a shrunken, war-ravaged tax base made these Republican regimes inviting targets. So did the presence in them of northerners, who were derisively called carpetbaggers.* The Redeemers railed against the wasteful excesses of "carpetbag" governments that, they said, had spent once responsible states to the brink of bankruptcy. Most of all, though, the Redeemers played on the deeply held

---

Ku Klux Klan Acts: Passed in Congress in 1870 and 1871, these acts resulted from overwhelming evidence of widespread white terrorism against blacks. They gave the president new powers to put down such violence, including the detention of whites.

Habeas corpus: The legal right of jailed persons to be brought before a court to determine whether they should be charged with a crime or released.

Carpetbaggers: The label applied by white southerners to northerners in the South during Reconstruction. The term was used to suggest that these "Yankees" carried their worldly goods in their carpetbags (suitcases) and therefore had no roots in the community. Because some of the northerners were involved in Reconstruction politics, the label also implied that they were corrupt—that is, out to enrich themselves at the public's expense.

racism of the white southerners. "Ignorant" blacks, they charged, had been taken advantage of by grasping "Yankees," and the result was a disgraceful riot of incompetence and theft. With its black-majority legislature, South Carolina was especially vulnerable to this charge. In 1874, *New York Tribune* reporter James Pike wrote an influential book titled *The Prostrate State: South Carolina Under Negro Government,* in which he referred to the actions of the legislature as a "shocking burlesque upon legislative proceedings" and to the black legislators themselves as an "uncouth and untutored multitude."

"NOTHING MORE TO DO WITH HIM"

These developments did not bode well for Smalls or Reconstruction. They set the stage, though, for Wade Hampton to lead the Democratic "redemption" of South Carolina, one of only three states where Republicans were still in control. As white Democrats became more assertive, prominent members of the state's Democratic Party turned to Hampton to accept its nomination for governor in 1876. Running against the incumbent Republican, Hampton enjoyed the backing of less "respectable" whites: the Red Shirts and members of Democratic rifle clubs, who frequently disrupted Republican rallies and intimidated black voters with whippings, assaults, and murders. **[See Source 6.]** Even as he promised blacks equal treatment under his administration and distanced himself from the "type of South Carolinian ... who killed negroes [*sic*] without provocation," Hampton tolerated widespread violence against blacks during the election, perhaps the bloodiest in the state's history. To mobilize white voters, many of whom had not voted since Republicans took control of the state, he even went on a triumphal tour of the state accompanied by hundreds of armed supporters.

Like the presidential election that year, the election for governor in South Carolina ended in a deadlock with disputed votes on each side. For six months, the state had two legislatures and two governors. The deadlocked presidential election of 1876, however, gave Hampton and his supporters their opening. The Democratic candidate, Samuel J. Tilden, won the popular vote, but twenty electoral votes in the Deep South were in dispute. When a special commission appointed by Congress met to resolve the issue, it awarded all twenty electoral votes—and the presidency—to the Republican candidate, Rutherford B. Hayes. The Democrats lost the presidency by one electoral vote, but they had gained something, too. Although Republicans retained control of the presidency, Democrats were able to end the protection provided to blacks by federal troops in the remaining Republican states in the South. Without it, the Republican governments in South Carolina, Florida, and Louisiana were doomed. In 1877, Hampton became the undisputed governor. At the same time, the Democratic Redeemer assembly named Benjamin Butler, the man who led the white assault in the Hamburg massacre, the state's new U.S. senator. With the so-called Compromise of 1877,[*] conservative Democratic rule was restored across the South. Reconstruction was over.

The meaning of Hampton's victory quickly became clear, especially for blacks. Although Hampton appointed freedmen to some minor state offices and for now they maintained the right to vote, Redemption proved disastrous for blacks. What protection

---

[*]*Compromise of 1877:* The political deal struck between Republicans and Democrats to break the deadlocked presidential election of 1876. In exchange for keeping control of the presidency, Republicans agreed to end military protection for Republican voters in three southern states, thereby ensuring an end to Reconstruction across the South.

federal force had provided to safeguard their civil rights was gone. Intimidation, voter fraud, and gerrymandering left the Republican Party in shambles. It was the same across the South. As one black Southerner put it, "Every state in the South had got into the hands of those who kept us as slaves."

After winning control of the state, Hampton and the Democrats in South Carolina moved to purge Republicans from important offices. One way was to prove the corruption of the prior Republican regimes. In his second term in Congress, Smalls became a prime target of their investigations. While serving in the state senate, he had chaired the Printing Committee, which oversaw the government's printing contracts. Now the Democrats accused him of accepting a bribe in connection with those contracts. Smalls said that he was innocent, but he was convicted by a jury and sentenced to three years in prison "with hard labor." He appealed the verdict before the state supreme court and lost, but the Democratic governor pardoned him when the Republicans promised to drop their investigation into Democratic election fraud. In reality, Smalls probably had overstepped the bounds of legality, but the evidence was scanty, others also were involved, and his crime paled in comparison to those committed by other politicians of the day. It was obvious that Smalls had been a political target and that the Democrats wanted control of his congressional district.

The Democrats had not seen the last of the determined Smalls, however. In 1878, he ran for reelection to Congress. As they had done throughout the South, the Democrats influenced the election by frightening voters away from the polls. Smalls lost, but he was undeterred. Two years later, he ran for Congress again. Despite all their advantages, the Democrats realized that it would be a close race. To counter Smalls's popularity among black voters, the Democrats stuffed the ballot boxes. The fraud was so obvious that Smalls was awarded the victory when he challenged the results. By the time he took his seat, however, his term was almost over. To ensure their victory when Smalls ran again in 1882, the Democrats in control of the state legislature redrew the boundaries of his congressional district so that he was unable even to win the Republican primary. Denied the nomination, he would regain his seat in 1884 when the Republican winner died in office and a party convention selected him to finish out the term. Later that year, he was reelected. The Democrats were still determined to have his seat, however, and in 1886 they once again resorted to violence, tossing out Republican ballots and forcing black voters away from the polls to defeat Smalls for good. Appointed a collector of customs for the port of Beaufort when the Republicans won the presidency in 1888, he served in that position on and off until 1913, one of the few black officeholders in the South. Until the day he died in 1915, however, he was convinced that Reconstruction had been a failure.

Meanwhile, Wade Hampton's political career had also been cut short. He won a second term as governor in 1878, but days after his reelection as governor in 1878, the state assembly named him to the U.S. Senate. There he continued in his role of spokesman for the South during two terms, even if it meant defending the Ku Klux Klan from northern attacks. His popularity, though, would not last. Hampton had won office with the support of less "respectable" upcountry whites who did not often share the gentry's paternalistic attitude toward blacks. Ironically, he lost office when the forces of racial violence that he had ridden into office turned on him. In 1890, the upcountry followers' of Benjamin Tillman, a populist, anti-black Democrat who had played an important role in the Hamburg massacre in 1876, launched a race-baiting campaign for control of the South Carolina government. As hard times hit southern farmers in the late nineteenth century, the Tillmanite campaign revealed a class divide within the "solid" Democratic South. The "natural" leader Hampton became one of the Tillmanites' targets, and in 1890, they denied him a third term in the Senate. Hampton's political career was over.

He went on to serve as a U.S. Railroad Commissioner for five years and then spent his remaining days at home in South Carolina.

Like Smalls, Hampton never doubted that Congressional Reconstruction was a failure. For Smalls, of course, it had failed by abandoning the freedmen; for Hampton, Congressional Reconstruction should never have happened at all. If judged by the second-class legal status of the freedmen and their economic and political condition, surely it *had* failed. In 1877, most blacks remained impoverished and tied to the land. By the time Hampton died in 1902, South Carolina and most other southern states had legally stripped the freedmen of the right to vote and hammered into place a rigid system of racial segregation enforced by lynching and other forms of violence. In South Carolina, this racial caste system stood as the ultimate bitter fruit of the Hampton-led redemption of the state. There and beyond, the predication of one publication had come to pass. "The Negro," The *Nation* magazine had declared in 1877, "will disappear from the field of national politics. Henceforth, the nation, as a nation, will have nothing more to do with him." Addressing that legal and political abandonment would be left for future generations. Only in the civil rights era of the next century would their efforts bear fruit. Then, in a "second Reconstruction," the nation began to finish the work of the first.

• PRIMARY SOURCES •

Source 1: Zion Presbyterian Church, *"Memorial to the Senate and House of Representatives"* (1865)

The freed people of the South were at the heart of Reconstruction. In this document, African Americans from Zion Presbyterian Church in Charleston, South Carolina, present a list of demands to the U.S. Congress. What do these demands reveal about the people's desires? What does the tone of this document suggest about those who wrote it and, in particular, the position in which they found themselves at the time?

Gentlemen:

We, the colored people of the State of South Carolina, in Convention assembled, respectfully present for your attention some prominent facts in relation to our present condition, and make a modest yet earnest appeal to your considerate judgment.

We, your memorialists, with profound gratitude to almighty God, recognize the great boon of freedom conferred upon us by the instrumentality of our late President, Abraham Lincoln, and the armies of the United States.

"The Fixed decree, which not all Heaven can move,

Thou, Fate, fulfill it; and, ye Powers, approve."

We also recognize with liveliest gratitude the vast services of the Freedmen's Bureau together with the efforts of the good and wise throughout the land to raise up an oppressed and deeply injured people in the scale of civilized being, during the throbbings of a mighty revolution which must affect the future destiny of the world.

SOURCE: Reprinted in James S. Allen, RECONSTRUCTION: THE BATTLE FOR DEMOCRACY, 1865–1876 (New York; International Publishers, 1937), appendix, pp. 228–229; originally from South Carolina African Americans' Petition, November 24, 1865.

Conscious of the difficulties that surround our position, we would ask for no rights or privileges but such as rest upon the strong basis of justice and expediency, in view of the best interests of our entire country.

We ask first, that the strong arm of law and order be placed alike over the entire people of this State; that life and property be secured, and the laborer free to sell his labor as the merchant his goods.

We ask that a fair and impartial instruction be given to the pledges of the government to us concerning the land question.

We ask that the three great agents of civilized society—the school, the pulpit, the press—be as secure in South Carolina as in Massachusetts or Vermont.

We ask that equal suffrage be conferred upon us, in common with the white men of this State.

This we ask, because "all free governments derive their just powers from the consent of the governed"; and we are largely in the majority in this State, bearing for a long period the burden of onerous taxation, without a just representation. We ask for equal suffrage as a protection for the hostility evoked by our known faithfulness to our country and flag under all circumstances.

We ask that colored men shall not in every instance be tried by white men; and that neither by custom nor enactment shall we be excluded from the jury box.

We ask that, inasmuch as the Constitution of the United States explicitly declares that the right to keep and bear arms shall not be infringed and the Constitution is the Supreme law of the land—that the late efforts of the Legislature of this State to pass an act to deprive us of arms be forbidden, as a plain violation of the Constitution, and unjust to many of us in the highest degree, who have been soldiers, and purchased our muskets from the United States Government when mustered out of service.

We protest against any code of black laws the Legislature of this State may enact, and pray to be governed by the same laws that control other men. The right to assemble in peaceful convention, to discuss the political questions of the day; the right to enter upon all the avenues of agriculture, commerce, trade; to amass wealth by thrift and industry; the right to develop our whole being by all the appliances that belong to civilized society, cannot be questioned by any class of intelligent legislators.

We solemnly affirm and desire to live orderly and peacefully with all the people of this State; and commending this memorial to your considerate judgment.

Thus we ever pray.

Charleston, S.C. November 24, 1865
Zion Presbyterian Church.

Source 2:   *Wade Hampton Protests to the President* (1866)

Acting as a spokesman for the white South, Wade Hampton wrote Andrew Johnson a widely read letter in August 1866 that expressed his views about Reconstruction under the president's plan. What are his chief complaints about Reconstruction? What does the tone of this letter suggest about the willingness of Hampton or other former Confederate leaders to accept political or social changes in the South under Reconstruction?

SOURCE: Charles E. Cauthen, ed., FAMILY LETTERS OF THE THREE WADE HAMPTONS, 1782–1901 (Columbia: University of South Carolina Press, 1953), pp. 124–125, 128–129, 130–131, 139–140.

[W]hilst we acknowledge to their fullest extent our obligations to you, we think, that owing to the misrepresentations of the true condition and feelings of the Southern people made to you by interested and mischievous parties, you have not exercised all the power in your hands, to restore to the South as fully and as speedily as might have been done peace—quiet and the inestimable rights of civil government. We do not at all question, Mr. President, your earnest disposition to extend to us all these blessings and to bring back the South to the Union with all her rights as well as all her duties intact and unimpaired. Nor are we insensible of the great difficulties which have met you at every step, nor of the bitter opposition which *fanaticism* has arrayed against you, in your efforts to accomplish this laudable purpose. You have given too many unequivocal evidences of your ardent desire to bring about this result, for us to doubt either the earnestness of your wishes or the sincerity of your convictions upon this vital point. And if your efforts have not been crowned with the success they deserve and if the hopes and expectations of the South have been disappointed, we attribute these results to no fault of yours, but solely to the inherent difficulties of your position and to that malignant spirit of fanaticism, which demands as the price of reunion, the complete degradation and the absolute ruin of the South....

The close of the war—or to speak more accurately—the cessation of active hostilities, found the South in the conditions I have but feebly portrayed. Clothed in sackcloth and ashes, with her desecrated fanes and her desolated hearths on all sides, she had to commence life anew. If stern Justice demanded that she should be punished, surely that Justice should have been tempered by mercy. The North professed to fight solely for the reestablishment of a fraternal union. When the sword was sheathed, what policy could so well have effected this result as conciliation. Look back, Mr. President at the events which have marked this, to the South, most bitter and mournful year and say if the retrospect shows one effort made to conciliate her—one act of legislation that is not calculated to gall and irritate her—or one evidence that the dominant party at the North does not still cherish towards her, feelings of the bitterest and most vindictive hatred. The very first act of *peace,* consisted in pouring into our whole country a horde of barbarians— your brutal negro troops under their no less brutal and more degraded Yankee Officers. Every licence was allowed to those wretches and the grossest outrages were committed by them with impunity. Their very presence amongst us at such a time, was felt as a direct and premeditated insult to the whole Southern people. Confederate soldiers returning home, weary and travel-stained, were seized by these negro soldiers, and the buttons of that grey jacket, under which perhaps was beating as heroic and as patriotic a heart as ever gave *its all* to a bleeding country—were roughly and ignominiously torn off. No armed foe being in the field, the great armies of the North, waged active and honorable warfare against Confederate grey and its brass buttons! Noble occupation for brave soldiers! It at least brought them into nearer contact with those hated emblems of Southern Soldiery, than they had ventured to assume, during the past four years....

The next step in the process of reconstruction was quite as unfortunate as that of garrisoning the South with negro troops. This was the establishment of that incubus,— that Hydra-headed Monster, the Freedman's Bureau. When the North had given freedom to four millions of stolen slaves, it was hoped that this generous offering which she had laid on the Altar of Liberty, would have terminated forever that baleful agitation of the negro question, which has deluged the land with blood and has ruined the fairest portion of this continent. The South acquiesced in the decree—though she was so blind as not to see the justice of it—which by one despotic stroke of a pen stripped her of more than a moiety of her property and she promptly and honestly endeavoured to adapt herself to the new relations between the two races, which this decree had brought about.

The Southern people, amongst whom the negro had lived for generations, naturally imagined that they were fully competent to direct, to instruct, and to protect him. Humanity and interest, which so seldom point in the same direction, in this case impelled the South to do all in its power to fit the negro for his new condition. The strong, but paternal hand which had controlled him through centuries of slavery, having been suddenly and rudely withdrawn, the only hope of rendering him, either useful, industrious or harmless, was to elevate him in the scale of civilization and to make him appreciate not only the blessings, but the duties of freedom. This was the prevalent, I may say the universal sentiment of the South and that much more not been done to carry this sentiment into effect, is due solely to the pernicious and mischievous interference of that most vicious institution, the Freedman's Bureau....

I have endeavoured, Mr. President, to lay before you fully and frankly those points wherein the South regards herself as injured and wronged and it only remains for me to state what I believe to be the prevailing sentiments of the people. That they felt the keenest disappointment at the failure of their attempt to separate from the North, there can be no question, and that they regarded this failure as a great misfortune, I do not pretend to deny. But while they were almost unanimous in their feelings on these points, they were perfectly sincere in their acceptance of the terms upon which they surrendered. They accepted those terms in good faith—without reservation—and they were and are prepared to abide them to the letter. Upon the main question, that most materially affecting their interests—the abolition of slavery—I honestly believe there is no desire to reverse the decree which has gone forth. I do not think that they would remand the negro to slavery, if they had the power to do so without question. The negro, whilst he was a slave, was happy, useful, honest, and industrious. But his unfortunate association with the Yankee, has corrupted him to such a degree that we should now be very loath to own him, or to be responsible for his rascalities. While he was *ours,* we did all in our power to ameliorate his condition, but since he has been withdrawn from our care, we feel no longer responsible for him, except as one who is to live amongst us and we turn him over willingly to those who imported him from Africa, sold him to us, and then stole him to make him free. We are perfectly aware what his fate will be, but we feel no longer responsible for it. I am sure that the Southern States would protect him and give him all the rights he is capable of enjoying, if he is left to their care. Northern interference has already entailed certain extermination on the race and a continuation of that interference will but hasten the fulfillment of this doom....

Source 3:   *A Northerner Assesses Southern Attitudes* (1866)

Sidney Andrews was one of a number of northern journalists and observers who traveled through the South during Reconstruction. Andrews, whose dispatches appeared in Boston and Chicago newspapers, spent considerable time in South Carolina and commented extensively on the conditions and attitudes he found there. How does he characterize the attitudes of what he calls the "ruling class" in the state? What impact do you think his reports would have on northerners?

SOURCE: Sidney Andrews, THE SOUTH SINCE THE WAR (Boston, Houghton Mifflin Company, 1971; originally published in 1866).

The indifference which so many of the people feel and express as to the fate of the negro is shocking and to the last degree revolting to me. He is actually to many of them nothing but a troublesome animal; not a human being, with hopes and longings and feelings, but a mere animal, valuable, but altogether unlovable. "I would shoot one just as soon as I would a dog," said a man to me yesterday on the cars. And I saw one shot at in Columbia as if he had been only a dog,—shot at from the door of a store, and at midday! "If I can only git shet of 'em I don't care what becomes of 'em," said one of my two stage companions in the ride from Columbia to Winnsboro, while speaking of the seventy negroes on his plantation. Of course he means to "git shet of 'em" as soon as possible. There are others who will follow his example....

Education never was general in the State, and for the last two or three years it has been almost entirely neglected. The ignorance of the great body of the whites is a fact that will astonish any observer conversant with the middle classes of the North. Travel where you will, and that sure indication of modern civilization, the school-house, is not to be found. Outside half a dozen of the larger towns I have not seen a dozen in over six hundred miles of travel. A few persons express the hope that the Legislature will do something to set the College once more at work; but, generally speaking, the indifference of the masses to the whole subject of education is as startling as it is painful.

The negroes, on the other hand, though in a very ignorant manner, are much interested in the matter. They all seem anxious to learn to read,—many of them appearing to have a notion that thereby will come honor and happiness. Schools for their benefit have already been established at some of the principal points, and the intent of the Freedmen's Bureau is that there shall be at least one in each district before spring. The disposition of the whites toward the negro schools is not good, and in many localities the teachers would be subject to insult, and probably to outrage, but for the presence of the military....

Where there is such a spirit of caste, where the ruling class has a personal interest in fostering prejudice, where the masses are in such an inert condition, where ignorance so generally prevails, where there is so little ambition for betterment, where life is so hard and material in its tone, it is not strange to find much hatred and contempt. Ignorance is generally cruel and frequently brutal. The political leaders of this people have apparently indoctrinated them with the notion that they are superior to any other class in the country. Hence there is usually very little effort to conceal the prevalent scorn of the Yankee,— this term being applied to the citizen of any Northern State. Any plan of reconstruction is wrong that tends to leave these old leaders in power. A few of them give certain evidence of a change of heart,—by some means save these for the sore and troubled future; but for the others, the men who not only brought on the war, but ruined the mental and moral force of their people before unfurling the banner of Rebellion,—for these there should never any more be place or countenance among honest and humane and patriotic people....

In South Carolina there is very little pretence of love for the Union, but everywhere a passionate devotion to the State; and the common sentiment holds that man guilty of treason who prefers the United States to South Carolina. There is no occasion to wonder at the admiration of the people for Wade Hampton, for he is the very exemplar of their spirit,—of their proud and narrow and domineering spirit. "It is our duty," he says, in a letter which he has recently addressed to the people of the State,—"it is our duty to support the President of the United States so long as he manifests a disposition to restore all our rights as a sovereign State." That sentence will forever stand as a model of cool arrogance, and yet it is in full accord with the spirit of the South-Carolinians. The war has taught them that the physical force of the nation cannot be resisted, and they will be obedient to the letter of the law; but the whole current of their lives flows in direct antagonism to its spirit....

Prior to the war we heard continually of the love of the master for his slave, and the love of the slave for his master. There was also much talk to the effect that the negro lived in the midst of pleasant surroundings, and had no desire to change his situation. It was asserted that he delighted in a state of dependence, and throve on the universal favor of the whites. Some of this language we conjectured might be extravagant; but to the single fact that there was universal good-will between the two classes every Southern white person bore evidence. So, too, during my trip through Georgia and the Carolinas they have generally seemed anxious to convince me that the blacks behaved well during the war,—kept at their old tasks, labored cheerfully and faithfully, did not show a disposition to be lawless, and were rarely guilty of acts of violence, even in sections where there were many women and children, and but few white men.

Yet I found everywhere now the most direct antagonism between the two classes. The whites charge generally that the negro is idle and at the bottom of all local disturbance, and credit him with most of the vices and very few of the virtues of humanity. The negroes charge that the whites are revengeful, and intend to cheat the laboring class at every opportunity, and credit them with neither good purposes nor kindly hearts. This present and positive hostility of each class to the other is a fact that will sorely perplex any Northern man travelling in either of these States. One would say, that, if there had formerly been such pleasant relations between them, there ought now to be mutual sympathy and forbearance, instead of mutual distrust and antagonism. One would say, too, that self-interest, the common interest of capital and labor, ought to keep them in harmony; while the fact is, that this very interest appears to put them in an attitude of partial defiance toward each other. I believe the most charitable traveller must come to the conclusion that the professed love of the whites for the blacks was mostly a monstrous sham or a downright false pretence. For myself, I judge that it was nothing less than an arrant humbug.

Source 4:   *Wade Hampton Testifies Before a Congressional Committee* (1871)

In 1871, a Joint Congressional Committee took testimony in South Carolina regarding conditions in the state under Congressional Reconstruction. In this excerpt, Wade Hampton is questioned by the Republican chairman, Senator John Scott of Pennsylvania, and Democratic representative Philadelph Van Trump of Ohio. In particular, they ask Hampton about the violence against blacks and about his views regarding blacks in the state. What does this source reveal about Hampton's attitudes? Do you think he was a credible witness, or that this testimony reflects what Sidney Andrews, the author of the previous source, called "a proud narrow, and domineering spirit"?

By Rep. Van Trump:

QUESTION. Is it your opinion then, general, or not, that negro suffrage unrestricted by education, and general participation with the white race in State legislation, and the holding of civil, State, and local offices, culminating

SOURCE: U.S. Congress, *Report of the Joint Select Committee to Inquire into the Condition of Affairs in the Lake Insurrectionary States*, vol. 4, South Carolina, (Washington, D.C.: Government Printing Office, 1872), pp. 1222–1223, 1227–1228, 1235–1236).

in a hostile supremacy on the part of the inferior race, is a decided failure in South Carolina, as now exhibited?

ANSWER. Yes, sir, I think it is.

QUESTION. In your intercourse with the people of South Carolina and the South generally, have you observed any marked or systematic hostility among any considerable part of the white population against a fair and reasonable system, honestly administered, of education for and among the negroes as a separate class?

ANSWER. No, sir; I think the people are very much impressed with the propriety of educating them, and would willingly give all the aid in their power to do so. I mean the white people generally, as a class. Of course, there are violent men in all parties.

QUESTION. Notwithstanding these sectional—and I mean by sectional, portions of the State—notwithstanding these sectional exhibitions of lawlessness, and the violations of law, have you ever known a single instance in South Carolina, since the war, of resistance to the service of legal process?

ANSWER. No, sir; it has never come under my observation at all.

QUESTION. Then, in your opinion, is the reason why these violences, committed by men in disguise, are unpunished, because the offenders cannot be identified or discovered, or is it a laxity in the administration of law, or imperfection in the process of law, by which these men in disguise escape?

ANSWER. I really do not know as to that all. I know nothing of these outrages except what I have seen in the papers, and how any one made his escape I do not know. But I think it would be very difficult to identify any men who disguise themselves as I am told they have done in more than one case.

QUESTION. What is your opinion, as a citizen of South Carolina, and noticing these things as far as you can notice them, as to this organization called the Ku-Klux organization?

ANSWER. As far as I know, I have never seen any man that was identified with that organization, if one exists. I have never been approached upon the subject at all, and I do not know that there is an organization of that kind at all. The outrages have been committed, I have no question, for that I have been stated; but whether this is done by any organization extending through the State or merely from some local outbreak, I do not know; but I am inclined to think it is the latter....

By the Chairman:

QUESTION. In the counties where these outrages exist, if they go to the extent of taking negroes out of their beds and whipping them to the number of one hundred and fifty or two hundred persons in a county, within five or six months, is it your idea that such a state of things could grow into toleration if the public sentiment of the leading men condemned it, and was actively at work to repress it?

ANSWER. I do not know. In the first place, while I have never heard of outrages committed to anything like that extent in any county, I should not think that punishment to as great an extent as that could be administered without a large number of persons being engaged in it, certainly.

QUESTION. Have you any idea that any portion of the democratic organization in this State is silently acquiescing in such a state of things, with the idea that it will ultimately, by the terror produced upon the colored people, prevent them from exercising the elective franchise?

ANSWER. No, sir. I do not believe that it was intended, or has ever been tried as a system extensively, to intimidate the colored vote. That is my honest conviction; I have never seen it, and I know I have heard always in this committee that we should never resort to anything of the sort, but try, on the contrary, to enlighten them. The only instances of intimidation—at least, I have no doubt the great majority of instances of intimidation in this State, as far as the colored population are concerned, have come from men of their own race, acting against those who voted, or wanted to vote, against the radical ticket. I have seen that myself. I saw two instances in which a deliberate attempt was made to murder colored people for no other reason in the world than because they expressed a desire of going with the democratic party.

QUESTION. Was that openly made?

ANSWER. Yes, sir; openly. One was over at Aiken, where there was a meeting during the presidential contest, and an old man—a very excellent man—a colored man, who had always borne a good character, was president of a democratic club—a negro club. He went over there and made a speech. I was sitting in the hotel when the meeting was over, and he was walking back, with two others, to get on a train; a large crowd followed him; we did not apprehend anything serious, but when they approached him, one man stepped out of the crowd and struck him with a large stick, knocking him down. General Butler[*] was present, and it was with great difficulty that we prevented a fight on the spot. A great many men were there, highly excited, and they procured arms, and for a few moments it was imminent that there would be a fight between the whites and the blacks.

QUESTION. Were there no arrests made after that occurrence?

ANSWER. No, sir. The other occasion was in the fall, at Charleston. General Butler was candidate for lieutenant governor. He asked me to speak, and I said a few words. They called on a colored man to speak. He got up on the stand, when some one in the crowd threw a large rock at him on the stand. It was thrown from the negroes, and there again we came very near having another collision....

QUESTION. One question I am prompted to ask by some sentiments which I have found in this State, and I ask for your opinion in regard to them. Is it your belief that the people of South Carolina will continue to yield obedience to the State government if the present majority of negro

---

[*]*General Matthew C. Butler:* General Butler, who served in the Hampton Legion during the Civil War, would be Hampton's colleague in politics for many years.

voters continues the republican party in power, or will the existing discontent increase and involve a contest between the races?

ANSWER. I am very much at a loss to pronounce an opinion upon that. I have been very much afraid of a collision—so much so that I wrote a letter to President Grant some years ago on that subject....

In that letter I remember expressing my fears that there would be a collision of the races in the State. Those fears are not yet removed; and that has been the main reason why I have deprecated rousing any antagonism between the two races. What would be the result, I do not know. I do not believe that the white people can now, or will, live under a rule where persons so entirely ignorant, so venal, so corrupt, have the management of their State government. I do not see how it is possible. I think they will bear as long as they can, but there will be a point beyond which they cannot bear.

QUESTION. In that very point of view I put the question, for it is one of great interest, certainly a perplexing one, and you being so much better acquainted with the state of sentiment among the white people than it is possible for the committee to be, I wish to know if the present negro majority continue the republican party in power, do you believe there will be submission, or will the feeling, which you have described, culminate in resistance to the State government?

ANSWER. If it was merely the negro majority to continue, I do not think it would produce a conflict. In other words, if they were to choose good men and have the government administered economically, I think the people would submit and bear it, in the hope that peaceful remedies and agencies would eventually restore their rights—the rights of the white people. But if they go on as they have been going on, taxing the State to this enormous extent, and being so venal and corrupt as they unquestionably are, for there can be no doubt of it. I have been told that no measure of any importance passes the legislature without the members being bought up regularly; that it is a notorious thing that money is placed upon the desks before them by parties who want measures carried through, and they are not paying any taxes themselves, but impose these enormous taxes, and that they have an exaggerated opinion of their power, as they do have. I am afraid it may end in a collision. The negro has an exaggerated opinion of his own power. You gentlemen do not know the negro at all, and there is the great difficulty. You all think the negroes are actuated by the same feeling as the white men, but that is a mistake. I do not pretend to say why it is but they are not. They have been dependent for a long time; they have no provision; they have no forethought at all; they are content to live from hand to mouth; they do not pretend to lay up anything; they are very credulous; they have an exaggerated opinion of their own power. I have known them to express the opinion, and I have no doubt they have the idea, that but for them the southern cause would have been successful; that they were the parties to whom success was due. I have heard them say so; that it was not until their aid was called for. More than once I have heard them express that opinion; that the Federal Army was triumphant, and they believe that they are strong enough, not only to defeat all the southern people, but all the northern people combined with them. I am not speaking of the more intelligent ones, but of the great mass of laborers. I have had a great deal to do with the negroes. I have spoken very kindly to them always, and all the negroes that I have living with me now, or the larger number of them, are my old slaves. I talk very freely with them. I give them the best advice I can. They talk very freely to me: and either they tell very wonderful lies or have been badly informed. I will give you one instance. My property was taken possession of by some hanger-on of the Federal Army while I was out of the way. He had hands there. When I went back after the war, I proposed to make a contract with them. They came up to see me. They went down to see this man, who had moved away, and came back and asked me for the truth. They said this man, who had been in the Federal Army and had worked them, had told them that if they hired to me they would all be branded and be put back into slavery for five years. I said, "Are you fools enough to believe that!" A man answered, "I don't know; this man told us so." I asked them, "Did I ever tell you a lie in my life!" They said, "No sir; you never did." I assured them it was not so. They actually told me that.

Source 5:   Representative Robert Smalls Protests the Withdrawal of Federal Troops (1876)

In the face of rising vigilante action against blacks in South Carolina, Robert Smalls introduced an amendment to a bill in Congress that would have reduced federal military forces in the state. What does Smalls's testimony reveal about the threat to Republican rule in the state? How would you compare the letter in this source to the appeal to Congress a decade earlier in Source 1?

I offer the amendment which I send to the desk. The clerk read as follows:

Add to the first section the following:

Provided, That no troops for the purposes named in this section shall be drawn from the State of South Carolina so long as the militia of that State peaceably assembled are assaulted, disarmed, and taken prisoners, and then massacred in cold blood by lawless bands of men invading that State from the State of Georgia.

I hope the House will adopt that proviso as an amendment to the bill. As I have only five minutes I send to the desk a letter published in one of the newspapers here from an eye-witness of the massacre at Hamburgh [*sic*], and I ask the Clerk to read it.

The Clerk read as follows:

The origin of the difficulty, as I learn from the best and most reliable authority, is as follows: On the Fourth of July the colored people of the town were engaged in celebrating the day, and part of the celebration consisted in the parade of the colored militia company. After marching through the principal streets of the town, the company came to a halt across one of the roads leading out of the town. While resting there two white

SOURCE: *Congressional Record,* 44th Congress, 1st sessions, 1876, 5, pt. 5: 4641–42.

men drove up in a buggy, and with curses ordered the company to break ranks and let them pass through. The captain of the company replied that there was plenty of room on either side of the company, and they could pass that way. The white men continued cursing and refused to turn out. So the captain of the militia, to avoid difficulty, ordered his men to break ranks and permit the buggy to pass through....

Late in the afternoon General M. C. Butler, one of the most malignant of the unreconstructed rebels, rode into the town, accompanied by a score of well-armed white men, and stated to the leading colored men that he came for the purpose of prosecuting the case on the part of the two white men, and he demanded that the militia company should give up their arms and also surrender their officers. This demand the militia was ready to comply with for the purpose of avoiding a difficulty if General Butler would guarantee them entire safety from molestation by the crowd of white desperadoes. This Butler refused to do, and persisted in his demand for the surrender of the guns and officers, and threatened that if the surrender was not immediately made he would take the guns and officers by force of arms. This threat aroused the militia company to a realizing sense of their impending danger, and they at once repaired to a large brick building, some two hundred yards from the river, used by them as on armory, and there took refuge. They numbered in all about forty men and had a very small quantity of ammunition. During this time, while the militia were taking refuge in their armory the white desperadoes were coming into the town in large numbers, not only from the adjacent county of Edgefield, but also from the city of Augusta, Georgia, until they numbered over fifteen hundred well-armed and ruffianly men, who were under the immediate command and direction of the ex-rebel chief, M. C. Butler. After the entire force had arrived, the building where the militia had taken refuge was entirely surrounded and a brisk fire opened upon it. This fire was kept up for some two hours, when, finding that the militia could not be dislodged by small arms, a messenger was sent to Augusta for artillery. During all this time not a shot had been fired by the militiamen. The artillery arrived and was posted on the bank of the river and opened fire on the building with grape and canister.

[An attempt to interrupt reading fails.]

The militia now realized that it was necessary to evacuate the armory at once. They proceeded to do so, getting out of a back window into a cornfield. They were soon discovered by the ruffians, and a rush was made for them. Fortunately, by hiding and hard fighting, a portion of the command escaped, but twenty-one were captured by the bushwhackers and taken immediately to a place near the railroad station.

Here a quasi-drumhead court-martial[*] was organized by the blood-hunters, and the last scene of the horrible drama began. It must now be remembered that not one of the twenty-one colored men had a pistol or gun about them. The moment they were captured their arms were taken from them, and they were absolutely defenseless. The orderly sergeant of the militia company was ordered to call the roll, and the first name called out to be shot in cold blood was Allan T. Attaway, the first lieutenant of the company, and holding the position of county commissioner of Aiken County, in which county Hamburgh is situated. He pleaded for his life, as only one in his position could plead, but his pleading were met with curses and blows, and he was taken from the sight of his comrades and a file of twelve men fired upon him. He was penetrated by four balls, one entering his brain, and the other three the

---

[*]*Drumhead court-martial:* A court-martial held in the field for the purpose of trying offenses during military operations.

lower portion of his body. He was instantly killed and after he was dead the brutes in human shape struck him over the head with their guns and stabbed him in the face with their bayonets. Three other men were treated in the same brutal manner. The fifth man when taken out made a dash for his life, and luckily escaped with only a slight wound in his leg.

In another portion of the town the chief of police, a colored man named James Cook, was taken from his house and while begging for his life brutally murdered. Not satisfied with this, the inhuman fiends beat him over the head with their muskets and cut out his tongue.

Another colored man, one of the marshals of the town, surrendered and was immediately shot through the body and mortally wounded. He has since died....

Are the southern colored citizens to be protected or are they to be left at the mercy of such ruffians as massacred the poor men of Hamburgh? Murdered Attaway was a man of considerable prominence in the republican party of the county. He was a law-abiding citizen, held a responsible office, and was well thought of by very many people. The other murdered men were good citizens and have never been known to infringe the law. The whole affair was a well and secretly planned scheme to destroy all the leading republicans of the county of Aiken living in Hamburgh. M. C. Butler, who lost a leg while fighting in the ranks of the rebels, and who is to-day the bitterest of Ku-Klux democrats, was the instigator of the whole affair and the blood-thirsty leader of the massacre. He boasted in Hamburgh during the fight that that was only the beginning; that the end should not be until after the elections in November. Such a man should be dealt with without pity or without hesitation. The United States Government is not powerless, and surely she will not be silent in an emergency like this, the parallel of which pen cannot describe. In this centennial year will she stand idly by and see her soil stained with the blood of defenseless citizens, and witness the bitter tears of women and children falling upon the murdered bodies of their loved ones? God forbid that such an attitude will be assumed toward the colored people of the South by the "best Government the world ever saw." Something must be done, and that quickly, or South Carolina will shed tears of blood and her limbs be shackled by democratic chains.

What I have written in this letter are facts which I vouch for entirely, and are not distorted in any degree. It's a "plain, unvarnished" narration of painful and horrible truths.

Source 6:   *Instructions to Red Shirts* (1876)

During the campaign for governor of South Carolina in 1876, the Democratic Executive Committee of Edgefield County adopted a plan for the intimidation of Republican voters. Often referred to as the "Edgefield plan" or the "shotgun plan," it declared that every Democrat should be a member of Democratic club and that each club or of member should follow certain procedures to ensure a Republican defeat. What do these instructions reveal about the means the Hampton forces employed to bring about his election victory? What light do they shed on the Congressional testimony of Robert Smalls and Wade Hampton in the previous sources?

SOURCE: From Robert K. Ackerman, WADE HAMPTON III (Columbia: University of South Carolina Press, 2007).

Each club should have a roster of every voter, white and black, in the township or region the club represented.

Every club member should be armed [the clubs often became synonymous with the rifle clubs]. The clubs should have a military organization and supplies for three days' action.

The clubs should demand that at least one of the three election managers be a Democrat.

The clubs should have a representative present when the votes are counted and demand a duplicate of the results.

The clubs should send a committee to Columbia with the duplicates to ensure an accurate count by the State Board of Canvassers.

Every club should provide transportation for voters to the polls.

The clubs should be alert to prevent underage blacks from voting and to prevent multiple voting.

Every Democrat should control the vote of one black, either by intimidation, by purchase, or by keeping him from voting.

Democrats should attend every Republican meeting to demand a division of time to challenge their statements, call them liars, cheats, or thieves.

Democrats should realize that argument serves no purpose with blacks; they can only be influenced by fear and cupidity ("treat them so as to show them you are the superior race and that their natural position is that of subordinates to the white man").

Clubs should let it be known that they will hold radical leaders responsible for any bloodshed, any house burnings, and voting irregularities.

Members of the county executive committees will visit the area clubs.

There should be five mass meetings in the counties, concentrating on July and August.

The counties should choose good candidates, preferring native whites to carpetbaggers.

There will be no financial assessments until the cotton harvest.

All transactions should be secret.

The clubs should enroll boys from age sixteen and up.

The watch word would be "Fight the devil with fire."

Organize black Democratic clubs or pretend to have organized such clubs.

The uniform is the red shirt.

QUESTIONS TO CONSIDER

1. What does the career of Robert Smalls reveal about the goals of blacks at the end of the Civil War? To what extent were they fulfilled under Congressional Reconstruction?

2. How would you account for the triumph of Wade Hampton and the Democrats in South Carolina in 1876? What would have to have changed to prevent the triumph of the Redeemers in that state and elsewhere in the South?

3. Based on the essay and sources in this chapter, what role do you think the racial or other attitudes of white southerners played in determining the way Reconstruction turned out? Which of Hampton's arguments do you think whites outside the South would have found most appealing?

4. Robert Smalls and Wade Hampton likely never met one another. If they had, what do you think each would have said to the other to attempt to get him to see his point of view regarding Congressional Reconstruction in South Carolina? What would have Smalls emphasized about its accomplishments? What would have Hampton said about its failures?

FOR FURTHER READING

Robert K. Ackerman, *Wade Hampton III* (Columbia: University of South Carolina Press, 2007), offers a recent and largely sympathetic biography of Hampton.

Eric Foner, *Reconstruction: America's Unfinished Revolution, 1863–1877* (New York: Harper & Row, 1988), offers a synthesis of the Reconstruction era. Foner argues that Reconstruction provided opportunities for reform that were not taken and correctly places African Americans at the center of the story.

Edward A. Miller Jr., *Gullah Statesman: Robert Smalls from Slavery to Congress, 1839–1915* (Columbia: University of South Carolina Press, 1995), provides a useful biography of the African American leader.

Kenneth M. Stampp, *The Era of Reconstruction, 1865–1877* (New York: Random House, 1965), remains a starting point for studies that present Reconstruction as a positive and successful policy.

Richard Zuczek, *State of Rebellion: Reconstruction in South Carolina* (Columbia: University of South Carolina Press, 1996), offers a thorough examination of the politics of Reconstruction in the Palmetto State.

2

Culture and Conflict on the Late Nineteenth-Century Plains: Sitting Bull and Richard Henry Pratt

Sitting Bull wanted nothing to do with the white man. In the summer of 1888, he also wanted nothing to do with the meeting of white men and Sioux at Standing Rock in the Dakota Territory. They had gathered there to discuss the fate of Sioux lands. Sitting Bull, however, had already seen enough. For years whites had encroached on Sioux land with unrelenting force. They had destroyed the buffalo on which his people depended. They had cut down Sioux warriors and undercut the Sioux way of life. They had taken the children and put them in their schools to learn white ways. Uncompromising, Sitting Bull had fought back for years. He even fled to Canada for a time to avoid the "prison" of the white man's world. He wanted his people to be free—to be left alone to roam the Black Hills and the plains as their ancestors always had. "I would rather die an Indian," he announced, "than live a white man." Now he was weary. At the Standing Rock council, he sat alone outside the deliberations. Other Sioux leaders would speak to the white men who had come armed with papers that would allow them to seize even more Sioux land.

The leader of the white commission at Standing Rock was Richard Henry Pratt, an army captain and founder and superintendent of the Carlisle Indian School in Pennsylvania. Just as much as Sitting Bull, Pratt was determined and uncompromising. His cause, however, was far different than the Sioux chief's. Just as Sitting Bull wanted to hold on to the Sioux way of life, Pratt wanted to destroy it. The only way to save the Indian, Pratt believed, was to replace his savagery with civilization—in effect, to turn him into

Sitting Bull   Richard Henry Pratt

a white man fully integrated into American society. Just as firmly, Pratt believed that no institution was more important in civilizing the Indian than the school. In 1888 at Standing Rock his task was different, but related to the larger cause of transforming and uplifting the Indian. Pratt and other reformers believed that the tribal lands of the reservation anchored Indians to a nomadic, "uncivilized" way of life. Attaching Indians to a small plot of land as tillers of the soil while sending their children to white schools would extinguish that way of life. At Standing Rock, Pratt was determined to implement allotment of reservation lands to individual Sioux families. That required Sioux support for a congressional act that turned over to white settlers and speculators nine million acres of left over Sioux land, half of their reservation.

For days, Sitting Bull refused to participate in the council meetings. Instead, he communicated behind the scenes, encouraging the other Sioux leaders to hold firm. Only after the talks had dragged on for days and began to grow rancorous did the great chief finally appear. His words were not inflammatory, as some observers had expected. "Talk to each other in a pleasant, quiet manner," he counseled. When Pratt and the other commissioners continued to insist on Sioux support for the act, however, Sitting Bull lost his patience. "I want to know how many months you expect us to stay here," he declared. After nearly a month, the council finally ended. Pratt realized that he had failed to secure enough Sioux support for the act. His commission's final report castigated the Sioux chiefs for rigidly refusing to see that the law was in their own best interests. It also recommended that allotment and revision of reservation boundaries be implemented without Sioux consent. In less than two years, the white man had won. He had achieved the breakup of Sioux lands and gained millions of acres of tribal land. By then, the captain was back at Carlisle, continuing with undiminished zeal his work of saving the Indian through education. After Sitting Rock, Sitting Bull went home as well. His worst fears had been confirmed yet again. The way of life he had known as a boy and young man was over. Perhaps fittingly, within months of the final approval of allotment the great Sioux chief's life was, too.

"TATANKA-IYOTANKA HE MIYE"

The details of Sitting Bull's early years are sketchy; his background and the culture of his people less so. He claimed to have been born along the Missouri River, but his birthplace may have been along one of its tributaries in what later became the Dakota Territory (the present-day states of North and South Dakota). He was probably born in 1831—the Sioux, of course, did not mark time the same way as the white man. He was a member of the Lakotas, one of seven tribes making up the very large Sioux[*] confederacy. The Sioux had originally lived in Minnesota, but in the late eighteenth century had been pushed onto the Great Plains by other tribes. Four of those tribes, the Dakotas, lived along the Minnesota River to the east. To the west were two more Dakota tribes, also living east of the Missouri in the Dakota Territory. Further west still, on the other side of the Missouri, were the Lakotas, who had also broken into seven tribes. Sitting Bull's tribe, the Hunkpapas, and the other Lakotas occupied the arid grassland, lands between the Missouri River and the Big Horn mountains in present-day North and South Dakota, Montana, and Wyoming. Like the other Lakota tribes, the Hunkpapas followed vast herds of buffalo that also occupied the plains from Canada to Oklahoma and Texas. Horses were the key to this nomadic life. Introduced originally by Spanish explorers and settlers to the south, they transformed the plains Indians' way of life, including that of the Lakotas, who fully adapted to horses only in the early nineteenth century. The animal made it possible to travel greater distances, more easily transport tipis and other necessities, and hunt far more effectively the buffalo, on which they had come to depend for food, fuel, clothing and shelter, tools, and weapons. By the time Sitting Bull was born, the Lakota were living in what some observers have called the golden age of the plains Indians—the period between the introduction of horses and the coming of the white man. For the Lakota, this age had begun only a generation before Sitting Bull's birth. In his lifetime, it came to a devastating end.

Sitting Bull's youth gave no hint of that. Rather, the great chief came of age at a time of relative cultural stability. Lakota villages may have moved from place to place on tribal lands. Life, however, followed certain rhythms, especially those tied to the seasons, and movement of the buffalo, and the hunt. The villages reflected that stability. Here, life centered on the tipi. Sitting Bull's mother, Her-Holy-Door, and other Sioux women cooked, prepared buffalo hides, and made clothing, tools, and utensils. Women were also responsible for packing the tipi and other possessions on *travois*—the frame

---

[*]*Sioux:* The name applied to the Lakotas and to the tribes to the east who called themselves Dakotas, which meant "ally." Sioux was a corruption of the Chippawa word meaning enemies and would also come to be used by the Dakotas and Lakotas as well.

connecting two poles that would be pulled by horses across the plains. Such tasks, mostly involving hard labor, indicated clearly prescribed gender roles within the culture. That work, however, did not indicate that women were inferior. In fact, they dominated life in the tipi and owned it and all family possessions. They also had control over raising the children, who were considered a gift from *Wakantanka*, the Great Mystery. With their children, Sioux parents were affectionate, indulgent, and gentle. Punishment was never physical. They were also persistent in their instruction. Sitting Bull's parents were no different. They also took pains to instill the four Lakota virtues: bravery, endurance or fortitude, generosity, and wisdom. Of the four, bravery was the paramount virtue and for good reason.

The plains Indians' golden age, in truth, was also one of continuous conflict. As the Lakota and other tribes had been pushed further westward, they collided with western tribes already in the area. The Lakota, for instance, battled the Crows for valuable hunting grounds along the Yellowstone River. As guns passed from white traders in the north and east into the hands of Indians, the conflicts grew more intense. Sometimes aligned with friendly Northern Cheyennes, the Lakota fought their enemies for horses and other prizes, for revenge, and sometimes just for honor. In other words, well before the coming of white soldiers, prospectors, railroads, and settlers, the plains were already a battleground. No tribe was more adept in battle than the Lakota, whose fierce reputation was well-deserved. Life for them had come to revolve around not only the buffalo, but the battle as well. It was the Lakota, the westernmost of the Sioux, who had pushed from the Minnesota River all the way to the foot of the Big Horn Mountains, clearing out one adversary after another, from the Kiowas, Poncas, and Omahas to the Pawnees, Mandans, and Crows. As one student of the Lakota put it, "A century of conquests had made them a proud, arrogant, and demanding people, and continuing hostilities … kept them a finely tuned war machine." Even more than the hunt, their life was based on war. Theirs was, above all, a warrior culture.

At an early age, Sitting Bull (whose name was Jumping Badger as a boy) demonstrated his prowess in the martial arts of his culture. In time, he would be given the name of his father, also a Hunkpapa chief. That name would be fitting. It connoted not inactivity, but a strong and determined animal that, when cornered, sat on its haunches to fight back. While still a boy, Jumping Badger became adept on a horse and skilled with a bow and arrow. At age ten, he killed his first buffalo. In time, he also demonstrated his courage, the prime Lakota virtue. At fourteen, he insisted on joining a party to explore for horses and to kill Crows. Penetrating Crow lands beyond the Powder River, the Sioux descended on a small band of mounted Crow warriors. Jumping Badger pulled alongside one and smashed him with a tomahawk, permitting another Hunkpapa to kill him. After the Sioux party returned to their encampment, a feast marked the boy's coming of age. His father presented him with a shield, a proud possession of every Sioux warrior. He also gave him his own name—Sitting Bull. Then his father, who would now be called Jumping Bull, placed a white feather in Sitting Bull's hair, the symbol of his first coup* or act of valor.

Coup: Pronounced *koo*, a common means among Native American tribes of marking bravery on the battlefield. Scoring first coup meant striking an adversary at close range, as Sitting Bull had done, as opposed to scoring second coup, as did the warrior who had slain the boy's target. Thus, first coup, striking an adversary up close, demonstrated more courage than striking from a distance or after a victim had already been injured.

In a battle with the Flatheads north of the Yellowstone River the next year, he won a red feather, indicating a wound suffered in battle. By the time he became a young man, Sitting Bull had participated in many battles and won a wide reputation among the Lakota and their allies as a fierce warrior. Pictographs drawn later by Sitting Bull as a visual autobiography record his numerous encounters with enemy warriors in close combat. **[See Source 1.]** In fact, Lakota warriors soon learned that his very name caused fear among enemy warriors. Going into battle, the Lakota often intimidated the enemy by shouting *Tatanka-Iyotanka he miye!* ("Sitting Bull, I am he!")

Sitting Bull's courage on the battlefield earned him standing as a war chief. His mastery of another Lakota virtue—wisdom—won him standing as a *Wichasha Wakan*, a holy man. A *Wichasha Wakan* understood the mysterious power (*wakan*) that existed in *Wakantanka* as well as everywhere in the physical world. For the Lakota, nature and *Waken* were one. As Her-Holy-Door, Jumping Bull, and others had taught Sitting Bull, nature in all its forms—creatures, plants, clouds, or stars—had to be observed very carefully to understand the powers of good and evil. Even as a young man, Sitting Bull developed a deep sense of spirituality, that is, a keen appreciation of nature's messages. Criticized once for aiding an injured meadowlark during a feast, he told the others to "teach our boys to be kind to all the birds, especially to our meadowlark friends that speak to us in our language." The Lakota also believed that *Waken* was revealed in dreams or visions. While still a boy, Sitting Bull set out on a vision quest, first seeking instruction from a *Wichasha Wakan* and then retreating to an isolated spot to fast and await a vision, which often appeared in the form of an animal or bird. Usually the same holy man would then help interpret the vision, which endowed the recipient with a special power throughout life. The vision would remain a highly personal possession, shared only with a few. The *Wichasha Wakan* would also help the recipient design an emblem or token—probably a thunderbird in Sitting Bull's case—to summon the special power of the vision when needed as a source of strength.

Not yet in his thirties, Sitting Bull clearly demonstrated exceptional qualities. Among the Lakota, it was unusual for a *Wichasha Wakan* also to be a war chief. He was both—destined, he believed, to use both his spiritual and war-making powers to help his people. To Hunkpapas, Sitting Bull possessed other appealing traits as well. He dressed plainly and by all accounts he was generous and never put on airs. He spoke infrequently, quietly, and with conviction. He was, in other words, a natural leader. Starting in the 1850s, the Hunkpapa and other Lakotas would need such a leader. By then, they faced a common threat in the *Waischus*—the white man.

Earlier, it had not been so. When Sitting Bull was born in the early 1830s, few whites ever reached the upper Missouri River. What little contact that took place between the *Waischus* and the Hunkpapas and other Lakota occurred at Fort Pierre on the banks of the Missouri in present-day South Dakota. Founded earlier in the century during the fur trade's heyday, it still served as a trading center. The white traders there were a rough bunch, hard-drinking, and usually illiterate. They cut down trees for firewood, trespassed on Lakota land, and their livestock ate the prairie grass. They did not act as people were supposed to. The Lakota, however, were perfectly willing to deal with these crude men. In exchange for buffalo robes, they supplied the Lakota with trade goods, including guns and ammunition, on which they had come to depend. In the 1830s, whites in significant numbers lived more than five hundred miles to the east and the Lakota could not perceive the bigger danger that the *Waischus* would come to pose.

By the late 1840s, though, the United States extended to the Pacific and more whites descended on the plains and Lakota Territory. They came in the wagon trains headed to Oregon, California, or other destinations. Then the "Long Knives"* appeared, sent to keep the peace and protect the emigrants. The Civil War slowed the flow of emigrants and diverted the soldiers and the nation's attention from the plains, but only for a time. When that war ended and the nation turned its attention once again to the West, Sitting Bull and the Lakota faced an unprecedented threat and the Great Plains was transformed into a bloody battleground. Sitting Bull and his people would face the full force of the white man.

"IMPRISONED ON ... TRIBAL RESERVATIONS"

Richard Henry Pratt had much in common with Sitting Bull. Like the great Sioux chief, Pratt was a warrior. He joined the U.S. Army at the age of twenty-one and would wear an army uniform for more than four decades. Like Sitting Bull, Pratt proved adept at organizing and maneuvering fighters on the plains. Pratt's particular skill, in fact, was leading units that included Indian scouts to reconnoiter and occasionally engage the enemy. Most important, like Sitting Bull, Pratt was a visionary. Just like the Lakota warrior, he devoted most of his life and energies to one mission—saving the Indians. And like him, Pratt carried to the end a deep and unwavering conviction about how to do that. Just as much as Sitting Bull, he entertained no doubts about the best life for the Indians. He even shared the chief's contempt for reservations. That, however, was where their similarity ended. Unlike Sitting Bull, Pratt was absolutely certain that the best life for the Lakota and other Native American tribes was not the one they knew before the coming of the white man. For Pratt, saving the Indians meant "civilizing" them. *His* life's work was to ensure that every trace of Native American culture and way of life was erased.

If Sitting Bull seemed marked as a leader of his people from an early age, nothing in Pratt's early years hinted at his later role as a leader in his nation's effort to solve the "Indian problem" in the late nineteenth century. He was born into quite ordinary circumstances in Rushford, New York, a small town about sixty miles southeast of Buffalo. He was only five when his father heard the siren call of the West, first settling his family in Delphi, Indiana, in 1846 and then leaving it three years later to seek his fortune in the California gold rush. He won his fortune, but on the way back to Indiana he was murdered by a fellow prospector. The oldest of three sons, young Richard left school at thirteen to help support his mother and brothers. He went to work as a printer's apprentice and split rails on the side to earn extra money. At eighteen, he became a tinsmith apprentice and within three years had mastered his craft. In the spring of 1861, however, the outbreak of the Civil War changed the trajectory of his life. Pratt enlisted eight days after the firing on Fort Sumter. During the war, he saw action in battles in Kentucky, Tennessee, and Georgia. Back in Indiana in the winter of 1863 and 1864 to recruit soldiers, Sergeant Pratt met Anna Mason, a girl from New York visiting relatives in Delphi. They were married that spring and eight days later, Pratt, by then a first lieutenant in the Indiana Cavalry, headed south again. He was mustered out about two months after the

---

Long Knives: The nickname of Native Americans in the West for soldiers because of the swords often carried by officers.

end of the war and, now twenty-five, settled back in Indiana, where he opened a hardware store. The business did not do well, though, and the army was still in his blood. Applying for commission in the U.S. Army, in 1867 he was appointed second lieutenant in the Tenth United States Cavalry.

Without knowing it, Pratt had found the vehicle to achieve his life's work. His regiment, newly organized, was made up of African American volunteers, so-called buffalo soldiers. They were stationed at Fort Arbuckle in the Indian Territory on the southern plains in present-day Oklahoma. Much like the troops that the Sioux and other northern plains Indians would confront in ever larger numbers after the Civil War, Pratt and his men were stationed there to keep the peace and enforce the reservation policy of the United States that dated to the time of Thomas Jefferson and Andrew Jackson. Confining Indians to reservation lands freed up large portions of traditional hunting grounds and removed the Indian from the inevitable white advance across the continent. Reservations, in short, were an instrument to help fulfill Manifest Destiny—Americans' self-proclaimed, God-given right to occupy land to the Pacific. In the Medicine Lodge Treaty of 1867 and the Fort Laramie Treaty of 1868, the United States established two large reservations, a northern one on the lands of the Sioux and other northern plains tribes and a southern one, the Indian Territory where Pratt now found himself, for the southern plains tribes. On the post–Civil War plains, the reservation policy would be enforced by the military. It would be administered by reservation agents of the Bureau of Indian Affairs, usually political appointees who knew little about the Indians and were often interested in opportunities for personal gain. In the Indian Territory of Oklahoma and elsewhere on the southern plains, that policy would effect tribes such as the Cherokee, displaced from the Southeast earlier in the nineteenth century by Andrew Jackson, as well as the Comanche, Kiowa, Pawnee, Arapaho, and others. Stationed in Oklahoma, Pratt would thus play a small part in much larger dramas: the American conquest of the plains and the "Indian Wars" that had raged on American soil since the seventeenth century.

Yet Pratt was no typical cog in the American machinery to subdue the Indians. True, like other soldiers after the Civil War, he found in the West a path to military promotion. In fact, once in Oklahoma, he was quickly elevated to first lieutenant. Because of his meritorious service in the Civil War, he had also received brevet rank* as captain, which he would be addressed as during his eight years of frontier service. Yet Pratt also went to the plains with critical eyes and an open mind. He applied both to the black soldiers under his command, the Indians he was there to subdue and oversee, and his own government and its policies. On the plains, in fact, Pratt had the opportunity open to few Americans at the time: a close working association with both African Americans and Native Americans. That association influenced his views about the condition of both groups and shaped an unshakable conviction about the rightful place of each in American society. At the time, the Fourteenth Amendment to the Constitution, which established citizenship for black Americans and provided for equal protection under the law, had been passed by Congress and was awaiting ratification by the states. By then, too, Pratt had experience with the black soldiers and Indian scouts under his command. He had been impressed by the abilities of both and could not reconcile the segregation of black troops with this amendment. Nor could he reconcile the amendment or the sentiments expressed in the Declaration of Independence with the realization that Indian scouts performed

---

*Brevet rank: A commission that promotes a military officer without an increase in pay.

"the very highest functions of citizens" while their people were "imprisoned on separate tribal reservations." **[See Source 2.]**

Nothing in Captain Pratt's subsequent experience on the plains would change his views about the Indians' proper place in American society. In fact, much of what witnessed about the Native Americans and their treatment within the reservation system strengthened his conviction that the Indian was fully capable of functioning within white society if given the opportunity. He could see the bravery and skill of the Indians. Without condescension, he marveled at the Pawnees' ability to work with and break horses. He decried the impact of whiskey on the Indians and the invidious comparisons with whites that resulted. The Indians' behavior under its influence was "broadcast as indicating their alleged savage qualities," he observed, even though it had no less effect on the white man. He also came to understand the devastating impact of the destruction of the buffalo, whose vast thundering herds had thickened the plains before the Civil War. Their numbers, perhaps thirteen to fifteen million before the war, diminished rapidly in a systematic destruction launched by white hunters and soldiers in the 1870s, abetted by the spread of the railroad and the insatiable demand of American industry for buffalo hides and bones. As he noted, the Indians "resented" this destruction, which contributed to the "fatal collisions between them and the white buffalo hunters" and drove them onto reservations.

Above all, Pratt was capable of seeing the humanity of the Indians. They were human beings, with whom he often became friends. He could also feel their anguish. In his journal, written many years after his service on the plains, Pratt recalled a "most miserable and repulsive" Kiowa squaw's visit to the Pratt home at Fort Arbuckle. Passing through the open door of the couple's home, she picked up the Pratt's little baby girl and held it in her arms. "You horrid, dirty thing," Anna Pratt yelled at her, snatching the baby from the Indian woman's arms. Then with a "mournful cry" and tears running down her cheeks, the Kiowa woman "made a sign that her [own] baby had died." Pratt's wife then passed their little girl back to the squaw. The bereaved Indian mother tenderly and carefully "passed her hands over the plump little limbs." After a few moments, she handed the Pratts's baby back "with a grateful look." A "strong mother love," the captain was moved to note, existed "in all races."

If Pratt's eight years of frontier service left him impressed by the Indians, it did nothing to lift his views regarding the Bureau of Indian Affairs. The bureau, he observed, did not keep its treaty obligations, leaving the Indians aggravated. "The white man did not keep his promises," he concluded. "Why should they keep theirs?" In the meantime, he observed, the Kiowas and other Indians under his "care" were "often greatly depressed and morose." In the face of what he called "obnoxious prison reservation policies," it was only "human" for the Indians to wish to "maintain their freedom and to hold on to their primitive life" when that was the only other alternative they saw available. Yet Pratt's frontier service also left him with a deep conviction that there was a better path for the Indian than their former "primitive life" *or* the reservation. As he put it to some Comanches with whom he met, the only "safe course" for the Indian was to "quit being tribal Indians" and live in white society "as individual men."

When the southern plains Indians were subdued by 1875, Pratt would have an unexpected opportunity to put these convictions into practice. Federal officials decided to move the most stubborn of the defeated Kiowas, Cheyennes, and Comanches to Fort Marion in St. Augustine, Florida. Pratt drew the assignment to escort seventy-one Indians to Florida and remained there as their jailor. There, he embarked on an experiment to demonstrate that the "savage" Indians could be transformed through education and assimilated into white society as peaceful and productive citizens. The prisoners cleared land, handled lumber, and performed other menial jobs. Pratt's main emphasis, however, was education. He had the help of female teachers, including for a time Harriet Beecher Stowe, author of the abolitionist novel *Uncle Tom's Cabin*. Like many other prominent abolitionists, Stowe turned her attention to Indian education after the Civil War and helped broadcast the results of Pratt's experiment in northern publications. Pratt also sent numerous reports of his own to his superiors detailing the progress at Fort Marion. As he proclaimed in one, they "will learn anything Washington wants them to." When the prisoners were released after three years, Pratt had made his point. In the face of a common view that Indians were simply unable to throw off their "savagery," he had convinced important people in the government that his experiment in Indian education should be conducted on a larger scale. He would finally have the opportunity to demonstrate to the nation, as he put it, the "righteousness" of his "contentions."

"THE LIFE OF WHITE MEN IS SLAVERY"

Pratt's opportunity to promote Indian education on an even bigger scale had much to do with the fate of the Lakota and other northern plains tribes in the late 1870s. After the Civil War, Sitting Bull watched more white settlers pass through Sioux land on the upper Missouri helping themselves to game, grass, and timber. At the same time, the army initiated a series of campaigns against the northern plains Indians to confine them to reservations. Sitting Bull responded quickly. A chief for eight years by 1865, he had already tasted battle with the Long Knives sent to protect the white trespassers on their way to mineral strikes or land further west. He had also come to realize that whites posed a fundamental threat. He was now convinced that they needed to get off Sioux land. On this, he would not compromise. Instead, he would fight for his people's land and their way of life. For the next sixteen years, Sitting Bull and the Lakota waged almost continuous war with the white man. The northern plains tribes would fall one by one, creating wider opportunities for Pratt and other Indian education advocates to "civilize" them. Before his people's resistance was broken, however, Sitting Bull came to embody the intransigence of all the plains tribes.

Immediately after the Civil War, the Sioux took on the military on several fronts. While Sitting Bull led raids on army outposts on the upper Missouri in present-day North Dakota, other Sioux waged a larger fight to the west. In a typical pattern, trouble started with a mineral strike.

In 1866 and 1867, Red Cloud, an Oglala Sioux chief, waged war against the army, which planned to build forts along the Bozeman Trail from Fort Laramie in southeastern Wyoming, northwest to the newly opened gold fields of Montana. After ambushing Captain William Fetterman in northern Wyoming in 1866, killing him and eighty-one men under his command, Red Cloud got the United States to back down. In the Treaty of Fort Laramie in 1868, it agreed to abandon its forts along the Bozeman Trail and guarantee the boundaries of Sioux lands. After his victory, Red Cloud called for peace and told his people to submit to life on the reservation. The treaty, however, said nothing about forts on Hunkpapa land along the upper Missouri extending into southeastern Montana. It also called for the Sioux to settle on a large reservation encompassing all of the land in present-day South Dakota west of the Missouri River, an area that was not even Hunkpapa land. Sitting Bull would have none of it.

Instead, he continued to launch guerrilla attacks against the forts on the upper Missouri. He also gained allies, including an unyielding Oglala Sioux warrior named Crazy

Horse. In 1869, Sitting Bull's supporters anointed him supreme chief of the Sioux confederation, a position that had not existed before. Through the first half of the next decade, he skillfully used that title to rally the "hostiles"—Lakotas who remained outside reservation lands year round rather than follow Red Cloud's path of compromise and life on the reservation. In those same years, a new threat appeared—the Northern Pacific Railroad. It planned to lay track right through the heart of the Lakota homeland in the Yellowstone River valley in southeastern Montana, through what General William T. Sherman called "probably, the most warlike nation of Indians on the continent, who will fight for every foot of the line."

He was right. When Long Knives appeared in the valley to protect railroad surveyors, Sitting Bull fired the opening shot, attacking an army encampment near the Yellowstone in 1872. The same year, the Northern Pacific reached the upper Missouri, giving birth there to a new town, Bismarck, and a nearby post, Fort Abraham Lincoln. Stationed there was the Seventh Cavalry, commanded by Lieutenant Colonel George Armstrong Custer, whose long, flowing locks led the Sioux to name him "Long Hair." That summer as Custer and his men marched westward into Montana, Sitting Bull and the Hunkpapas were encamped directly in his path. After outrunning the Long Knives, Sitting Bull organized a counterattack and then fled to the south, up the Bighorn River. It would be the last Lakota battle waged against the Northern Pacific, which was halted not by Sioux guns, but by bankruptcy brought on by a financial panic in 1873.

The threat posed by the Long Knives and other white trespassers, however, only grew. In the 1870s, their attention turned to the Black Hills, which lay in the western third of the Great Sioux Reservation. Considered sacred by the Sioux, they were rumored to contain gold. In 1874, Custer led troops, accompanied by miners and newspaper reporters, to explore the Black Hills. Before they were done, news of a gold discovery sent fortune seekers rushing there. Given the continuing threat posed by "hostiles" like Sitting Bull who refused to submit to the reservation system, generals and top political officials decided the next year that they needed to be neutralized with force. The army launched its war against these "hunting bands" in 1876, leading to the climactic battle of the Indian wars on the northern plains. In June, a large group of Sitting Bull's Hunkpapas, Oglalas loyal to Crazy Horse, Northern Cheyenne—the Lakotas' staunchest ally—and a smattering of Indians from other "hunting" tribes were encamped in a village along the Little Big Horn Creek in southeastern Montana. Sitting Bull and Crazy Horse agreed that they would only fight a defensive war, but if attacked they would fight to the death. Later that month, they were attacked. After uncovering the large village, George Custer and his Seventh Cavalry descended on it, firing into tipis and killing some women and children. Led by Sitting Bull and Crazy Horse, the defenders repulsed the outnumbered attackers and then counterattacked, leaving "Long Hair," 263 of his men, and maybe 40 Indians dead.

Sitting Bull had given his people a great victory. The chief had foreseen the outcome in a vision, which only increased his stature as a holy man and a warrior. The Lakota, however, would never see another triumph like it. Their war, like that of other Native Americans in the West, was already lost. By the late 1870s, fighting and disease had ravaged their ranks. The buffalo were disappearing, forcing more tribes to depend on the reservation agencies,[*] which provided supplies to reservation Indians. After the Battle of Little Big Horn, the army hunted down and decimated the "hostiles" who refused to

---

[*]*Reservation Agencies:* Headed by Bureau of Indian Affairs agents, outposts on the reservation that distributed rations and other forms of assistance to reservation Indians.

submit to the reservation. Their numbers had never been large, perhaps thirty-four hundred Lakotas and Cheyennes. Stung by Little Big Horn, that fall the army launched the "Great Sioux War." It destroyed a Sioux village near the Black Hills. Later, it struck the Northern Cheyenne village on the Powder River in Wyoming, destroyed tipis and blankets, leaving many of those not killed to freeze to death. "Wherever we went," one Sioux warrior said later, "soldiers came to kill us." Crazy Horse surrendered the next spring and before year's end was fatally stabbed by a soldier at an army camp in Nebraska. In 1877, the Sioux also watched the sacred Black Hills lopped off from their reservation.

Meanwhile, Sitting Bull fled. While newspapers ran profiles of his holdout against "civilization," whites called for his head, and many of his people left for the supplies offered by reservation agents, the great chief moved north into Canada rather than accept life on the reservation. With him was a small band of followers and his family, including his mother and his two wives. Vowing that he would never settle on one spot to farm, he continued to have faith that *Wakantanka* would never permit the buffalo to disappear. Life, however, proved little better in Canada, where the buffalo had also been thinned. Hungry, tired, and poorly clad against the cold, in 1881 Sitting Bull and his band recrossed the boundary to surrender. He agreed to live on the reservation, but insisted that it be without restraints. The Indians, he said, do not like to stay in the same place and "dig in the ground" as do white people. Whites, he believed, were "prisoners" of farms and towns. The Indians liked to hunt. By contrast, he concluded, "The life of the white man is slavery."

With nearly 170 of his followers, Sitting Bull was taken as a prisoner of war to Fort Randall in the southern Dakota Territory. Only after the secretary of the interior interceded in 1883 were he and his followers released. They were transported to the Standing Rock Agency on the Great Sioux Reservation in the northern Dakota Territory. There, Sitting Bull began a life that he had never known and for which he was ill-suited. Insisting that he wanted no government rations from the agency, he initially refused to learn farming, which many white reformers perceived as a powerful means to "individualize" and "civilize" the Indian. Yet, however reluctantly, Sitting Bull also came to realize the need to learn the white man's ways. When a Senate committee sent to investigate the condition of the Indian tribes met with the Sioux in 1883, Sitting Bull told the committee before walking out, "You have conducted yourselves like men who have been drinking whiskey." The next day, however, he came back to testify. He now had to consider the future of his children, he told the senators, and "my children's children, too." **[See Source 3.]** The next year, Sitting Bull and his family joined some sixty other Hunkpapa families already settled about thirty-five miles south of the Standing Rock Agency. They moved into a log cabin and under the guidance of the reservation agent he took up life as a farmer, raising animals and crops. This spot, across the Grand River from where he was born fifty-three years earlier, would be his last residence.

"CIVILIZATION OUT OF SAVAGERY!"

By the time Sitting Bull submitted to the "slave" life of the white man, changes far from the plains brought another assault on the Sioux and other plains Indians. In 1879, while Sitting Bull and his Hunkpapas avoided capture in Canada, Richard Henry Pratt had launched his ambitious plan to "save" the Indians. With the backing of the Interior Department, he established the Carlisle Indian School in old army barracks in Carlisle,

Pennsylvania. It represented the fruits of his lobbying efforts to conduct Indian education on a grander scale than anyone had attempted previously. His timing was perfect. By the time Pratt's school opened its doors to the first class of two hundred students in 1879, the collapse of the Sioux and other tribes in the West shifted the nation's attention from conquering the Indians to "saving" them. In the 1880s, influential reformers launched a two-pronged effort to "civilize" the Native Americans. One was embodied in the Dawes Severalty Act of 1887. It called for the breakup of the reservations, to which many Indians had already been confined, into small parcels to be farmed by individual families. Pratt and other white Indian reformers believed that severalty would uplift the Indian by turning him into a yeoman farmer, replacing the tribe with the family and old nomadic life on tribal land with one based on ownership of private property The other prong of the assault was education. As one white Indian commissioner expressed it, "As a savage we cannot tolerate him any more than as a half-civilized parasite, wanderer, or vagabond. The only alternative left is to fit him by education for civilized life."

The idea of educating the Indian was not new, of course. As early as the colonial period, missionaries took it upon themselves to educate the Indians and instill the white man's religion. Later, Thomas Jefferson and others who thought about the "Indian problem" advocated steps to transform him, in effect, into a white man. In the nineteenth century, the idea gained U.S. government backing with small appropriations for education inserted in treaties with various tribes. What schooling did take place was on the reservations and funding, it faced stiff resistance from a public skeptical about the Indians' innate abilities to learn. By the 1880s, however, attitudes shifted dramatically. Fueled by concern about the fate of Indians decimated by disease, the buffalo's destruction, and the army's withering assault, eastern humanitarian groups and philanthropists launched an Indian reform movement. Its primary focus was Indian education. Believing the adults beyond hope, they targeted children. Rather than reservation schools, however, the reformers preferred Indian schools away from the contaminating familial and tribal influences of the reservation. As the experience of Sitting Bull and his Hunkpapas amply demonstrated by the 1880s, the Sioux and other Native American tribes—their resistance broken, confined to reservations, and dependent on government rations—were in no position to resist a stepped-up effort to instill the white man's culture in their children. Pratt's moment had arrived.

Carlisle's curriculum reflected the intent of the reformers. From the beginning in 1879, the school emphasized both academic subjects and manual learning. As at Fort Marion, much effort was directed at learning English, the essential step for adjusting to white society. In addition, students studied such subjects as basic mathematics, geography, and history. Pratt also made sure that students received instruction in various trades, such as carpentry, blacksmithing, or farming. Girls, meanwhile, learned various homemaking skills. Yet Pratt's approach had less to do with academics or "manual arts" than with forced acculturation. As he put it, he believed "in immersing the Indians in our civilization and when we get them under[,] holding them there until they are thoroughly soaked." The students' experience at Carlisle reflected this approach from the moment they arrived. Assigned new names, they promptly received haircuts, uniforms, a new diet, and stiff discipline. Students caught speaking their native tongue were punished. **[See Source 4.]**

Retaining his military commission, Pratt ran Carlisle with rigid discipline and faced its critics with fixed determination. Confronting hostility from opponents of Indian education, he saw himself in battle with the "enemies of civilization." As he wrote to President Rutherford B. Hayes, he sought to bring "Civilization out of savagery! Cleanliness out of filth!" Not one to question his own views, Pratt told the president that because he knew he was "supremely right, it would be wicked to falter." The experience of the "Negro race," he remained convinced, provided the model. "Under the care and authority of individual of the higher race," he declared, "they learned self-support and something of citizenship." **[See Source 5.]** Such determination bore fruit. The publicity surrounding Pratt's work at Carlisle helped swing public opinion behind Indian education and federal appropriations for it soared in the 1880s. Though reservation education remained the predominate approach, off-reservation schools modeled on Carlisle spread from Kansas to Oregon. Meanwhile, enrollment at Carlisle grew steadily, reaching more than twelve hundred students by 1903. By the time Pratt stepped down as superintendent that year, it had educated nearly five thousand students.

Even after the Bureau of Indian Affairs closed Carlisle in 1918, Pratt continued to champion his cause. Convinced of his own righteousness, he never saw the limitations of his approach. Until he died in 1924, he never questioned his assumptions about the Indians' cultural "inferiority." Nor did he understand the shock of cultural "immersion" for students, who sometimes fell ill and even died in their new surroundings. He could not acknowledge that Carlisle's graduates, alienated from the reservation and the ways of their parents, were usually not fully prepared to succeed in the white man's world. More immediately, he could not see the human suffering caused by ripping apart families and systematically destroying their way of life. Sitting Bull's Hunkpapas might have taught him something about that. In 1882, while Sitting Bull and his Hunkpapa followers were still held as prisoners at Fort Randall, Carlisle recruited ten of their children. Pratt sensed the positive publicity for his school presented by these students. Sitting Bull himself would come to accept the idea of Indian education, eventually sending the five children living under his roof to a local day school. The Hunkpapa parents of the children ordered by the military to Pratt's school, however, would have none of Pratt's plan, which was quickly dropped. Meanwhile, Pratt could have looked even closer to home to understand the effects of his program on Native American families. The art created by his own students about the same time vividly captured the trauma involved in removing children from families to attend Carlisle. **[See Source 6.]**

Most of all, Pratt and other white reformers never understood the perspective of their Native American subjects. Unable to appreciate the enduring hold of culture, Pratt could not comprehend what one historian called the "shadow world, neither white, nor Indian" in which Indian students found themselves after leaving Carlisle. Native American culture could not simply be washed away as "filth," and nowhere was its resilience more evident than with their religion. Carlisle and local missionary schools may have taught Indian students English and other academic or vocational subjects, but they were far less successful at replacing Native American beliefs. Their lingering hold was evident in the Ghost Dance phenomenon, which originated in the 1880s with a visionary Nevada Paiute named Wovoka, who foresaw the return of the Indians' way of life, preached a return to traditional beliefs, and taught his followers songs and dance steps known as the Ghost Dance. The Ghost Dance spread and by 1890 the Sioux had embraced it with deadly consequences. In 1890, the same Seventh Cavalry that Sitting Bull had fought at Little Big Horn gunned down three hundred Sioux at Wounded Knee in an outburst of violence triggered by the Ghost Dance. Early the next year, a young Sioux man named Plenty Horses, a Carlisle graduate, was accused of killing an army officer during the Ghost Dance disturbances. During his trial, he explained that he had acted to wash off the mark that Pratt's school had left on him and to win a place back with his people.

By then, the longing to remain true to the old way of life had also swept away Sitting Bull. When his cabin became a focal point for Ghost Dance leaders, he came under pressure from frightened reservation authorities to stop the ceremonies. Proclaiming that the dance threatened no one and that his religion was his own business, he refused. The authorities ordered Sitting Bull arrested a few weeks before the Wounded Knee massacre. When police arrived to take him in, he refused to surrender. A scuffle broke out and he was fatally shot. As determined as Richard Henry Pratt was to wash away the culture of the Lakotas and other Native Americans, Sitting Bull had been stubbornly committed to saving it. He had vowed that he would rather die as an Indian than live as a white man. In the end, he got his wish.

•PRIMARY SOURCES•

Source 1:   *Scenes from Sitting Bull's Pictorial Autobiography* (1882)

While a prisoner at Fort Randall shortly after he surrendered, Sitting Bull illustrated important scenes in his life. The top drawing shows him in 1859 on his horse, wearing a headdress and a long sash and carrying his shield, charging a Crow chief. "Here is where I got wounded in leg and got off of horse and killed this man," he said. "No prisoners in that fight." In the bottom drawing, Sitting Bull, wearing a feather headdress, kills another Crow with a lance. What aspects of his earlier life does he emphasize in these drawings? What do they reveal about why Sitting Bull lamented after his surrender that "now it is all over, a hard time I have"?

Manuscript 1929B, National Anthropological Archives, Smithsonian Institution

Manuscript 1929B, National Anthropological Archives, Smithsonian Institution

---

Source 2: *Richard Henry Pratt Discusses the Fate of Blacks and Indians* (ca. 1923)

Richard Henry Pratt wrote his memoir late in life. In the following passage, he recounts the conversation he had with another officer shortly after arriving at Fort Arbuckle in the Indian Territory. Based on this passage, how would you characterize his views of blacks and Indians? Do you think Pratt's account of an event that happened so long before he wrote about it may have been influenced by his experiences in the intervening years?

The Major proved to be a jolly traveling companion, and as we rode the remaining days we discussed the Civil War, in which we both had participated, from the beginning to the end, and then the portent of our new life, in the regular service against hostile Indians. We became well acquainted with the Indian sergeant and his Indians and our confidence in them was greatly increased. Our Negro troopers grew in our estimate by their ready obedience and faithful performance of duty.

One thing the Major and I discussed freely. Being sworn as army officers "to support and defend the Constitution of the United States against all enemies foreign and domestic," we gave consideration to our immediate duties. The fourteenth and fifteenth amendments to the Constitution then pending before the states provided that "All persons born or naturalized in the United States, and subject to its jurisdiction, are citizens thereof." We talked of these high purposes and the Declaration of Independence, which affirmed that "all men are created equal with certain inalienable rights," etc., and then contrasted these declarations and the proposed amendment with the fact that the Indian scouts, who were enlisted to perform the very highest functions of citizens, even giving their lives if need be to enforce these American purposes, were imprisoned on reservations throughout the country and were thus barred from these guaranteed opportunities which they only needed in order to develop, become equal, and able to compete as citizens in all the opportunities of our American life. In considering the case of the Negro, we were agreed that when the fourteenth amendment became a part of the Constitution, the Negro would be entitled to be treated in every way as other citizens, and we were unable to reconcile that two regiments of cavalry and two of infantry then being inducted into the army of the United States, the enlisted men of which were to be Negros and the officers white, would accord with the amendment which provided that there must be no distinction. It seemed plain that under this amendment the Negro could not be relegated in army service to the Negro units of enlisted men solely, and the Indian could not be continued imprisoned on separate tribal reservations. The rights of citizenship included fraternity and equal privilege for development. None of our people were held under as severe "jurisdiction" by the United States as our Indians.

This first discussion and experience in my regular army service aroused an interest in my mind for the two races which became more absorbingly intense as the years enlarged my knowledge of them. Now, after more than fifty-four years of widest experience with them, I cannot see otherwise than that all the gross injustices to both races which have followed and become indurated policies are primarily the result of national neglect to give the opportunities and enforce the safeguards of our Declaration and Constitution.

SOURCE: Richard Henry Pratt, *Battlefield and Classroom: Four Decades with the American Indian, 1867–1904* (New Haven: Yale University Press, 1964), pp. 7–8.

Source 3:   *Sitting Bull Testifies Before a Senate Committee* (1883)

When a senate committee was sent to investigate conditions among the Indians on the upper plains, the five-member group heard numerous complaints from the Lakotas, including those of Sitting Bull. What were his main grievances? What does this source reveal about his state of mind by the time he had surrendered?

If a man loses anything, and goes back and looks carefully for it he will find it, and that is what the Indians are doing now when they ask you to give them the things they were promised them in the past. And I do not consider that they should be treated like beasts, and that is the reason I have grown up with the feelings I have.

Whatever you wanted of me I have obeyed, and I have come when you called me. The Great Father sent me word that what ever he had against me in the past had been forgiven and thrown aside, and he would have nothing against me in the future; and I accepted his promises and came in. And he told me not to step aside from the white man's path, and I told him I would not, and I am doing my best to travel in that path.

I feel that my country has gotten a bad name, and I want it to have a good name. It used to have a good name, and I sit sometimes and wonder who it is that has given it a bad name. You are the only people now who can give it a good name, and I want you to take care of my country and respect it.

When we sold the Black Hills we got a very small price for it, and not what we ought to have received. I used to think that the size of the payments would remain the same all the time, but they are growing smaller all the time.

I want you to tell the Great Father everything I have said, and that we want some benefits from the promises he has made to us. And I don't think I should be tormented with anything about giving up any part of my land until those promises are fulfilled. I would rather wait until that time, when I will be ready to transact any business he may desire.

I consider that my country takes in the Black Hills, and runs from the Powder River to the Missouri, and that all of this land belongs to me. Our reservation is not as large as we want it to be, and I suppose the Great Father owes us money now for land he has taken from us in the past.

You white men advise us to follow your ways, and therefore I talk as I do. When you have a piece of land, and anything trespasses on it, you catch it and keep it until you get damages, and I am doing the same thing now. And I want you to tell this to the Great Father for me. I am looking into the future for the benefit of my children, and that is what I mean, when I say I want my country taken care of for me.

My children will grow up here, and I am looking ahead for their benefit and for the benefit of my children's children, too; and even beyond that again. I sit here and look around me now, and I see my people starving, and I want the Great Father to make an increase in the amount of food that is allowed us now, so that they may be able to live. We want cattle to butcher — I want you to kill 300 head of cattle at a time. That is the way you live and we want to live the same way. This is what I want you to tell the Great Father when you go back home.

SOURCE: 48th Congress, 1st Session. Senate rep. No. 283, Serial 2164, 80–81.

If we get the things we want, our children will be raised like the white children. When the Great Father told me to live like his people I told him to send me six teams of mules, because that is the way white people make a living, and I wanted my children to have these things to help them to make a living. I also told him to send me two spans of horses with wagons, and everything else my children would need. I also asked for a horse and buggy for my children. I was advised to follow the ways of the white man, and that is why I asked for those things.

I never ask for anything that is not needed. I also asked for a cow and a bull for each family, so that they can raise cattle of their own. I asked for four yokes of oxen and wagons with them. Also a yoke of oxen and a wagon for each of my children to haul wood with.

It is your own doing that I am here. You sent me here, and advised me to live as you do, and it is not right for me to live in poverty. I asked the Great Father for hogs, male and female, and for male and female sheep for my children to raise from. I did not leave out anything in the way of animals that the white men have; I asked for every one of them. I want you to tell the Great Father to send me some agricultural implements, so that I will not he obliged to work bare-handed.

Whatever he sends to this agency our agent will take care of for us, and we will be satisfied because we know he will keep everything right. Whatever is sent here for us he will be pleased to take care of for us. I want to tell you that our rations have been reduced to almost nothing, and many of the people have starved to death.

Now I beg of you to have the amount of rations, increased so that our children will not starve, but will live better than they do now. I want clothing, too, and I will ask for that, too. We want all kinds of clothing for our people. Look at the men around here and see how poorly dressed they are. We want some clothing this month, and when it gets cold we want more to protect us from the weather.

That is all I have to say.

Source 4:   *Luther Standing Bear Recalls Carlisle* (1933)

In 1879, when he was eleven years old, Plenty Kill, the son of Standing Bear, left his South Dakota home with other Sioux boys and girls to enroll at Carlisle, where he received a new name: Luther Standing Bear. Later, he recalled his experiences as a student there. What does this account reveal about Pratt's methods at the school and their impact?

At the age of eleven years, ancestral life for me and my people was most abruptly ended without regard for our wishes, comforts, or rights in the matter. At once I was thrust into an alien world, into an environment as different from the one into which I had been born as it is possible to imagine, to remake myself, if I could, into the likeness of the invader.

By 1879, my people were no longer free, but were subjects confined on reservations under the rule of agents. One day there came to the agency a party of white people from the East. Their presence aroused considerable excitement when it became known that these people were school teachers who wanted some Indian boys and girls to take away with them to train as were white boys and girls....

Source: *Luther Standing Bear*, Land of the Spotted Eagle (Lincoln: University of Nebraska Press, 1933), pp. 230, 232–234.

At last at Carlisle the transforming, the 'civilizing' process began. It began with clothes. Never, no matter what our philosophy or spiritual quality, could we be civilized while wearing the moccasin and blanket. The task before us was not only that of accepting new ideas and adopting new manners, but actual physical changes and discomfort has to be borne uncomplainingly until the body adjusted itself to new tastes and habits. Our accustomed dress was taken and replaced with clothing that felt cumbersome and awkward. Against trousers and handkerchiefs we had a distinct feeling — they were unsanitary and the trousers kept us from breathing well. High collars, stiff-bosomed shirts, and suspenders fully three inches in width were uncomfortable, while leather boots caused actual suffering. We longed to go barefoot, but were told that the dew on the grass would give us colds. That was a new warning for us, for our mothers had never told us to beware of colds, and I remember as a child coming into the tipi with moccasins full of snow. Unconcernedly I would take them off my feet, pour out the snow, and put them on my feet again without any thought of sickness, for in that time colds, catarrh, bronchitis, and *la grippe* were unknown. But we were soon to know them. Then, red flannel undergarments were given us for winter wear, and for me, at least, discomfort grew into actual torture. I used to endure it as long as possible, then run upstairs and quickly take off the flannel garments and hide them. When inspection time came, I ran and put them on again, for I knew that if I were found disobeying the orders of the school I should be punished. My niece once asked me what it was that I disliked the most during those first bewildering days, and I said, 'red flannel.' Not knowing what I meant, she laughed, but I still remember those horrid, sticky garments which we had to wear next to the skin, and I still squirm and itch when I think of them. Of course, our hair was cut, and then there was much disapproval. But that was part of the transformation process and in some mysterious way long hair stood in the path of our development. For all the grumbling among the bigger boys, we soon had our heads shaven. How strange I felt! Involuntarily, time and time again, my hands went to my head, and that night it was a long time before I went to sleep. If we did not learn much at first, it will not be wondered at, I think. Everything was queer, and it took a few months to get adjusted to the new surroundings.

Almost immediately our names were changed to those in common use in the English language. Instead of translating our names into English and calling Zinkcaziwin, Yellow Bird, and Wanbli K'leska, Spotted Eagle, which in itself would have been educational, we were just John, Henry, or Maggie, as the case might be. I was told to take a pointer and select a name for myself from the list written on the blackboard. I did, and since one was just as good as another, and as I could not distinguish any difference in them, I placed the pointer on the name Luther. I then learned to call myself by that name and got used to hearing others call me by it, too. By that time we had been forbidden to speak our mother tongue, which is the rule in all boarding-schools. This rule is uncalled for, and today is not only robbing the Indian, but America of a rich heritage. The language of a people is part of their history. Today we should be perpetuating history instead of destroying it, and this can only be effectively done by allowing and encouraging the young to keep it alive. A language, unused, embalmed, and reposing only in a book, is a dead language. Only the people themselves, and never the scholars, can nourish it into life.

Of all the changes we were forced to make, that of diet was doubtless the most injurious, for it was immediate and drastic. White bread we had for the first meal and thereafter, as well as coffee and sugar. Had we been allowed our own simple diet of meat, either boiled with soup or dried, and fruit, with perhaps a few vegetables, we should have thrived. But the change in clothing, housing, food, and confinement combined with lonesomeness was too much, and in three years nearly one half of the children from the Plains were dead and through with all earthly schools. In the graveyard at Carlisle most of the graves are those of little ones.

Source 5:   *Richard Henry Pratt on the Indian and Indian Education* (1892)

Richard Henry Pratt offered his assessment of the effects of Indian education at Carlisle to a gathering of reformers in 1892. What is his view of the Indians' natural state? What is his argument for educating Indian students off the reservation? What light does the experience of the student in Source 4 shed on Pratt's justification for off-reservation education?

… A great general has said that the only good Indian is a dead one, and that high sanction of his destruction has been an enormous factor in promoting Indian massacres. In a sense, I agree with the sentiment, but only in this: that all the Indian there is in the race should be dead. Kill the Indian in him, and save the man.…

"Put yourself in his place" is as good a guide to a proper conception of the Indian and his cause as it is to help us to right conclusions in our relations with other men. For many years we greatly oppressed the black man, but the germ of human liberty remained among us and grew, until, in spite of our irregularities, there came from the lowest savagery into intelligent manhood and freedom among us more than seven millions of our population, who are to-day an element of industrial value with which we could not well dispense. However great this victory has been for us, we have not yet fully learned our lesson nor completed our work; nor will we have done so until there is throughout all of our communities the most unequivocal and complete acceptance of our own doctrines, both national and religious.…

Inscrutable are the ways of Providence. Horrible as were the experiences of its introduction, and of slavery itself, there was concealed in them the greatest blessing that ever came to the Negro race,—seven millions of blacks from cannibalism in darkest Africa to citizenship in free and enlightened America; not full, not complete citizenship, but possible—probable—citizenship, and on the highway and near to it.

There is a great lesson in this. The schools did not make them citizens, the schools did not teach them the language, nor make them industrious and self-supporting. Denied the right of schools, they became English-speaking and industrious through the influences of association. Scattered here and there, under the care and authority of individuals of the higher race, they learned self-support and something of citizenship, and so reached their present place. No other influence or force would have so speedily accomplished such a result. Left in Africa, surrounded by their fellow-savages, our seven millions of industrious black fellow-citizens would still be savages. Transferred into these new surroundings and experiences, behold the result. They became English-speaking and civilized, because forced into association with English-speaking and civilized people; became healthy and multiplied, because they were property; and

SOURCE: Francis Paul Prucha, ed., *Americanizing the American Indians: Writings* by the "Friends of Indians," 1880–1900 (Cambridge: Harvard University Press, 1973), pp. 260–261, 262, 263–264, 269; originally from an extract of the Official Report of the Nineteenth Annual Conference of Charities and Correction (1892), pp. 46–59.

industrious, because industry, which brings contentment and health, was a necessary quality to increase their value.

The Indians under our care remained savage, because forced back upon themselves and away from association with English-speaking and civilized people, and because of our savage example and treatment of them....

This ponderous Indian question relates to less than two hundred and fifty thousand people, numerically less than double the population of this city. They are divided into about seventy tribes and languages. Their plane of life has always been above that of the African in his native state. That they have not become civilized and incorporated in the nation is entirely our fault. We have never made any attempt to civilize them with the idea of taking them into the nation, and all of our policies have been against citizenizing and absorbing them. Although some of the policies now prominent are advertised to carry them into citizenship and consequent association and competition with other masses of the nation, they are not, in reality, calculated to do this....

As we have taken into our national family seven millions of Negroes, and as we receive foreigners at the rate of more than five hundred thousand a year, and assimilate them, it would seem that the time may have arrived when we can very properly make at least the attempt to assimilate our two hundred and fifty thousand Indians, using this proven potent line, and see if that will not end this vexed question and remove them from public attention, where they occupy so much more space than they are entitled to either by numbers or worth.

The school at Carlisle is an attempt on the part of the government to do this. Carlisle has always planted treason to the tribe and loyalty to the nation at large. It has preached against colonizing Indians, and in favor of individualizing them. It has demanded for them the same multiplicity of chances which all others in the country enjoy. Carlisle fills young Indians with the spirit of loyalty to the stars and stripes, and then moves them out into our communities to show by their conduct and ability that the Indian is no different from the white or the colored, that he has the inalienable right to liberty and opportunity that the white and the negro have. Carlisle does not dictate to him what line of life he should fill, so it is an honest one. It says to him that, if he gets his living by the sweat of his brow, and demonstrates to the nation that he is a man, he does more good for his race than hundreds of his fellows who cling to their tribal communistic surroundings....

Source 6:   *Taking a Crow Child to Carlisle* (1891)

According to a Bureau of Indian Affairs clerk at the Crow reservation, this drawing was made by Carlisle school boys. His notes on the drawing read: "Major Wyman, U.S. Ind[ian] Agent at Crow Agency Mont. With his chief of Police 'Boy that Grabs' trying to get Indian children for the school. A Crow Indian squaw leads her little girl by the hand to deliver her to the Capt. Of Police." What do the facial expression of the Indian agent and the gesture and facial expression of the mother as well as her stance next to her daughter indicate about the situation?

Boys from Carlisle Indian School/Montana State University Library

QUESTIONS TO CONSIDER

1. What does the life of Sitting Bull and the experience of the Lakotas reveal about the impact on Native Americans of American expansion into the West in the decades after the Civil War? What threats did they face? How did they respond to them?

2. How would you describe the program of Richard Henry Pratt and other white Indian reformers in the late nineteenth and early twentieth centuries to "save" the Indians? What was Pratt's rationale for it? What do the sources in this chapter reveal about its impact on Native Americans?

3. Different as they were, Sitting Bull and Richard Henry Pratt shared some character traits and fixed assumptions about a proper way of life. How would you compare their views about their own culture or way of life? How would you compare their personal qualities?

4. Faced with the loss of a way of life, Sitting Bull was unyielding in his desire to maintain it. Other Lakotas, including Chief Red Cloud, who annihilated William Fetterman and his forces in 1866, were not. Red Cloud compromised, seeking to carve out a new life on the reservation. Considering Sitting Bull's life and the circumstances confronting the Sioux in the decades after the Civil War, whose path would you have followed? Why?

5. One student of Richard Henry Pratt's life concluded that, given the assumptions of his own time about race and culture, he was a "determined, courageous, selfless worker in behalf of justice to a people suffering from four centuries of oppression by the dominant culture." Considering the information and sources in this chapter, how would you assess that statement?

FOR FURTHER READING

David Wallace Adams, *Education for Extinction: American Indians and the Boarding School Experience, 1875–1928* (Lawrence: University of Kansas Press, 1995), examines Carlisle and other Indian boarding schools as one aspect of the nation's program to assimilate the Indians through education.

Susan Betttelyoun and Josephine Waggoner, *With My Own Eyes: A Lakota Woman Tells Her People's History* (Lincoln: University of Nebraska Press, 1998), relates the experience of the Sioux from a female Lakota's perspective.

Richard Henry Pratt, *Battlefield and Classroom: Four Decades with the American Indian, 1867–1904* (New Haven: Yale University Press, 1964), tells the story of Pratt's long engagement with Native Americans from his point of view.

Luther Standing Bear, *My People the Sioux* (Lincoln: University of Nebraska Press, 2006), provides account of one Lakota's life before, during, and after his time as a student at the Carlisle Indian School.

Robert M. Utley, *The Lance and the Shield: The Life and Time of Sitting Bull* (New York: Henry Holt and Company, 1993), offers a detailed though highly readable account of the life of the famous Lakota chief.

Robert M. Utley, *The Last Days of the Sioux Nation* (Yale University Press, 1963), is an overview of the multifaceted assault on the Sioux in the late nineteenth century.

Organizing Labor in the Age of Industry: Terence Powderly and Samuel Gompers

Samuel Gompers could feel the tension in the meeting hall. Peering over the delegates jammed into the convention of the New York Workingman's Assembly, he saw two groups primed for a fight. On one side stood supporters of his recently organized American Federation of Labor (AF of L); on the other, members of Terence Powderly's Knights of Labor, the nation's largest union. When it came time to determine who was entitled to sit as delegates, tempers flared. Gompers, who presided over the convention, sensed trouble and ordered visitors to clear the galleries. For one irate delegate, that demand was too much. Rushing from the rear of the room, he jumped on the platform where Gompers stood and pointed a gun at the union leader's chest. Gompers smiled. Then he stepped next to the gunman, threw his arms around him, and pinned the man's arms to his body. Carefully moving his arms down to the gun, he grabbed it, put it in his pocket, and told the would-be assassin, "Now beat it, while the going is good."

This incident in Albany, New York, in 1887 revealed much about the strong-willed Gompers. It also reflected the deep animosity between his AF of L and Terence Powderly's Knights of Labor. That hostility was no wonder. Powderly and Gompers were equally interested in elevating the swelling ranks of American workers, but they were almost completely at odds about how to do it. Powderly believed workers' best hope lay in dramatically reforming society. Gompers instead insisted that workers must focus on immediate, concrete gains—on "more, more, here and now." Powderly believed the nation's workers needed allies wherever they could find them and threw open membership in the Knights to practically anyone. Gompers limited membership in the AF of L to workers, and mostly skilled ones at that. Powderly concluded that

Bettmann/Corbis

Bettmann/Corbis

Terence Powderly   Samuel Gompers

strikes were "suicidal" after watching striking workers suffer disastrous defeats in the railroad and other industries in the 1870s. Gompers had no problem with them. Strikes, he said, were a sign that workers were willing to fight for "their honor and their independence."

The differences between Powderly and Gompers, however, cut much deeper. They were also personal. As it happened, these two men had little in common. Powderly, native born, Roman Catholic, and a nondrinker, was cautious and quiet. Essentially a middle-class reformer, he did not like to talk about class. The Jewish immigrant Gompers was an aggressive extrovert who spoke often about class conflict. He also spent many hours drinking with workingmen at clubs or saloons. The teetotaling Powderly frequently made disparaging comments about "men who indulge to excess," and his disdain for Gompers would be returned in kind. Gompers had little use for what he called "visionary" reforms or organizations that pursued them. As American workers waged a bitter struggle against powerful business in the late nineteenth century, Powderly's and Gompers's unions fought their own war to the death. Though deeply personal, their battle would shape the future of millions of American workers for generations to come.

"GRAND MASTER WORKMAN"

It would have been easy for the compact, powerfully built Gompers to look at Terence Powderly and conclude that he was weak. As a scrawny boy, however, Powderly's looks belied his toughness. Born in Carbondale, Pennsylvania, in 1849, the eleventh of twelve children of Irish immigrants, young Terence gave up his formal education at thirteen to go to work as a switch operator for a small Pennsylvania railroad. He was soon promoted to brakeman and then served an apprenticeship in the company's locomotive shop under a master machinist. Amid the pounding noise of the shop, the young apprentice learned a trade and absorbed the pride that the artisan class had in its skills. He soon discovered, however, that many employers did not value their employees' work.

In the growing industrial economy after the Civil War, the spread of machine production was fast eroding the position of the skilled artisan class. Increasingly, skilled craft workers were simply employees who were paid for their time. Often, too, they were merely appendages of machines. Mass production divided the labor process into small tasks, requiring workers to perform the same actions over and over. Thus, a worker in a shoe factory might be required only to nail the heels to the soles of shoes. One company's standards called for twenty-four hundred pairs of shoes to be completed each day. Moreover, as industrialization spread, the workday—often ten hours or more—was divided into shifts. Each shift included workers who were interchangeable. That way, each employee could perform the same tasks in the same way, producing at the same level. As one machinist put it in the 1870s, mechanization was "fast rendering trades useless." Wage levels reflected the machine's assault on skill levels. Wages, many workers found, were too low to make ends meet.

Powderly got his introduction to the emerging industrial order when his company laid him off a few months after he became a regular machinist. He remained unemployed for nearly a year before finally finding a position in Scranton, Pennsylvania, with the Delaware, Lackawanna and Western Railroad. Meanwhile, Powderly observed the violent strikes in the coal mines that eventually resulted in the hanging of several members of the Molly Maguires,[*] a militant labor group blamed for the unrest. The strikes had an impact on Powderly, and by the time he joined the Machinists' and Blacksmiths' Union in 1871 and was elected president of the local two years later, he was convinced that strikes were dangerous. Throughout his career, Powderly would prefer peaceful negotiation and persuasion to agitation and violence.

Even that approach met with limited success, though. In the late nineteenth century, the owners of companies typically regarded unions as interfering with the natural laws of supply and demand that ruled the business world and set wages. Employees, they believed, needed to negotiate with employers on an individual, rather than on a collective, basis, as they always had. Workers found little sympathy for their pleas for better wages and shorter hours. Hard times made matters worse. As business declined and companies went under, increased competition for jobs sent union activity spiraling downward. During the depression that followed the Panic of 1873, Powderly was blacklisted for his union activities. Forced to become a wandering tradesman, he traveled from place to place seeking whatever employment he could find. All the while, he continued to work for the Machinists' and Blacksmiths' Union.

At the same time, Powderly was attracted to a budding movement to create a national labor organization. Before the Civil War, labor unions represented workers in var-

---

[*]*Molly Maguires:* A secret organization of miners with roots in Ireland that promoted labor violence in Pennsylvania mines starting in the 1860s. By the mid-1870s, two dozen members had been convicted in connection with the violence and ten had been executed.

ious locales. After the war, some craft unions representing the same skill joined together to form national trade organizations. In 1866, these trade organizations joined with others to form the National Labor Union (NLU), a nationwide union representing numerous crafts. Powderly was quickly drawn into the NLU. Unable to maintain unity among various workers, however, the union dissolved in 1873.

Through the NLU, Powderly came under the influence of labor reformer Ira Steward. A champion of the eight-hour workday, Steward believed that increasing wages and shortening the workday would allow laborers to escape the factory jobs that turned them into commodities. It also would permit them to become self-employed. Every worker could be a "capitalist" either by owning his own business or by being a member of a cooperative. Owned by their members, cooperatives would allow workers to be property owners in the face of industrialization, the rising power of corporations, and the spread of skill-eroding machine production. In short, Steward's aspirations for workers were for them to become middle-class property owners. This was an appealing idea, especially to artisans who spent years learning their trades. And it conformed perfectly to widespread assumptions about opportunity and upward social mobility in the nineteenth century. In the pre–Civil War economy of farms and small shops, ambitious workers often had not been permanent wage earners. Rather, they eventually joined the employer or propertied class by rising naturally from apprentices to journeymen to craftsmen. As master craftsmen, they would own their own shops and employ upwardly mobile apprentices and journeymen of their own. In an expanding industrial economy in which the factory was rapidly expanding the class of permanent wage earners, Steward and other labor reformers assumed that many workers could continue to join the propertied class.

Powderly, like Steward, emphasized the goal of economic independence for workers and moderate political and social reforms to achieve it. He took up the call for social reforms such as graduated property taxes,[*] women's rights, temperance, and cooperatives. These reforms had less to do with changing the workplace than with changing the larger society, and Powderly soon came to believe that the only solution to labor's problems was political power. After his union activity made him Scranton's foremost labor leader, he naturally turned to politics. In 1878, he easily won election as the city's mayor. In office, he pursued a course of moderate reform that included the establishment of a board of health, tax reform, expanded fire and police departments, and a public works program that paved streets and built sewers. Powderly's program appealed to many workers, and he won reelection twice. Like other workers, however, he eventually realized that politics alone would not solve the mounting problems of low wages, long hours, and the erosion of skills posed by machines.

In the face of these threats, many workers were already turning to secret organizations for help. One of them was the Noble and Holy Order of the Knights of Labor. Founded in Philadelphia in 1869 by a tailor named Uriah S. Stephens, it quickly began to appeal to a wide spectrum of wage earners. The order's secrecy offered protection to members, while its fraternal rituals instilled loyalty and a sense of community. Stephens and many of his followers also shared a widespread assumption dating back to pre–Civil War artisans that workers were independent producers, much like farmers. Their labor added value to commodities by transforming them from raw materials to finished products. In this view, society was divided into two great classes: the wealth producers, and

---

[*]*Graduated property taxes:* Taxes structured so that people with substantial property holdings pay taxes at a higher rate than those with less property.

those who lived off them. Unlike Karl Marx,* who saw private property itself as the problem facing workers, the Knights defined "non-producers" as the enemy. It was a compelling notion in the expanding commercial and industrial economy of the nineteenth century. Many people found themselves increasingly dependent on distant markets that they only vaguely understood. It was easy for them to see far-off bankers, brokers, and others who manipulated those markets for their own benefit as "non-producers." Thus Stephens, too, was an advocate of workers' cooperatives. In the long run, they were the only way to free the "wealth producers" from "wage slavery."

Like many skilled craftsmen, Powderly shared this "producer" ideology, and in 1876, he became a member of the Knights. The following year, the charismatic and articulate Powderly helped found a local in Scranton, and in 1879, he replaced Stephens as "grand master workman." As a devout Catholic, he was troubled by the church's rejection of the order's secrecy and rituals. So he quickly moved to transform the secret society into a public union. He also opened it up to a wide membership. In an age when most unions excluded blacks, the Knights welcomed them, and by 1886, the Knights claimed nearly sixty thousand African American members. Powderly compromised on the race issue when it was clear that white members of the union would not accept integrated locals. Grasping the reality of entrenched racism, he accepted segregated locals, which would allow African Americans to participate in the union. Yet he refused to back down at the national level, and the Knights included black members in national and regional organizations. Powderly also insisted that the nobility of work entitled all workers—male and female—to certain rights. He expanded the union's definition of work to include domestic servants and even housewives. Powderly's stand for women's rights was unparalleled. Most unions of the day were exclusively male and often fought against women working outside the home in order to protect men's jobs from further competition. He recognized, though, that the inclusion of women helped build a sense of community by uniting families in labor activities.

All the while, the Knights continued to reflect a "producer" ideology. The union excluded from membership only "non-producers"—lawyers, gamblers, bankers, and liquor sellers—and its rhetoric emphasized the nobility and independence of labor. Alarmed by the accumulation and concentration of wealth in the hands of the few, it decried the exploitation of the "toiling masses." Instead of revolution, the Knights offered a program of moderate reform and individual self-improvement. It promoted temperance and urged workers to make morality and hard work, rather than money, the standards for success. It demanded that the government preserve public land for homesteading by settlers rather than give it to railroads in massive land grants. It called for legislation to require corporations to pay their employees weekly. It supported the eight-hour workday. **[See Source 1.]** Higher wages and fewer hours, however, were merely short-run solutions to workers' problems. Above all, Powderly emphasized, the Knights needed to work for the reform of society through cooperatives. As he put it in 1880, they "will eventually make every man his own master." **[See Source 2.]** To many workers facing uncertain futures in the new industrial order, it was an appealing prospect, and by 1885, the union claimed one hundred thousand members. Powderly had emerged as the voice of the American worker and the leader of the nation's largest

---

*Karl Marx: The German-born economic philosopher who argued that human labor rather than capital added economic value to goods. Marx concluded that because capitalists unfairly claimed a portion of this value, private property and capitalism itself should be abolished.

and most powerful union. Behind him was what he called an "Army of the Discontented." Shortly, he would lead it into its biggest fight.

"THE UNION IS NOT A SUNDAY SCHOOL"

Like Terence Powderly and many other working-class children in the nineteenth century, Samuel Gompers grew up fast. Born in London in 1850, Gompers was the son of a cigar maker who had earlier emigrated from Holland. Young Sam grew up in East London, where the family of seven shared one room. After attending a Jewish free school from ages six to ten, Gompers went to work as a shoemaker's apprentice to supplement the family income. Switching after a short time to his father's craft, he apprenticed as a cigarmaker and then went to work with his father. Meanwhile, on the narrow, mean streets of East London, Gompers learned lessons about life. Although small, he became a hardened street fighter capable of defending himself and his mates. Convinced that "the strong rule," he displayed a fierce temper that in time he would learn to restrain. He also learned that ends justified means.

At home and work, young Gompers learned another important lesson, one that shaped the course of his life. As a cigarmaker, young Sam entered a tight community of skilled immigrant workers who were alienated from British society. Engaged in quiet work, cigarmakers often hired someone to read aloud in the shop, often sparking intense discussions on wide-ranging topics. The practice furthered the bright, young Gompers's education even as it reinforced a sense of community among the workers. That comrade ship was reinforced by the Cigarmakers Society, a craft union[*] that provided unemployment and sickness benefits and fought for better wages and conditions. Sam's father was a passionate union member and passed that feeling on to his son. As Gompers later wrote in his autobiography, early in life he "accepted as a matter of course that every wage earner should belong to the union of his trade."

Gompers carried that conviction to America. Like other European Jews who immigrated to Britain, Gompers's father never felt at home there, and in 1863, the family moved to the United States. Landing in New York, the family settled in a tenement in lower Manhattan, and young Gompers went to work rolling cigars by his father's side. Within a year, he had joined a union, and two years later, he became a journeyman and left home. The next year, at age seventeen, he married. All the while, he continued his self-education, attending plays and lectures and feeding his "mental hunger" by studying history, biography, geography, and astronomy. Gompers was getting on in his new home. Within a few years, though, his work would be threatened and his commitment to unions strengthened even further.

Like Powderly, Gompers was to learn about the threat to skilled craft work posed by the spread of machine production after the Civil War. In Gompers's case, it was the introduction in 1869 of a machine that automatically formed the cigar molding, allowing unskilled workers to perform that job. Facing a potential flood of unskilled workers into his craft, Gompers dove into union activities. As he did, he learned lessons that would guide him in his entire life. When the cigarmakers' union unsuccessfully went on strike to protest the introduction of the machinery, Gompers realized that resisting the spread of machine production was useless. When the economy slid into a depression in the

---

[*]*Craft union:* A union whose members practice a particular craft. Craft unions are thus organized by skill rather than industry.

1870s, he learned even more lessons. First, striking in hard times was futile. Employers could always hire replacements from the ranks of the unemployed. Far better, he concluded, to embrace the fight for an eight–hour day so that available work could be spread among more workers. He also saw how hard times stimulated a myriad of protest groups, from socialists and anarchists to Greenbackers[*] and prohibitionists, each with its own panacea for labor's ills. Witnessing a brutal police assault on one gaggle of protesters in New York in 1874, Gompers realized that the labor movement had to separate itself from agitators who peddled pie-in-the-sky nostrums or frightened powerful interests in society. In particular, he developed a deep animosity toward radicals, whose protests promised only to bring down on workers the wrath of the establishment. Most of the people peddling utopian schemes to improve society, he concluded, were not workers, and "entangling alliances" with them were to be avoided.

In the 1870s, Gompers also met two men, Adolph Strasser and Karl Ferdinand Laurrell, who helped him develop an approach to building a powerful union. He met Strasser in the cigarmakers' union and Laurrell in the shop where they worked. Both men, like Gompers, were European immigrants, and both were refugees: Strasser from socialist politics and Laurrell from a Marxist[*] labor organization. The two were tired of the endless philosophical debates of socialists and Marxists and impressed on Gompers the need for a pragmatic, concrete plan for elevating the condition of workers through unions. By the end of the 1870s, the plan had taken shape. Later labeled "business unionism," Gompers's plan envisioned a federation of semi-independent national unions organized by their trades. Because these unions, like the cigarmakers, were organized along craft lines, their members would be largely skilled workers. They would pay high union dues because employers facing a union with a fat strike fund would be more likely to negotiate. Their goals would be achieved without the inclusion of political parties—an approach Gompers later called "pure and simple" unionism. And those goals would be "immediate" and "practical" improvements: more wages, fewer hours, and better job conditions. [See Source 3.] Here was a formula that accepted the existing order of things: industrialism, big corporations, and even capitalism. It was also an easier one, in turn, for the political and economic powers to accept.

Gompers's approach fit the times. In the 1870s, capital poured into machinery and factories. Manufacturing output soared, but so did the threat to jobs of skilled craft workers. As Terence Powderly learned, that threat would be a big spur to trade union activity. While Powderly joined and eventually rose to the top of the Knights of Labor, Gompers began to chart a different course. First, while retaining membership in the existing cigarmakers' local, he formed a new union that he, Strasser, and Laurrell dominated. Gompers had committed a cardinal sin in the labor movement: dual unionism—creating a union in a trade where one already existed. Gompers's union, however, would take all cigarmakers, skilled and unskilled. For Gompers, it made no sense to exclude certain workers in a trade. In his mind, the dual union sin was justified by the end—building a viable union in the face of mechanization. In short order, Gompers's local gained recognition by the Cigarmakers' International Union. By 1877, he and Strasser, his lifelong confidant, had effectively gained control of the

---

[*]*Greenbackers:* Supporters of the Greenback Party, organized in 1877. Greenbackers called for expansion of the money supply, immigration restrictions, and legislation limiting the hours of labor.

[*]*Marxist:* The philosophy advanced by Karl Marx in the nineteenth century. It called for the abolition of capitalism and private property.

entire union. Gompers persuaded the union's other locals to embrace his "business union" strategy, in part by getting the national union to pool funds that any local could draw from in time of need. Within a few years, he was ready to reach out with his "business union" approach to other trades besides cigarmaking. When representatives of 31 trade unions gathered in Pittsburgh in 1881, Gompers gained control of the meeting and emerged as the vice president of the new labor organization that arose from it, the Federation of Organized Trades and Labor Unions.

For the next five years, the determined Gompers fought off socialists in the Federation of Trades and those who sought political solutions for labor's ills, such as those proposed by the Greenback Party. Though possessed of enormous political skills, he remained convinced for years that turning to politics involved "dabbling in that cesspool of corruption commonly known as party politics." To Gompers, socialists in the labor movement were an even bigger threat, for their course was suicide. With angry disdain, he bared his knuckles to minimize their influence, even overriding democratic union procedures if need be. As he put it later, "The trade union is not a Sunday School."

In the 1880s, however, Gompers faced an even more formidable enemy in the Knights of Labor. At first, Gompers watched this rival suspiciously. Then, when the Knights invaded his home turf, his suspicions blossomed into open hostility. Not content to annex existing unions, the Knights began to commit the sin of duel unionism, just as Gompers had years before. When the Knights did so in Gompers's own cigarmaking trade, he responded ruthlessly. When cigarmakers who had joined the Knights went on strike, for instance, his local supplied strikebreakers. Powderly charged Gompers's union with treachery and declared that he had "never had the pleasure of meeting with Mr. Gompers when he was sober." By 1886, though, the Knights had been driven out of the cigar trade. And in Gompers's mind, Powderly's union had come to represent a threat to his work, his ambitions, and the entire trade union movement. Soon, he would launch an all-out campaign to undermine it.

"FLOATING LIKE A SCUM"

By the time Gompers set his sights on Powderly, millions of workers toiled for long hours and low wages in factories, mines, and mills. Taking virtually all comers, the Knights held out to workers a compelling vision of a future in which they could once again be their own bosses. To workers suffering from poor conditions and a loss of independence, it seemed an alluring antidote to spreading machine production and rising corporate power. The Knights drew members, moreover, using familiar language from the past: that virtuous "producers" must restrain the non-producers arrayed against them.

The appeal of the Knights soared higher after it pulled off a dramatic victory over one of the most notorious businessmen of the era. In 1886, when financier and railroad operator Jay Gould cut wages on his Wabash line during an economic downturn, the Knights responded with a strike against the Wabash. Gould countered by locking out the Wabash workers, but the Knights then threatened to launch a strike against Gould's other railroads. The action would have a crippling impact similar to the Great Railroad Strike of 1877. Involving thousands of workers, the strike of 1877 resulted in the deaths of nearly one hundred people and the shutdown of two-thirds of the nation's rail system. Realizing the danger, Gould agreed to meet with Powderly. The result was shocking: the bare-knuckled Gould capitulated. Rather than face a strike, he backed down and reinstated locked-out employees. Workers across the country rejoined over "Brother Powderly's" great victory. In less than a year, about six hundred thousand more workers flocked to join the Knights of Labor. With roughly three-quarters of a million members, the Knights had suddenly emerged as the nation's biggest union by 1886 and Powderly as its most important labor leader.

Within months, however, the Knights would be slammed by a dramatic turn of events. One of them involved Jay Gould, who quickly began to fire members of the Knights on a railroad line serving the Southwest. The Knights responded by demanding that he hire back the discharged men and pay unskilled workers at least $1.50 a day or face a strike. But, Powderly knew that the union was nearly broke and could not afford to pay strike benefits if a major walkout occurred. Though praised for his stunning victory over Gould, Powderly opposed further action against Gould's line. The union's local leadership, however, overrode Powderly's objections and ordered another strike after Gould rejected the Knights' demands. Powderly was forced to go along with the action. This time, though, it turned out differently. The strike quickly disintegrated into widespread violence and chaos as enraged Knights destroyed railroad property worth hundreds of thousands of dollars. Meanwhile, the entire Southwest had slipped into commercial paralysis and a frightened public began to turn against the strikers. In early May, as Powderly's rivals within the Knights seized the opportunity to attack Powderly for weak leadership and lack of support, the union capitulated to Gould, calling off the strike.

A second blow fell in Chicago the day after the Knights ended their strike against Gould. In response to a strike at the McCormick reaper works, one of the city's biggest employers, management had called on strikebreakers and police to protect them. When strikers attacked a group of strikebreakers outside the plant, police attacked the strikers, killing or wounding six of them. Unions, including the Knights, called for a protest rally the following evening at Haymarket Square. That protest also spun out of control. When police arrived to break up the crowd, a bomb exploded, killing seven policemen. Although the bomb throwers were never positively identified, the Haymarket bombing brought the trial and conviction of eight anarchists. No officer of the Knights had spoken at the Haymarket gathering, but many Americans' fears about organized labor had been confirmed. As the nation's biggest union, the Knights were associated in many Americans' minds with murder and violence.

Meanwhile, with organized labor reeling after the Haymarket bombing, Gompers was feeling the heat as well. Besieged by the Knights's duel union tactics and public hostility, he launched his own offensive. First, at a national trade union conference a couple of weeks after the bombing, he accused Knights of selling out workers. Too many of its leaders, he charged, were not even workers, but people "floating like a scum on the top of a part of the labor movement." The Knights, he demanded, should withdraw from the labor movement to engage in educational and reform activity. Powderly angrily rejected the demand and, in turn, accused Gompers of his allies of losing their heads to "an excess ... of intoxicants." Determined to do battle with the Knights, Gompers then moved to replace the Federation of Trades with a tighter, more disciplined organization. The AF of L would be, as he put it, "more than a paper organization." Formed out of the Federation of Trades later in 1886 with Gompers as its president, the AF of L girded for battle with Powderly's Knights.

Neither Powderly nor Gompers realized it, but the Knights had already passed the peak of its power. For the next several years, though, Gompers was unsparing in his efforts to destroy the union's influence. Those efforts included limiting the Knights's role in such labor gatherings as the Workingman's Assembly of New York State, where in 1887 Gompers faced down the angry gun-wielding member of the Knights and, after order was restored to the gathering, effectively wrestled control of the body from members of Powderly's union. Gompers's battle with the Knights in various trades lasted for another decade, but his opponent was already crippled. After the disastrous battle with Gould and the Haymarket bombing, hundreds of thousands of disillusioned members fled the Knights. By the early 1890s, local and regional Knights organizations carried out strikes and violent attacks in open defiance of Powderly's orders. In 1893, he was forced to resign, and the following year, he was expelled from the order. By then, the union's ranks had fallen to fewer than one hundred thousand members. In 1894, representatives of the Knights proposed a plan for united action with the AF of L and other organizations, but Gompers knew he could stand his ground. Unyielding in his insistence that trade unions had to operate "unmolested" by "obstructionists," he rebuffed the dwindling Knights, who would soon be virtually absorbed by the Populist movement of the 1890s.

"PRACTICALLY EVERY MAN WORE A SILK HAT"

In the end, Jay Gould and the Haymarket bombing probably did more to destroy Powderly's dream of "one big union" than did Gompers's attacks. Powderly's own vision for labor played a big role, too. Millions of workers in the late nineteenth century labored under wretched conditions for abysmal wages. As alluring as was Powderly's dream of reforming society so workers could rise into the owner ranks or control the means of production, it had little to do with millions of employees in an age of gigantic enterprise. Meanwhile, most workers' strikes had to do with concrete gains regarding hours, wages, and working conditions. Achieving the Knights' reform goals through politics, moreover, would have required the organization of the entire labor force. Workers, though, were divided in so many ways—skill level, race, ethnicity, religion, and gender—and the romantic Powderly never understood how difficult unity would be. Indeed, his later career reflected how removed he became from the concerns of most workers. After his ouster from the Knights, he returned to politics, studied law, and became an attorney. Later, he took up the cause of high tariffs because he believed that protection from foreign imports benefited workers. He even joined the protariff and probusiness Republican Party. In fact, before he died in 1924, he received numerous appointments to federal positions, mostly at the hands of Republicans.

For his part, Gompers never forgot or forgave Powderly's attacks on him. He denounced President William McKinley's appointment of Powderly as Superintendent of Immigration in 1897 as an insult to the labor movement. When Powderly sought an appointment from President Theodore Roosevelt in the Department of Commerce six years later, he wrote to Gompers to have him put in a good word about him to the president. "Were the situations reversed," Powderly told him, "I would do it for you." Gompers never said anything.

With the Knights virtually gone by 1900, Gompers's union stood as the nation's largest and most powerful. Impressively, its membership numbered more than one million workers. With ranks filled mostly with skilled craft workers, it had skimmed the cream off the American labor force. Its members were almost exclusively white and male and overwhelmingly native born. In fact, neither African Americans nor female workers were welcome. **[See Source 4.]** The AF of L had also organized workers in trades that were less affected by factory production. As machine production spread in the late nineteenth century, more and more workers were unskilled and often immigrants, but Gompers's "business union" plan never did anything to help them.

The AF of L had triumphed by 1900, but more than 90 percent of the nation's workers remained outside unions. Facing long hours and low pay, their situation was bleak. **[See Source 5.]** Making matters worse, they often labored anonymously as unskilled workers in industries run by managers working for distant owners. For such managers and owners, control was everything. Gompers's union had organized workers in trades dominated by owner-managers. Those proprietors often knew many of their workers personally and, as owners, viewed union demands as a matter of cost, not power. The same turmoil at the McCormick reaper works in 1886 that helped lead to the Knights' demise, in fact, illustrated labor's bleak future under the new industrial regime. The McCormick works were part of an enormous industrial combine called International Harvester, a trust* formed by the merger of several farm-equipment manufacturers. Its factories were managed not by proprietors, but by managers who saw unions as a direct challenge to their right to run the company as they saw fit. In their minds, here was an issue more basic than money: the right of control inherent in private property. As in other labor disputes, these managers had powerful weapons at their disposal. They could simply fire and replace unskilled strikers. They could also rely on the government for police and militia support. Finally, they could turn to the courts, which repeatedly upheld the rights associated with corporate property in the late nineteenth century.

Judged narrowly, Gompers's union succeeded. Unlike Powderly's Knights, it survived and, in fact, in altered form survives to this day. In the meantime, it won for its members more pay, shorter hours, and better conditions. With his belief in upward mobility and pride in fulfilling his childhood dream of home ownership, Gompers made it possible for millions of its members to elevate their living standards and enjoy middle-class amenities. As did no other by early twentieth century, Gompers's union brought labor into the American mainstream. Never ceasing to enjoy hobnobbing with industrialists and presidents, he also brought its leaders into the establishment. In fact, the aspirations of Gompers and the labor elite that he represented were nicely captured by one observer at a meeting between Gompers and other trade union leaders in the 1880s. "Practically every man," he noted, "wore a silk hat."

Considered more broadly, though, Gompers's union failed. Forged in battle with socialists and the Knights, the AF of L was unprepared for the new age of management and mechanization. Gompers never took his union into the industrial future—to the millions of workers outside the small shops and craft industries. Until he died in 1924, he remained atop the AF of L. In later years, though, Gompers's early determination to organize all American workers gave way to the goal of protecting his craft unions and his own position in the union. Later in the twentieth century, more militant labor organizations would lead the often violent and bloody fights to unionize the mass of unskilled wage earners in industries such as steel, automobiles, and rubber. With the backing of the federal government during the New Deal, other labor leaders spearheaded these drives with industrial unions, which organized workers along industry rather than craft lines. In doing so, they defied Gompers's successors in the AF of L. In coming decades,

---

Trust: A combination of several firms in a single industry for the purpose of limiting or ending competition and cut-throat price cutting.

though, their unions would bring their members higher wages, shorter hours, and better conditions. In other words, they succeeded in bringing Gompers's goal of "more, more, here and now" to millions of workers so long ignored by his union.

• PRIMARY SOURCES •

Source 1:   Terence Powderly, *Preamble to the Constitution of the Knights of Labor* (1878)

The Knights of Labor was formed as a secret society in 1869, but Terence Powderly turned the organization into an open trade union. In 1878, he helped write a new constitution for the Knights. This excerpt is the preamble to that constitution. What issues does it address? How do the Knights propose to improve the condition of workers?

The recent alarming development and aggression of aggregated wealth which, unless checked, will invariably lead to the pauperization and hopeless degradation of the toiling masses, render it imperative, if we desire to enjoy the blessings of life, that a check should be placed upon its power and upon unjust accumulation, and a system adopted which will secure to the laborer the fruits of his toil, and as this much-desired object can only be accomplished by the thorough unification of labor, and the united efforts of those who obey the divine injunction that "in the sweat of thy brow shalt thou eat bread," we have formed the [Knights of Labor] with a view of securing the organization and direction, by cooperative effort, of the power of the industrial classes, and we submit to the world the object sought to be accomplished by our organization, calling upon all who believe in securing "the greatest good to the greatest number" to aid and assist us:

    I.   To bring within the folds of organization every department of productive industry, making knowledge a standpoint for action, and industrial and moral worth, not wealth, the true standard of individual and national greatness.

    II.   To secure to the toilers a proper share of the wealth that they create, more of the leisure that rightfully belongs to them, more societary advantages, more of the benefits, privileges, and emoluments of the world, in a word, all those rights and privileges necessary to make them capable of enjoying, appreciating, defending, and perpetuating the blessings of good government.

    III.   To arrive at the true condition of the producing masses in their educational, moral, and financial condition, by demanding from the various governments the establishment of bureaus of Labor Statistics.

    IV.   The establishment of co-operative institutions, productive and distributive.

    V.   The reserving of the public lands, the heritage of the people, for the actual settler—not another acre for railroads or speculators.

    VI.   The abrogation of all laws that do not bear equally upon capital and labor, the removal of unjust technicalities, delays, and discriminations, in the

SOURCE: From Terence V. Powderly, THIRTY YEARS OF LABOR (Philadelphia, 1890).

administration of justice and the adopting of measures providing for the health and safety of those engaged in mining, manufacturing, or building pursuits.

VII. The enactment of laws to compel chartered corporations to pay their employees weekly, in full, for labor performed during the preceding week, in the lawful money of the country.

VIII. The enactment of laws giving mechanics and laborers a first lien on their work for their full wages.

IX. The abolishment of the contract system of national, state, and municipal work.

X. The substitution of arbitration for strikes, whenever and wherever employers and employees are willing to meet on equitable grounds.

XI. The prohibition of the employment of children in workshops, mines, and factories before attaining their fourteenth year.

XII. To abolish the system of letting out by contract the labor of convicts in our prisons and reformatory institutions.

XIII. To secure for both sexes equal pay for equal work.

XIV. The reduction of the hours of labor to eight per day so that the laborers may have more time for social enjoyment and intellectual improvement, and be enabled to reap the advantages conferred by the labor saving machinery which their brains have created.

XV. To prevail upon governments to establish a purely national circulating medium based upon the faith and resources of the nation, and issued directly to the people, without the intervention of any system of banking corporations, which money shall be a legal tender in payment of all debts, public or private.

Source 2:   *Terence Powderly Calls for Cooperatives* (1880)

In his first annual address to the General Assembly of the Knights of Labor, Terence Powderly discussed the long-range goals of the Knights, including the reform of the "present order of things" through worker-controlled cooperatives. Why were Powderly and many craft workers drawn to the idea of transforming society in this way? Was it realistic?

The wage system, at its inception; was but an experiment, and for a time doubts were entertained as to its adoption; but the avaricious eye of the Shylock of labor saw in it a weapon with which he could control the toiler, and today that system has so firm a hold upon us that every attempt at shaking off the fetters, by resorting to a strike, only makes it easier for the master to say to his slave, *You must work for lower wages.*

We must teach our members, then, that the remedy for the redress of the wrongs we complain of does not lie in the suicidal strike; but in thorough, effective organization. Without organization we cannot accomplish anything; through it we hope to forever banish that curse of modern civilization—wage slavery.

SOURCE: Terence V. Powderly, THE PATH I TROD: THE AUTOBIOGRAPHY OF TERENCE V. POWDERLY (1940 reprint, New York: AMS Press, 1968).

But how? Surely not by forming an association and remaining a member; not by getting every other worthy man to become a member and remain one; not by paying the dues required of us as they fall due. These are all important factors in the method by which we hope to regain our independence, and are vitally important; they are the elements necessary to complete organization.

Organization once perfected, what must we do? I answer, study the best means of putting your organization to some practicable use by embarking in a system of which will eventually make every man his own master—every man his own employer; a system which will give the laborer a fair proportion of the products of his toil. It is to coopera- tion, then, as the lever of labor's emancipation, that the eyes of the workingmen and women of the world should be directed, upon cooperation their hopes should be cen- tered, and to it do I now direct your attention. I am deeply sensible of the importance, of the magnitude, of the undertaking in which I invite you to engage. I know that it is human nature to grow cold, apathetic, and finally indifferent when engaged in that which requires deep study and persistent effort, unattended by excitement; men are apt to believe that physical force is the better way of redressing grievances, being the shorter remedy; but even that requires patience and fortitude as well as strength…. The laboring man needs education in this great social question, and the best minds of the Order must give their precious thought to this system. There is no good reason why labor cannot, through cooperation, own and operate mines, factories, and railroads.

Source 3:   *Samuel Gompers on Trade Unions* (1898)

In these excerpts from his Annual Reports to the American Federation of Labor Conventions in 1890 and 1898, Samuel Gompers reminds delegates of his organization's goals. How does he define them? What does he say about workers unhappy with the progress of the labor movement?

There are those who, failing to comprehend the economic, political and social tendencies of the trade union movement, regard it as entirely "too slow," "too conservative," and desire to hurl it headlong into a path which, while struggling and hoping for the end, will leave us stranded and losing the practical and beneficial results of our efforts. I main- tain that the working people are in too great a need of immediate improvements in their condition to allow them to forego them in the endeavor to devote their entire energies to an idealistic end however beautiful to contemplate. I maintain further, that the achievement of present practical improvements for the toilers places them on so much vantage ground gained and renders them more capable to deal with the various problems it is their mission to solve. In the language of that foremost of economic and social thin- kers, Ira Steward, "The way out of the wage system is through higher wages, resultant only from shorter hours…."

It has been charged that I am trying to drive the socialists out of the movement, that I am intolerant of others' opinions. I desire to take this opportunity of saying that I have ever held that the trade unions are broad enough and liberal enough to admit of any and all shades of thought upon the economic and social question; but at the same time the

SOURCE: Samuel Gompers, LABOR AND THE COMMON WELFARE (Freeport, New York: Books for Libraries Press, 1969, originally published in 1919), pp. 2–3, 6–9.

conviction is deeply rooted in me that in the trade union movement the first condition requisite is good-standing membership in a trade union, regardless of to which party a man might belong.

Those who have had any experience in the labor movement will admit the great work and forbearance, tact and judgment requisite to maintain harmony in organization. The trade unions are no exception to this rule. In the trade union movement I have ever endeavored to attain that much-desired end, and recognize that that in itself is of a sufficiently important nature and requirement as to preclude the possibility of jointly acting with organizations based upon different practical workings or policy.

I am willing to subordinate my opinions to the well being, harmony and success of the labor movement; I am willing to sacrifice myself also in the furtherance of any action it may take for its advancement; I am willing to step aside if that will promote our cause, but I cannot and will not prove false to my convictions that the trade unions pure and simple are the natural organizations of the wage-workers to secure their present material and practical improvement and to achieve their final emancipation....

The trade unions are the legitimate outgrowth of modern societary and industrial conditions. They are not the creation of any man's brain. They are organizations of necessity. They were born of the necessity of the workers to protect and defend themselves from encroachment, injustice, and wrong. They are the organizations of the working class, for the working class, by the working class; grappling with economic and social problems as they arise, dealing with them in a practical manner to the end that a solution commensurate with the interests of all may be attained.

From hand labor in the home to machine and factory labor witnessed the transition from the trade guilds to the trade unions; with the concentration of wealth and the development of industry, the growth from the local to the national and the international unions, and the closer affiliation of all in a broad and comprehensive federation.

There are some who, dissatisfied with what they term the slow progress of the labor movement, would have us hasten it by what they lead themselves to believe is a shorter route. No intelligent workman who has passed years of his life in the study of the labor problem, expects to wake up any fine morning to find the hopes of these years realized over night, and the world on the flood-tide of the millennium. With the knowledge that the past tells us of the slow progress of the ages, of trial and travail, mistakes and doubts yet unsolved; with the history of the working class bedewed with the tears of a thousand generations and tinged with the life-blood of numberless martyrs, the trade unionist is not likely to stake his future hopes on the fond chance of the many millions turning philosophers in the twinkling of an eye.

Much of our misery as enforced wage-workers springs, not so much from any power exerted by the "upper" or ruling class, as it is the result of the ignorance of so many in our own class who accept conditions by their own volition. The more intelligent, realizing their inability to *create* a millennium, will not descend to trickery or juggling with terms. They seek to benefit themselves and their fellow men through trade unions and trade union action, and, by bearing the brunt, be in the vanguard in the cause, and hasten on the process of education that will fit humanity even to recognize the millennium when it arrives.

The trade unions not only discuss economics and social problems, but deal with them in a practical fashion calculated to bring about better conditions of life today, and thus fit the workers for the greater struggles for amelioration and emancipation yet to come.

No one having any conception of the labor problems—the struggles of life—would for a moment entertain the notion, much less advise the workers, to abstain from the exercise of their political rights and their political power. On the contrary, trade union action upon the surface is economic action, yet there is no act which the trade unions can take but which in its effect is political.

But, in the exercise of the political power of the workers, that is, the casting of the ballot, we are sometimes urged to throw to the winds the experience and the tangible results of ages, and to hazard the interests of labor in a new era of political partisanship....

Our movement is of the wage-earning class, recognizing that class interests, that class advancement, that class progress is best made by working class trade union action....

The toilers of our country look to you to devise the ways and means by which a more thorough organization of the wage-earners may be accomplished, and to save our children in their infancy from being forced into the maelstrom of wage slavery. Let us see to it that they are not dwarfed in body and mind, or brought to a premature death by early drudgery; give them the sunshine of the school-room and playground, instead of the factory and the workshop. To protect the workers in their inalienable rights to a higher and better life; to protect them, not only as equals before the law but also in their rights to the product of their labor; to protect their lives, their limbs, their health, their homes, their firesides, their liberties as men, as workers, and as citizens; to overcome and conquer prejudice and antagonism; to secure to them the right to life, and the opportunity to maintain that life; the right to be full sharers in the abundance which is the result of their brain and brawn, and the civilization of which they are the founders and the mainstay; to this the workers are entitled beyond the cavil of a doubt. With nothing less ought they, or will they, be satisfied. The attainment of these is the glorious mission of the trade unions. No higher or nobler mission ever fell to the lot of a people than that committed to the working class—a class of which we have the honor to be members.

Source 4:   *Samuel Gompers on Female Workers* (1906)

By the turn of the twentieth century, roughly five million women were employed full time. In this piece from a trade union publication, Samuel Gompers discusses the impact of women working outside the home. What harmful effects does he see in such work? How do you think Powderly would have argued against him?

In undertaking to answer the question as to whether the wife should help to support the family, I take it that what is meant is the wife of a mechanic, a laborer, a workman, not the well-to-do or the fairly well-to-do, for among the latter there is not even the false pretense of necessity. Taking, then, my conception of what is implied by the question, I have no hesitancy in answering, positively and absolutely, "No." I take it, also, that the inference from the question is that the help which is implied is the help which finds its expression in work for wages, and to that, with added emphasis, I again answer, "No."

Modern industrial conditions have made it decidedly uneconomical for any great amount of work to be done other than in factories, workshops, or other industrial plants, where steam and electric power are used and the best and most highly developed machinery is employed; in which labor in its different branches is so divided, subdivided, and specialized that each worker performs a very small part of the complete product.

SOURCE: Samuel Gompers, "Should the Wife Help to Support the Family," THE LEATHER WORKERS' JOURNAL VIII, No. 9 (May 1906).

The workers in each case are dependent, and wait upon those employed in the preceding branch, so that it requires constant application, immediate attention, and the close proximity of all. This requires that the workers must generally begin and close the day's work together. It therefore necessarily requires the worker to leave home early in the morning, absent himself or herself from the home during the working hours and the time necessary to go to and from the place of employment. Imagine the wife leaving her home and children unprotected and uncared for during the working hours, which among women generally, by reason of their comparative lack of organization, are much longer than the day's work of men.

In some of the factory towns I have seen—and it can easily be seen even now— wifes [sic] and mothers have taken their nursing babes with them to the factory and mill, with all the humdrum of machinery, and in their highly nervous state undertaken to nurse their babes. A friend informed me that recently a woman, hiding from the foreman, let herself down on a rear elevator, that she might rush home and see the children, whom she had left ill in the morning. Who can tell the awful agony a mother endures from the uncertainty of her unprotected, uncared-for children?

Nor do I wish to be understood to be opposed to the full and free opportunity of woman to work whenever and wherever necessity requires. It has been the policy of my associates and myself to throw open wide the doors of our organizations and invite the working girls and working women to membership for their and our common protection. It is in the unions of labor that the full rights of the working women are proclaimed and asserted, defended and contended for; and many a contest has been waged by union men to secure for women equal wages and conditions for equal work performed.

It is not for any real preference for their labor that the unscrupulous employer gives work to girls and boys and women, but because of his guilty knowledge that he can easily compel them to work longer hours and at a lower wage than men. It is the so-called competition of the unorganized, defenseless woman worker, the girl and the wife, that often tends to reduce the wages of the fathers and husband, so that frequently in after years, particularly in factory towns, the combined wages of the husband and wife, the father and daughter, have been reduced to the standard of the wages earned by the father or husband in the beginning.

I contend that the wife or mother, attending to the duties of the home, makes the greatest contribution to the support of the family. The honor, glory, and happiness that come from a beloved wife and the holiness of motherhood are a contribution to the support and future welfare of the family that our common humanity does not yet fully appreciate.

It is with keen gratification that observers have noticed in recent years that the wife of the wage-earner, where the husband has been a fair breadwinner for the family, has taken up beautiful needlework, embroidery, and the cultivation of her better, but heretofore latent, talents.

There is no reason why all the opportunities for the development of the best that woman can do should be denied her, either in the home or elsewhere. I entertain no doubt but that from the constant better opportunity resultant from the larger earning power of the husband the wife will, apart from performing her natural household duties, perform that work which is most pleasurable for her, contributing to the beautifying of her home and surroundings.

In our time, and at least in our country, generally speaking, there is no necessity for the wife contributing to the support of the family by working—that is, working as here understood, by wage labor. In our country, rich and fertile as any in the world, producing wealth in such prodigious proportions, the wife as a wage-earner is a disadvantage economically considered, and socially is unnecessary.—By Samuel Gompers.

Source 5:   *An Investigator Reports on Steel Workers* (1910)

John A. Fitch's The Steel Workers *was part of a multivolume sociological study of the conditions in Pittsburgh, Pennsylvania, published in 1910. Fitch's volume examined conditions in the steel industry there. The following tables from that study present statistical evidence regarding those conditions in the years immediately after the collapse of the Homestead Strike at the Carnegie Company's massive iron and steel complex. The failure of that strike helped set back the unionization of industrial workers in the steel and other "heavy" industries in the United States for decades. What do these tables reveal about the post-strike working conditions in the steel industry? What light do they shed on Gompers's interest in organizing skilled craft workers rather than steel and other industrial workers?*

TABLE 3.1   195 Fatalities in Steel Plants of The Pittsburgh District, July 1, 1906–June 30, 1907.—By Causes

Cause	Number of Fatalities
Hot metal explosions.	22
Asphyxiation by furnace gas.	5
Operation of rolls.	<u>10</u>
Total.	37 (19 per cent)
Operation of broad gauge railroad.	18
" " narrow gauge railroad	13
" " cranes.	<u>42</u>
Total.	73 (37 per cent)
Falling from height or into pit.	24
Electric shock.	7
Loading and piling of steel and iron products	<u>8</u>
Total.	39 (20 per cent)
Due to miscellaneous causes.	<u>46</u> (24 per cent)
Total number killed in steel making.	195

57%

SOURCE: John A. Fitch, THE STEEL WORKERS (New York: Charities Publication Committee, 15 pp. 64, 156, 171, 196).

TABLE 3.2   Showing Reduction in Daily Earnings and in Labor Cost For Certain Positions on Plate Mills at Homestead, 1892–1907

Position	Average Daily Earnings per Position					Labor Cost per Position in 24 Hours				
	May 1892, 119-inch Mill (8 Hours)	1907, 84-inch Mill (12 Hours)	Per cent of Decline, 1892-1907	Oct. 1, 1907, 128-inch Mill (12 Hours)	Per cent of Decline, 1892–1907	May 1892, 119-inch Mill, 3 Crews	1907, 84-inch Mill, 2 Crews	Per cent of Decline, 1892–1907	Oct. 1, 1907, 128-inch Mill, 2 Crews	Per cent of Decline, 1892–1907
Roller . . .	$11.84	$9.90	16.39	$8.44	28.72	$35.52	$19.80	44.26	$16.88	52.48
Screwdown .	8.74	7.39	15.45	....	....	25.22	14.78	41.40	....	....
Heater. . .	8.16	7.72	5.39	7.21	11.64	24.48	15.44	36.93	14.42	41.09
Heater's helpers	5.80	4.50	22.41	4.09	29.48	17.40	9.00	48.28	8.18	52.99
Tableman. .	7.75	5.91	23.74	....	....	23.25	11.82	49.16	....	....
First shearman	9.49	....	....	5.58	41.20	28.47	....	....	11.16	60.80

TABLE 3.3   Working Day of Employees in a Steel Mill, October, 1907—By Length of Working Day

Duration of Working Day	Number of Employees	Per cent in Each Group
Eight hours	9	0.24
Ten hours	721	19.31
Eleven hours	68	1.82
Twelve hours.	2,935	78.63
Total	3,733	100.00

TABLE 3.4   Compensation Paid By Employers to Dependents of 168 Married Men Killed in Work-Accidents in Allegheny County, July 1, 1906 to June 30, 1907

Name of Employees	Nothing	$100 or less of funeral expenses	$101– $500	$501– $1000	$1001– $2000	$2001– $3000	Unknown	Total
American Steel and Wire Co. .	..	..	4	1	..	..	..	5
National Tube Co. .		6	3	1	1	..	2	13
Carnegie Steel Co. .	10	17	8	3	2	2	..	42
Jones & Laughlin Steel Co. .	7	10	4	3	2	2	..	28
Pressed Steel Car Co. . . .	3	3	3	..	..	..	1	10
Other Companies	30	23	14	1	..	..	2	70
Total. . .	50	59	36	9	5	4	5	168

QUESTIONS TO CONSIDER

1. How would you compare the approaches of Terence Powderly and Samuel Gompers to solving the problems facing workers in the late nineteenth century? What were the strengths and weaknesses of each?

2. Although Powderly's and Gompers's roots were in skilled crafts, these two men thought very differently about how to protect skilled workers in the late nineteenth century. How do you account for the difference? What experiences, factors, or ideas

most influenced Powderly's and Gompers's views about the organization of workers into unions?

3. How do you account for the fact that the Knights of Labor, unlike the American Federation of Labor, failed to survive? What did Powderly's and Gompers's strategies have to do with the failure of one union and the success of the other? Was one more realistic? How so?

4. What do the lives of Powderly and Gompers as well as the primary sources in this chapter reveal about the conditions confronting labor in the late nineteenth century? What do they reveal about the obstacles confronting unions?

FOR FURTHER READING

Ilene A. DeVault, *United Apart: Gender and the Rise of Craft Unionism* (Ithaca: Cornell University Press, 2004), provides a recent study showing how craft unions dealt with female workers in the years marked by the triumph of the American Federation of Labor over the Knights of Labor.

Harold C. Livesay, *Samuel Gompers and Organized Labor in America* (Boston: Little, Brown and Company, 1978), offers a short, highly readable account of Gompers's life and influence in the labor movement.

David Montgomery, *The Fall of the House of Labor: The Workplace, the State, and American Labor Activism, 1865–1925* (New York: Cambridge University Press, 1987), details the changing fortunes of organized labor in the late nineteenth and early twentieth centuries.

Craig Phelan, *Grand Master Workman: Terence Powderly and the Knights of Labor* (Westport, CT: Greenwood Press, 2000), offers a recent and well-researched biography of Powderly.

Jonathan Rees, *Industrialization and the Transformation of American Life: A Brief Introduction* (Armonk, NY: M.E. Sharpe, Inc., 2013), provides a brief survey of the impact of industrial growth on American society, including labor, in the late nineteenth and early twentieth centuries.

4

Monopoly, Money, and Power in Progressive America: John D. Rockefeller and Ida Tarbell

Ida Tarbell was nervous as she slipped into the pew at Cleveland's Euclid Avenue Baptist Church. The young magazine writer had been on the trail of Standard Oil's John D. Rockefeller for some time, digging into his life and the gigantic web of companies that operated under the Standard name. She had already published several of her scathing articles on Rockefeller and Standard. Yet Tarbell had never seen the man. Anxious about public exposure, Rockefeller rarely mingled in crowds, except in church. Now in the fall of 1903, Tarbell had learned that he was scheduled to give a talk at his Ohio church. She knew that Pinkerton detectives accompanied him to such appearances and she assumed that some of them were scattered in the Sunday crowd. She also knew that this might be her only opportunity to see the man she had vilified in print as ruthless, greedy, and predatory.

Tarbell's anxiety was understandable. Rockefeller was one of the most hated and feared men of his day, and Tarbell shared that fear and loathing. Her father had been ruined by Standard and cautioned her not to probe into Rockefeller's personal life or his company's history, suggesting that Standard might retaliate by having her maimed or possibly murdered. "Don't do it, Ida," he warned. For the determined Tarbell, however, the work was personal. Armed only with a pen, she had taken up a fight with one of the richest and most powerful men in the world. Now as she looked around the packed Sunday school room, she was afraid that Rockefeller would spot her—the woman he derisively called "Miss Tarbarrel."

As Rockefeller entered the room, Tarbell's research assistant jabbed her ribs and whispered, "There he is." Tarbell was struck by his appearance. His voice was strong, but he was bald and had "an awful age in his face." Later during the Sunday service

John D. Rockefeller   Ida Tarbell

she continued to spy on the sixty-four-year-old oil baron. She noticed that he fidgeted in his seat and constantly looked around the room. Rockefeller, she later concluded, was on the lookout for assassins. Suddenly, she felt sorry for him. For all his power, Tarbell thought, he was afraid. The lesson she drew for her readers was clear. No matter how powerful he might be, this man she regarded as evil was unable to escape a guilty conscience and enjoy his own wealth.

It was a satisfying story line. Yet it may not have explained much about Rockefeller's behavior at all. In fact, the oil millionaire routinely handed out envelopes with cash to needy congregants in his church. It was just as likely, as one biographer concluded, that he continually glanced around at the crowd to spot that Sunday's worthy recipients. Tarbell's conclusion, though, is instructive. So much written about John D. Rockefeller and Standard Oil was open to competing interpretations. Indeed, few of the business titans of Rockefeller's day would prove as controversial. In the public's mind in the early twentieth century, however, the case against Rockefeller and his creation was virtually closed. Even today, perhaps no company is more closely identified with the misdeeds of the no-holds-barred, buccaneering capitalism of the industrial age than Standard Oil. Few people had more to do with sealing the case against Rockefeller—and also the fate of his gigantic enterprise—than the woman who sat anxiously in the Cleveland church that fall Sunday eager only for a glimpse of him.

"AN ANGEL OF MERCY"

John D. Rockefeller was his own worst enemy. Suspicious of the press, wary of crowds, he spoke sparingly in public. Far more comfortable with numbers than words, he left historians a meager written record. And he professed not to care what people said about him. "You can abuse me, you can strike me," he said early on, "so long as you let me have my own way." As a result, others shaped the public's view of him and, like Tarbell in the Cleveland church pew, assigned their own motives to his actions. Students can understand much about the man and his motives, however, by examining his own past.

Born in 1839 in an upstate New York farming hamlet, Rockefeller was the oldest son of five children. His mother Eliza was a frugal, pious Baptist. His father William could not have been more different. Broad shouldered and quick-witted, "Big Bill," unlike his wife and their neighbors, was not thrifty, hardworking, or steady. He certainly was not pious. Handsome and charming, he was a natural-born con man. Mysteriously disappearing for long stretches, Bill took the road as "Doc" Rockefeller, peddling to gullible rural folk various herbal remedies and potions that he touted as cures for numerous maladies, including cancer. Often he returned with new clothes on his back and a wad of cash in his hand. Only later did it come out that he was a bigamist who, under an assumed name, was living in South Dakota with another woman. Meanwhile, the stoic Eliza and the children endured a threadbare existence. Later in life, Rockefeller reminisced fondly about his childhood. His memories of it were not always accurate, but there is little doubt about its impact on him. From his mother, he absorbed enduring values: piousness, sobriety, steadiness, and an obsession with stability. Not the least, she taught him the value of thrift. "Willful waste," she told her children, "makes woeful want." From his wheeler-dealer father, he learned the value of the dollar and how to drive a hard bargain. When Bill loaned his children money, he charged them the going interest rate and insisted that they respect contracts. He also cheated his sons. "I skin 'em every time I can," he boasted. "I want to make 'em sharp." Without realizing it, of course, his parents had in their own ways prepared John well to succeed in the rough-and-tumble world of late nineteenth-century industry.

Though an unexceptional youngster, Rockefeller exhibited qualities that would later serve him well. He was only an average student, but determined and steady in his work. In 1853, when Rockefeller was fourteen, his father boarded his family on a train bound for Cleveland, where he figured he would be closer to his customers—all of the unsuspecting marks flocking optimistically West. In high school there, John was serious and had few friends, but already cared little what others thought. When not in school, he was drawn to Cleveland's bustling commercial center along the lakefront. Amid the docks and warehouses along Lake Erie, ships came and departed and stevedores and merchants went about their work. Rockefeller often stood alone and watched the hustle and bustle, as if lured by commerce and possibilities it held for making money. One day when a schoolmate asked him what he wanted to be when he grew up, Rockefeller quickly replied, "I want to be worth a hundred thousand dollars, and I'm going to be, too."

Besides commerce and money, Rockefeller was drawn to the Baptist church. His Bible-reading mother took her children to church and encouraged them to place their pennies in the collection plate. Later in life, he credited her influence in encouraging his philanthropy. In fact, Rockefeller never considered that making money and doing

God's work were at odds. He learned in church that God wanted people to earn money and give it away. "I was trained from the beginning to work and save," he wrote late in life. He regarded it as his duty to "get all I could honorably and to give all I could." His religion, in short, was a key to his character. His puritanical attitudes toward alcohol, theater, dancing, and ostentatious excess stemmed from his Baptist upbringing. So did a lifelong inclination toward self-control, self-improvement, and a nearly obsessive concern for making money. It would be easy for Rockefeller to believe all his life that he did God's work seven days a week. As he once declared, "The power to make money is a gift from God."

Whatever its source, he had the gift. After high school and a brief stint at a commercial college to study bookkeeping, he "tramped" the streets for weeks knocking on doors before landing a job as a bookkeeper at a commission firm. Nerve centers in an expanding commercial economy, these firms handled bulk orders for factory and farm products, on which they charged commissions, arranged shipments with railroad and shipping companies, and extended loans. Rockefeller arrived at work every morning at 6:30 to sit hunched over his ledger book, working often by whale oil lamp. It was a perfect position to get a bird's eye view of the way goods moved around the country. He learned that success involved timely purchases and securing preferential treatment from shipping firms, including railroads. At the same time, he impressed his employers with his discipline and close attention to details, especially those involving money. It was how he ordered his own life. His personal ledger book carefully tracked to the penny—his income, expenditures, contributions, and investments. Until 1864, when he married Laura Spelman, the daughter of a successful Cleveland merchant and abolitionist, his only activity outside of work was the local Baptist church. His self-denial, thrift, and careful budgeting would serve him well when he went into business for himself.

After three years, Rockefeller and another clerk pooled their savings to start their own commission firm, Clark and Rockefeller. Their timing was perfect. With the outbreak of the Civil War, war orders poured in and the partners' profits soared. Rockefeller's younger brother, who lied about his age, served in the Union army. Rockefeller, though, never did, explaining later that he wanted to do his part, but had "no one to take my place" at the firm. He profited handsomely from the decision. By the time the partnership dissolved in 1865, he was a well-off young man. Meanwhile, his decision proved fortunate in another way. In 1859, oil had been discovered nearby in western Pennsylvania. From his Ohio perch, Rockefeller observed the brutally competitive drilling business. He saw its boom and bust cycles with shortages giving way to oversupply and falling prices. Refining, he concluded, was a far more stable end of the business. Already small refineries were sprouting up all over Cleveland, turning oil into kerosene and other products. In 1863, Rockefeller entered a partnership with Clark and Samuel Andrews, an acquaintance from his church, to purchase one of them. After the sale of the commission business, he devoted his full attention to this new business. About the same time, he and Andrews bought out Clark. Now in charge, Rockefeller was determined that Cleveland, well positioned with water and rail transportation, would become a major refining center. He was just as determined that he would control the industry.

Rockefeller shrewdly charted the partners' course. Their refinery was already the biggest in Cleveland, but he believed the key to success was expansion. With high volume, secured with large purchases of crude oil, he kept the refinery going full tilt. High output, he knew, meant lower costs, which could be passed on as lower prices to customers that his competitors could not match. At the same time, he sought out trusted associates. He brought his brother (and Civil War veteran) William into the firm and sent him to New York to handle exports. Expansion also required more capital, so Rockefeller decided to incorporate the firm as the Standard Oil Company of Ohio. Finally, from his days in the commission business, he knew that favorable railroad rates were crucial. They could be secured with rebates, under-the-table payments that railroads made to large-volume shippers. For the railroad, rebates attracted valued shippers, while they gave Standard another key cost advantage over competitors. To handle negotiations, he turned to Henry Flagler, another trusted assistant, who skillfully played one railroad line against another to secure rebates on carloads of refined products. To make sure that he could fill all those cars, Rockefeller got dozens of small refiners to sell out to him.

Rockefeller's drive to consolidate refiners revealed his heavy-handed tactics. By 1870, the postwar boom had gone bust and Rockefeller was driven into the arms of the Pennsylvania Railroad, a key link in the oil business. In the face of declining traffic, the railroad, Standard, and several other refiners established a secret dummy firm, the South Improvement Company. Standard and the other refiners received rebates from the railroad and it secured steady business from them. Rockefeller, his brother, and Flagler together held more stock in the dummy firm than anyone else, and Rockefeller cleverly viewed his participation in the scheme as a way to eliminate refiners in Cleveland who were not part of it. One after another, he sat down with the owners and quietly laid out their simple choice: sell out to Standard or go it alone and be crushed with higher shipping costs. To make matters worse, Rockefeller offered Standard stock to leading Cleveland bankers, who would deny loans to the refiners who held out. One by one, the refiners saw the light. In just one month, twenty-three of them threw in with Standard. Rockefeller virtually eliminated competition in Cleveland and controlled a quarter of the nation's refining capacity.

The scheme had less happy consequences for Standard in Pennsylvania's oil regions. When word of the cartel[*] and its members' rebates leaked out, the producers there panicked. Earlier, they had formed their own cartels to prop up oil prices. Fearful that this powerful combination of refiners would now squeeze *them* by paying lower prices for crude oil, they protested with torchlight parades and petitions to the legislature. When the names of Rockefeller and the other schemers came out, the secretive Cleveland refiner and his creation entered the public consciousness. Standard represented something new and dangerous, a devious and destructive "octopus." Meanwhile, Rockefeller was unruffled, even when he was later accused of practically stealing one of the Cleveland refineries from a widow whose husband had owned it. He did what was right, he said later, "between me and my God." He never altered his view. "The conditions were so chaotic and uncertain," he declared, "that most of the refiners were very desirous to get out of the business." **[See Source 1.]**

Even after the Pennsylvania Railroad dissolved the South Improvement Company in the face of public outcry, Rockefeller and Standard came out of the episode in a far stronger position. He was little concerned with the oil region producers. They were too undisciplined to restrain their own production. The area's numerous refiners, who had the advantage of proximity to the oil, were another matter. Going on the offensive, he convinced the largest refiners in Pittsburgh, Philadelphia, and New York to join him, using Standard stock rather than cash as the lure. These mergers were secret, so that the

---

[*]*Cartel:* A combination of independent business created to control prices, production, or marketing.

newly merged firms could continue to buy up rivals in the oil region and elsewhere, the owners unaware that they were actually selling to Standard. When Rockefeller was done, Standard had gobbled up seventy refiners and only it remained. By 1880, it had cornered the market, controlling 95 percent of the nation's refining capacity. Rockefeller would say later that Standard was like "an angel of mercy" to smaller companies. The company had "reached down from the sky and said, 'Get into the ark.'"

He did not rest there. Standard moved to control tank cars, which transported oil and refined products. Then, when pipelines threatened to undermine their role, it sought control of that link, using the same bare-knuckled tactics. It also extended its reach forward to the consumer with aggressive marketing. Standard wagons fanned out on city streets, selling kerosene by the gallon and driving thousands of small distributors out of business. Only after securing control of refining, marketing, and transportation would Standard move into production, aggressively buying one oil lease after another. The company's reach would extend from the oil well to the customer's kerosene lamp. As Standard's operations grew, however, it had become a sprawling, splintered organization difficult to manage. The problem was state incorporation laws, which prohibited corporations from owning property outside the state. Standard pioneered a solution. First, it created a Standard Oil company in each state to control all operations there and then a board of trustees in New York City. Stockholders in the various Standard units around the country exchanged their stock for trust certificates, which paid a handsome dividend. To skirt state laws, the board held these shares "in trust" for the stockholders, but it actually controlled and coordinated all the Standard Oil operations. One of nine trustees, Rockefeller owned nearly half the stock transferred to the board, which he dominated. In 1882, the Standard Oil Trust was born. By 1890, Rockefeller was worth $37 million, only a fraction of the wealth he would come to amass.

"A MORE SUBTLE FORM OF SLAVERY"

Rockefeller struck quickly. By the time he had achieved control of the refining industry it was too late to stop him. Yet he also left many angry people in his wake. One of them was from Hatch Hollow, ramshackle settlement not far from the birthplace of Pennsylvania's oil boom. Born in a log cabin 1857, only two years before the boom started, Ida Tarbell was a child of the oil fields. Her father Franklin and mother Esther scraped by on a small farm, supplementing income from the soil with occasional school teaching and welding work. The work was sometimes unsteady, but not Franklin's self-reliance and spirit of independence. Nor was Esther's determination to learn and to work, despite the restrictions on education and employment facing women in the nineteenth century. Growing up in a Methodist family that encouraged female education, Esther attended a seminary in western New York and a private academy in Pennsylvania. At eighteen, eight years before she married Franklin in 1856, she became a schoolteacher. After their marriage and with Esther pregnant with her first child, the couple looked to the West, as had Rockefeller's father, for greater opportunities. Franklin struck out to buy a farm in Iowa, planning to come back later for his wife. Returning finally in 1859 to retrieve Esther and Ida—born while he was away—the couple's plans suddenly changed. The discovery of oil in Titusville, some forty miles from Hatch Hollow, sparked an oil rush much like those set off by mineral strikes in the West. The Tarbells decided to stay.

Oil would be good to them. Traveling to Titusville, Franklin witnessed oil gushing out of the ground faster than the drillers could contain it. He quickly realized how he could play the boom. Employing his carpentry and welding skills, he would produce barrels and tanks to store the oil. Demand was brisk and within months he employed dozens of men working around the clock. The next year, the family moved to the boomtown of Rouseville, just outside Titusville, to be nearer to the business. The Civil War brought no interruption to the boom. Like Rockefeller, Franklin avoided wartime service by paying for a substitute to take his place so he could tend to his growing business. Meanwhile, the family, including a son born in 1861 and another daughter born two years later, enjoyed more comfortable circumstances. Moving into a bigger house on a hillside, they found refuge from the raucous boomtown atmosphere, the ugly forest of drilling equipment, and the oil stench below. At the same time, Ida found her own refuge. Her parents stressed the importance of education and Ida was an apt pupil. Rouseville lacked a grammar school, so Esther taught her daughter at home. The Tarbell home, unlike most in the oil patch, had books, a piano, and other marks of refinement. There, Ida could read the *New York Tribune*, *Harper's Weekly*, and other publications. A curious, observant child, Tarbell learned quickly. In 1870, Franklin moved the family again, this time into a large home in Titusville that he had built for the family. A village of three hundred people before the boom, the town now had sixty-three thousand residents, railroad connections, an opera house, and schools. There, Ida attended primary and high school, where she developed an interest in geology and biology.

She was also old enough to notice changes in the oil fields. Her father's business had expanded through the previous decade as orders for tanks and barrels poured in from around the area. By the end of the decade, however, large iron tanks produced by bigger and better financed concerns began to replace his wooden ones. Franklin adjusted, moving into oil production by buying and leasing wells. That move, though, put him face-to-face with a far bigger threat—John D. Rockefeller. As Standard Oil was consolidating oil refining, it took aim in 1872 at Pennsylvania's oil region through the South Improvement Company. When word of the scheme to squeeze the small refiners got out, small producers like Franklin Tarbell were also fearful. The South Improvement scheme raised the possibility they would soon have only one buyer for their oil—Standard. In response, thousands of angry oil region residents rallied in the Titusville opera house, where speakers angrily denounced Rockefeller and other conspirators. The protesters vowed that they would not sell to Standard and moved to create a Petroleum Producers' Union. Protests, torchlight rallies, and newspaper attacks against the conspiracy went on for weeks. By the time the South Improvement scheme was dropped and the protests ended, a deep impression had been left on the fourteen-year-old Ida. Like so many other residents of the oil region, she had been suddenly made aware of John D. Rockefeller. Years later, she could recall the "night when my father came home with a grim look on his face" and told how he and other producers had signed a pledge not to sell to the "Cleveland ogre." **[Source 2.]**

Rockefeller remained characteristically unruffled throughout South Improvement protests, but small operators like Ida's father had plenty to be worried about. They could try to counter Standard's power by forming a producers' association, but Rockefeller knew such organizations inevitably fell apart. He called them "ropes of sand" because they had no power to enforce production agreements and members always broke them. Meanwhile, the world of Franklin Tarbell and other independent operators faced an unprecedented threat. In the 1870s, American industries were still dotted with numerous small, competing firms. With roots in a pre–Civil War farm and small-shop economy, this postwar economic landscape nourished longstanding and widely held notions about American society. Free competition was the natural state of things. So too were opportunities to rise up in life through the ownership of productive property. People like Franklin Tarbell who owned these small firms had often worked for someone else before joining the owner class and they prided themselves on their independence. As his daughter Ida later wrote, "Dignity and success lay in being your own master." In such a landscape, it was easy to believe the myth of the self-made man that anyone who had talent and who worked hard had a good chance to achieve independence and respect. In fact, to many Americans, widespread opportunities to succeed in this very way set their nation apart.

In the last decades of the nineteenth century, large-scale corporations tore up that landscape. A small number of firms would come to control industry after industry, eliminate competition, and shatter Americans' dreams of independence. The railroads, the nation's first big business, had never supported thousands of small firms. The oil business, however, was different. Numerous small operators in production, refining, or marketing were, like Ida's father, among the first of the small propertied class to face the harsh reality of industrial consolidation and the ensuing loss of independence. Franklin probably could have thrown in with Standard and done very well. In fact, as Rockefeller was quick to remind audiences, many did. One of Franklin Tarbell's biggest complaints about Standard, though, was the way it turned business owners in the oil region into employees—"mighty prosperous hired men, some of them, but nonetheless taking orders." Even as a girl, Ida could see what this grim realization did to him. She watched his easygoing nature vanish, replaced by a quiet somberness. And she listened to the attacks in the Tarbell home on privilege and, in particular, on Standard.

The changes wrought by Rockefeller's company made Ida aware of a world beyond Titusville. They also fueled her growing determination to participate in it. In 1875, she enrolled at Allegheny College in Meadville, New York, not far from the Tarbell home. Affiliated with the Methodist Church, the college recently moved to accept women and reflected a strong belief in female education. Tarbell planned to study biology, but realized that she had a talent for writing. After graduation, she took up school teaching in a nearby village. Though teaching was one of the few professions open to women, she was unsatisfied and unable to live on the low salary. After two years, at twenty-four, Tarbell quit and returned home feeling like a failure. She was not there long. In 1882, a Methodist minister who edited *The Chautauquan*, the national magazine of the Chautauqua Assembly, visited her parents' home and offered Ida a job as an editor's assistant. Founded in 1874, the Chautauqua movement provided opportunities for religious instruction outside the church and continued learning beyond high school. That summer, it conducted its first educational gathering on the shores of Chautauqua Lake. The Chautauqua movement satisfied a growing middle-class hunger for self-improvement and in coming years thousands of families, including the Tarbells, trekked to Chautauqua Lake to hear lectures and attend classes.

Based in nearby Meadville, *The Chautauquan* delivered a strong dose of moral uplift to its readers and proved a useful training ground for Tarbell. She edited, wrote brief items, and eventually took on longer articles. She learned to ground her writing on evidence. At the same time, she wrote with moral conviction. In one article on the arts and industries of Cincinnati, she reported on the beer bottling display in the most prominent space at an industrial exhibition and found it "horrifying" that the only sign outside the hall advertised the same beer. Moral commentary would run through all of Tarbell's work. It would always be supported, though, with research and hard facts. When she left *The Chautauquan* in 1890 after a falling out with the editor, she realized that she had found her passion. As she put it, an "absorption in rocks and plants had veered to an intense interest in human beings."

Determined now to be a writer (and to stay single), Tarbell moved to Paris the next year. With three friends from Titusville, she rented a cheap apartment. She intended to write about the life of Madam Roland,[*] a prominent figure in the French Revolution. To support herself, she also wrote dispatches to American publications, including a syndicate[*] owned by a crusading Irish immigrant named Samuel S. McClure. Impressed by her work, McClure visited Tarbell on a trip to Europe. McClure had just started a new publication, New York City–based *McClure's Magazine*, and wanted to interest Tarbell in writing for it. McClure took the unusual step of hiring full-time staff writers for the magazine and finally persuaded Tarbell to return home to work for it. She would be one of the few full-time magazine staff writers in the country. Tarbell came back in 1894 to a nation in crisis. The country was in the grip of a severe depression, the worst it had seen. Visiting Titusville, she saw its effects. Her father struggled to meet his obligations and one of his business partners had taken his own life. Her brother Will helped to keep the family afloat as the treasurer of the Pure Oil Company, which had integrated production, transportation, refining, and marketing and competed directly with the far larger Standard. The work at *McClure's* quickly refocused her attention and in coming years she turned out serialized biographies of Napoleon Bonaparte, Madame Roland, and Abraham Lincoln. The biographies boosted the magazine's circulation and later sold well as books. Yet the conditions in the society around her were impossible to ignore. In particular, she thought more about the oil industry and the way Rockefeller had come to dominate it—subjects, in truth, that had never been far from her mind.

An exposé of the Standard Oil Trust would be timely. Since pioneered by Standard in 1882, trusts had spread to meat packing, sugar refining, tobacco processing, and other major industries. Confronting an unprecedented concentration of economic power, the elimination of competition, and the specter of diminished opportunity, many Americans had come to a disturbing realization regarding industrial capitalism: unchecked free markets could become unfree. Already in 1881, a reform-minded journalist named Henry Demarest Lloyd had published "The Story of a Great Monopoly" in *The Atlantic Monthly* detailing abuses committed by Standard as it moved to control the oil refining industry. Responding to rising public outrage about "the trusts," Congress passed the Sherman Antitrust Act in 1890, which prohibited mergers that reduced competition within an industry. The act, though, was difficult to enforce and had little effect in slowing the consolidation of American industry—or in diminishing the public's fears. Four years later, Lloyd struck an ever bigger public nerve with the publication of *Wealth Against Commonwealth*, which focused on the unrestrained power of large corporations, primarily Standard Oil. Men like Rockefeller, he suggested, were "gluttons of luxury and power" whose very power had made them "public enemies." By the end of the century, such attacks had made Standard synonymous with monopolistic abuse.[*]

---

[*]*Madam Roland:* Madam Manon Marie-Jeanne Phillipon Roland was a vocal supporter of the French Revolution and advocate for women in the French republic who was led to the guillotine in 1793.

[*]*Syndicate:* A company that sells articles or photographs to a number of publications simultaneously.

[*]*Monopolistic Abuse:* Behavior related to a single firm's control of an entire industry.

A shifting public temperament at the turn of the century lent added urgency to another investigation of Standard Oil. Depression had given way to renewed prosperity,
but the festering social, political, and economic ills associated with unrestrained urban
and industrial growth remained. At the beginning of the new century, a rising sense of
urgency to address these ills fueled the rise of progressive reform.* For progressive-
minded Americans, few developments seemed more alarming than the unprecedented
concentration of wealth and power in the hands of a new industrial elite. Tarbell's own
magazine, along with *Scribner's, The Atlantic,* and others, had much to do with stirring
progressive reform sentiment. Landing in the parlors of the growing urban middle-class,
these mass circulation publications had turned to investigative journalism in addition to
their usual fare of general interest stories or fiction. McClure, in fact, started his magazine
with a mission to document social ills and expose corruption. He went on to assemble a
stable of investigative reporters, including Ray Stannard Baker, who wrote about labor
relations in the Pennsylvania coal fields, and Lincoln Steffens, who exposed corrupt political bosses in a series called "The Shame of the Cities."

In 1900, McClure and his staff decided to launch a series on the Standard Oil
Trust. Tarbell's background made her the logical choice to do it. Her work on Lincoln
had left her with the feeling that trusts like Standard threatened to bring "a more subtle
form of slavery." To give the complex issue and human face, she decided to focus on
Rockefeller as well as Standard. Tarbell set to work, pouring through previously published material, company sources, and testimony of Standard officials in various government inquiries. She even got a few Standard executives and Rockefeller's brother to
talk to her. Unlike *Wealth Against Commonwealth,* long on colorful prose and short on
accuracy, Tarbell's series would be grounded in solid research. The first installment
came out in November 1902. The nineteenth (and final) installment appeared two
years later, about the same time as an expanded, best-selling book version, *The History
of the Standard Oil Company.* Armed with overwhelming factual evidence, Tarbell laid
bare the story of Rockefeller and Standard, presenting in mostly clinical prose a story of
intimidation and unsavory business practices. **[See Source 3.]** In 1905, however,
Tarbell dropped any pretense of objectivity, portraying Rockefeller in a two-part character study of Standard's founder as a "living mummy"—a repulsive, money-mad ogre.
"From him we have received no impulse to public duty," she concluded, "only lessons
in evading it for private greed." **[See Source 4.]**

"IS THE PEN MIGHTIER THAN THE MONEY-BAG [?]"

When Tarbell's work appeared, Rockefeller was publically silent. Years later, he claimed
that he never read her book, only that he "may have skimmed it." Tarbell, he said, was
driven by jealousy due to the inability of her father and brother to compete with Standard. Nonetheless, the work clearly rankled him. He told one of his friends, at the mention of Tarbell's name, that times had changed since they were boys. "The world," he
said, "is full of socialists and anarchists." Strolling on his Cleveland estate one day with
an acquaintance who suggested that he respond to Tarbell, Rockefeller pointed to a

---

Progressive Reform: Reforms at the turn of the twentieth century to make government
more responsive to the people, improve working and living conditions, and restrain
corporate power.

worm in their path and said, "If I step on that worm I will call attention to it. If I ignore it, it will disappear."

In truth, Rockefeller had no compelling reason to fight Tarbell's accusations. Standard had always found a way to deal with public excitement—and investigations—about its methods. The company hired the best legal talent. And Rockefeller *was* cunning. His father, who cheated his sons to "make 'em sharp," taught the oil baron well. In state after state, Standard found ways to bat down prosecution and investigations. In 1888, for example, a New York state senate committee, responding to intense public criticism of the trusts, looked into Standard's affairs. Before he testified, Rockefeller was coached by a prominent lawyer, who quickly discovered that his client could take care of himself. Denying on the stand that Standard was a trust, Rockefeller submitted the names of 111 competing refining companies. When the senate interrogator brought up Standard's efforts to quash competitors in the Pennsylvania oil region through the South Improvement Company, he asked Rockefeller if he had ever been in the *Southern* Improvement Company. Rather than correct the counsel's mistake, Rockefeller pounced on the verbal slip, responding, "I was not." The counsel was dumbfounded, but as Rockefeller later mused, "I never undertake to instruct the man who asks me questions."

Standard had even found a clever way to evade the Sherman Antitrust Act. When the Ohio Supreme Court ruled in 1892 that Standard Oil of Ohio was controlled by Standard's trustees in New York and ordered the trust agreement revoked, a company attorney declared that the ruling was a minor "inconvenience" and the trust arrangement was "not really necessary." In fact, Rockefeller had already looked into a recent New Jersey law that allowed corporations based in the state to hold stock in other corporations. In other words, they could organize as holding companies that actually operated nationwide. In a meeting in 1892 at the company's New York headquarters chaired by Rockefeller, the trust was dissolved and Standard Oil Company of New Jersey, one of the old trust's operating companies, would now also serve the holding company for stock in all the others. As if nothing had happened, the various Standard interests continued to operate as a single unit. The members of the trust's executive committee lost their titles only to emerge as the presidents of the twenty Standard operating companies and, as one Rockefeller biographer noted, they did not even have "to switch seats at the lunch table."

Behind clever legal maneuvering, however, lay Rockefeller's utter certainty about the righteousness of his actions. Some trusts or holding companies may have cut production and raised prices to line the pockets of owners. Rockefeller knew, however, that Standard's consolidation had never been about mere price manipulation. Rather the aim was the greater efficiency and lower costs that could be achieved with the economies of scale.* Having imbibed his mother's lessons about economy, Rockefeller applied them ruthlessly to every aspect of Standard's business. His obsession often led him to drop in on Standard plants to jot down how even the smallest savings might be realized. Once when inspecting how tin cans for kerosene were constructed, he found out that forty drops of solder were used to seal them. Rockefeller suggested that fewer drops be tried and in the future only thirty-nine drops were used. He knew, of course, that in large-scale production, even the drops of solder added up. As he later said with a smile, "A fortune. That's what we saved. A fortune." The result, Rockefeller also understood

---

Economies of Scale: The reduction of manufacturing, distribution, or selling costs per unit with large-scale production or processing.

very well, was dramatic reductions in the costs of operating Standard refineries—and lower, not higher, prices for consumers. In fact, accumulating money, he insisted, had never been his aim. Instead, he sought to bring stability, order, and efficiency to a vast industry. Only large-scale production could achieve that. As he asserted when the trusts again came under attack after the publication of Tarbell's work, "the day of individual competition in large affairs is past and gone." **[See Source 5.]**

Whatever his aim in consolidating the industry, Rockefeller's wealth piled up at an astounding rate. By the turn of the twentieth century, when the average industrial worker's pay was barely more than $1.25 a day and even lower for women, Rockefeller pulled in $3 million in dividends a year. Still counting every penny and living less ostentatiously than other industrial titans, he was well on his way to becoming the richest man in the world. In addition to his Standard holdings, he had investments in railroads and steamship lines, steel, banks, and other businesses. The Rockefeller family enjoyed sprawling estates in Cleveland and New York as well as a home in New York City. Yet Rockefeller had never forgotten the charitable impulse instilled in him by his mother. Now, however, the problem was giving away the money fast enough. As with all matters having to do with money, he proceeded carefully, choosing only "worthy" recipients for his largesse. Educational institutions and medical research were prominent among them. Rockefeller money virtually built the University of Chicago, and supported Atlanta's Spelman College, which had been founded earlier to educate black students and came to bear his wife's name. His money funded the Rockefeller Institute for Medical Research and efforts to eradicate hookworm in the South. Through the Rockefeller Foundation, established in 1909, it would continue to flow to projects to "promote the well-being" of Americans for generations to come.

Despite his generosity, though, Rockefeller was a conspicuous target. It mattered little that he had retired from active management of Standard in 1897 at sixty-one. In the early years of the twentieth century, he and his company were in the spotlight as never before. **[See Source 6.]** Tarbell's work, a publishing sensation, portrayed Rockefeller as the supreme villain of his time. One publication was even moved to ask, "Is the pen mightier than the Money-Bag.... Is Ida M. Tarbell, weak woman, more potent than John D. Rockefeller millionaire?" Moreover, whatever Standard's earlier successes in fending off investigations and prying politicians, the nation's political climate had changed in the first years of the new century. When Theodore Roosevelt rose to the presidency after the assassination of William McKinley in 1901, progressives had a powerful champion in the White House. TR may have labeled some investigative journalists "muckrakers"[*] in 1906, but he shared many Americans' concerns about concentrated wealth and power. Already he had railed against what he called "the wealthy criminal class." As the former governor of New York, he was especially familiar with Standard and targeted Rockefeller for special criticism. Giving away fortunes, TR declared, would never "compensate for the misconduct in acquiring them." When Tarbell's series appeared, he was so impressed that he sent her an approving note.

Tarbell had handed Roosevelt a prime target. In fact, TR believed that big business was not necessarily bad. Much like Rockefeller, he realized that it was a fact of life and actually

---

[*]*Muckrakers:* An unflattering label applied by TR in a speech in 1906 in which he suggested that too many journalists wrote sensationalist accounts that attacked "good men." Although he had only a few journalists in mind, the term came to be applied to Progressive-Era investigative reporters in general.

brought greater efficiency. Yet, as a politician, he sensed the direction of the political breezes. And he knew that there was no more high-profile—or unpopular—target for trust-busting than Standard. A sportsman who hunted big game, Roosevelt took aim at Standard in 1906, filing an antitrust suit against it. Rockefeller's company was a big target, of course, but proved difficult to bring down. It was armed with its high-profile team of legal talent that had plenty of experience fending off legal challenges and it mounted a vigorous defense. Rockefeller believed that the suit was nothing but a vendetta by Roosevelt. A government report the next year, however, documented the extent of Standard's control of the industry. It controlled 87 percent of all kerosene production and was more than twenty times bigger than Pure Oil, the company's biggest competitor.

Rockefeller was about to realize that the Standard Oil monolith's time was almost up. Even before the federal court announced its verdict, a court in Illinois decided another case against Standard Oil of Indiana, accused of taking rebates after they had been made illegal by federal legislation. In exchange for Rockefeller's testimony, the judge extended to him immunity from criminal prosecution. In ruling against Standard of Indiana in 1907, however, he compared Standard to a common criminal, denounced its attorneys for their "studied insolence," and slapped a fine of more than $30 million on the company, the biggest in history until then. At a steep price and much to TR's chagrin, Rockefeller had won what he really wanted—immunity. That did not protect Standard, however, in the federal case. In 1909, a federal court ruled that Standard Oil of New Jersey and its subsidiary corporations were in violation of the Sherman Antitrust Act. Appealed immediately by Standard, the decision was upheld in 1911 by the U.S. Supreme Court, which ruled that thirty-three of its companies had to be severed from the New Jersey parent.

Rockefeller's creation would be dismembered. Although no longer president, TR had triumphed. In her own way, so had Ida Tarbell. In fact, in a three-part series published during the trial for *The American Magazine*, she explained how the government sought to prove that Standard should be broken up. Although she described it as "the most magnificent example of efficient organization" and "a thing of which we ought to be able to be proud," she went on to write that it had become "a synonym for commercial depravity." Ironically, the breakup of Standard came at the very time that its market share had begun to decline, as Texaco and other new companies began to tap new oil fields faster than it could respond. Stung by Tarbell and the Illinois case, Rockefeller finally spoke up in 1909 with the publication of his memoirs, *Random Reminiscences of Men and Events* (while the federal antitrust case lay before the Supreme Court). **[See Sources 1 and 5.]**

Rockefeller's wealth actually increased vastly after that adverse decision. He received a substantial portion of stock in all the post-breakup companies, which grew rapidly as the automobile began to stimulate the demand for gasoline. Until he died in 1937 at the age of ninety-seven, Rockefeller continued to be mostly concerned with how to give away the bulk of his growing fortune. Meanwhile, after the publication of *The History of the Standard Oil Company*, Tarbell continued to write about such progressive issues as the tariff and working conditions. Yet she did not forget about Standard. Acknowledging the ambiguous results of Progressive-Era trust-busting, she wrote in 1923 that the price consumers paid for gasoline "is the price fixed by the Standard Oil Company." In fact, if the example of Standard Oil illustrates the ambiguity of progressive reform, Tarbell's later work also demonstrated the complex attitudes of many Progressive-Era reformers. Like trust-busting, women's suffrage is usually associated with progressivism in the early twentieth century. Yet in turning her attention in the 1920s to the roles of women, Tarbell questioned women's suffrage and revealed many traditional views about women and their work. That did little, though, to affect her reputation as a Progressive-Era reformer. In the decades after her death in 1944 at eighty-six, Tarbell's reputation would continue to rest squarely on her investigation of John D. Rockefeller, whose own reputation she had done so much to shape and whose company she had helped bring down.

• PRIMARY SOURCES •

Source 1: *Rockefeller Discusses Consolidation and Rebates* (1909)

In the early twentieth century, John D. Rockefeller discussed his actions in the initial stages of Standard Oil's growth. In the following source , he defends Standard's consolidation of oil refining in Cleveland, including his treatment of the widow he was often accused of fleecing, and the practice of extracting railroad rebates. How does Rockefeller defend Standard's record in consolidating refineries and securing rebates?

Character the Essential Thing

In speaking of the real beginning of the Standard Oil Company, it should be remembered that it was not so much the consolidation of the firms in which we had a personal interest, but the coming together of the men who had the combined brain power to do the work, which was the actual starting point. Perhaps it is worth while to emphasize again the fact that it is not merely capital and "plants" and the strict material things which make up a business, but the character of the men behind these things, their personalities, and their abilities; these are the essentials to be reckoned with.

Late in 1871, we began the purchase of some of the more important of the refinery interests of Cleveland. The conditions were so chaotic and uncertain that most of the refiners were very desirous to get out of the business. We invariably offered those who wanted to sell the option of taking cash or stock in the company. We very much preferred to have them take the stock, because a dollar in those days looked as large as a cart wheel, but as a matter of business policy we found it desirable to offer them the option, and in most cases they were even precipitate in their choice of the cash. They knew what a dollar would buy, but they were very skeptical in regard to the possibilities of resurrecting the oil business and giving any permanent value to these shares.

These purchases continued over a period of years, during which many of the more important refineries at Cleveland were bought by the Standard Oil Company. Some of the smaller concerns, however, continued in the business for many years, although they had the same opportunity as others to sell. There were always, at other refining points which were regarded as more favorably located than Cleveland, many refineries in successful operation.

The Backus Purchase

All these purchases of refineries were conducted with the utmost fairness and good faith on our part, yet in many quarters the stories of certain of these transactions have been told in such form as to give the impression that the sales were made most unwillingly

SOURCE: John D. Rockefeller, *Random Reminiscences of Men and Events* (Tarrytown, NY: Sleepy Hollow Press, 1985), pp. 67–70, 74–76; originally published in *The World's Work* (Doubleday, Page & Co.), 1908–1909.

and only because the sellers were forced to make them by the most ruthless exertion of superior power. There was one transaction, viz., the purchase of the property of the Backus Oil Company, which has been variously exploited and I am made to appear as having personally robbed a defenseless widow of an extremely valuable property, paying her only a mere fraction of its worth. The story as told is one which makes the strongest appeal to the sympathy and, if it were true, would represent a shocking instance of cruelty in crushing a defenseless woman. It is probable that its wide circulation and its acceptance as true by those who know nothing of the facts has awakened more hostility against the Standard Oil Company and against me personally than any charge which has been made.

This is my reason for entering so much into detail in this particular case, which I am exceedingly reluctant to do, and for many years have refrained from doing.

Mr. F. M. Backus, a highly respected citizen of Cleveland and an old and personal friend of mine, had for several years prior to his death in 1874 been engaged in the lubricating oil business, which was carried on after his death as a corporation known as the Backus Oil Company. In the latter part of 1878, our company purchased certain portions of the property of this company. The negotiations which led to this purchase extended over several weeks, being conducted on behalf of Mrs. Backus, as the principal stockholder, by Mr. Charles H. Marr, and on behalf of our company by Mr. Peter S. Jennings. I personally had nothing to do with the negotiations except that, when the matter first came up, Mrs. Backus requested me to call at her house, which I did, when she spoke of selling the property to our company and requested me to personally conduct the negotiations with her with reference to it. This I was obliged to decline to do, because, as I then explained to her, I was not familiar with the details of the business. In that conversation I advised her not to take any hasty action, and when she expressed fears about the future of the business, stating, for example, that she could not get cars to transport sufficient oil, I said to her that, though we were using our cars and required them in our business, yet we would loan her any number she needed, and do anything else in reason to assist her, and I did not see why she could not successfully prosecute her business in the future as in the past. I told her, however, that if after reflection she desired to pursue negotiations for the sale of her property, some of our people, familiar with the lubricating oil business, would take up the question with her. As she still expressed a desire to have our company buy her property, negotiations were taken up by Mr. Jennings, and the only other thing that I had to do with the matter was that when our experts reported that in their judgment the value of the works, goodwill, and successor ship which we had decided to buy were worth a certain sum, I asked them to add $10,000, in order to make doubly sure that she received full value. The sale was consummated, as we supposed, to the entire satisfaction of Mrs. Backus, and the purchase price which had been agreed upon was paid....

So far as I can see, after more than thirty years have elapsed, there was nothing but the most kindly and considerate treatment of Mrs. Backus on the part of the Standard Oil company. I regret that Mrs. Backus did not take at least part of her pay in Standard certificates, as we suggested she should do.

The Question of Rebates

Of all the subjects which seem to have attracted the attention of the public to the affairs of the Standard Oil Company, the matter of rebates from railroads has perhaps been uppermost. The Standard Oil Company of Ohio, of which I was president, did receive rebates from the railroads prior to 1880, but received no advantages for which it did not give full compensation. The reason for rebates was that such was the railroad's method of business. A public rate was made and collected by the railroad companies, but, so far as my knowledge extends, was seldom retained in full; a portion of it was repaid to the shippers as a rebate. By this method the real rate of freight which any shipper paid was not known by his competitors nor by other railroad companies, the amount being a matter of bargain with the carrying company Each shipper made the best bargain that he could, but whether he was doing better than his competitor was only a matter of conjecture. Much depended upon whether the shipper had the advantage of competition of carriers.

The Standard Oil Company of Ohio, being situated at Cleveland, had the advantage of different carrying lines, as well as of water transportation in the summer; taking advantage of those facilities, it made the best bargains possible for its freights. Other companies sought to do the same. The Standard gave advantages to the railroads for the purpose of reducing the cost of transportation of freight. It offered freights in large quantity, carloads and trainloads. It furnished loading facilities and discharging facilities at great cost. It provided regular traffic, so that a railroad could conduct its transportation to the best advantage and use its equipment to the full extent of its hauling capacity without waiting for the refiner's convenience. It exempted railroads from liability for fire and carried its own insurance. It provided at its own expense terminal facilities which permitted economies in handling. For these services it obtained contracts for special allowances on freights.

But notwithstanding these special allowances, this traffic from the Standard Oil Company was far more profitable to the railroad companies than the smaller and irregular traffic, which might have paid a higher rate.

To understand the situation which affected the giving and taking of rebates it must be remembered that the railroads were all eager to enlarge their freight traffic. They were competing with the facilities and rates offered by the boats on lake and canal and by the pipelines. All these means of transporting oil cut into the business of the railroads, and they were desperately anxious to successfully meet this competition. As I have stated, we provided means for loading and unloading cars expeditiously, agreed to furnish a regular fixed number of carloads to transport each day, and arranged with them for all the other things that I have mentioned, the final result being to reduce the cost of transportation for both the railroads and ourselves. All this was following in the natural laws of trade.

Source 2:   *Ida Tarbell Reflects on the Oil War* (1939)

In this excerpt from her autobiography, Ida Tarbell recounts the impact in the early 1870s of the South Improvement Company's rebate scheme on her hometown of Titusville, Pennsylvania, and on her father. What lessons does Tarbell draw from this episode? How and why do you think her perspective may have changed nearly seven decades after the South Improvement Company rebate scheme?

Things were going well in father's business; there was ease such as we had never known, luxuries we had never heard of. Our first Christmas in the new home was celebrated lavishly. Far away was that first Christmas in the shanty on the flats when there was nothing but nuts and candy and my mother and father promising, "Just wait, just wait, the day will come." The day had come—a gorgeous Christmas tree, a velvet cloak, *and* a fur coat for my mother. I haven't the least idea what there was for the rest of us, but those coats were an epoch in my life—my first notion of elegance.

SOURCE: Ida M. Tarbell, *All in the Day's Work: An Autobiography* (Urbana: University of Illinois Press, 2003), pp. 22–24, 25–26; originally published by Macmillan, 1939.

This family blossoming was characteristic of the town. Titusville was gay, confident of its future. It was spending money on schools and churches, was building an Opera House.... More and more fine homes were going up. Its main street had been graded and worked until fine afternoons, winter and summer, it was cleared by four o'clock for the trotting of the fast horses the rich were importing. When New Year's Day came every woman received—wine, cakes, salads, cold meats on the table—every man went calling. That is, Titusville was taking on metropolitan airs, led by a few citizens who knew New York and its ways....

There was reason for confidence. In the dozen years since the first well was drilled the Oil Creek Valley had yielded nearly thirty-three million barrels of crude oil. Producing, transporting, refining, marketing, exporting, and by-products had been developed into an organized industry which was now believed to have a splendid future.

Then suddenly this gay, prosperous town received a blow between the eyes. Self-dependent in all but transportation and locally in that through the pipe lines it was rapidly laying to shipping points, it was dependent on the railroads for the carrying of its crude oil to outside refining points and for a shipping of both crude and refined to the seaboard—a rich and steady traffic for which the Oil Region felt the railroads ought to be grateful; but it was the railroads that struck the blow. A few refiners outside the region—Cleveland, Pittsburgh, Philadelphia—concocted a marvelous scheme which they had the persuasive power to put over with the railroads, a big scheme by which those in the ring would be able to ship crude and refined oil more cheaply than anybody outside. And then, marvelous invention, they would receive in addition to their advantage a drawback on every barrel of oil shipped by any one not in the group. Those in the South Improvement Company, as the masterpiece was called, were to be rewarded for shipping; and those not in, to be doubly penalized. Of course it was a secret scheme. The Oil Region did not learn of it until it had actually been put into operation in Cleveland, Ohio, and leaked out. What did it mean to the Oil Region? It meant that the man who produced the oil, and all outside refiners, were entirely at the mercy of this group who, if they would, could make the price of crude oil as well as refined. But it was a plan which could not survive daylight. As soon as the Oil Region learned of it a wonderful row followed. There were nightly antimonopoly meetings, violent speeches, processions; trains of oil cars loaded for members of the offending corporation were raided, the oil run on the ground, their buyers turned out of the oil exchanges; appeals were made to the state legislature, to Congress for an interstate commerce bill, producers and refiners uniting for protection. I remember a night when my father came home with a grim look on his face and told how he with scores of other producers had signed a pledge not to sell to the Cleveland ogre that alone had profited from the scheme—a new name, that of the Standard Oil Company, replacing the name South Improvement Company in popular contempt.

There were long days of excitement. Father coming home at night, silent and stern, a sternness even unchanged by his after-dinner cigar, which had come to stand in my mind as the sign of his relaxation after a hard day. He no longer told of the funny things he had seen and heard, during the day....

Out of the alarm and bitterness and confusion, I gathered from my father's talk a conviction to which I still hold—that what had been undertaken was *wrong*. My father told me it was as if somebody had tried to crowd me off the road. Now I knew very well that, on this road where our little white horse trotted up and down, we had our side, there were rules, you couldn't use the road unless you obeyed those rules, it was not only bad manners but dangerous to attempt to disobey them. The railroads—so said my father—ran through the valley by the consent of the people; they had given them a right of way. The road on which I trotted was a right of way. One man had the same right as another, but the railroads had given to one something they would not give to another. It was wrong. I sometimes hear learned people arguing that in the days of this historic quarrel everybody took rebates, it was the accepted way, If they had lived in the Oil Region through those days in 1872, they would have realized that, far from being accepted, it was fought tooth and nail. Everybody did not do it. In the nature of the offense everybody could not do it. The strong wrested from the railroads the privilege of preying upon the weak, and the railroads never dared give the privilege save under promise of secrecy.

In walking through the world there is a choice for a man to make. He can choose the fair and open path, the path which sound ethics, sound democracy, and the common law prescribe, or choose the secret way by which he can get the better of his fellow man. It was that choice made by powerful men that suddenly confronted the Oil Region. The sly, secret, greedy way won in the end, and bitterness and unhappiness and incalculable ethical deterioration for the country at large came out of that struggle and others like it which were going on all over the country—an old struggle with old defeats but never without men willing to make stiff fights for their rights, even if it cost them all they ever hoped to possess.

Source 3:   Ida M. Tarbell, *The History of the Standard Oil Company* (1904)

In this excerpt from Ida Tarbell's classic account of Standard Oil's rise, she discusses the response in Pennsylvania's oil region to the formation of the South Improvement Company and consolidation of refining in Cleveland. Elsewhere in Tarbell's History, she rebutted the long-standing accusation that Standard had blown up a competitor's refinery in New York, but repeats here the persistent—and dubious—charge that Rockefeller had virtually stolen a Cleveland refinery inherited by a widow, Mrs. Fred Backus. How does Tarbell characterize Rockefeller? How does her portrayal of Standard's actions in consolidating of independent refiners such as that belonging to Backus compare to Rockefeller's in Source 1? Do you think she portrays this episode fairly?

It was inevitable that under the pressure of their indignation and resentment some person or persons should be fixed upon as responsible, and should be hated accordingly. Before the lifting of the embargo this responsibility had been fixed. It was the Standard Oil Company of Cleveland, so the Oil Regions decided, which was at the bottom of the business, and the "Mephistopheles of the Cleveland company," as they put it, was John D. Rockefeller....

Before the Oil War the involving the South Improvement Company Standard Oil company had been known simply as one of several successful firms in that city. It drove close bargains, but it paid promptly, and was considered a desirable customer. Now the Oil Regions learned for the first time of the sudden and phenomenal expansion of the company. Where there had been at the beginning of 1872 twenty-six refining firms in Cleveland, there were but six left. In three months before and during the Oil War the Standard had absorbed

SOURCE: Ida M. Tarbell, *The History of the Standard Oil Company* (Gloucester, Mass., Peter Smith, 1963), Vol. I, pp. 97–98, 99, 102–103, 156–157, 202, 203, 207; originally published by the MacMillan Company, 1904.

twenty plants. It was generally charged by the Cleveland refiners that Mr. Rockefeller had used the South Improvement scheme to persuade or compel his rivals to sell to him....

If Mr. Rockefeller had been an ordinary man the outburst of popular contempt and suspicion which suddenly poured on his head would have thwarted and crushed him. But he was no ordinary man. He had the powerful imagination to sec what might be done with the oil business if it could be centered in his hands—the intelligence to analyse the problem into its elements and to find the key to control. He had the essential clement of all great achievement, a stead fastness to a purpose once conceived which nothing can crush. The Oil Regions might rage, call him a conspirator, and all those who sold him oil, traitors; the railroads might withdraw their contracts and the Legislature annul his charter; undisturbed and unresting he kept at his great purpose....

... This lack of comprehension by many men of what seems to other men to be the most obvious principles of justice is not rare. Many men who are widely known as good, share it. Mr. Rockefeller was "good." There was no more faithful Baptist in Cleveland than he. Every enterprise of that church he had supported liberally from his youth. He gave to its poor. He visited its sick. He wept with its suffering. Moreover, he gave unostentatiously to many outside charities of whose worthiness he was satisfied. He was simple and frugal in his habits. He never went to the theatre, never drank wine. He gave much time to the training of his children, seeking to develop in them his own habits of economy and of charity. Yet he was willing to strain every nerve to obtain for himself special and unjust privileges from the railroads which were bound to ruin every man in the oil business not sharing them with him. He was willing to array himself against the combined better sentiment of a whole industry, to oppose a popular movement aimed at righting an injustice, so revolting to one's sense of fair play as that of railroad discriminations. Religious emotion and sentiments of charity, propriety and self-denial seem to have taken the place in him of notions of justice and regard for the rights of others.

Unhampered, then, by any ethical consideration, undismayed by the clamour of the Oil Regions, believing firmly as ever that relief for the disorders in the oil business lay in combining and controlling the entire refining interest, this man of vast patience and foresight took up his work....

... The system of "predatory competition" was no invention of the Standard Oil Company. It had prevailed in the oil business from the start. Indeed, it was one of the evils Mr. Rockefeller claimed his combination would cure, but until now it had been used spasmodically. Mr. Rockefeller never did anything spasmodically. He applied underselling for destroying his rivals' market with the same deliberation and persistency that characterised all his efforts, and in the long run he always won. There were other forms of pressure. Sometimes the independents found it impossible to get oil; again, they were obliged to wait days for cars to ship in; there seemed to be no end to the ways of making it hard for men to do business, of discouraging them until they would sell or lease, and always at the psychological moment a purchaser was at their side....

As this work of absorption went on steadily, persistently, the superstitious fear of resistance to proposals to lease or sell which came from parties known or suspected to be working in harmony with the Standard Oil Company, which had been strong in 1875, grew almost insuperable. In Cleveland this was particularly true. A proposal from Mr. Rockefeller was certainly regarded popularly as little better than a command to "stand and deliver."...

The feeling is admirably shown in a remarkable case still quoted in Cleveland—and which belongs to the same period as the foregoing cases, 1878—a case which took the deeper hold op the public sympathy because the contestant was a woman, the widow of one of the first refiners of the town, a Mr. B——, who had, begun refining in Cleveland in 1860. Mr. B——'s principal business was the manufacture of lubricating oil. Now at the start the Standard Oil Company handled only illuminating oil, and accordingly a contract was made between the two parties that Mr. B—— should sell to Mr. Rockefeller his refined oil, and that the Standard Oil Company should let the lubricating business in Cleveland alone. This was the status when in 1874 Mr. B—— died. What happened afterwards has been told in full in affidavits....

It is undoubtedly true, as Mr. Rockefeller avers, that Mrs. B—— was not obliged to sell out, but the fate of those who in this period of absorption refused to sell was before her eyes. She had seen the twenty Cleveland refineries fall into Mr. Rockefeller's hands in 1872. She had watched the steady collapse of the independents in all the refining centres. She had seen every effort to preserve an individual business thwarted. Rightly or wrongly she had come to believe that a refusal to sell meant a fight with Mr. Rockefeller, that a fight meant ultimately defeat, and she gave up her business to avoid ruin.

Source 4:   Ida M. Tarbell, "John D. Rockefeller: A Character Study" (1905)

The year after the publication of Tarbell's History of the Standard Oil Company, *she wrote a character study of Rockefeller. How would you compare the tone of the two works? According to Tarbell, what was Rockefeller's primary motivation in building Standard? What are her conclusions about his charitable giving?*

WHEN the late ohio Senator mark Hanna said of John D. Rockefeller, "Money mad, money mad, sane in every other respect but money mad," he gave the true biographic clue to the man's character. No candid study of his career can lead to the conclusion that he is a victim of perhaps the ugliest, the least reasonable of all passions, that for money, money as an end—a victim, for the passion has mastered all other ambitions and cravings—has made itself supreme and is in his eyes worthy of what it has cost him.

It is not a pleasant picture that such a reflection arouses—not the portrait of a gentleman one would like to know—this money-maniac secretly, patiently, eternally plotting how he way add to his wealth. Nor is the man himself pleasanter to look upon....

The impression he makes on one who sees him for the first time is overwhelming. Brought face to face with Mr. Rockefeller unexpectedly, and not knowing him, the writer's immediate thought was "this is the oldest man in the world—a living mummy." But there is no sense of feebleness with the sense of age; indeed there is one of terrific power....

Devoted as he is to his church, Mr. Rockefeller makes much more impression by his charities which are indeed one expression of his religion. Mr. Rockefeller has always held that methodical giving was a part of a Christian's duty. Again and again he has stated this view in his Sunday school talks. "I believe it is a religious duty to get all the money you can fairly and honestly;" he told young men one day, "to keep all you can and to give away all you can." Will they (the people of the future) say of us, we accumulated wealth" he remarked in a little Cleveland address a few years ago: "No, that will all be forgotten. They will want to know what we did with it. Did we spend it for the benefit of our fellow man? Of that we ought to think" Such expression are often on his tongue They are but reflections of his

SOURCE: Ida M. Tarbell, "John D. Rockefeller: A Character Study," *McClure's Magazine* (August 1905).

practice of fifty years. Never since the time when he was accustomed to enter in "Ledger A" "10 cents for foreign missions," 12 cents for Five Point Missions," has he failed in methodical giving. It is evident that his giving is governed by some theory of the percent due to the Lord, though it is evident that he never has gone as high as ten percent! Whatever the percentage he has decided on he distributes it cautiously and reverentially, and it is not probable that he often exceeds it, for those who have dealings with Mr. Rockefeller in charities frequently are met with the plea "I cannot afford it." The spirit in which he gives is one of plain, hard duty. It is an investment on which he has determined, an investment in the Kingdom of Heaven; and he means to get all possible out of it. He himself has stated his theory—"According as you put something in, the greater will be your dividends of salvation!"...

If Mr. Rockefeller thinks on these things and the care with which he scrutinizes his gifts, would lead one to think he does, may he not come to realize finally the utter impossibility of justifying by charity the injustice which such an accumulation as his has cost? Today he can not give away more than a pittance of his great total income without doing harm. In a few years he will die and the colossus he has erected will be left to others to administer. Can they do better than he has done? Impossible. May not Mr. Rockefeller come to see finally that the injustice and wrong it takes to build such a fortune as his are only equaled by the weakened manhood and the stimulated greed engendered in its spending? Is it too much to hope that Mr. Rockefeller may finally understand how much more good he would have done the world if, thirty-five years ago, he had turned his great ability to bringing order with justice into the industry in which he was the leader, instead of bringing order with injustice. How many more men he would have helped if he had set his face towards equalizing opportunities instead of restricting them. Is it too much to hope that even Mr. Rockefeller will see, at last, that what we need in society is not charity but fair play, and that he who attempts to substitute the one for the other handles a sword which deals fatal blows in two directions. It may even be that it is because Mr. Rockefeller has begun to see vaguely that he will never be able to give away enough to drown the wrong he has done that his face has taken its terrible pathos....

He has led a life devoted to charity and the church. True, And the principles of the religion he professes are so antagonistic to the principles of the business he practices that the very world which emulates him has been turned into hypocrites and cynics under his tutelage. While, in the world which look on, charity itself has become hateful to many a man—a cloak to cover a multitude of sins. Others actually withdraw their bequests from institutions which accept his funds. (It has been stated on the best authority that three wills making bequests to one of our leading universities have been changed because this institution has accepted money from Mr. Rockefeller). Not only has charity been tainted by the hypocrisy of his life, the church itself has been polluted and many a man has turned away from its doors because of the servile support it gives to the men of whom Mr. Rockefeller is the most eminent type. Does all this pay?

There is no shirking the answer. It does not pay. Our national life is on every side distinctly poorer, uglier, meaner for the kind of influence he exercises. From him we have received no impulse to public duty, only lessons in evading it for private greed; no stimulus to nobler ideals, only a lesson in the further deification of gold; no example of enlarged and noble living; only one of concealment and evasion; no impulse to free thinking, only a lesson in obscuring vital ethical issues by dressing them in the garbs of piety and generosity. None of those higher things which the public has a right to demand from the man to whom the public permits great power are returned to it by Mr. Rockefeller. For Mr. Rockefeller has none of these things to give. He has nothing but Money, and never was there a more striking example of the impotency of money! He has neither taste nor cultivation, ideals nor potent personality. He is not a great man, not a "human man." He is a machine—a money machine—stripped by his overwhelming passion of greed of every quality which makes a man worthy of citizenship. He has not made good. He cannot make good. It is not in him. He has nothing the aspiring world needs. On the contrary, that for which he stands is a menace to our free development not only or chiefly our free development in commerce, but, vastly more important, our free development in citizenship and in morals....

It is this threatening saturation of all forms of American life with commercial Machiavellism which forces a study of John D. Rockefeller on those interested in our ethical and intellectual tendencies. He symbolizes the thing—is, as far as we can see, the very essence of the thing. Admit him to be the unconscious victim of his time—the inevitable result of the qualities he inherited—or did not inherit—explain him as you will, justify him if you can, there still remains the fact so tragic for Mr. Rockefeller that he is the founder of a creed charged with poison.

Source 5:   *Rockefeller Discusses Large-Scale Enterprise (1909)*

In this source, John D. Rockefeller confronts a growing public distrust of large corporations. How does he justify large "industrial combinations"? How does he think the government should respond to them?

Beyond question there is a suspicion of corporations. There may be reason for such suspicion very often; for a corporation may be moral or immoral, just as a man may be moral or the reverse; but it is folly to condemn all corporations because some are bad, or even to be unduly suspicious of all, because some are bad. But the corporation in form and character has come to stay—that is a thing that may be depended upon. Even small firms are becoming corporations, because it is a convenient form of partnership.

It is equally true that combinations of capital are bound to continue and to grow, and this need not alarm even the most timid if the corporation, or the series of corporations, is properly conducted with due regard for the rights of others. The day of individual competition in large affairs is past and gone—you might just as well argue that we should go back to hand labor and throw away our efficient machines—and the sober good sense of the people will accept this fact when they have studied and tried it out. Just see how the list of stockholders in the great corporations is increasing by leaps and bounds. This means that all these people are becoming partners in great businesses. It is a good thing—it will bring a feeling of increased responsibility to the managers of the corporations and will make the people who have their interests involved study the facts impartially before condemning or attacking them.

On this subject of industrial combinations I have often expressed my opinions; and, as I have not changed my mind, I am not averse to repeating them now, especially as the subject seems again to be so much in the public eye.

The chief advantages from industrial combinations are those which can be derived from a cooperation of persons and aggregation of capital. Much that one man cannot do alone two can do together, and once admit the fact that cooperation, or, what is the same thing, combination, is necessary on a small scale, the limit depends solely upon the

SOURCE: John D. Rockefeller, *Random Reminiscences of Men and Events* (Tarrytown, NY: Sleepy Hollow Press, 1985), pp. 12–13; originally published in *The World's Work* (Doubleday, Page & Co.), 1908–1909.

necessities of business. Two persons in partnership may be a sufficiently large combination for a small business, but if the business grows or can be made to grow, more persons and more capital must be taken in. The business may grow so large that a partnership ceases to be a proper instrumentality for its purposes, and then a corporation becomes a necessity. In most countries, as in England, this form of industrial combination is sufficient for a business co-extensive with the parent country, but it is not so in America. Our federal form of government, making every corporation created by a state foreign to every other state, renders it necessary for persons doing business through corporate agency to organize corporations in some or many of the different states in which their business is located. Instead of doing business through the agency of one corporation they must do business through the agencies of several corporations. If the business is extended to foreign countries, and Americans are not today satisfied with home markets alone, it will be found helpful and possibly necessary to organize corporations in such countries, for Europeans are prejudiced against foreign corporations, as are the people of many of our states. These different corporations thus become cooperating agencies in the same business and are held together by common ownership of their stocks.

It is too late to argue about advantages of industrial combinations. They are a necessity. And if Americans are to have the privilege of extending their business in all the states of the Union, and into foreign countries as well, they are a necessity on a large scale, and require the agency of more than one corporation.

The dangers are that the power conferred by combination may be abused, that combinations may be formed for speculation in stocks rather than for conducting business, and that for this purpose prices may be temporarily raised instead of being lowered, These, abuses are possible to a greater or less extent in all combinations, large or small, but this fact, is no more of an argument against combinations than the fact that steam may explode is an argument against steam. Steam is necessary and can be made comparatively safe. Combination is necessary and its abuses can be minimized; otherwise our legislators must acknowledge their incapacity to deal with the most important instrument of industry.

In the hearing of the Industrial Commission in 1899, I then said, that if I were to suggest any legislation regarding industrial combinations it would be: First, federal legislation under which corporations may be created and regulated, if that be possible. Second, in lieu thereof, state legislation as nearly uniform as possible, encouraging combinations of persons and capital for the purpose of carrying on industries, but permitting state supervision, not of a character to hamper industries, but sufficient to prevent frauds upon the public. I still feel as I did in 1899.

Source 6:   *Standard Oil as an Octopus* (1904)

The rising public concern about Standard Oil in the early twentieth century, particularly after the publication of Tarbell's History, *can be seen in cartoons in the popular press. In the following image, Standard Oil, pictured as an oil tank octopus, reaches its tentacles to the federal and state government and various industries. What public concerns about Standard's dominance of the oil industry did this cartoon reflect—and likely enhance? Does Rockefeller address some aspects of this cartoon in Source 5?*

Source: Udo Joseph Keppler, Next! from Puck (September 1904); Library of Congress.

Keppler, Udo J., 1872–1956/N.Y.: J. Ottmann Lith. Co., Puck Bldg., 1904 September 7/Library of Congress Prints and Photographs Division [LC-USZC4-435]

QUESTIONS TO CONSIDER

1. How did John D. Rockefeller triumph as he did in the oil industry? Citing the essay and sources in this chapter, explain what important factors account for Standard's success. What did Rockefeller's personality, as opposed to other factors, have to do with it?

2. How did John D. Rockefeller justify Standard's actions in consolidating the oil refining business? How does his explanation compare to that offered by Ida Tarbell in her history of Standard Oil and her later profile of Rockefeller? Whose explanation seems more accurate?

3. How did Ida Tarbell's and John D. Rockefeller's backgrounds influence their later actions in life? Specifically, how did their early circumstances influence Rockefeller's attitudes toward business and money, and Tarbell's toward Standard and Rockefeller? Which sources support your conclusions in each case?

4. What do the essay and sources in this chapter reveal about why Americans in the late nineteenth and early twentieth centuries were so concerned about big business? In the case of the oil refining industry, what effects did consolidation have? Why was Standard Oil such a prominent target? Taking Standard as one example, did Progressive-Era trust-busting have consequences that reformers may not have intended?

FURTHER READING

Ron Chernow, *Titan: The Life of John D. Rockefeller* (New York: Random House, 1998), is a comprehensive, highly readable biography of Rockefeller and history of Standard Oil.

Steven J. Diner, *A Very Different Age: Americans of the Progressive Era* (New York: Hill and Wang, 1997), offers a fine, short overview of the Progressive Era, including the transformation of business enterprise.

Matthew Josephson, *The Robber Barons: The Great American Capitalists, 1861–1901* (New York: Harcourt, Brace and Company, 1934), presents a classic and highly critical look at the misdeeds of the post–Civil War era's new industrial elite.

Ida Tarbell, *All in the Day's Work: An Autobiography* (New York: The MacMillan Company, 1939), provides insights into the influence of Tarbell's background on her and her work, and the impact of Standard Oil on her family.

Steve *Weinberg, Taking on the Trust: The Epic Battle of Ida Tarbell and John D. Rockefeller* (New York: W. W. Norton & Company, 2008), is a useful introduction to the lives of Tarbell and Rockefeller and the conflict between them.

Progressives at War: Randolph Bourne and George Creel

As he entered the House of Representatives on the evening of April 2, 1917, President Woodrow Wilson was greeted with loud applause. Everyone in the chamber knew why he was there. A beleaguered Germany, worn down after nearly three years of war with Britain, France, and Russia, had announced only two months earlier that its submarines would strike American neutral ships trading with Britain or the other Allies. In the last month, German torpedoes had sunk four American merchant ships. Now a reluctant Wilson stood before a joint session of Congress asking that it "formally accept the status of belligerent." The somber president had no illusions about the magnitude of the task before the nation. Waging war against Germany would require far more than raising and equipping an army. The Allies and the principal Central Powers—Germany, Austria-Hungary, and Turkey—had already lost millions of men. World War I demanded, as Wilson put it, the "mobilization of all the material resources of the country." Wilson also knew that war would require the enlistment of Americans' hearts and minds. Less than two weeks after his call for American intervention, he signed an executive order creating the Committee on Public Information, the nation's first full-scale propaganda agency. Then he quickly appointed journalist, reformer, and ardent Wilson supporter George Creel to head it.

Like Wilson, Creel called himself a progressive. For nearly two decades in the early twentieth century, progressive reformers had battled many ills plaguing America's urban, industrial society. Now they saw Wilson's crusade abroad as an extension of the battle they had waged in this country to democratize politics and increase the power of the government to improve living and working conditions. Progressives like Creel believed that public power should be used to curb private interests. War would bring new opportunities to do just that. The defeat of the Central Powers, they assumed, would make the world "safe for democracy." And unprecedented wartime controls over private property would help usher in a bright progressive future for American society.

Randolph Bourne

George Creel

Randolph Bourne thought otherwise. As Creel eagerly sold Wilson's cause to the American people, Bourne set his impressive mind to a different task. Like Creel, Bourne had enthusiastically embraced many progressive assumptions about the need for social planning and the greater use of state power. Far removed from the centers of power, however, he was convinced that progressives' faith in the war's positive effects was tragically misplaced. If Creel assumed that war would further progressive reform, Bourne feared that it would overwhelm those who thought they could control its consequences. Bourne was not alone in his antiwar views. The depth of his critique, however, placed his dissent in a class by itself. No one would offer a more scathing indictment of progressive assumptions about the war—or more chilling predictions about its consequences.

"LOLLIPOPPED WITH HALF-TRUTHS"

In his autobiography, George Creel declared his distaste for biographies that "prattle along through infancy and adolescence." Fortunately, one can make sense of Creel's life without committing that sin. Born in Missouri in 1876, Creel was the youngest of three sons of a former Confederate officer who failed as a farmer before moving his family to Kansas City. There Creel's father drank "as an escape from his failure," while his mother ran a boarding house and imparted to young George a "fair knowledge of history and the classics." He attended high school for one year, where he wrote for the school paper. After a brief stint working at odd jobs, he went to work for the *Kansas City World* in 1894. Refusing to report on a private scandal in a prominent Kansas City family soon got him fired, but Creel had already set his sights on a larger world. Riding freight trains to New York City, he landed a job at William Randolph Hearst's *New York Journal*. It was 1898, and the Spanish-American War would soon make Hearst and the *Journal* household names. Yet Creel was not happy working for the foremost practitioner of sensational journalism. Seeing himself as "the cheapest sort of hack," he returned to Kansas City to start the *Independent*, a weekly journal, with the backing of a New York acquaintance.

Beginning with its first issue in 1899, the *Independent* offered readers poetry, short stories, and discussions of social and economic issues. With the slogan "A Clean, Clever Paper for Intelligent People," the publication demonstrated a certain high-mindedness. As the *Independent's* slogan suggested, Creel was no opponent of conventional morality. In fact, he later declared that he was "repelled" by communists because of their "derision" of middle-class respectability. At the same time, he was no opponent of reform, and he used the *Independent* to promote a progressive agenda. Serving as editor and publisher, Creel took on the political machine of Kansas City boss Tom Pendergast and even promoted Woodrow Wilson for the presidency in 1905, seven years before Wilson became the Democratic Party candidate. As a high school student, Creel had heard Wilson speak about "the cultivation of the mind and the reading of books" and was instantly won over by the Princeton professor. Imbued with the spirit of reform, the young editor championed everything from the regulation of public utilities to the liberation of women from a "hermetically sealed home."

After selling the *Independent* in 1909, Creel took an assignment as a writer for the *Denver Post*, where he demonstrated the same crusading zeal, campaigning for such progressive reforms as the initiative, referendum, and recall;* effective railroad regulation; an income tax; and municipal ownership of public utilities. Disillusioned by the *Post's* half-hearted commitment to reform, Creel jumped to the rival *Rocky Mountain News*, where he did battle with Denver's political machine and, in one editorial, suggested that eleven state legislators be lynched. (At the subsequent libel trial, Creel testified that he meant exactly what he said.) When a reform mayor was elected in 1912, the newspaperman was appointed police commissioner in the new regime. Creel closed down the red-light district, rounded up prostitutes, and pushed a plan to rehabilitate them. Amid a public outcry, he took away policemen's nightsticks and guns and refused to arrest "Big Bill" Haywood and other Industrial Workers of the World* (IWW) agitators when they arrived in Denver. "Happening to believe in free speech," he declared, "I gave the wobblies the right to talk their heads off."

Such controversial policies helped end his career as commissioner after only several months. Continuing for a time as a muckraker* at the *Rocky Mountain News*, Creel supported Wilson as the "bosses' foe" in the 1912 presidential campaign. The year after Wilson's election, he quit the *Rocky Mountain News* and moved to New York. There he wrote for *Harper's Weekly*, *Century*, *Everybody's Magazine*, and other muckraking magazines and coauthored *Children in Bondage* (1914), an attack on "the great American cancer" of child labor. Creel's muckraking often supported Wilson's New Freedom* program. It also put him in touch with men who would play an important role in the

---

Initiative, referendum, and recall: Political reforms adopted in a number of states in the early twentieth century. They were intended to give voters more power by allowing them to initiate their own legislation, vote on proposed laws or amendments, and recall elected officials before their terms had expired.

Industrial Workers of the World: A radical labor union formed in 1905 whose members were nicknamed "Wobblies."

Muckraker: An investigative reporter in the early twentieth century who helped promote progressive reform by reporting on corruption in government and business.

New Freedom: The reforms advanced by Wilson in the 1912 presidential campaign, including trust-busting and lower tariffs.

Wilson administration, including Cleveland mayor Newton D. Baker, the future secretary of war. About the same time, Creel's circle of acquaintances was further broadened by his marriage to the actress Blanche Bates. The star of *Madame Butterfly*, *The Darling of the Gods*, and other stage hits counted among her friends Margaret Wilson, the president's daughter.

Creel took up his pen even more directly in Wilson's cause in 1916. During the president's reelection campaign, he wrote *Wilson and the Issues*, which posed the election as a choice between a "government of the people" and "the rule of the self-elected few." He was a loud defender of Wilson's secretary of the navy, Josephus Daniels, who had come under heavy Republican attack for accusing private contractors of overcharging the navy. During the campaign, Creel assembled a group of "publicists" and authors, including muckrakers Ray Stannard Baker, Lincoln Steffens, and Ida Tarbell,[*] to issue endorsements and write pamphlets. Wilson was so delighted by Creel's contributions to his campaign that he offered him a position in his administration, which Creel declined. With a growing family, "Setting up a home in Washington," he later confessed, "called for more money than I had."

Creel soon changed his mind about government service. He knew that although Wilson's call for war was met with virtually unanimous approval in Congress, his support fell far short of that in the country at large. Many Americans opposed involvement in the war because of the absence of a direct German attack on the United States. Others had ethnic ties to Germany, Austria-Hungary, or even anti-British Ireland and thus disagreed with Wilson's war policy. Still others pointed to the distance of the "European war" from American shores as the reason for their opposition. Meanwhile, many socialists considered the war nothing more than a struggle between capitalist nations. By the time the United States entered the war, Creel was eager to head any government agency charged with wartime publicity. He even suggested himself for the job to Secretary Daniels, telling Daniels that any such agency should be less concerned with censorship, which he called "criminally stupid," than with efforts to "arouse ardor and enthusiasm" for the war. In April 1917, Wilson appointed him to head the Committee on Public Information (CPI) shortly after it was created.

Under Creel, the CPI worked to influence public opinion in a variety of ways. Creel and his three assistant directors—the secretaries of war, state, and the navy—oversaw both the Foreign Section, which maintained offices in more than thirty countries, and the Domestic Section, which disseminated war news at home. Through its News Division, the CPI eventually issued some six thousand press releases. To inform the public about the government's activities during the war, it also started the *Official Bulletin*, the first daily newspaper put out by the federal government. The News Division, Creel observed, "presented the facts without the slightest trace of color or bias." Typical of many press releases, however, was *Pershing's Crusaders*, a newsreel that purported to show "the very latest news of what our boys are doing in the front line trenches." Opening with a scene of two American soldiers standing beside a medieval Crusader, it declared, "The men of America are going out to save Civilization."

At the beginning of the war, Creel told Wilson that "*expression, not suppression, was the real need.*" Later, he boasted that the American people received "a daily diet of our material." Yet Creel found that influencing news content involved more than issuing an

---

[*]*Ray Stannard Baker, Lincoln Steffens, and Ida Tarbell:* Baker wrote about the plight of African Americans, Steffens exposed corruption in city government, and Tarbell took on John D. Rockefeller in an expose of his Standard Oil Company.

avalanche of press releases. Less than two months after the United States entered the war, Creel also put out guidelines for coverage of the war by the press. Declaring that all "questionable" material should be voluntarily submitted to the CPI for approval, he reminded journalists that "the term traitor is not too harsh in application to the publisher, editor, or writer who wields ... power without full and even solemn recognition of responsibilities." Although Congress placed serious curbs on free expression with the Espionage Act[*] in 1917 and the Sedition Act[*] the following year, the CPI had no statutory authority to engage in censorship. Still, as a member of the Censorship Board, established to oversee the government's numerous censorship efforts, Creel had the power to review all magazine articles prior to publication, ban publications from the mail, and recommend that editors be prosecuted. Armed with this power, he not only suppressed radical publications but also received widespread cooperation from the press.

Influencing the content of war news was one thing, but Creel envisioned an even broader role for his agency. To arouse Americans' "ardor" for the war, the CPI developed a publicity and advertising offensive that included cartoons, posters, newspaper advertisements, pamphlets, and films. Creel called on the services of hundreds of writers, journalists, academics, artists, and advertising men. In addition to Tarbell, Baker, and Steffens, Creel recruited muckrakers John Spargo[*] and Upton Sinclair,[*] reformer Jane Addams[*], and movie director D. W. Griffith[*] to work for the CPI. While the Bureau of War Expositions displayed exhibits of captured German war equipment in twenty cities, the Bureau of State Fair Exhibits emphasized the need for wartime conservation in displays that attracted some seven million people at sixty fairs. Meanwhile, the Four-Minute Men organized seventy-five thousand volunteer speakers who gave four-minute talks to perhaps four hundred million people on topics such as German militarism and the dangers of treason. The Division of Women's War Work mobilized women by mailing approximately fifty thousand letters and producing several thousand news and feature stories to demonstrate what women could do to aid the war effort. The Bureau of Cartoons offered guidance to the nation's cartoonists, while the Picture Division and the Film Division showed Americans the government's war activities through the "exploitation of the camera."

It was with printer's ink, however, that the CPI primarily carried on its war for Americans' hearts and minds. Working through its Division of Civic and Educational Publications, which was supposed to "educate" the public about American democracy, Creel's organization blanketed the country with millions of pamphlets, posters, and advertisements designed to promote patriotism and create support for Wilson's war policy. Much of the CPI's attention was concentrated on the nation's classrooms, where youngsters could be taught, as one CPI official put it, "the more virile virtues of duty and effort and sacrifice." The CPI's main vehicle for instilling these values was the *National School Service*, a bulletin sent to thousands of schools to help teachers bring the war home to their pupils. Filled with stories about the war, the *National School Service*'s goal was to

---

[*]*Espionage Act:* Authorized jail sentences and fines for individuals found guilty of interfering with the draft or encouraging disloyalty to the United States.

[*]*Sedition Act:* Extended similar penalties to those whose published writings attacked the government.

[*]*John Spargo:* Investigated and wrote about child labor.

[*]*Upton Sinclair:* The author of an influential expose of the meatpacking industry (see Chapter 7).

[*]*Jane Addams:* The founder of Hull House, a Chicago settlement house.

[*]*D. W. Griffith:* Produced *The Birth of a Nation* (1915), a silent movie that glorified the Ku Klux Klan's efforts to overturn Reconstruction in the South.

create "unswerving loyalty" among children by making "every school pupil a messenger for Uncle Sam" and every teacher "an officer of the state."

Through the Division of Civic and Educational Publications, the CPI also published some seventy-five million pamphlets and "Loyalty Leaflets." These publications were intended to promote American democratic ideals, but they often reflected a growing concern about national unity and immigrants who allegedly threatened to undermine it. *American and Allied Ideals*, written by a University of Illinois English professor, declared that unassimilated immigrants were "enemies of the American republic." Meanwhile, *Friendly Words to the Foreign Born*, written by a federal judge, warned that the problem with immigrants "is not the fact of the hyphen, but whether a man's heart is at the American end of the hyphen." Other CPI pamphlets addressed the problem of loyalty among the nation's workers with messages designed to prevent labor unrest and increase productivity. In *Why Workingmen Support the War*, for instance, University of Wisconsin economist John R. Commons declared that labor would come out of the war with a "universal" eight-hour day and "as much power to fix its own wages … as employers have."

CPI literature also sought to justify American involvement in the war by presenting German militarism "in all its horror." Its pamphlets pictured enemy soldiers as bloodthirsty beasts who had been "cold-bloodedly programmed" for years by their leaders. The CPI's visual images of the enemy were even more damning. If the CPI was, as Creel declared, "a vast enterprise in salesmanship," it was only natural that its chairman turned "almost instinctively" to Madison Avenue for assistance in selling the war. Dozens of advertising men, as eager to demonstrate the power of their craft as they were to promote the war, came to work for Creel's Division of Advertising. In conjunction with artists such as Charles Dana Gibson, creator of the famous Gibson girl* posters at the turn of the century, they churned out posters and advertisements for numerous government agencies. Gibson believed that it was impossible to "create enthusiasm for the war on the basis of rational appeal." Instead, wartime art had to "appeal to the heart." Guided by such thinking, the CPI produced some of the war's most memorable propaganda images. **[See Sources 1 and 2.]** Like many of the CPI's pamphlets, some of these images emphasized German atrocities. Other pointed to the dangers that German militarism posed to America. **[See Source 3.]** The CPI often relied on dubious accounts of the Germans' rape, enslavement, and execution of civilians and the enemy's use of human shields. Nonetheless, Creel believed that his agency's work represented the "most sober and terrific indictment ever drawn by one government of the political and military system of another government." Ever sure of his own convictions, he entertained no doubts about his agency's efforts to create "national unity" during the war. "From the first," he said after the war, "nothing stood more clear than the confusion and shapelessness of public opinion." If anything, Creel's efforts to shape public opinion reflected perfectly his own progressive and democratic ideals. As the former muckraker observed, "Before a sound, steadfast public opinion could be formed, it had to be *informed*." And informing the public, Creel concluded, was exactly what the CPI had done. After all, he said, "A free people were not children to be … lollipopped with half-truths," because in a democracy, war is not just a fight of generals but also "the grim business of a whole people."

Gibson girl: One of the young women portrayed in posters created by Charles Dana Gibson. In contrast to the traditional portraits of corseted Victorian women, Gibson girls were often depicted enjoying athletic and outdoor activities and came to symbolize the rejection of older styles and ideas.

"WAR IS THE HEALTH OF THE STATE"

Randolph Bourne agreed with Creel that war was "grim business." Yet he rejected outright the progressive belief that World War I was a struggle to make the world safe for democracy. Instead, he focused on the war's dark reality. Far from expanding reform, the fight against Germany and its allies would only choke it off. When the war was over, he predicted, the intellectuals who supported this holy crusade would be swept aside. Creel may have believed that the war was not only for generals, but Bourne had no such faith. As much as in Germany, he argued, the conduct of war in the United States would reflect not the will of the people, but the needs of the state.

Bourne's unorthodox views arose naturally from a profound alienation whose roots reached deep into his childhood. Born in 1886 into a declining yet comfortable family in Bloomfield, New Jersey, Bourne grew up in a three-story house with large grounds that included a tennis court and a small golf course. Yet his childhood circumstances were not as fortunate as this idyllic setting might suggest. His birth was, as he later put it, "terribly messy." The umbilical cord was wrapped around his left ear, leaving it deformed. The physician's forceps did more damage, scarring his face and twisting it into a permanent grimace. Then, at age four, he was struck by spinal tuberculosis, which retarded his growth and left him afflicted with double curvature of the spine. In short, Bourne would live his life as a hunchbacked dwarf with a grossly deformed face that rarely failed to elicit initial shock.

Most of Bourne's adult friends, once they had engaged his remarkable mind, claimed they quickly forgot what one called his "misshapen body." But childhood acquaintances were often less kind, and Bourne's early years were full of despair. His condition quickly made him an outsider. "I suffered tortures," he later confessed, "in trying to learn to skate, to climb trees, to play ball, to conform in general to the ways of the world." Although he later claimed that childhood had "nothing to offer him," young Randolph took up the piano and reading. At age two, he began to read grocery labels, and by the time he started school, he could read the Bible and other books. Nonetheless, the precocious youngster was often frustrated by the "passivity" into which he was forced. Unable to join directly in activities, he studied other people and became adept at sizing them up. He was not without friends and was even elected class president in high school. At the same time, he showed signs of increasing estrangement from his family and its environs.

The Bournes traced their ancestry back to Bloomfield's seventeenth-century Puritan founders. Embodiments of middle-class Protestant respectability, they counted themselves among the town's leading citizens. For Randolph, however, neither Bloomfield nor his family offered much stimulation. The impoverishment of both seemed to be symbolized by the family's set of classics, "stiffly enshrined behind glass doors that were very hard to open." The works of Nathaniel Hawthorne, Alfred Tennyson, and Sir Walter Scott sat there, Bourne reported, "but nobody ever discussed them or looked at them." The failure of Bourne's father to live up to Bloomfield's code of respectability reinforced Randolph's sense of alienation. Like the elder Creel, Bourne's father drank too much, paid too little attention to business, and eventually abandoned his family. Whereas Creel went on to defend conventional values, Bourne longed to escape from Bloomfield's provincialism and his family's middle-class puritanism. "I am constantly confronted there," he confided to a friend, "by the immeasurable gulf between my outlook and theirs."

Bourne's experiences after high school only deepened his disaffection. He realized that he would never enter the world of "dances and parties and social evenings and boy-and-girl attachments." He also knew that he could not attend college. Though admitted to Princeton, he could not enroll due to the family's dwindling resources. After working several months at odd jobs, he found employment working on a machine that punched out music rolls for player pianos. The mind-numbing work helped him "fix the terms" by which he saw the world. When his employer cut his pay, Bourne protested and threatened to quit. Then fear gripped him, and he returned quietly to his workbench. "This was my only skill," he confessed. When his employer's business eventually folded, Bourne had tended a machine so long that his love of literature was nearly dead. Two years spent looking for work in New York City only deepened his sense of estrangement. He endured this period of "mental torture" that arose from the "repeated failure even to obtain a chance to fail" by immersing himself in Greek and Roman classics and social criticism. His reading eventually led him to socialism.[*] With the enthusiasm of a convert, Bourne became convinced that he never would have embraced "this radical philosophy" were it not for his deformity. He could now comfort himself in the knowledge that "the price has not been a heavy one to pay."

Bourne worked at more odd jobs until 1909. Then, despairing over his unfitness for "the business world," he applied for admission to Columbia University and was accepted with a scholarship, the first of many. After the deadening routine of factory work and the narrow-minded conformity of Bloomfield, Bourne found the atmosphere at Columbia liberating. "One's self respect," he declared, "can begin to grow like a weed." Delighting in "the pure pleasure of thought," he quickly caught the attention of his professors. He had little trouble making close friends, and he discovered that writing for campus publications allowed him to express his radical views. When a detective who was frequently employed by corporations to investigate labor unrest spoke to several campus clubs, for instance, an indignant Bourne lashed out. "Better a thousand times," he declared, "that Emma Goldman[*] should address a club of students."

Such commentary soon landed Bourne a spot on the *Columbia Monthly*, a campus journal, and the next year he was named its editor. He made an even bigger splash when the *Atlantic Monthly* published his response to an article attacking youth for their vulgar tastes, poor command of English, socialist leanings, and general lack of "character." In "The Two Generations," Bourne declared that many young men faced the unpleasant prospect of "being swallowed up in the routine of a big corporation." It was understandable, he concluded, that young people had grown "impatient with the conventional explanations of the older generation." In another *Atlantic Monthly* article and in his first book, *Youth and Life* (1913), Bourne returned to a defense of his generation. Youth, he declared, would never believe that "the inertia of older people is wisdom." Arguing that youth felt an overpowering urge "toward self-expression," he advised young people to resist the destruction of the spontaneity that their elders saw as irresponsible hedonism and lack of self-control.

Bourne's call for his generation to resist conformity reflected the influence on him of John Dewey, the champion of what came to be known as "progressive education." At Columbia, Dewey launched a frontal assault on traditional conceptions of childhood and learning. Nineteenth-century methods of instruction were rooted in a long-standing view that children must be transformed into little adults. Educators went about that task

---

[*]*Socialism:* The doctrine that calls for public rather than private ownership of the means of production. Socialists in the early twentieth century often concluded that many progressive solutions to the nation's social and economic ills were inadequate.

[*]*Emma Goldman:* An anarchist who for a time embraced violence as a means to radically restructure society and was later imprisoned and deported to Russia.

with heavy doses of discipline, morality, memorization, and instruction in Greek and Latin, subjects traditionally associated with an aristocratic ideal of education. Dewey called for a more "democratic" education that recognized the individuality of children and was related to life rather than sealed off from it. Instead of making little adults in school, he argued, "for certain moral and intellectual purposes, adults must become as little children." Bourne received Dewey's ideas as manna from heaven. The Columbia educator, he believed, was "the most significant thinker in America," for his theories provided nothing less than a way to reshape conservative institutions, remove old habits of thought, and remake society. Education itself could be an instrument of reform. Rather than merely indoctrinate students and produce conformists—"the conventional bigoted man," as Bourne put it—schools could develop self-expressing individuals.

Later in the twentieth century, Bourne's views about his generation earned him a reputation as the first spokesman for a youth rebellion. For the time being, his writing helped increase his celebrity on campus and, after graduation in 1913, led to a fellowship that allowed him to travel to Europe. In England, he found a class-bound society stymied by its conservatism. In Germany, Bourne was struck by a sense of community, by the country's cleanliness and order, and by a certain "lack of critical sense" among Germans. His views about German conformity were no doubt tempered by his arrival there at a "tense and tragic moment." In the opening days of the war, Bourne stood on a street in Berlin and watched endless columns of soldiers march by. Two weeks later, he was on a ship bound for the United States, convinced that European civilization was about to be "torn to shreds."

When Bourne arrived in New York City at the end of the summer, he "never expected to be so glad to come back to America." He moved into an apartment near Greenwich Village,* where he took to wearing a black cloak that covered his hunched back. Hoping to put his experience "to some useful purpose," he also began to support himself by writing for the *Atlantic Monthly*, *Lippincott's Magazine*, and the *New Republic*, a progressive magazine founded in 1914. Over the next four years, Bourne wrote at least three hundred literary essays and articles on a variety of social issues, particularly Dewey's ideas on education. Increasingly, though, his writing would be bound up with the war he had only glimpsed in Berlin.

Even before 1917, Bourne was distressed by calls for military preparations, especially when they were accompanied by demands for the "Americanization" of immigrants. He was repelled by the "poison" of mindless chauvinism he had seen in Europe. Fearful that war would only bring regimentation and conformity to American life, he became a vocal champion of diversity. Responding to calls that immigrants shed their native cultures, he declared that "there is no distinctly American culture." Immigrants leavened American life with new ideas, he said, while those who insisted on "national unity" only created "hordes of men and women without a spiritual country."

After the U.S. entry into the war, Bourne took up his pen against a fight he thought unjust and misguided. Much of his criticism was aimed at the progressive professors and writers who supported the war and often worked for the Committee on Public Information and other government agencies. In particular, he scorned such progressive thinkers as his onetime hero Dewey and *New Republic* editors Herbert Croly and Walter Lippmann. These intellectuals dismissed suggestions that the war would breed intolerance or that "liberty of thought and speech," as Dewey put it, "would suffer … in any lasting way."

Greenwich Village: A neighborhood in New York City that was a haven for writers, artists, and intellectuals.

Instead, they justified support for American intervention with the belief that the war, like a classroom, provided a marvelous setting for remaking society. In Dewey's words, the war would demonstrate "the supremacy of public need over private possessions." In fact, it had brought unprecedented government controls to the economy. The War Industries Board, for instance, coordinated the nation's industrial production, while the Food Administration oversaw the production and distribution of foodstuffs. Meanwhile, the National War Labor Board imposed regulations on labor to make sure production continued uninterrupted. Altogether, some five thousand government agencies controlled production, rationalized industry, and enlisted private interests in the cause. Dewey and other reformers were heartened by the unprecedented opportunity these wartime agencies created to reshape society along more "scientific" and "rational" lines. Bourne countered that societies, unlike schools, were "not rational entities" and thus not suitable laboratories for social control and experimentation. He believed that linking themselves to the "beast" of war would not make these intellectuals any better able to control its ends. **[See Source 4.]**

Bourne paid a steep price for his dissent. He soon found the pages of the *New Republic* closed to him. With his ability to earn a living severely curtailed, he had to give up his apartment for a room in a basement. Though impoverished and depressed, he continued to write for the *Seven Arts*, a short-lived radical journal that was harassed by federal agents for publishing articles critical of the war. His experience led him to think even more deeply about the impact of war on society. In 1918, he began a study of the modern state, whose nature had been brought "into very clear relief by the war. The state, he insisted, was simply "the organization of the herd to act offensively or defensively against another herd similarly organized." By coercing cooperation, war was bad for creativity and individualism but good for the state. In fact, he concluded, "War is the health of the State." **[See Source 5.]**

"GHOST IN A BLACK CLOAK"

Bourne never finished his essay on the state. Only weeks after the armistice ending World War I, he became one of the more than half million Americans carried away in the influenza epidemic of 1918. Meanwhile, the Committee on Public Information lived on until 1919, when Congress shut it down along with the other wartime regulatory agencies. The next year, George Creel published the "amazing story" of the CPI, which told how it had spread the "gospel of Americanism" and "weld[ed]" Americans into "one white-hot mass instinct." **[See Source 6.]**

Even before Creel told his agency's story, some of the effects of the CPI's work were already evident. Its efforts to heat up Americans' "instincts" had helped create the very climate of intolerance and repression that Bourne had predicted. In this atmosphere, the Wilson administration had found it easy to support the Sedition Act and other moves to repress minority opinion. Meanwhile, rising nativism—the belief that native-born Americans should be favored over immigrants—had led to numerous wartime vigilante attacks on German Americans. One of the most notorious cases of mob action took place near St. Louis in 1918 when a young German American (who had tried unsuccessfully to enlist in the U.S. Navy) was stripped, dragged through the streets, and lynched. In their zeal to achieve national unity, "patriots" across the nation attempted to eradicate all traces of German culture from American life. They removed German books from libraries and schools (and frequently burned them), demanded that orchestras stop performing the works of German composers, and even renamed such familiar items as sauerkraut (Liberty cabbage) and hamburgers (Liberty sandwiches). Nor were Germans their only targets. In the drive to create national unity, all immigrant groups were suspect in the eyes of "100 percenters." In 1917, Congress imposed a literacy test on immigrants, which was sustained over a presidential veto. Four years later, the Immigration Restriction Act established quotas that limited the number of European immigrants allowed to enter the country.

Nativism, in turn, fed rising antilabor and antiradical sentiment. After all, many workers were immigrants, and socialism seemed to many Americans a foreign ideology. As CPI chairman, Creel understood the vulnerability of workers to the no-strike policy advanced by the National War Labor Board. He even sympathized with labor's view that its sacrifices regarding wages and hours should be matched by employers' "concessions in the matter of profits." During the war, however, charges of disloyalty against workers by management proved a very effective tool in muzzling unions. Moreover, workers who were opposed to the war often had the full weight of government authority dropped on them. Federal authorities raided meeting halls of the antiwar IWW in 1917 and tried IWW leaders under the Espionage Act. Dozens of other dissenters met a similar fate, including socialist leader Eugene Debs, whose antiwar speech earned him a ten-year prison sentence. Such repression did not end with the armistice in 1918. The next year, the Wilson administration had federal agents round up thousands of radicals and alleged radicals and then jailed or deported them in what came to be known as the Red Scare.

By the time the Red Scare died down in 1920, the war had provoked still other unexpected responses. Creel defended both Wilson and the Treaty of Versailles[*] after the war, but many Americans were quickly disillusioned with Wilson's idealistic rhetoric about saving the world for democracy. In the coming years, they would conclude that the United States should stay out of other nations' conflicts. Something else had gone wrong as well. Many progressives had entered World War I with great hopes of using government to restrain private interests for the public good. In 1920, they watched as voters elected Republican presidential candidate Warren G. Harding, who promised not a golden age of reform, but "normalcy." In the coming decade, few Americans shared John Dewey's concern for "public need." Instead, many settled down to enjoy unprecedented prosperity, often by purchasing the new consumer goods pouring from the nation's factories. Suddenly, the Progressive Era seemed far away.

Before Creel died in 1953 after a long career as a popular history writer and columnist, he would find new enemies to fight. He ran against former muckraker and socialist Upton Sinclair for the Democratic nomination in California's gubernatorial race in 1934. After World War II, he accused liberals of being duped by a vast communist conspiracy. Long before Creel became obsessed with the specter of communism, however, other former progressives were disturbed by something else. Entering World War I with such high hopes, they were haunted by an apparition at its end. Writer John Dos Passos described the figure this way in his 1932 novel *1919*:

> A tiny twisted ... ghost in a black cloak hopping along the grimy old brick and brownstone streets still left in downtown New York, crying out in a shrill soundless giggle: *War is the health of the State.*

---

[*]*Treaty of Versailles:* The treaty negotiated by Wilson and European leaders in 1919 that ended World War I, imposed heavy penalties on Germany, and created the League of Nations.

• P R I M A R Y   S O U R C E S •

Source 1:   Bachelor of Atrocities

Enlisted in the Wilson administration's efforts to finance the war, the CPI created posters and advertisements to encourage the purchase of war bonds. This advertisement, an example of CPI "target marketing," reminds readers of the German attack on the University of Louvain, destroyed with much of the rest of the Belgian city in 1914. (The Hohenzollerns were the German ruling family.) Do you think the CPI's use of that event and this ad's characterization of it would have been effective?

Bachelor of Atrocities

IN THE vicious guttural language of Kultur, the degree A. B. means Bachelor of Atrocities. Are you going to let the Prussian Python strike at your Alma Mater, as it struck at the University of Louvain?

The Hohenzollern fang strikes at every element of decency and culture and taste that your college stands for. It leaves a track so terrible that only whispered fragments may be recounted. It has ripped all the world-old romance out of war, and reduced it to the dead, black depths of muck, and hate, and bitterness.

You may soon be called to fight. But you are called upon right now to buy Liberty Bonds. You are called upon to economize in every way. It is sometimes harder to live nobly than to die nobly. The supreme sacrifice of life may come easier than the petty sacrifices of comforts and luxuries. You are called to exercise stern self-discipline. Upon this the Allied Success depends.

Set aside every possible dollar for the purchase of Liberty Bonds. Do it relentlessly. Kill every wasteful impulse that America may live. Every bond you buy fires point-blank at Prussian Terrorism.

BUY U. S. GOVERNMENT BONDS FOURTH LIBERTY LOAN

Contributed through Division of Advertising   United States Govt. Comm. on Public Information

This space contributed for the winning of the war by

SOURCE: Stephen Vaughn, HOLDING FAST THE INNER LINES: DEMOCRACY, NATIONALISTM, AND THE COMMITTTE ON PUBLIC INFORMATION. Chapel Hill: The University of North Carolina Press, 1980, p. 167; originally from the National Archives.

Source 2:   *Committee on Public Information Army Recruitment Poster* (1917)

This iconic image of "Uncle Sam" was created in 1916 by illustrator and portrait artist James Montgomery Flagg for a magazine cover and used by the CPI in an army recruiting poster during World War I. With four million copies distributed during the war, it was, in the words of Flagg, "the most popular poster in the world." What do you think Creel and Bourne would say about this image and its popularity?

Library of Congress Prints and Photograph Division

Source 3:   *An Advertisement for Publications of the Committee on Public Information* (1918)

Much of the Committee on Public Information's work attempted to illustrate that the United States could not remain isolated from the German threat. What does this source suggest about George Creel's intention to use rational appeals to mold public opinion?

THE HOHENZOLLERN DREAM

Germany is a war-made,—a war-making state.

She believes the sword the only satisfactory arbiter of international questions,—blood the only food for a growing state.

With Germany in the ascendancy, war will remain the world's chief business.

The longer she is permitted to retain her "might" idea, the more ruthless her methods, the wider her conquests.

The next war will come *right* on to our own shores unless we crush the War idea—unless we crush Germany.

Know the essential war facts! Your government itself will give them to you. Any two of the following named pamphlets sent free upon request.

The President's Flag Day Speech. With evidence of Germany's plans. 32 pages.
The War Message and the Facts Behind It. 32 pages.
The Nation in Arms. 16 pages.
Why We Fight Germany.

War, Labor and Peace.
Conquest and Kultur. 160 pages.
German War Practices. 96 pages.
Treatment of German Militarism and German Critics.
The German War Code. 16 pages.

Address, COMMITTEE ON PUBLIC INFORMATION, 8 Jackson Pl., Washington, D.C.

Contributed through Division of Advertising

U. S. Gov't Comm. on Public Information

This space contributed for the Winning of the War by

Source 4:   Randolph Bourne, *"The War and the Intellectuals"* (1917)

In this article, written shortly after the American entry into the war, Randolph Bourne expresses his opposition to progressive intellectuals' assumptions about the war. On what grounds does he reject them?

We go to war to save the world from subjugation! But the German intellectuals went to war to save their culture from barbarization! And the French went to war to save their beautiful France! And the English to save international honor! And Russia, most altruistic and self-sacrificing of all, to save a small State from destruction! Whence is our miraculous intuition of our moral spotlessness? Whence our confidence that history will not unravel huge economic and imperialist forces upon which our rationalizations float like bubbles? ...

The task of making our own country detailedly fit for peace was abandoned in favor of a feverish concern for the management of the war, advice to the fighting governments on all matters, military, social and political, and a gradual working up of the conviction that we were ordained as a nation to lead all erring brothers towards the light of liberty and democracy....

The results of war on the intellectual class are already apparent. Their thought becomes little more than a description and justification of what is going on. They turn upon any rash one who continues idly to speculate. Once the war is on, the conviction spreads that individual thought is helpless, that the only way one can count is as a cog in the great wheel. There is no good holding back. We are told to dry our unnoticed and ineffective tears and plunge into the great work. Not only is everyone forced into line, but the new certitude becomes idealized.... The pacifist is roundly scolded for refusing to face the facts, and for retiring into his own world of sentimental desire. But is the realist, who refuses to challenge or criticise facts, entitled to any more credit than that which comes from following the line of least resistance? The realist thinks he at least can control events by linking himself to the forces that are moving. Perhaps he can. But if it is a question of controlling war, it is difficult to see how the child on the back of a mad elephant is to be any more effective in stopping the beast than is the child who tries to stop him from the ground.

Source 5:   Randolph Bourne, *"The State"* (1919)

In this unfinished essay, published after his death, Randolph Bourne contrasts the "State" with the nation and the government. The State, Bourne concludes, is a "mystical conception." The nation represents the people in a country, while the government is the power exercised by its leaders. What impact does the State have on individuals during a war, according to Bourne?

As the Church is the medium for the spiritual salvation of m[a]n, so the State is thought of as the medium for his political salvation. Its idealism is a rich blood flowing to all the

SOURCE 4: Reprinted in Carl Resek, ed., WAR AND THE INTELLECTUALS: ESSAYS BY RANDOLPH S. BOURNE, 1915–1919 (New York: Harper & Row, 1964), pp. 7, 10, 12. Originally from Seven Arts, June 1917.

SOURCE 5: Reprinted in Carl Resek, ed., WAR AND THE INTELLECTUALS: ESSAYS BY RANDOLPH S. BOURNE, 1915–1919 (New York: Harper & Row, 1964), pp. 69, 70–71. Originally from James Oppenheim, ed., Untimely Papers (New York: B. W. Huebsch, 1919).

members of the body politic. And it is precisely in war that the urgency for union seems greatest, and the necessity for universality seems most unquestioned. The State is the organization of the herd to act offensively or defensively against another herd similarly organized. The more terrifying the occasion for defense, the closer will become the organization and the more coercive the influence upon each member of the herd....

The classes which are able to play an active and not merely a passive role in the organization for war get a tremendous liberation of activity and energy.... Every individual citizen who in peacetimes had no function to perform by which he could imagine himself an expression or living fragment of the State becomes an active amateur agent of the Government in reporting spies and disloyalists, in raising Government funds, or in propagating such measures as are considered necessary by officialdom. Minority opinion, which in times of peace, was only irritating and could not be dealt with by law unless it was conjoined with actual crime, becomes, with the outbreak of war, a case for outlawry. Criticism of the State, objections to war, luke-warm opinions concerning the necessity or the beauty of conscription, are made subject to ferocious penalties, far exceeding in severity those affixed to actual pragmatic crimes. Public opinion, as expressed in the newspapers, and the pulpits and the schools, becomes one solid block. "Loyalty," or rather war orthodoxy, becomes the sole test for all professions, techniques, occupations. Particularly is this true in the sphere of the intellectual life. There the smallest taint is held to spread over the whole soul, so that a professor of physics is *ipso facto* disqualified to teach physics or to hold honorable place in a university—the republic of learning—if he is at all unsound on the war. Even mere association with persons thus tainted is considered to disqualify a teacher. Anything pertaining to the enemy becomes taboo. His books are suppressed wherever possible, his language is forbidden. His artistic products are considered to convey in the subtlest spiritual way taints of vast poison to the soul that permits itself to enjoy them. So enemy music is suppressed, and energetic measures of opprobrium taken against those whose artistic consciences are not ready to perform such an act of self-sacrifice....

War is the health of the State. It automatically sets in motion throughout society those irresistible forces for uniformity, for passionate cooperation with the Government in coercing into obedience the minority groups and individuals which lack the larger herd sense. The machinery of government sets and enforces the drastic penalties, the minorities are either intimidated into silence, or brought slowly around by a subtle process of persuasion which may seem to them really to be converting them.... Other values such as artistic creation, knowledge, reason, beauty, the enhancement of life, are instantly and almost unanimously sacrificed, and the significant classes who have constituted themselves the amateur agents of the State are engaged not only in sacrificing these values for themselves but in coercing all other persons into sacrificing them.

Source 6:   *George Creel on the Committee on Public Information* (1920)

In George Creel's account of the activities of the Committee on Public Information published after the armistice, he demonstrates his firm faith in its work. On what grounds does he defend the actions of the CPI and, in particular, its efforts to arouse the "war-will" of the people?

SOURCE: George Creel, HOW WE ADVERTISED AMERICA (1920; reprint, New York: Arno Press, 1972), pp. 3–5.

The Committee on Public Information was called into existence to … plead the justice of America's cause before the jury of Public Opinion…. *In no degree was the Committee an agency of censorship, a machinery of concealment or repression. Its emphasis throughout was on the open and the positive. At no point did it seek or exercise authorities under those war laws that limited the freedom of speech and press.* In all things, from first to last, without halt or change, it was a plain publicity proposition, a vast enterprise in salesmanship, the world's greatest adventure in advertising.

Under the pressure of tremendous necessities an organization grew that not only reached deep into every American community, but that carried to every corner of the civilized globe the full message of America's idealism, unselfishness, and indomitable purpose. We fought prejudice, indifference, and disaffection at home and we fought ignorance and falsehood abroad…. We did not call it propaganda, for that word, in German hands, had come to be associated with deceit and corruption. Our effort was educational and informative throughout, for we had such confidence in our case as to feel that no other argument was needed than the simple, straightforward presentation of facts.

There was no part of the great war machinery that we did not touch, no medium of appeal that we did not employ. The printed word, the spoken word, the motion picture, the telegraph, the cable, the wireless, the poster, the sign-board—all these were used in our campaign to make our own people and all other peoples understand the causes that compelled America to take arms. All that was fine and ardent in the civilian population came at our call until more than one hundred and fifty thousand men and women were devoting highly specialized abilities to the work of the Committee, as faithful and devoted in their service as though they wore the khaki.

While America's summons was answered without question by the citizenship as a whole, it is to be remembered that during the three and a half years of our neutrality the land had been torn by a thousand divisive prejudices, stunned by the voices of anger and confusion, and muddled by the pull and haul of opposed interests. These were conditions that could not be permitted to endure. What we had to have was no mere surface unity, but a passionate belief in the justice of America's cause that should weld the people of the United States into one white-hot mass instinct with fraternity, devotion, courage, and deathless determination. The *war-will,* the will-to-win, of a democracy depends upon the degree to which each one of all the people of that democracy can concentrate and consecrate body and soul and spirit in the supreme effort of service and sacrifice. What had to be driven home was that all business was the nation's business, and every task a common task for a single purpose.

QUESTIONS TO CONSIDER

1. Although both George Creel and Randolph Bourne considered themselves progressives, they held very different views about World War I. What do the primary sources reveal about those views? How did their backgrounds influence their perceptions of the war?

2. In a democracy, Creel argued, winning a war depends on the degree to which people commit "body and soul and spirit" to it. How did the Committee on Public Information attempt to elicit such a commitment? Did its efforts subvert Woodrow Wilson's goal of waging a war for "democracy"?

3. Bourne argued that the progressives who took the United States to war would not be able to control its consequences. What were the war's most important effects on American society? Did they validate Bourne's analysis?

4. Some historians have argued that as Americans grew disillusioned with World War I after the armistice, they also lost interest in reform. What does the work of Creel and the Committee on Public Information reveal about the impact of the government's efforts to control Americans' hearts and minds during the war? What role did Creel's agency play in a backlash against reform after the war?

5. Citing specific sources, explain whether Bourne or Creel offered a more cogent analysis of the war. What does their work reveal about the wisdom of Wilson's decision to take the nation to war without a direct attack on the country?

FOR FURTHER READING

Alan Axelrod, *Selling the Great War: The Making of American Propaganda* (New York: Palgrave Macmillan, 2009), offers a recent appraisal of the CPI's work and its impact.

George Creel, *Rebel at Large: Recollections of Fifty Crowded Years* (New York: G. P. Putnam's Sons, 1947), demonstrates Creel's ability to tell a story and provides insight into his background and activities as the head of the Committee on Public Information.

Louis Filler, *Randolph Bourne* (New York: Citadel Press, 1966), remains one of the most engaging of the many studies of Bourne's life and work.

David Kennedy, *Over Here: The First World War and American Society* (New York: Oxford University Press, 1980), provides an excellent survey of World War I's impact on American society.

Carl Resek, ed., *War and the Intellectuals: Essays by Randolph S. Bourne, 1915–1919* (New York: Harper & Row, 1964), provides a brief collection of Bourne's writings on World War I. These essays formed the basis of his reputation later in the twentieth century.

Stephen Vaughn, *Holding Fast the Inner Lines: Democracy, Nationalism, and the Committee on Public Information* (Chapel Hill: University of North Carolina Press, 1980), offers a thorough account of the CPI's efforts to control news and encourage nationalism during World War I.

6

Science, Religion, and "Culture Wars" in the 1920s: William Jennings Bryan and Clarence Darrow

It was hot and humid in Dayton, Tennessee, when Clarence Darrow called William Jennings Bryan to the witness stand. Bryan confidently stepped forward, took an oath, sat down, and gazed at a sea of three thousand spectators. They were gathered in July 1925 for the trial of John Scopes, the town's high school science teacher. The twenty-four-year-old Scopes stood accused of violating a new law that prohibited the teaching of evolution in the state's public schools. Sensationalism drew many curious onlookers to Dayton, but invisible and unnamed codefendants, not ballyhoo alone, explain the phenomenal public interest in the trial. To millions of Americans, Scopes stood on the side of enlightened, modern thought. To millions of others, he stood for everything threatening and dangerous to traditional values and religious ideals.

Whatever brought the spectators to Dayton, the courtroom could no longer hold them all, so the judge decided to move the proceedings to the courthouse lawn, where Bryan took his seat under a blazing afternoon sun. The sixty-five-year-old witness needed no introduction. He had been catapulted into the national spotlight in 1896 when he captured the Democratic presidential nomination with a rousing speech at his party's convention. Bryan lost the election, but remained an important figure in national politics. In coming years, he exercised his impressive oratorical skills in speeches around the country. In many of them, he denounced the theory of evolution as a "conspiracy among the atheists and agnostics against the Christian religion," and by the early 1920s, he was the leader of a nationwide antievolution movement.

Clarence Darrow and William Jennings Bryan

A lawyer by training, Bryan came to Dayton as a member of the prosecution team. But in an unusual move, the defense called him as an "expert witness" on the Bible. Sitting in his shirt sleeves, this "defender of the faith" was an eager combatant in what he called a "duel to the death" between Christianity and science. He was not prepared, though, for Clarence Darrow. The most famous lawyer of his day, Darrow had racked up an impressive string of courtroom victories defending underdogs. Bryan may have been a peerless orator, but Darrow's ability to examine witnesses in the courtroom was unsurpassed. For two hours, the sixty-eight-year-old attorney subjected the bewildered Bryan to a withering barrage of questions. Frustrated, Bryan finally lashed out at Darrow, proclaiming that he was out to ridicule "every Christian who believes in the Bible." "We have the purpose," Darrow retorted, "of preventing bigots and ignoramuses from controlling the education of the United States."

The Scopes Trial brought face to face two leading combatants in the culture wars raging across the United States in the 1920s. While Bryan spoke for an older, rural society dominated by traditional morals and ideas, Darrow represented a modern, urban society characterized by new beliefs, manners, and values. Products of the old order, Bryan and Darrow traced their roots to the same side in this contest. But like many other Americans, they were divided by social, cultural, and intellectual currents sweeping over the nation in the early twentieth century. Thus, the two old warriors, representing millions of others, found themselves facing off in Dayton.

"THE ARMOR OF RIGHTEOUS CAUSE"

William Jennings Bryan's very presence at the Scopes Trial was a testament to the enduring impact of his upbringing. Bryan was born in 1860 in Salem, Illinois, the fourth of six surviving children of Silas and Mariah Bryan. Planted squarely in the nation's farm belt, Salem counted some two thousand residents. Its small shops and mills served those who, as Bryan's father put it, worked up "a sweat of the face in agricultural pursuits." Young Will knew exactly what that meant. Shortly after he was born, Bryan's family moved to a farm just outside town. Earning most of his income as a lawyer and judge, Silas was only a gentleman farmer. Nonetheless, Will was subjected to his share of physical work. What he called the drudgery of farm chores left him with abiding respect for those who earned a living behind a plow.

The Bryan household was intensely religious. A devout Baptist deacon, Silas Bryan prayed three times a day and gathered the family every Sunday afternoon for hymn singing. Because Mariah was a committed Methodist, Will attended Sunday school every week at each of his parents' churches. Raised in two Protestant churches, he found it easy to join yet another. After attending a Presbyterian revival in Salem when he was fourteen, Bryan became a member of the church. Will had already imbibed a strong disdain for swearing, drinking, gambling, dancing, and other activities of "questionable moral tendency." As he later wrote, having grown up in a "Christian home," his conversion did not represent any change in "habits of life or habits of thought."

If Bryan shared his parents' Protestant piety, he also embraced his father's political views. Active in local politics, Silas was a staunch Democrat. His was the party of Thomas Jefferson and Andrew Jackson. Like these party founders, Silas firmly believed in the people's ability to govern themselves. Common people were the best judges of their own interests and possessed enough wisdom to govern themselves as they saw fit. The danger was a government that promoted the interests of the few. Along with these views, young Bryan inherited a love for politics itself. As a twelve-year-old, Will accompanied his father while he campaigned unsuccessfully for Congress, and from then on, Will's life's course was set. Like his father, Bryan had little difficulty mixing politics with piety or turning numerous political causes into moral crusades.

Exposed early on to both pulpit and stump, Bryan was attracted to oratory. He joined the debating club in high school and later participated in speech contests as a student at Illinois College in nearby Jacksonville, Illinois. Bryan was drawn to the study of law as preparation for a career in politics, and after graduating as the head of his class in 1881, he went off to Union Law School in Chicago, where he continued to compete in speech contests. Degree in hand, he returned to Jacksonville two years later, married his college sweetheart Mary Baird, and settled down to practice law and enter politics. After several years, though, he was frustrated by the scant political opportunities for a Democrat in heavily Republican Jacksonville. So in 1887, he headed west with Mary and the first of their three children to settle in Lincoln, Nebraska.

It was a good choice, given Bryan's political aspirations, oratorical skills, and reverence for common people. And the timing could not have been better. By the late 1880s, many farmers were caught in a vise of overproduction, falling prices, and high debt. In 1890, their worsening plight gave birth to the Populist Party[*]. The same year, Bryan took advantage of the rising agrarian unrest to win a seat in Congress. Meanwhile, his

---

[*]*Populist Party:* The political party organized in 1890 that called for nationalization of railroads, a graduated income tax, and coinage of silver.

oratory gained him wider attention. Across the rural South and West, stricken farmers demanded the coinage of silver in the belief that increasing the amount of money in circulation would cause farm prices to rise. A supporter of silver, Bryan won reelection in 1892 with Populist and Democratic votes. He lost a bid to become a senator two years later, but his political career was not over. As the economy skidded into a deep depression and farmers' woes mounted, the pro-silver Bryan was flooded with invitations to speak around the country, including at the Democratic Convention in 1896.

Bryan's moment arrived at the Chicago convention. This son of Salem understood the outlook and shared the values of millions of hard-pressed rural Americans. He knew they faced a threat from powerful corporate interests centered in distant eastern cities. And he believed in their strength and virtue. He reminded the gathering that, "the humblest citizen in all the land, when clad in the armor of righteous cause, is stronger than all the hosts of error." He also demonstrated his ability to mix Protestant piety with politics. Assaulting a gold-based money system, he dramatically spread his arms wide and proclaimed, "You shall not crucify mankind upon a cross of gold!" The "Cross of Gold" speech rocked the convention hall, and the electrified delegates awarded Bryan their party's presidential nomination. In the end, however, silver and rural support could not defeat Republican William McKinley, who captured the urban, industrial Northeast with the support of the gold standard and tariff policies favorable to business.

Bryan's sterling oratory kept him in the spotlight as he continued to speak out on important issues after the election. During the Spanish-American War, he was a vocal opponent of America's acquisition of overseas territory. If common people in this country were capable of governing themselves, he believed, those in Cuba and the Philippines were as well. Once more capturing the Democratic nomination in 1900, Bryan attacked imperialism in the presidential campaign. He lost to McKinley again, but continued to reach a wide audience. He returned to Lincoln to start the *Commoner*, a newspaper whose mission was to "aid the common people in protection of their rights." Its favorite targets were big business and banks, and within a year, it boasted a circulation of one hundred forty thousand. In coming years, Bryan reached even more people through public speaking. Most summers, he lectured before Chautauqua* gatherings in hundreds of small towns across the country. He often made the same points: the importance of faith in God and the right of the people "to have what they want in legislation." During the Progressive Era, many people wanted legislation that put restraints on corporate power, and in 1908, Bryan's ability to articulate these concerns won him the Democratic presidential nomination for a third time; he faced Republican William Howard Taft and once again fell short.

Bryan quickly found other crusades, though. One was a resurgent temperance movement, fed by a progressive desire to uplift people by controlling their behavior. Like many Protestants, Bryan, a lifelong teetotaler, associated alcohol consumption with sin. Non-Protestant immigrants crowding the nation's cities attached no such stigma to drink. In fact, the growing debate over alcohol in the early twentieth century reflected a deep cultural divide between middle-class, native-born, mostly rural Protestants and growing numbers of poor Catholic and Jewish immigrants in the cities. Like other temperance advocates, though, Bryan could not see religious bigotry in support for prohibition. It was just another "righteous cause," and in coming years, he watched with satisfaction as Nebraska and many other rural states went dry.

Chautauqua: An institution with roots in religious meetings at Chautauqua Lake in New York State. It sponsored lectures on religious and educational topics and public issues in small towns in the late nineteenth and early twentieth centuries.

Bryan approached the cause of peace with the same fervor. When Woodrow Wilson named him secretary of state in 1915, soon after the outbreak of war in Europe, Bryan applied the Christian message of peace to diplomacy, but resigned the next year after concluding that the Wilson administration sided with the Allies. Campaigning against American entry into World War I, he defined the problem much as he had in 1896. Arrayed against the peace-loving common people were predatory concentrations of wealth headquartered in the East: the "money power" of Wall Street, the "tariff barons," and the "trust magnates," who would drag the nation to war for profit.

Bryan looked to the future with optimism when peace finally came in 1918. He called the postwar period a "glorious" time. It would be so for many Americans, especially the well-off residents of cities. Primary beneficiaries of a prolonged postwar economic expansion, they enjoyed unprecedented prosperity and wide opportunities to buy new consumer goods and indulge in new forms of entertainment. They eagerly embraced other changes as well: new technology, new values, and new standards of morality and behavior. The result was a seismic shift in American culture. Bryan and millions of other mostly rural Americans, however, were not prepared for it. One last time, therefore, the "Great Commoner" donned "the armor of righteous cause" to defend common people. This time the foe had little to do with concentrated economic power. Rather, it was the modern ideas and dangerous cultural influences emanating from eastern cities. In the 1920s, Bryan and many others targeted a concrete and potent symbol of this elusive threat to the old life: the theory of evolution. They also found a very able opponent in one of its most outspoken defenders: the man who squared off against Bryan in Dayton.

"THIS VILLAGE RELIGIOUS STUFF"

Clarence Darrow entered the world in an Ohio village that some casual observers might easily have mistaken for Salem, Illinois. Nestled in the northeastern corner of the state, the farming community of Kinsman numbered some four hundred people when Darrow was born there in 1857. Growing up in Kinsman, he enjoyed experiences that he remembered fondly all his life: fishing, playing baseball, and tobogganing down snow-covered hills. Looking back much later on the circumstances of his birth, though, he observed that he would have chosen to be born in a "noisy city" instead of a tiny village.

He most certainly would have chosen more elevated economic circumstances. The fifth child of Amirus and Emily Eddy Darrow, the famous attorney was born to a family that traced its roots to the seventeenth-century Plymouth Pilgrims. Yet the Darrows were poor, and young Clarence, who cared little about ancestry, inherited very limited prospects. Amirus eked out a living as a carpenter and furniture maker, while Emily kept house and struggled to make the growing family's ends meet.

Clarence later realized, however, that his parents bequeathed to him something more important than economic advantage. Amirus and Emily had been drawn to one another by a love of books, and their home in Kinsman was piled high with them. Those books provided one of young Clarence's first childhood memories. "The house was small, the family large, the furniture meager," he later wrote, "but there were books whichever way one turned." Clarence became an avid reader in this environment. Here was an inheritance that eventually carried him far from Kinsman.

Like young Bryan, Darrow also inherited his father's views about politics and religion. As a student in Pennsylvania, Amirus had studied theology, apparently with the intention of becoming a minister. By the time he graduated, however, he had lost his faith, and in a sea of rural Protestant piety, Amirus stood alone. "My father," Darrow observed later, "was the village infidel." He stood apart in other ways, too. In heavily Republican northeast Ohio, Amirus was a Democrat. In a Yankee culture that valued practicality and achievement, he remained unconcerned with material success. Amirus gloried in his reputation as an outsider who defied popular opinion. He had a profound impact on young Clarence, who also learned to stand up for his convictions no matter how unpopular. All his life, he would emulate his father.

The results were obvious in his experiences at school and church. For all his love of books, Clarence was not a good student. Though eager to learn, he never cared for formal schooling. Like his father, he came to view schools as institutions that instilled orthodox views, encouraged conventional morality, and suppressed independent thinking. Looking back on his own experience, he concluded that school was "an appalling waste of time." He came to feel much the same about organized religion. Despite Amirus's unorthodox views, Emily made sure that the Darrow children were marched off to church on Sundays. It was not a pleasant experience for the boy, who never forgot the "tortures of listening to an endless sermon."

Besides views about education and religion, Amirus imparted to his son a belief that he should strive to succeed and gain influence. By fits and starts, he did. After completing high school in 1873, Darrow enrolled at Allegheny College, his father's alma mater. Still only a mediocre student, he dropped out after one year, returned to Kinsman, and went to work in his father's furniture shop. He quickly discovered that carpentry did not suit him, so he tried his hand at school teaching in a nearby village. Despite his feelings toward his own formal schooling, he managed to stay for three years before he enrolled in the University of Michigan's law school, where a college degree was not yet required for admission. He stayed only one year. Concerned about the strain on his family's finances, Darrow left to study in a lawyer's office in Youngstown, Ohio, where he passed the bar examination after only several months.

At age twenty-one, he was ready to fulfill his father's dream for him. Returning to Kinsman, Darrow hung out his lawyer's shingle. He also courted Jessie Ohl, a longtime acquaintance and daughter of a prosperous mill owner. He married her in 1880. The couple soon moved to nearby Andover and then to the larger town of Ashtabula as Darrow searched for clients. Like Bryan, he got involved in the Democratic Party and developed an appetite for public speaking. Unlike Bryan, however, he grew tired of life in a "farming section with farmers' ideas." As he later put it, he "read himself out" of the countryside. So Darrow moved his family again several years later, this time to a mecca for ambitious young men in the rural Midwest: Chicago.

He could not have made a better choice. Chicago in 1887 was one of the fastest-growing cities in the country—a commercial, financial, and industrial hub of nearly a million people. It was also a focal point of many of the changes transforming American society in the late nineteenth century: industrial expansion, a flood of immigrants from southern and eastern Europe, the rise of organized labor and industrial strife, and the growing specter of political radicalism. Darrow was not in the Windy City long before its vibrant environment had, in the words of one biographer, "blown the straw out of his hair."

Darrow had no money or connections when he moved to Chicago. Within a decade, he was one of the city's best-known attorneys. More than anyone, he owed his rapid rise to John Peter Altgeld. A German immigrant, Altgeld was a Cook County judge and rising star in the Illinois Democratic machine. As Altgeld rose to the governorship in 1892, Darrow was at his side as a friend and advisor. Altgeld shared Darrow's radical sympathies and was equally contemptuous of popular opinion, as he demonstrated in

1893 when he pardoned three anarchists convicted in the fatal Haymarket Square bombing[*] in 1886. As Darrow worked to advance his mentor's political career, Altgeld opened doors for his young protégé with various appointments, including one as corporate attorney for the Chicago and Northwestern Railway, which had a keen interest in Chicago politics and the means to provide Darrow with financial security.

Darrow was on the railroad's payroll for six years, but guilt over his work there eventually led him to take up the cause of labor. At a time of unprecedented labor unrest, he built a thriving practice defending unions. In 1895, he successfully defended Eugene Debs, the socialist leader of the American Railway Union who was charged with criminal conspiracy during the Pullman Strike[*] of 1894. With Debs's acquittal, Darrow had no problem attracting clients. In 1902, the United Mine Workers union called on him to arbitrate a strike in the coal fields of Pennsylvania. Later, he won the acquittal of William "Big Bill" Haywood and two other leaders of the Western Federation of Miners accused of murdering the former governor of Idaho. In these cases and others, the cantankerous Darrow perfected his devastatingly effective courtroom style: a combination of logic and verbal abuse designed to diminish opponents and undercut their arguments.

These cases made Darrow famous, but fame took a toll on his marriage. His wife Jessie longed for a quiet, domestic life, just as she had in Kinsman. Clarence, on the other hand, was seduced by the city. Fond of the public spotlight, he relished his growing celebrity. He reveled in opportunities to participate in lectures, debates, and dinner parties, where he discussed the great issues of the day and enjoyed new friends. His fame also offered opportunities to mingle with admiring women—and carry on adulterous affairs with some of them. Only seven years after moving from the country, Darrow filed for divorce.

In the city, Darrow found liberation from social conventions and the opportunity to flout traditional morality. Although he remarried in 1903, he preached and occasionally practiced free love. He defied conventional political views by espousing socialism and advocating numerous reforms, including black rights. After taking up the cause of workers' rights, he proclaimed that labor was oppressed by an exploitive economic and political system, a view expressed during numerous trials, including his defense of three radical labor leaders accused of blowing up the *Los Angeles Times* building in 1910, killing twenty people. He also flouted conventional morality with attacks on the idea of individual responsibility for behavior. In many cases, he argued that defendants' actions were determined by their environment. That view was the basis of his defense of two young men from wealthy Chicago families, Nathan Leopold and Richard Loeb, who were accused of kidnapping and murdering a fourteen-year-old neighbor boy in 1924. Many observers called it the "crime of the century," and Darrow's clients were found guilty, but he saved them from execution by arguing that their environment had made them mentally abnormal.

Darrow's conspicuous rejection of traditional morality, politics, and ideas was matched by his vocal attacks on religion. He made his religious views public as early as 1899, when he published a pamphlet titled *Why I Am an Agnostic.* Darrow associated religion, especially evangelical Protestantism, with everything he had escaped from in

---

[*]*Haymarket Square Bombing:* A bombing incident that occurred after police attempted to disperse a labor protest in Chicago's Haymarket Square against the McCormick reaper company. The bombing left seven people dead and resulted in the trial and conviction of eight anarchists, even though those who threw the bombs were never identified.

[*]*Pullman Strike:* A strike led by Debs's American Railway Union against the Pullman Company, the manufacturer of railroad sleeping cars. The strike spread to the rails and crippled the nation's transportation system.

leaving Kinsman. And in his mind, no one came to embody the narrow-minded and re-pressive religion of the countryside more than William Jennings Bryan. Darrow and Bryan actually stood on the same side of many reform causes in the early twentieth cen-tury, including the regulation of business. But since the 1890s, Darrow had maintained a simmering dislike for the Great Commoner. Political differences fed much of his animos-ity. Bryan's agenda for reform and his popularity in the Democratic Party reflected his rural base. He appealed to voters with silver, prohibition, and piety. Darrow, on the other hand, had moved to the city and aligned himself with a big-city Democratic Party machine and industrial workers. Like many city dwellers, he associated Bryan and his moralistic appeals with provincial Protestant bigotry. After he ran unsuccessfully for a seat in Congress in 1896, Darrow blamed his defeat on Bryan, who had alienated many urban voters. In an encounter with the former Democratic presidential candidate the next year, Darrow told Bryan that he was not ready to lead his party. "You'd better go back to Lincoln," he exploded, "and study science, history, [and] philosophy … and quit this village religious stuff." Twenty-eight years later in Dayton, Darrow would have the opportunity to do battle with Bryan and his "village religious stuff."

THE "MONKEY TRIAL"

By the time Clarence Darrow gained nationwide fame defending the perpetrators of the "crime of the century," William Jennings Bryan's influence in politics had diminished. His influence in religious affairs, however, had soared. By 1924, Bryan marched at the head of a Protestant religious movement known as fundamentalism. Based on the doc-trine of the Scripture's infallibility, fundamentalism was organized as a movement in 1919 by conservative Christians in response to "modernists" who believed that readers of the Bible had to understand its historical context and its allegorical and symbolic nature. In the early 1920s, fundamentalism brought together millions of Methodists, Baptists, and other mostly rural Protestants in a militant religious crusade centered in the southern Bible Belt. It also identified an evil to battle: Darwinian evolution.

Evolutionary theory, of course, was not new in the 1920s. The English biologist Charles Darwin first advanced his theory of evolution through natural selection in the mid-nineteenth century. Although modified by some since Darwin's day, the theory was universally embraced by scientists and widely accepted by the public in the 1920s. Already by the late nineteenth century, school textbooks had replaced the notion of man's divine creation with Darwinian explanations. Many Christian theologians, more-over, adapted their views to it. For those swept up in the fundamentalist movement, however, evolution was an outrage. It suggested a randomness to existence that contra-dicted a Christian worldview. More to the point, it flew in the face of a literal reading of Scripture, especially the creation accounts in the Book of Genesis.

Yet the appeal of antievolutionism went deeper than that. For many Americans in the 1920s, this modern idea was a highly charged unifying symbol for all that was wrong with their society. And plenty seemed to have gone wrong in the postwar Jazz Age. A revolt against traditional Victorian morality was in full swing, reinforced by such modern ideas as Sigmund Freud's* psychoanalytic theories, which many Americans understood as

---

Sigmund Freud: The Austrian psychoanalyst who in the early twentieth century argued that the exploration of the unconscious mind was the key to understanding behavior and that the sex drive was the most important component of one's psychological makeup.

a call to overthrow sexual inhibitions. Respectability suddenly seemed to have been discarded in favor of loose morals and shocking behavior. In alcohol-sodden speakeasies, patrons flouted prohibition, which had been enacted nationwide with the ratification of the Eighteenth Amendment in 1919. On dance hall floors, young people moved suggestively to the rhythms of shocking new music. Flappers—single and sexually free young women—openly rejected traditional Victorian ideals regarding gender, sexuality, and self-control. Dangerous "modernism," it seemed, had taken hold everywhere.

Many Americans had little difficulty locating the source of these disturbing trends. They were manifestations of the powerful new culture emanating from the nation's rapidly expanding cities, which now claimed more residents than the countryside. This urban culture's influences were everywhere: in movies, radio programs, music, and the hedonistic, live-for-the-day messages of advertising. As the locus of a pervasive new morality, urban America was more threatening than ever. Fears of the city were further heightened by other changes, such as the influx of African Americans into northern cities. Sparked by a labor shortage during World War I, this Great Migration of blacks out of the South transformed the racial makeup of urban America. It also reinforced the association between cities and such dangers as race mixing and loose morals. These fears were reflected in widespread condemnations of jazz, increasingly popular among urban whites, as too "sensuous" and "African." The urban landscape was also transformed by a new wave of immigration that washed millions of newcomers onto the nation's shores. Huddled in urban tenements, they made the city a confusing Tower of Babel to many native-born, rural Americans.

Faced with this rising threat, rural America fought back. One obvious counterattack was Prohibition. The Eighteenth Amendment was an attempt by mostly native-born, small-town, and rural Americans to impose traditional Protestant morality on besotted, city-dwelling immigrants. In a postwar environment of rising nativism, it was also no accident that the door to massive European immigration slammed shut with the passage of the Johnson-Reed Act in 1924. The new law established annual quotas for immigration that favored northern European immigrants over non-Protestant southern and eastern Europeans. Nor was it coincidence that the Ku Klux Klan enjoyed a resurgence during the Jazz Age. Promising to battle Jews, Catholics, immigrants, "flapperism," violations of Prohibition, and other manifestations of immorality, the Klan attracted millions of mainly small-town and rural Americans. **[See Source 1.]**

In the early 1920s, many Americans saw the theory of evolution as the religious counterpart to a dangerous new urban culture. Nobody reflected that view better than Bryan. The Great Commoner, of course, had been long concerned about various threats emanating from the city, including Darwinism. He believed that the idea of the survival of the fittest was a convenient argument by conservative social Darwinists* to undermine reform. Darwin's theory, he declared in 1904, was a "merciless law by which the strong crowd out and kill off the weak." He was even convinced that German militarism was fostered by the belief that a "struggle for survival" applied to nations. Most important, though, Darwinism posed a threat to Christianity. The teaching of evolution caused young people "to lose faith in the Bible." As dangerous social, cultural, and intellectual trends threatened society, defending the faith and the traditional morality it upheld was more imperative than ever. Favoring old-time religion and old-fashioned music, art, and literature, Bryan never

---

Social Darwinists: Late nineteenth-century social commentators who applied Darwin's
theory of evolution through natural selection to society to defend unrestricted
competition and justify the position of powerful corporations and the wealthy.

wavered in his beliefs or cultural preferences. And like many other Americans, he believed that Darwinism undermined them all. As he declared in 1924, "All the ills from which America suffers can be traced back to the teaching of evolution."

When fundamentalists turned their attention to the teaching of evolution in the 1920s, they had a powerful champion in Bryan. And they soon had their first victory. Bills to ban the teaching of evolution were introduced by 1925 in several southern states, including Tennessee. That state's bill made it a crime to teach in the public schools "any theory that denies the story of the Divine creation of man as taught in the Bible." Although one lawmaker jokingly proposed legislation to "require teachers to teach that the world is not round," the antievolution bill passed in 1925. The vote in the legislature's lower house was seventy-one to five.

The American Civil Liberties Union (ACLU) immediately sought a case to test the law's constitutionality. Founded during World War I in response to the Wilson administration's efforts to root out antiwar dissent, the ACLU waged a broader defense of civil liberties after the war. Its attorneys saw the Tennessee law as a violation of freedom of speech and a teacher's right to work without political interference. So they placed advertisements in newspapers seeking a plaintiff. With John Scopes's cooperation, the leading citizens of Dayton responded. Looking merely to generate publicity for their economically slumping town, they succeeded beyond their wildest dreams. Thousands of curious people, some with pet primates, and reporters from all over descended on Dayton to witness or report on the Scopes "Monkey Trial."

Public interest in the trial only increased when Bryan and Darrow entered the fray. For Bryan, it would be a chance to defend the faith. As he announced before the trial, this case boiled down to one question: "Is there a God?" For the Great Commoner, though, there was another issue, too. The man who battled to protect the people from powerful minority interests firmly believed that the majority had the right to determine what was taught to children in school and to protect them from dangerous ideas. For his part, Darrow knew this case could establish the unconstitutionality of the antievolution law. More important, the trial presented an opportunity to battle the "village religion" that was responsible for it. Brought to the defense by Scopes himself, Darrow had little faith in the wisdom of the people to determine what their children should be taught in school. He put his faith instead in a minority: established experts in a discipline.

In fact, each side's lead attorneys reflected the social and cultural division surrounding the battle over evolution. Two ACLU attorneys sat for the defense with the agnostic Darrow: one a Catholic, the other a Jew. All three men hailed from the big city. The two ACLU lawyers were from New York City. Darrow, of course, hailed from Chicago, a city synonymous with corruption and gangsterism. One ACLU attorney was a wealthy radical; the other a successful divorce lawyer and, in the words of one southern newspaper, a "slick city fellow." Darrow, meanwhile, had been divorced himself. And sitting beside them was young Scopes, a Kentucky native whose father, a labor organizer, had passed to his son a willingness to challenge orthodoxy. On the other side sat Bryan, ready to defend God and old-time religion. He got a standing ovation from the crowd as he entered the courtroom on the first day, but his attacks on the National Education Association, the American Library Association, and other organizations for "poisoning young minds" with "anti-Christian propaganda" made him a laughingstock to many Americans. The longtime "dry" on prohibition was in favor of immigration restriction and refused to take a stand against the Ku Klux Klan at the Democratic Convention in 1924. Beside him sat a young state attorney general who proudly proclaimed his fundamentalist faith and a retired attorney general who taunted the defense attorneys as "outsiders" and "agnostics." **[See Source 2.]**

The trial lasted seven days. The first six were occupied with jury selection and legal skirmishes on several fronts. The defense first contended that the law itself was a violation of the state constitution's separation of church and state. What Darrow called a "foolish, mischievous, and wicked act" resulted in the implementation of fundamentalist religious doctrine by the state. **[See Source 3.]** When the prosecution countered that the separation of church and state referred to a state's preference for one particular religious *denomination* over others, the judge rejected the dismissal of Scopes's indictment on constitutional grounds. The defense also argued that the antievolution law violated Scopes's right of free speech in the classroom, but the prosecution responded that a teacher has no such right there. If Scopes did not like the conditions laid down by his employer, Bryan declared, he was free to take a job at an "atheist school." When the defense sought to bring in experts in science and theology to testify that Christianity and evolution were compatible, Bryan argued that "the Word of God … does not take an expert to understand it." **[See Source 4.]** The defense was stymied again when the judge barred outside experts from testifying—a ruling that seemed to bring the trial to an end. But in a surprise move, the defense called Bryan himself to testify as an expert witness on the Bible. It wanted to demonstrate that even a fundamentalist like Bryan might not read the Bible literally and thereby prove that Scopes did not necessarily contradict Scripture in teaching evolution. Darrow, of course, was determined to have Bryan demonstrate what he considered to be the narrow-minded bigotry behind the fundamentalist assault on evolution. Just as eager to defend his faith, Bryan agreed to testify, against the wishes of the other prosecutors.

When the Great Commoner took the stand on the trial's seventh day, Darrow's questioning was relentless. Zeroing in on Bryan's literal reading of scripture, Darrow laid bare Bryan's astounding ignorance of basic scientific and historical information. He asked Bryan about biblical accounts of a whale swallowing Jonah, Joshua's ability to make the sun stand still, and God's creation of the universe in six days. His searing examination forced Bryan to admit that the Bible sometimes could not be read literally—a position supporting the defense's contention that evolution did not necessarily contradict biblical accounts. When Bryan jumped to his feet and objected to his opponent's "slurring of the Bible," his flash of anger only played into Darrow's hands. Shaking his fist at the witness, Darrow shot back, "I am examining you on your fool ideas that no intelligent Christian on earth believes." **[See Source 5.]**

After two hours, with both men enraged and shouting at one another, the judge suddenly adjourned for the day. An exhausted Bryan slumped in his chair, while a throng of bystanders crowded around Darrow to congratulate him. The next morning, the prosecution refused to let Bryan go back on the stand. Darrow countered by waiving his right to a closing statement, thereby denying Bryan the opportunity to deliver his. With that, the trial was over. In coming weeks, commentators across the country would weigh in on it. **[See Source 6.]**

The verdict was anticlimactic. After deliberating for nine minutes, the jury found Scopes guilty. He was later fined $100. Still seeking a constitutional ruling on the state's antievolution law, the defense appealed the verdict to the Tennessee Supreme Court. But it was foiled again. Although that court overturned Scopes's conviction on a technicality, it refused to issue a broader constitutional ruling on the law, which stayed on the books until the legislature repealed it in 1967.

After the trial, Bryan lingered in Dayton to make plans for the fight against evolution. Five days later, he laid down to take a nap from which he never woke. As thousands of mourners watched the train taking the Great Commoner's body to Washington, D.C., for burial, many of them blamed the "atheists" for carrying him away. The antievolution movement lived on, though. The next year, 1926, Mississippi banned the teaching of evolution, and the governor of Texas moved to purge mention of evolution from that state's textbooks. Nineteen state legislatures across the nation considered antievolution bills in 1927. Although none of those bills passed, Arkansas passed an antievolution law by referendum the next year. Meanwhile, many county boards of education in the South banned the teaching of evolution in public schools. In Georgia, the Ku Klux Klan took up the cause of removing evolutionists from the classroom. Publishers also revised science textbooks to eliminate mention of evolution from them—or began to offer two versions, one with and one without Darwin's theory. Only in 1930, when the nation's attention shifted to economic depression, did the antievolution movement wane.

In the face of these antievolution victories, Darrow battled on. In lectures and debates, he proclaimed his agnosticism and ridiculed the fundamentalists' literal reading of the Bible. He also continued to defend the theory of evolution and even served as a commentator in a movie about it in 1931. And until four years before his death in 1938 at age eighty-one, he was in court defending clients. Like his old adversary, Darrow lived long enough to see himself become a folk hero.

Neither Bryan nor Darrow, of course, survived to see the Supreme Court strike down Arkansas's ban on teaching evolution in a 1968 decision declaring it to be a violation of the First Amendment. Nor would they witness the emergence of a new antievolution movement in our own time. Its followers, known as "creationists," are not necessarily guided by a literal reading of Scripture, but proclaim the "intelligent design" of life by a Creator. And unlike earlier antievolutionists, they insist that this belief should be taught in schools *alongside* Darwinism. Eighty years after the Scopes Trial, creationists had introduced proposals challenging the supremacy of Darwinian evolution in the public schools in at least twenty states, and President George W. Bush had weighed in on the side of teaching intelligent design in school. Observing this new movement, William Jennings Bryan might be pleased. Clarence Darrow, on the other hand, would probably seek one more courtroom battle involving the teaching of religion and science in the schools.

• PRIMARY SOURCES •

Source 1:   *An "Imperial Wizard" Explains the Ku Klux Klan's Appeal (1926)*

The following source is from an article written by Hiram Wesley Evans, one of the leaders of the Ku Klux Klan in the 1920s. What does it reveal about the connection between the "culture wars" of the 1920s and other divisions in American society?

The Klan ... has now come to speak for the great mass of Americans of the old pioneer stock. We believe that it does fairly and faithfully represent them, and our proof lies in their support. To understand the Klan, then, it is necessary to understand the character and present mind of the mass of old-stock Americans....

SOURCE: Hiram Wesley Evans, "The Klan's Fight for Americanism," THE NORTH AMERICAN REVIEW, March 1926.

These are, in the first place, a blend of various peoples of the so-called Nordic race, the race which, with all its faults, has given the world almost the whole of modern civilization. The Klan does not try to represent any people but these....

In spite of it, however, these Nordic Americans for the last generation have found themselves increasingly uncomfortable, and finally deeply distressed. There appeared first confusion in thought and opinion, a groping and hesitancy about national affairs and private life alike, in sharp contrast to the clear, straightforward purposes of our earlier years. There was futility in religion, too, which was in many ways even more distressing. Presently we began to find that we are dealing with strange ideas; policies that always sounded well, but somehow always made us still more uncomfortable.

Finally came the moral breakdown that has been going on for two decades. One by one all our traditional moral standards went by the boards, or were so disregarded that they ceased to be binding. The sacredness of our Sabbath, of our homes, of chastity, and finally even of our right to teach our own children in our own schools fundamental facts and truths were torn away from us. Those who maintained the old standards did so only in the face of constant ridicule....

We are a movement of the plain people, very weak in the matter of culture, intellectual support, and trained leadership. We are demanding, and we expect to win, a return of power into the hands of the everyday, not highly cultured, not overly intellectualized, but entirely unspoiled and not de-Americanized, average citizen of the old stock.

Source 2: *A Preacher Defends Tennessee from Attack* (1925)

The author of this article was a popular fundamentalist minister who preached around the country in the 1920s against evolution and modernism. In his view, how does the defense team in the Scopes Trial reflect the threat facing Tennessee?

The real issue at Dayton and everywhere today is: "Whether the religion of the Bible shall be ruled out of the schools and the religion of evolution, with its ruinous results—shall be ruled into the schools by law." The issue is whether the taxpayers—the mothers and fathers of the children—shall be made to support the false and materialistic religion, namely evolution, in the schools, while Christianity is ruled out, and thereby denied their children.

And with this goes the even deeper issue of whether the majority shall really have the right to rule in America, or whether we are to be ruled by an insignificant minority—an "aristocracy" ... of skeptical schoolmen and agnostics.

That is the exact issue in this country today. And that it is a very real and urgent issue is proved by the recent invasion of the sovereign state of Tennessee by a group of outside agnostics, atheists, Unitarian preachers, skeptical scientists, and political revolutionists. These uninvited men—including Clarence Darrow, the world's greatest unbeliever, and Dudley Malone,* the world s greatest religious What-Is-It,—these and the

SOURCE: John Roach Straton, "The Most Sinister Movement in the United States," AMERICAN FUNDAMENTALIST, December 26, 1925.

---

*Dudley Malone was a divorce attorney from New York City and a member of the defense team.

other samples of our proposed "aristocracy" of would-be rulers, swarmed down to Dayton during the Scopes trial and brazenly tried to nullify the laws and overthrow the political and religious faiths of a great, enlightened, prosperous, and peaceful people.

And the only redeeming feature in all that unlovely parade of human vanity, arrogant self-sufficiency, religious unbelief, and anti-American defiance of majority rule was the courtesy, hospitality (even to unwelcome guests), forbearance, patience, and Christlike fortitude displayed by the noble judge, and the Christian prosecuting attorneys and people of Tennessee!

There was an element of profound natural irony in the entire situation. Darrow, Malone, and the other members of the Evolutionist Bund* vicariously left their own communities and bravely sallied forth, like Don Quixote, to defeat the windmills and save other communities from themselves.

They left New York and Chicago, where real religion is being most neglected, where law, consequently, is most defied, where vice and crime are most rampant, and where the follies and ruinous immoralities of the rising generation— debauched already by religious modernism and a Godless materialistic science—smell to high heaven, and they went to save from itself a community where women are still honored, where men are still chivalric, where laws are still respected, where home life is still sweet, where the marriage vow is still sacred, and where man is still regarded, not as a descendant of the slime and beasts of the jungle, but as a child of God, with the wisdom and love of a divine Revelation in his hands, to guide him on life's rugged road, to give him the knowledge of a Savior from his sins, and to plant in his heart the hope of heaven to cheer him on his upward way!

And that is the sort of community which Darrow, Malone, and company left Chicago and New York to save!

Think of the illogic of it! and the nerve of it! and the colossal vanity of it!

Little wonder it is recorded in Holy Writ that "He that sitteth in the Heavens shall laugh" at the follies of men! And surely the very battlements of Heaven must have rocked with laughter at the spectacle of Clarence Darrow, Dudley Malone, and their company of cocksure evolutionists going down to save the South from itself!

It is all the other way around! The religious faith and the robust conservatism of the chivalric South and the sturdy West will have to save America from the sins and shams and shames that are now menacing her splendid life!

Source 3:   *Clarence Darrow Attacks the Antievolution Law as Unconstitutional* (1925)

On the second day of the trial, Clarence Darrow argued that the Tennessee law prohibiting the teaching of evolution in the state's public schools was unconstitutional. On what grounds did he argue that it violates the state constitution's guarantee of religious freedom?

The people of Tennessee adopted a constitution, and they made it broad and plain, and said that the people of Tennessee should always enjoy religious freedom in

SOURCE: First seen in "The World's Most Famous Court Trial: State of Tennessee v. John Thomas Scopes" (National Book Co., 1925); reprinted by DaCapo Press, 1971.

*The Bund was a German-American political organization.

its broadest terms, so I assume, that no legislature could fix a course of study which violated that....

[T]he state of Tennessee under an honest and fair interpretation of the constitution has no more right to teach the Bible as the divine book than that the Koran is one, or the book of Mormons, or the book of Confucius, or the Budda [*sic*], or the Essays of Emerson, or any one of the 10,000 books to which human souls have gone for consolation and aid in their troubles....

What is the Bible? Your Honor, I have read it myself I might read it more or more wisely. Others may understand it better. Others may think they understand it better when they do not. But in a general way I know what it is. I know there are millions of people in the world who look on it as being a divine book, and I have not the slightest objection to it. I know there are millions of people in the world who derive consolation in their times of trouble and solace in times of distress from the Bible. I would be pretty near the last one in the world to do anything or take any action to take it away. I feel just exactly the same toward the religious creed of every human being who lives. If anybody finds anything in this life that brings them consolation and health and happiness I think they ought to have it whatever they get. I haven't any fault to find with them at all. But what is it? The Bible is not one book. The Bible is made up of sixty-six books written over a period of about one thousand years, some of them very early and some of them comparatively late. It is a book primarily of religion and morals. It is not a book of science. Never was and was never meant to be. Under it there is nothing prescribed that would tell you how to build a railroad or a steamboat or to make anything that would advance civilization. It is not a textbook or a text on chemistry. It is not big enough to be. It is not a book on geology; they knew nothing about geology. It is not a book on biology; they knew nothing about it....

[Y]our life and my life and the life of every American citizen depends after all upon the tolerance and forebearance of his fellowman. If men are not tolerant, if men cannot respect each other's opinions, if men cannot live and let live, then no man's life is safe, no man's life is safe.

Here is a country made up of Englishmen, Irishmen, Scotch, German, Europeans, Asiatics, Africans, men of every sort and men of every creed and men of every scientific belief; who is going to begin this sorting out and say, "I shall measure you; I know you are a fool, or worse; I know and I have read a creed telling what I know and I will make people go to Heaven even if they don't want to go with me, I will make them do it." Where is the man that is wise enough to do it?

Source 4:   *William Jennings Bryan Argues Against Expert Testimony* (1925)

Bryan was silent during the first four days of the Scopes Trial. On the fifth day, however, he spoke against admitting expert testimony. On what grounds did he do so? How does his argument reflect broader conflicts that divided the nation in the 1920s?

[W]hile Mr. Scopes knew what the law was and knew what evolution was, and knew that it violated the law, he proceeded to violate the law. That is the evidence before

SOURCE: First seen in "The World's Most Famous Court Trial: State of Tennessee v. John Thomas Scopes" (National Book Co., 1925); reprinted by DaCapo Press, 1971.

this court, and we do not need any expert to tell us what that law means. An expert cannot be permitted to come in here and try to defeat the enforcement of a law by testifying that it isn't a bad law and it isn't—I mean a bad doctrine—no matter how these people phrase the doctrine—no matter how they eulogize it. This is not the place to try to prove that the law ought never to have been passed. The place to prove that, or teach that, was to the legislature.... And, my friends, if the people of Tennessee were to go into a state like New York—the one from which this impulse comes to resist this law, or go into any state—if they went into any state and tried to convince the people that a law they had passed ought not to be enforced, just because the people who went there didn't think it ought to have been passed, don't you think it would be resented as an impertinence? ... The people of this state passed this law, the people of this state knew what they were doing when they passed the law, and they knew the dangers of the doctrine—that they did not want it taught to their children, and my friends, it isn't—your honor, it isn't proper to bring experts in here to try to defeat the purpose of the people of this state by trying to show that this thing that they denounce and outlaw is a beautiful thing that everybody ought to believe in.... These people want to come here with experts to make your honor believe that the law should never have been passed and because in their opinion it ought not to have been passed, it ought not to be enforced. It isn't a place for expert testimony. We have sufficient proof in the book—doesn't the book state the very thing that is objected to, and outlawed in this state? ...

The question is can a minority in this state come in and compel a teacher to teach that the Bible is not true and make the parents of these children pay the expenses of the teacher to tell their children what these people believe is false and dangerous? Has it come to a time when the minority can take charge of a state like Tennessee and compel the majority to pay their teachers while they take religion out of the heart of the children of the parents who pay the teachers? ... Now, your honor, when it comes to Bible experts, do they think that they can bring them in here to instruct the members of the jury, eleven of whom are members of the church? I submit that of the eleven members of the jury more of the jurors are experts on what the Bible is than any Bible expert who does not subscribe to the true spiritual influences or spiritual discernments of what our Bible says.

Voice in audience, "Amen!" ... And, when it comes to Bible experts, every member of the jury is as good an expert on the Bible as any man that they could bring, or that we could bring. The one beauty about the Word of God is, it does not take an expert to understand it.... That Bible is not going to be driven out of this court by experts who come hundreds of miles to testify that they can reconcile evolution, with its ancestor in the jungle, with man made by God in His image, and put here for purposes as a part of the divine plan. No, we are not going to settle that question here, and I think we ought to confine ourselves to the law and to the evidence that can be admitted in accordance with the law.

Source 5:   Clarence Darrow Questions William Jennings Bryan on the Bible (1925)

On the seventh day of the Scopes Trial, Clarence Darrow called Bryan to the stand to prove that a literal reading of the Bible was absurd and, therefore, John Scopes did not violate the Tennessee law forbidding the teaching of "the Divine creation of man as taught in the Bible." Do you think that

SOURCE: First seen in "The World's Most Famous Court Trial: State of Tennessee v. John Thomas Scopes" (National Book Co., 1925); reprinted by DaCapo Press, 1971.

Darrow succeeded in his goal? Given the outcome of the trial, how do you think the jury may have interpreted this exchange?

Mr. Darrow—[W]hen you read that Jonah swallowed the whale—or that the whale swallowed Jonah—excuse me please—how do you literally interpret that?

A—When I read that a big fish swallowed Jonah—it does not say whale.

Q—Doesn't it? Are you sure?

A—That is my recollection of it. A big fish, and I believe it, and I believe in a God who can make a whale and can make a man and make both do what He pleases.

Q—Mr. Bryan, doesn't the New Testament say whale?

A—I am not sure. My impression is that it says fish; but it does not make so much difference; I merely called your attention to where it says fish—it does not say whale.

Q—But in the New Testament it says whale, doesn't it?

A—That may be true; I cannot remember in my own mind what I read about it.

Q—Now, you say, the big fish swallowed Jonah, and he there remained how long—three days—and then he spewed him upon the land. You believe that the big fish was made to swallow Jonah?

A—I am not prepared to say that; the Bible merely says it was done.

Q—You don't know whether it was the ordinary run of fish, or made for that purpose?

A—You may guess; you evolutionists guess.

Q—But when we do guess, we have a sense to guess right.

A—But do not do it often.

Q—You are not prepared to say whether that fish was made especially to swallow a man or not?

A—The Bible doesn't say, so I am not prepared to say.

Q—You don't know whether that was fixed up specially for the purpose.

A—No, the Bible doesn't say.

Q—But do you believe He made them—that He made such a fish and that it was enough to swallow Jonah?

A—Yes, sir. Let me add: One miracle is just as easy to believe as another.

Q—It is for me.

A—It is for me.

Q—Just as hard?

A—It is hard to believe for you, but easy for me. Amiracle is a thing performed beyond what man can perform. When you get beyond what man can do, you get within the realm of miracles; and it is just as easy to believe the miracle of Jonah as any other miracle in the Bible.

Q—Perfectly easy to believe that Jonah swallowed the whale?

A—If the Bible said so; the Bible doesn't make as extreme statements as evolutionists do....

Q—Do you consider the story of Jonah and the whale miracle?

A—I think it is....

Q—Would you say that the earth was only 4,000 years old?

A—Oh, no; I think it is much older than that.

Q—How much?

A—I couldn't say.

Q—Do you say whether the Bible itself says it is older than that?

A—I don't think the Bible says itself whether it is older or not.

Q—Do you think the earth was made in six days?

A—Not six days of twenty-four hours.

Q—Doesn't it say so?

A—No, sir....

Q—Now, you refer to the cloud that was put in the heaven after the flood, the rainbow. Do you believe in that?

A—Read it.

Q—All right, Mr. Bryan, I will read it for you.

MR. BRYAN—Your honor, I think I can shorten this testimony. The only purpose Mr. Darrow has is to slur at the Bible, but I will answer his question. I will answer it all at once, and I have no objection in the world, I want the world to know that this man, who does not believe in a God, is trying to use a court in Tennessee—

MR. DARROW—I object to that.

MR. BRYAN—(Continuing) to slur at it, and while it will require time, I am willing to take it.

MR. DARROW—I object to your statement. I am exempting you on your fool ideas that no intelligent Christian on earth believes.

THE COURT—Court is adjourned until 9 o'clock tomorrow morning.

Source 6:   *A Black Intellectual Comments on the Scopes Trial* (1925)

Black historian, author, and journalist W. E. B. Du Bois commented on the Scopes Trial as the editor of Crisis, the official publication of the National Association for the Advancement of Colored People. What meaning does he assign to the trial and its verdict? Does his commentary point to another division within American society that was revealed by the antievolution controversy in the 1920s?

SOURCE: W. E. B. Du Bois, "Scopes," CRISIS, September 1925, p. 218.

One hundred per cent Americans are now endeavoring to persuade hilarious and sarcastic Europe that Dayton, Tennessee, is a huge joke and very, very exceptional.... The truth is and we know it: Dayton, Tennessee, is America: a great, ignorant, simple-minded land, curiously compounded of brutality, bigotry, religious faith and demagoguery, and capable not simply of mistakes but of persecution, lynching, murder and idiotic blundering, as well as charity, missions, love and hope.

That is America and America is what it is because we believe in Ignorance. The whole modern Nordic civilization of which America is a great and leading branch has sold its soul to Ignorance. Its leading priests profess a religious faith which they do not believe and which they know, and every man of intelligence knows, they do not and cannot believe....

The folk who leave white Tennessee in blank and ridiculous ignorance of what science has taught the world since 1859 are the same ones who would leave black Tennessee and black America with just as little education as is consistent with fairly efficient labor and reasonable contentment; who rave over the 18th Amendment and are dumb over the 15th,[*] who permit lynching and make bastardy legal in order to render their race pure. It is such folk who, when in sudden darkness they descry the awful faces of the Fanatic, the Fury and the Fool, try to hide the vision with gales of laughter.

But Dayton, Tennessee, is no laughing matter. It is menace and warning. It is a challenge to Religion, Science and Democracy.

QUESTIONS TO CONSIDER

1. How would you compare the backgrounds of William Jennings Bryan and Clarence Darrow? What aspects of each man's background were most important in shaping their positions regarding Darwinian evolution in the 1920s?

2. The trial in a small southern town of a young high school science teacher accused of teaching evolution would not at first glance seem worthy of nationwide attention. How do you explain the great interest surrounding the Scopes Trial in 1925? What do you see as its significance?

3. What broad social, cultural, and intellectual divisions among Americans do the sources reveal? How did cultural, sectional, religious, and social differences interact by the 1920s to support a fundamentalist antievolution movement? How did Bryan and Darrow reflect these differences?

4. William Jennings Bryan believed that the majority of people in a community had the right to determine what should be taught to their children in school. Clarence Darrow, on the other hand, believed that this should be decided by experts in a given discipline. Who do you think was correct? Are there dangers in each position? What do you think each man would say about the idea of teaching "intelligent design" or creationism alongside the theory of evolution in the nation's schools today?

---

[*]The Fifteenth Amendment, ratified in 1870, was intended to guarantee black males the right to vote.

FOR FURTHER READING

Robert W. Chery, *A Righteous Cause: The Life of William Jennings Bryan* (Boston: Little, Brown and Company, 1985), offers a concise overview of Bryan's life and career.

David J. Goldberg, *Discontented America: The United States in the 1920s* (Baltimore: Johns Hopkins University Press, 1999), examines numerous changes in postwar American society, including those that led to a backlash against evolution.

Edward J. Larson, *Summer for the Gods: The Scopes Trial and America's Continuing Debate Over Science and Religion* (New York: Basic Books, 1997), examines the roots of the antievolution movement in the 1920s that culminated in the Scopes Trial.

Roderick Nash, *The Nervous Generation: American Thought, 1917–1930* (Chicago: Ivan R. Dee, 1990), remains a useful overview of intellectual and cultural currents during the 1920s.

Kevin Tierney, *Darrow: A Biography* (New York: Thomas Y. Crowell, 1979), offers a comprehensive, though highly readable, account of Darrow's life.

Politics and the Big Screen in the Great Depression: Upton Sinclair and Louis B. Mayer

As the curtains parted and the lights dimmed, the Friday night patrons at Hollywood's El Portal theater settled back in their seats. Tonight's feature was *Chained*, starring Joan Crawford and Clark Gable. This Metro-Goldwyn-Mayer (MGM) release offered moviegoers a few hours of relief from the grim reality of life in 1934. The story of a young American woman who falls in love with an Argentine rancher on a cruise to South America, the movie portrayed lives that most Americans could only dream about. As usual, the El Portal's patrons sat through a cartoon and newsreel before the main feature. Tonight, however, they were also treated to a political short titled *California Election News*. The five-minute feature was a reminder that the gubernatorial election was only a few weeks away.

Normally, of course, a California governor's race was a subject unworthy of the big screen. These were not normal times, though. Since late 1929, the Great Depression had thrown millions of Americans out of work. Five years later, many of its victims continued to stand in relief lines, find shelter in shantytowns, and roam the nation's highways and railroads. In California, closed banks, foreclosed farms, shuttered businesses, and shattered lives stood as testaments to the Depression's devastation. So did the sudden political rise of a socialist named Upton Sinclair, who had won the Democratic Party's nomination for governor in 1934. Sinclair had been catapulted to fame with the publication of *The Jungle* (1906), his shocking Progressive-Era exposé of the meatpacking industry. Later, he had moved to southern California, where he wrote a stream of novels. Now he was on the verge of winning the governorship on a platform called End Poverty in California (EPIC), which proposed state-run enterprises, steep taxes on the rich, and a tax on the motion-picture industry.

Everett Collection Historical/Alamy

Bettmann/Corbis

Upton Sinclair   Louis B. Mayer

California's movers and shakers were alarmed. Louis B. Mayer, for one, was terrified at the prospect of a Sinclair victory. Like Sinclair, Mayer had been born poor. The head of MGM, however, was no socialist. A Republican Party state chairman, Mayer lived with his wife and daughters in a huge Santa Monica home overlooking the Pacific. As the most powerful movie mogul in Hollywood, he ran his studio with a tyrant's grip on his stars and an industry captain's cold eye on the bottom line. Mayer wanted Sinclair stopped, and as the boss of Hollywood's most successful studio, he was determined to bring the anti-Sinclair message right into California's movie theaters. Tonight, long before Clark Gable got the girl, the El Portal's patrons would be among the first to see and hear it.

As a map of the Golden State flashed on the screen and strains of "California, Here I Come" filled the theater, the *California Election News* narrator introduced himself as the "Inquiring Cameraman." His job, he explained, was to travel all over California and talk with voters. The faces of laborers, women, and businessmen appearing on the screen, he said, were not actors. "I don't rehearse them," he intoned, "I'm impartial." As even the dimmest viewer could see, these Californians' political preferences fell into a neat pattern. An African American in an old car, a Hispanic with shifty eyes, and an elderly man with no front teeth all pledged their support for Sinclair or "St. Clair." They were quickly countered by respectable-looking voters: an African American standing in front of a house, an elderly woman in a suburban yard, and two men in suits. All of the anti-Sinclair voters declared that the Democratic candidate and his EPIC plan were dangerous and radical. Later, some amused EPIC supporters were sure that some of the "Inquiring Cameraman's" voters were actors. Yet laughter would be a feeble defense against the likes of Louis B. Mayer. His studio's political short was the first attempt to use the enormous power of big-screen images to defeat a political candidate. And in the midst of one of the most vitriolic gubernatorial campaigns in American history, it was merely a preview of more to come.

"MOVIE WRITING ... INEVITABLY BECOMES TRASH"

If Upton Sinclair had a more worrisome enemy than Louis B. Mayer, it was Sinclair himself. By 1934, he had denounced the capitalist system as bankrupt, Wall Street as "bond slavery," and bankers as "parasites." He also had assaulted nearly every major institution in American life: colleges ("manned by intellectual prostitutes"), religion ("a mighty fortress of graft"), marriage ("prostitution"), medicine ("a thousand dollars [for] a few minutes work"), and the press ("the business of presenting the news of the day in the interest of economic privilege"). Even the Boy Scouts ("more warlike every day") were not immune. At least Sinclair realized that he was his own worst enemy. "I have written so much," he confessed during the campaign, "and not always temperately." He was also self-aware enough to understand the source of his attitudes toward money and power. "I diagnose my psychology," he declared in his *Autobiography*, "as that of a 'poor relation.'" It was his lot "from earliest childhood," he explained, "to live in the presence of wealth which belonged to others."

The "others" in Sinclair's case were his maternal grandfather, a railroad treasurer, and his aunt and her banker husband, members of Baltimore's business elite. Descended from a long line of naval officers, Sinclair's father looked and acted every bit the southern gentleman. In reality, though, he was a failed New York City salesman and a drunk who frequently disappeared, leaving Upton and his mother sleeping in hovels. The youngster's financially strapped parents periodically sent him to live in Baltimore, where he learned firsthand the difference between wealth and poverty. In his relatives' luxurious homes, Sinclair quickly came to resent his inferior position. He found his snobbish uncle insufferable and resolved "never to 'sell out' to that class."

Sinclair's parents reinforced his early prejudices. His father worshiped the Confederate general Robert E. Lee and other "Virginia gentlemen" because they rose above mere moneygrubbing, while his mother condemned even tea or coffee consumption. From them, young Upton inherited a lifelong abhorrence of business and alcohol— and a broad Puritan streak. With an ascetic's self-discipline, he subsisted for most of his life on rice and raw fruits and vegetables. Through all of it, he also displayed an amazing capacity for work. His mother also instilled in him a love of reading. In his uncle's library, young Sinclair found plenty of unread books, which provided an escape from both poverty and snobbery. They also left him with a rich imagination and an ability to spin a tale.

In 1892, the precocious fourteen-year-old entered the College of the City of New York, the same year he wrote and sold his first short story. Writing fourteen hours a day, Sinclair made enough money to move into his own apartment when he was seventeen. After graduation, he studied literature at Columbia University while supporting himself as a magazine writer. He was quickly disenchanted with both hack writing and graduate school, however. Convinced that he had the ability to write a great novel, he spent an entire summer holed up in a cabin by a lake in Quebec, where he wrote up to sixteen hours a day. By fall, he had a manuscript—and a bride. The eighteen-year-old daughter of family friends happened to be at the same lake that summer with her mother. Later that year, Meta Fuller and Upton Sinclair, then twenty-two, were married.

The couple's marriage began amid dreams of literary success, but they were soon dashed. When publishers rejected his manuscript, Sinclair immediately set to work on a novel about greed and unhappiness in high society. When publishers rejected it as well, Meta left with their infant son to live with her parents, convinced that her husband needed to find a real job. Living alone in an attic in New York, the desperate Sinclair ground out two more novels. The first earned no royalties. The second, a merciless attack on the rich, was wanted by no publishers. In his hour of despair, Sinclair found salvation. Introduced by an editor to a small circle of wealthy socialists, he was a ready convert. Though no stranger to social inequality, his reading had left him ignorant of socialism and its call for public ownership of the means of production. "It was like the falling down of prison walls about my mind," he declared. With financial support from his new friends, Sinclair finished another book while living in a tent. A romantic novel set in the years before the Civil War, it sold poorly, too. The book's treatment of slavery's horrors, however, intrigued the editor of an influential socialist weekly. When he asked Sinclair to write an exposé of modern-day wage slavery, the struggling author quickly agreed.

Published in 1906, *The Jungle* changed Sinclair's life. The book became a best seller as stunned readers ignored its socialist message and concentrated instead on the vivid descriptions of conditions in meatpacking plants. (In the novel, one worker falls into a vat and ends up as sausage.) The book helped spur the passage of the Pure Food and Drug Act in 1906, which prevented the sale of mislabeled or adulterated foods and drugs. Muckraking, though, had never been Sinclair's intention. Rather, he had spent seven weeks in Chicago's stockyards and slaughterhouses to provide a realistic setting for a story about capitalism's exploitation of workers. As he later put it, he had aimed at Americans' hearts and hit them "in the stomach." Nonetheless, at twenty-seven, Sinclair was famous, and for the first time in his life, he was also flush with money.

Determined to realize a Utopian vision, he used the royalties from *The Jungle* to establish a cooperative community of some forty like-minded writers, professors, and artists in New Jersey. Unfortunately, Sinclair's investment went up in smoke when the place burned down four months later. Sinclair soon joined a single-tax community* in Alabama, but communal living put a further strain on his marriage. At the New Jersey and Alabama communities, both Upton and Meta had extramarital affairs, and in 1911, the couple finally divorced. By then, Sinclair had been converted again. In 1909, he had visited a sanatorium run by Bernarr Macfadden, the Progressive Era's leading prophet of fitness. While Macfadden convinced him of the value of vegetarianism and fasting, Sinclair fell in love with another "patient," a Mississippi judge's daughter named Mary Craig Kimbrough. Despite his belief that marriage was merely a middle-class convention, in 1913 he married Mary Craig, a union that lasted until her death nearly five decades later. The couple's interest in health and fitness soon brought them to southern California, already home to many cultists and health faddists. They settled in Pasadena, where Craig dabbled in real estate while Upton pecked out an endless stream of books on his typewriter.

None of Sinclair's later works matched the success of *The Jungle*, but he never shied away from attacks on powerful, even sacred, institutions. Thus he wrote exposes of churches, the press, schools, and the arts—all institutions, he believed, corrupted by capitalism. At the same time, Sinclair eagerly sought wealth and social acceptance. An avid

---

Single-tax community: A community that imposed a tax on the appreciated value of real estate. The single tax had been proposed by the late nineteenth-century reformer Henry George and had sparked a popular reform movement.

tennis player, he enjoyed this "leisure-class recreation" at a socially exclusive Pasadena tennis club, even though off the court he was shunned by fellow members. Rejected by Pasadena's gentry, Sinclair kept company with a group of wealthy socialists that included actor Charlie Chaplin, one of Hollywood's richest men.

In Hollywood, he again found himself on the fringes of wealth and power, slighted yet longing to break in. *The Jungle* had been made into a silent film, and although it had not been a box-office success, it had left him with a nagging desire to hit it big in the movies. The feeling intensified when studios showed interest in some of his later work. In fact, much of Sinclair's work was for MGM, which paid him $20,000 for *The Wet Parade* (1931) and $10,000 to develop a plot and characters for another proposed movie. Even so, Sinclair felt that the studio executives were shunning him, and he believed their motives were political. The "masters of capitalist drama and screen," he complained, repeatedly broke contracts because of his socialist message—or forced him to break them when they "set to work to undo my efforts."

Like a scorned lover, he claimed not to desire what he could not have. "I refuse to do movie writing," he said, "because it inevitably becomes trash." Yet for decades, Sinclair actually sought such work, and at the outset of the Depression, he even bought a foreclosed Beverly Hills mansion to be closer to Hollywood. Determined that the big screen would be his ticket to success, he invested in a failed movie venture with the Russian filmmaker Sergei Eisenstein in the early 1930s. Later, he accepted $20,000 from William Fox to write the film producer's biography. Sinclair's anti-Semitic account pictured Hollywood as a bastion of Jewish gangsters. That did not prevent him, however, from giving his unlisted telephone number—one of his most guarded secrets—to a Jewish studio executive named Irving Thalberg in the hopes of getting more work. Thalberg, as it happened, was the right-hand man of another Jewish studio executive, Louis B. Mayer.

"MORE STARS ... THAN IN HEAVEN"

In 1934, Mayer, the head of MGM, was the highest-paid corporate executive in the country. This son of an immigrant peddler had come a long way. Although his energies were not directed to intellectual pursuits, like Sinclair he worked incessantly. As one early acquaintance testified, "He rarely slept ... and he rarely ate without talking business." More than anything, though, Mayer understood motion pictures, the public, and the economics of the film industry. Like many other Jewish immigrants, Mayer's parents came to the United States to escape czarist Russia. They arrived in steerage in 1888 with their three children. Louis, the middle child, was three years old. Shortly after arriving in New York, the family left for Canada, where Mayer's father worked as a door-to-door peddler and then as a scrap-metal dealer. Before long, he had an assistant. Less interested in book learning than in making money, Louis left school at age twelve to pull a wagon through the streets of St. John, New Brunswick, and collect metal. Two years later, the new sign above the business—J. MAYER & SON—indicated that the boy had already become a partner. The ambitious Louis prodded his father to take on larger salvaging jobs, including wrecked ships. By 1900, Mayer & Son had merged with an American salvage outfit, and Louis had become its northeastern representative. The job gave him the opportunity to travel throughout New England and see a larger world. Determined to leave St. John, he moved to Boston in 1904, taking a job with another scrap-metal merchant. Not long after that, he also found a bride, Margaret Shenberg.

Quickly striking out on his own, Mayer bought his own scrap-metal operation in Brooklyn, New York, only to see it wiped out in the Panic of 1907.* Discouraged and now the father of two daughters, he moved back to Boston to live with Margaret's parents and look for another line of work. He found one at a nickelodeon called the Hub. Nickelodeons showed short, inexpensive silent features—entertainment that even the working class could afford. And unlike the scrap-metal business, they did not appear to be affected by recession. After spending time at the Hub studying programs and films, he scraped together $600 to lease a vacant theater in Haverhill, a factory town north of Boston. Nickelodeons were frequently associated with suggestive entertainment, and everything about Mayer's venture seemed unsavory. Located in a seedy part of town, the run-down property had been the home of traveling burlesque shows. Yet Mayer thought that movies shown in the right setting could attract the middle class—and those who aspired to join it. The workers from Haverhill's numerous factories and mills, he believed, would be willing to pay for inexpensive, respectable entertainment.

Repaired, repainted, and renamed the Orpheum, the theater opened in late 1907. Like other theaters of the day, it booked moving pictures and vaudeville acts, and Mayer made sure that the theater, the images on its screen, and its live performances were clean. His hunch about his patrons' cultural aspirations paid off. By the end of the first year, Mayer had grossed $25,000. Within four years, he had opened a second Haverhill theater, a movie palace that seated twenty-five hundred people and cost $150,000 to build. Soon he had a monopoly on all of the city's theaters and had taken his movie houses into several nearby towns.

By then, Mayer realized that the future of the theater business was not vaudeville but motion pictures. He also knew that exhibitors had little control over the kinds of films produced or their rental rates. Exhibition, he discovered, was a low-margin proposition. The real money was in the other two segments of the business: production and distribution. In a succession of quick moves starting in 1913, Mayer climbed up the motion-picture chain, first getting into distribution and then into production. In 1915, he secured the New England distribution rights to *The Birth of a Nation*, D. W. Griffith's huge hit about the post–Civil War redemption of the South at the hands of the Ku Klux Klan. Mayer pocketed $150,000 from the deal—enough to persuade him to liquidate his theater interests and break into producing, potentially the most profitable end of the business. In 1917, he set up his own production company. His first picture, *Virtuous Wives*, was a big hit, and he immediately began work on a second film, *In Old Kentucky*, which was to be largely shot outdoors. Most of the other film producers had already set up studios in southern California, where the climate permitted year-round outdoor filming. *In Old Kentucky* was all the impetus Mayer needed to join them. In 1918, he moved his family in quick succession from Haverhill to Boston to a bungalow near the Hollywood district of Los Angeles.

For the next five years, Mayer's modest four-stage studio churned out comedies and melodramas. The films did well, but Mayer was constrained by the economics of the rapidly growing movie industry. As weekly theater attendance reached into the tens of millions, increasing competition had driven up the big stars' salaries. For instance, Charlie Chaplin was already under contract with another studio for a million dollars a year. To justify such huge contracts, studios had to put their stars in a lot of films—a difficult proposition for a small company like Louis B. Mayer Pictures. Meanwhile, large theater operators such as Marcus Loew, who had built a chain of more than one hundred theaters in the Northeast, were under increasing pressure to maintain a steady flow of films

---

*Panic of 1907: An economic downturn brought on by the collapse of the stock market and several bank failures.

into their theaters. As in other major industries, the solution was to achieve economy through vertical integration* and consolidation.

By the early 1920s, theater operators had moved into distribution and production, while producers had moved into exhibition. Mayer fell "victim" to this consolidation wave in 1925, when he sold his company to Marcus Loew's production company for $76,000. Like many motion-picture pioneers, Loew had started out in vaudeville. In 1920, the theater operator had bought Metro Pictures Corporation, a struggling production company. Four years later, he had combined it with Goldwyn Pictures, another fledgling outfit whose most notable feature was its trademark Leo the lion and the halo scroll reading *Ars Gratia Artis* (Art for Art's Sake). Already impressed by Mayer's operation, Loew turned to the young producer to run the new company, naming him first vice president and head of production at MGM. Mayer would get a weekly salary of $1500 and 10 percent of the studio's profits. Meanwhile, his young assistant, Irving Thalberg, became second vice president.

Although he now worked for someone else, Mayer was still in charge. After a ceremony at the company's new Universal City studios, where he read congratulatory telegrams from President Calvin Coolidge and Secretary of Commerce Herbert Hoover, Mayer got down to the business of producing movies. After all, Loew's expanding theater chain had nearly a quarter of a million seats to be filled every day. Mayer organized the studio into numerous departments and film production into an assembly line. Every assistant producer and department head was answerable to the studio head. Mayer also controlled the kinds of movies that MGM made. The films that filled seats, he believed, had strong characters whom viewers could root for and relate to. Moviegoers did not want to be confused or threatened, and they did not want their values challenged. Just like Haverhill's Orpheum theater, MGM's films would be clean: Adultery, lewdness, and infidelity were invariably condemned. "I'll never make anything that I wouldn't take my daughters to see," Mayer said.

Above all, MGM's boss also knew that big-name stars filled theater seats. In the silent-film era, his studio's stable included Lillian Gish, Greta Garbo, Lon Chaney, and Lionel Barrymore. After MGM switched to sound production in 1929, it laid claim to Judy Garland, Katharine Hepburn, and Spencer Tracy, as well as Joan Crawford and Clark Gable. By the early 1930s, MGM advertised that its films contained "more stars than there are in heaven." These big-name stars often commanded princely salaries and lived like royalty. Marion Davies's dressing room on the MGM lot, for instance, was a fourteen-room "bungalow." By the 1930s, this star system helped make Hollywood the third-biggest source of news in the nation—after New York City and Washington, D.C.—as studios released tidbits about their stars' lives to a ravenous public.

The glitter surrounding the stars also hid the dictatorial control that Mayer and other studio heads exercised over them. The stars, Mayer realized, were the studios' biggest asset. That meant they needed to be controlled. Contracts tied stars to a studio for seven years and gave it total control over their performances and roles. More than any other studio boss, Mayer rid his studio of performers who showed independence. His control extended to the stars' private lives. Responding to a growing public outcry about Hollywood's lax moral standards, the studios imposed censorship on themselves in 1930 with the establishment of a production code. Will Hays, president of the Motion Picture

---

Vertical integration: A form of business organization in which one firm controls all steps in the production process, from securing the raw materials to distributing the finished product.

Producers and Distributors of America, administered the code. In this atmosphere, Mayer would not tolerate even a hint of public scandal among his stars.

If no movie boss was more powerful than Mayer, no company prospered more under the studio system than MGM. By the early 1930s, Hollywood was dominated by five major firms that turned out the vast majority of motion pictures, cooperated on movie distribution, and controlled the most lucrative theaters. Of the so-called Big Five, MGM was the biggest and most profitable. Mayer's rationalized production system and absolute control proved a winning formula even in the depths of the Depression. Between 1930 and 1933, his studio produced nine of the twenty-four top-grossing films. Mayer spent lavishly, pouring on average far more money into each film than any other studio. He also knew that Depression-era movie audiences wanted to be entertained with fantasy, not reminded of their troubles. Although Warner Brothers and a few other studios produced gangster, crime, and other "social problem" films in the 1930s, MGM studiously avoided movies that dealt with the decade's social and economic issues. Rather, Mayer's studio was a dream factory that produced films conveying glitz, glamour, and luxury.

While MGM churned out celluloid fantasies, the Depression's stark reality was becoming all too clear. Between 1929 and 1932, the nation's economic output plummeted nearly 50 percent, more than fifty-five hundred banks went under, and unemployment swelled from only 3 percent to 25 percent. Not heavily industrialized in the early twentieth century, California initially felt the Depression's effects less than many other areas. By 1934, however, even the Golden State had withered under its impact. In that year, more than four hundred thousand Californians were unemployed, 1.5 million were on public relief or private charity, and thousands of desperate migrants streamed into the state every week. Many of these newcomers were former tenants or sharecroppers from the South who had been run off the land, victims of a prolonged agricultural slump. Others were victims of the drought that had turned much of the high plains into the Dust Bowl. These poor refugees—"Okies," as many Californians called them—usually found conditions in the Golden State little better than those they had fled. By 1934, there were not enough agricultural jobs to go around. Those lucky enough to find work in the fields often labored for as little as fifteen cents an hour. No wonder labor unrest and violence had spread from the state's farms to its canneries and docks in the past year.

By 1934, the Depression was even hitting uncomfortably close to the movie studios' star-studded lots. Since 1929, movie attendance had decreased by about twenty-five million, and thousands of movie houses had turned out their lights for good. At the same time, labor organizing spread to Hollywood, as hard times spawned a renewed interest in unions among workers nationwide. Membership in the Screen Actors Guild, a union formed in 1933 to battle the "professional slavery" of the studio contract system, grew dramatically in just its first year. Writers quickly followed suit by reviving the Screen Writers Guild, with several MGM writers taking the lead. Confronted with growing labor agitation, the studio heads were alarmed, and MGM even placed a number of its employees under surveillance, suspicious that they might be communists. Making matters worse, by the fall of 1934, Upton Sinclair appeared headed for victory in the governor's race.

"NONSENSE OFTEN RULES THE ROOST"

Only the year before, some disgruntled California Democrats had persuaded Sinclair to challenge the state party's conservative establishment by running for governor. The author launched his campaign in characteristic fashion, by writing *I, Governor of California: And How I Ended Poverty*, a futuristic story about a governor named Upton Sinclair. In this "true story of the future," Sinclair ends poverty in California by taking over idle farmland and factories and turning them over to cooperatives owned by unemployed farmers and workers. As the story made clear, production for use rather than profit was the heart of Sinclair's EPIC program. Sinclair also called for the repeal of the sales tax, steeply graduated income and property taxes, and stiff taxes on public utilities. In addition, needy individuals over age sixty would be able to collect a monthly pension of $50. In a series of pamphlets produced during the campaign, Sinclair further defined the EPIC program. He made clear that it was not just a temporary relief measure but a way to restructure the economy of California permanently through the introduction of socialism. [See Source 1.]

Sinclair's platform quickly gained widespread support among Californians disillusioned by the failure of FDR's New Deal to bring economic recovery. It was especially popular in the southern part of the state, where many recent transplants from the Midwest had settled. Many were lower-middle class and elderly who had looked forward to a warm and comfortable retirement. The Depression had taken away their jobs and, as banks and insurance companies went under, their retirement nest eggs as well. With their golden dreams shattered, these people found an outlet for their increasing disaffection by rushing into any number of reform movements. Thousands of them joined the Utopian Society of America, an organization dedicated to promoting a technocracy.* Others flocked to the movement led by Francis Townsend, a retired Long Beach physician and former midwesterner whose Townsend Plan proposed to rescue the elderly with a $200 monthly pension. Organized in early 1934, Townsend's movement spread rapidly through southern California and beyond. By the end of the year, it would claim a half million followers nationwide.

Utopians and Townsendites provided the EPIC movement with a large, enthusiastic, well-organized constituency. Many small farmers, blue-collar workers, and academics—and even some studio employees—were attracted to the EPIC crusade as well. By the summer of 1934, Sinclair's supporters had organized more than a thousand EPIC clubs, which held picnics, auctions, rummage sales, and other fund-raisers. They also had registered three hundred fifty thousand Democratic Party voters. In the August primary, Sinclair shocked the state's Democratic establishment—and himself—when the accelerating EPIC bandwagon crushed his opponent, George Creel, Woodrow Wilson's propaganda chief during World War I (see Chapter 5). Meanwhile, the winner of the Republican primary—archconservative incumbent Frank Merriam—had generated little excitement, even among Republicans, and Sinclair had out-polled him by nearly a hundred thousand votes.

Like most other Californians, Louis B. Mayer was surprised by Sinclair's sudden popularity. Only two years before, during the filming of Sinclair's book *The Wet Parade*, the MGM boss had ordered "that bum" kept off the studio's lot. After learning of Sinclair's victory, Mayer told reporters that if Sinclair won in the November election, "chaos" would reign in the state. "I am a Republican," he added, "only because I believe a Republican administration is better for the business and economic condition of our country." Mayer was not ready to concede the defeat of the economic system just yet. First, he quickly drafted his own employees into the anti-Sinclair cause by deducting one day's wages a week from the biggest stars down to the stagehands. Next, he rallied other

---

Technocracy: A society in which the government and economy are controlled by technocrats—scientists and engineers.

studio bosses to support the effort to stop the EPIC movement. Through MGM, they were linked to an anti-Sinclair front organization called United for California. It brought together Mayer, *Los Angeles Times* publisher Harry Chandler, the head of the huge agricultural cooperative Sunkist, and the bosses of other big firms such as Southern California Edison, Southern Pacific, and Standard Oil of California. United for California raised several hundred thousand dollars, much of it from Hollywood studios. Then, with the assistance of Lord & Thomas, an advertising agency brought in to run the Merriam campaign, it began to wage an all-out war on Sinclair. Lord & Thomas had previously convinced millions of Americans to consume California citrus products. Now, for the first time, an ad agency would run a political campaign. Bankrolled by United for California, the agency began filling the airwaves with anti-Sinclair radio spots, while anti-Sinclair groups blanketed the state with millions of pamphlets and leaflets. **[See Source 2.]**

To Sinclair, Mayer represented everything that was evil about a studio system dominated by the "masters of big business and special privilege." Now he had a chance to defy the studio boss. When Mayer issued a statement during the campaign that the studios would move to Florida if Sinclair won the election, the Democratic candidate dismissed the threat as "bunk." Then he countered Mayer with a threat of his own: Once elected, he would get the state into the movie business. Such pronouncements only made his opponents' task easier. The novice Democratic candidate also said too much in public, as when he jokingly remarked that if he were elected, "Half the unemployed of the United States will come to California." Raising the frightening specter of an invading army of unemployed people, the anti-Sinclair forces skillfully played on middle-class fears of social unrest and class conflict. For instance, the *Los Angeles Examiner* and other newspapers ran a picture of homeless people arriving in California by train in anticipation of a Sinclair victory. Readers did not know that the photo was a fake—a still from *Wild Boys of the Road*, a 1933 Warner Brothers movie about young men who rode the rails during the Depression. **[See Source 3.]**

Meanwhile, Mayer's assistant Irving Thalberg also worked to thwart the Sinclair movement. The result was *California Election News*, a series of film shorts that looked and sounded like newsreels but were merely anti-Sinclair propaganda. After the first *California Election News* trailer appeared in theaters in mid-October, some irate patrons protested. That did nothing, however, to stop the "Inquiring Cameraman" series. The second installment hit theaters later that month. It followed the format of its predecessor, but it lacked any subtlety at all. One man in the film said that he was going to vote for "St. Clair" because he "is the author of the Russian government." He was countered by an auto mechanic, wearing a bow tie and spotless clothes, who said, "Mr. Merriam will support all the principles America has stood for."

The Sinclair campaign protested that the *California Election News* shorts contained fake footage and that the Inquiring Cameraman created copy "to suit himself," but MGM kept roaring. The third film arrived in theaters the weekend prior to the election. This one abandoned the man-on-the-street format to present a shocking expose of hobos invading California. It was filled with scenes of men riding the rails, although some of the images were much sharper than others, a hint that they were probably cuts from feature films. Then it took viewers into the "jungle" of a "hobo camp." As the camera passed over the "hobos" (or movie extras), the narrator said ominously, "Look at them. Listen to them, and *think.*" **[See Source 4.]**

In the face of this barrage, Sinclair's campaign sputtered. California's newspapers lined up uniformly against the Democratic candidate and frequently reminded their readers of Mayer's threat to pull the motion-picture industry out of the state if Sinclair won. The *Los Angeles*

Times ran virtually no news stories on Sinclair's campaign, while emitting a daily drumbeat of anti-Sinclair editorials. A "maggot-like horde of Reds," it warned in one, was supporting the Sinclair campaign. "They are termites … secretly and darkly eating into everything that the American heart has held dear and sacred." Denied access to the state's media, the candidate was forced to campaign mostly at rallies of the faithful. They were no match for the frightening images that too many Californians saw in newspapers and on the big screen. When the votes were counted, Sinclair had lost. More than eight hundred seventy-nine thousand voters had cast ballots for him, but more than one million one hundred thirty-eight thousand had voted for Merriam. It did not help that Sinclair had failed to gain FDR's support. The president already had a wary eye on Francis Townsend and the other leaders of Depression-era crusades. By 1934, right-wing Michigan radio priest Charles Coughlin had won a large audience with calls for social justice. Meanwhile, Louisiana populist demagogue Huey Long had amassed a huge nationwide following with his Share Our Wealth program, which proposed to combat the Depression's effects with soak-the-rich taxes and wealth redistribution. Given these men's threats to his own popularity, Roosevelt was not about to go out on a limb for the eccentric Sinclair. The failure of George Creel and other California Democratic leaders to endorse their party's candidate also did not help. In addition, Sinclair had failed to persuade the Progressive Party candidate, who garnered more than three hundred thousand votes, to withdraw. Finally, Sinclair had refused to counter the charges leveled against him by his opponents. The accusations were merely "nonsense," he told a Screen Writers Guild organizer. "But nonsense," the writer replied, "often rules the roost."

"WE DID WIN"

On election night, Mayer threw a bash attended by some of Hollywood's biggest celebrities. The studio boss declared jubilantly that the "voters of California have made a fearless choice between radicalism and patriotism." Sinclair, too, met the election outcome in fitting fashion: He wrote a book about it. Titled *I, Candidate for Governor: And How I Got Licked*, it was a "revelation of what money can do in American politics [and] what it will do when its privileges are threatened." **[See Source 5.]**

Even though Mayer had helped defeat Sinclair, the nature of his victory became less clear as time went on. The MGM lion, of course, still roars on the big screen, while motion pictures remain a powerful form of popular cultural expression. Moreover, advertising and public relations have come to play an increasing role in American political campaigns as the line between entertainment and news becomes ever more blurred. The power of Mayer and other studio moguls, however, would diminish in the next two decades. Buoyed by the pro-labor Wagner Act[*], studio employees began to win independence from the bosses' iron grip. Later, as fear of communist subversion grew in the late 1940s, Hollywood became the target of congressional investigators. Although Mayer and other bosses solidified their reputations as red-baiters with blacklists against alleged communists, the "red scare" in Hollywood demonstrated the studios' vulnerability to outside political pressures. So did a major antitrust decision by the Supreme Court in 1948 that ordered the studios to get out of the film exhibition business, a ruling that hit MGM especially hard. Within a few years, the rise of television would further erode the studios' power. By the early 1950s, even the once-mighty MGM saw its sales and profits slump.

---

[*]*Wagner Act:* Legislation passed in 1935 that bolstered the right of labor unions to organize and bargain collectively for wages and benefits.

The demise of the studio system was paralleled by the deterioration of Mayer's personal life. Although MGM's films frequently upheld the sanctity of marriage, Mayer was not a faithful husband, and in 1946, Margaret Mayer sued for divorce. About the same time, when his young girlfriend decided to marry another man, Mayer took an overdose of sleeping pills. Although he remarried several years later, Mayer was increasingly out of touch with changing popular tastes in films. Six years before he died in 1957, MGM ousted its onetime master.

Meanwhile, Sinclair continued to churn out books until a few years before he died in 1968. Right after the California election, he attempted to take EPIC nationwide, but the crusade soon collapsed as unemployment began to decline with the help of the New Deal programs. Yet EPIC had left its mark. While governor, Frank Merriam signed a state income tax, one of the planks in EPIC's platform. Furthermore, the New Deal responded to EPIC and other popular movements by embracing a raft of new programs, including Social Security, steeper taxes on the rich, and massive work relief. Perhaps Sinclair had all that in mind when he answered a reporter's question in 1958 about how California would be different had he won in 1934. "We did win," he replied. "We gave California and all the other states an exciting awareness of what democracy really is."

• PRIMARY SOURCES •

Source 1:   Upton Sinclair, *"EPIC Answers"* (1934)

Following is an excerpt from one of four pamphlets that Sinclair published before the 1934 California gubernatorial election. What are his solutions to the Depression? Do they reflect socialist views? Are any of his proposed solutions in effect today?

In our State of California we have now more than a million persons dependent upon public charity for their existence. Many of our counties are already bankrupt. Our State will be more than a hundred million dollars "in the hole" by the end of 1934, and bankruptcy has only been averted by the Federal Government stepping in to take the burden of feeding the hungry. The Federal Government is now supporting the banks, the insurance companies, the railroads, the great industrial corporations; the home-owners, the farmers, the veterans, the unemployed. Bankruptcy for the Federal Government is only a question of months.

To this problem there can be but one solution. It is necessary to put the unemployed at productive labor. A million people in California must be made self-sustaining. They must have access to the land to grow their own food; they must have access to the factories to produce their own clothing and building materials, out of which to make their own homes. We must take them off the backs of the little tax-payers, and stop forcing the latter out of their homes and off their ranches. There must be prompt action, for the crisis is desperate and the next breakdown may lead to attempts at revolt and civil war....

The destitute people cannot get land or factories or raw materials for themselves. This can only be done by the credit of the State. The EPIC plan proposes that the State

SOURCE: Upton Sinclair, "EPIC Answers," pp. 3–A, 5–6 in Upton Sinclair, The EPIC Plan for California (1934).

shall purchase the idle land and factories at the present bankruptcy prices, and shall immediately institute a State system of production and exchange, whereby the unemployed may produce what they consume.

The "subsistence homesteads" now proposed as a solution of the problem constitute a step backward. When men live on small farms and produce only what they themselves consume, they can never escape poverty and drudgery. Modern production is mass production, both on farms and in factories. It requires great tracts of land, costly machinery, and expert direction.

The EPIC plan proposes that the State of California shall set up land colonies in which the unemployed farm workers shall live and produce the food required by the million destitute persons in our State. Operating thus upon a large scale, the farm workers can live in what will amount to new villages, with all the advantages of modern civilization: kitchens and cafeterias operated by the community, a social hall with opportunities for recreation, a church, a school-house, a store, a library, a motion picture theatre, etc....

The factories will be great productive units owned and managed by the State. There also will be social buildings with kitchens, cafeterias, lecture halls, libraries, etc. The State will maintain a system of distribution, whereby the food is brought into the cities and the manufactured products are taken out to the land colonies, and all the products of the system are made available at cost. Those who produce will receive the full social value of their product, so they will be able to buy what they have produced, and for the first time consumption will balance production....

People are now losing their homes and ranches because they can no longer pay their taxes. The tax system of the State is to be revised, and all homes occupied by the owners and ranches operated by the owners, which are assessed at less than $3000, are to be exempted from taxation. Taxes on the more valuable properties will be graduated, increasing at the rate of one-half of one per cent for each $5000 of additional value.

It is proposed to repeal the State sales tax, which is a tax on poverty, and to raise a portion of the money by means of a State tax upon stock exchange transactions. New York State imposes a tax of 4 cents per share on stock transfers, and there is no reason why California could not do the same. It is estimated that a million shares change hands in our State every gambling day. Let Wall Street pay the sales tax!

Next it is proposed to impose a State income tax. In the United States today an income of $25,000 per year pays 10%. In England, France, and Germany, such an income pays 30% to 40%. So there is ample margin for a graduated State income tax. It is also proposed to increase the State inheritance tax in the higher brackets, taking 50% of those great fortunes which are unearned and which are a menace to our society.

Finally, it is proposed to impose a graduated tax upon idle and unused land. Our cities and towns are ringed around with vacant lots held by speculators. If a person owns a lot assessed at not more than $1000, and wishes to build a home upon that lot, there will be a State building loan fund to make this possible. But persons who are holding large tracts of land out of use will be taxed for it, the tax being graduated according to the valuation held by each individual.

It is also proposed to include a tax on privately owned public utility corporations and banks, which are shamefully undertaxed at present.

The remainder of the EPIC program has to do with those persons who are unable to work. It promises that needy persons over sixty years of age who have lived three years within the State, shall receive a pension of $50 per month. It promises the same for the blind and disabled, and for the widowed mothers of dependent children. If there are more than two children, it proposes to add $25 per month for each additional child.

Source 2:   *Anti-Sinclair Leaflet* (1934)

Anti-Sinclair forces flooded California with millions of leaflets. What fears does this example reflect?

> # SINCLAIR
>
> ### DYNAMITER
> OF
> ### ALL CHURCHES
> AND
> ### ALL CHRISTIAN
> ### INSTITUTIONS
>
> ---
>
> ### ACTIVE OFFICIAL
> OF
> ### COMMUNIST
> ### ORGANIZATIONS
>
> ---
>
> ### COMMUNIST WRITER
>
> ---
>
> ### COMMUNIST AGITATOR
>
> ---
>
> THE MAN WHO SAID THE
> ## P. T. A.
> HAS BEEN TAKEN OVER
> BY THE
>
> # BLACK HAND
>
> Issued by
> California Democratic Governor's League
> M. J. Brown, Secy., 2000 Holly Drive, Los Angeles

SOURCE: Reprinted in Greg Mitchell, The Campaign of the Century: Upton Sinclair's Race for Governor of California and the Birth of Media Politics (New York: Random House, 1992), between pp. 332 and 333.

Source 3: *"California, Here We Come"* (1934)

This anti-Sinclair leaflet was distributed after Sinclair quipped that unemployed people would flock to California if he were elected. In what ways do you think this image would play on the fears of many Californians? Which one of these leaflets do you find more successful or compelling?

SOURCE: Reprinted in Greg Mitchell, The Campaign of the Century: Upton Sinclair's Race for Governor and the birth of Media Politics (New York: Random House, 1992) p. 333.

Source 4:   *"Hollywood Masses the Full Power of Her Resources to Fight Sinclair"* (1934)

This article, published in the New York Times *on the Sunday before election day, detailed the lengths to which the MGM-led forces in Hollywood went to ensure Sinclair's defeat. Do you think it is significant that a story such as this was published in an East Coast rather than a California newspaper?*

From a Staff Correspondent Hollywood.

The full force of the motion-picture industry overwhelming in this fabulous city, has been thrown into the crusade to keep Upton Sinclair out of the Governor's chair at Sacramento.

Under a plan of campaign accredited generally to Louis B. Mayer, Republican State chairman and head of the Metro-Goldwyn-Mayer Studios, the thirty-odd thousand people employed directly or indirectly in making pictures, as well as the talents and skill of the craft, have been drafted for the final multi-partisan assault upon the smiling Socialist who captured the Democratic nomination in the August primaries.

The higher salaried employes of each of the … seven major studios have either been assessed or "requested" a day's salary for the campaign fund of Governor Frank F. Merriam, whose Republican candidacy has now become the standard for the "Stop Sinclair" forces. All movie workers, high and low, have been called or circularized and either told or "advised" how to vote in the interest of maintenance of their jobs. Merriam literature, buttons and emblems have been distributed through all the lots.

★ ★ ★

The city of Los Angeles has turned into a huge movie set where many newsreel pictures are made every day, depicting the feelings of the people against Mr. Sinclair. Equipment from one of the major studios, as well as some of its second-rate players, may be seen at various street intersections or out in the residential neighborhood, "shooting" the melodrama and unconscious comedy of the campaign. Their product can be seen in leading motion-picture houses in practically every city or town of the State.

In one of the "melodramas" recently filmed and shown here in Los Angeles, an interviewer approaches a demure old lady, sitting on her front porch and rocking away in her rocking chair.

"For whom are you voting, Mother?" asked the interviewer.

"I am voting for Governor Merriam," the old lady answers in a faltering voice.

"Why, Mother?"

"Because I want to save my little home. It is all I have left in this world."

In another recent newsreel there is shown a shaggy man with bristling Russian whiskers and a menacing look in his eye.

"For whom are you voting?" asks the interviewer.

"Vy, I am foting for Seenclair."

"Why are you voting for Mr. Sinclair?"

"Vell, his system worked vell in Russia, vy can't it vork here?"

All these "releases" are presented as newsreels.

Another "newsreel" has been made of Oscar Rankin, a colored prizefighter and preacher who is quite a favorite with his race in Los Angeles county. Asked why he

SOURCE: THE NEW YORK TIMES, November 5, 1934, p. 5.

was voting for Governor Merriam, he answered that he likes to preach and play the piano and he wants to keep a church to preach in and a piano to play.

Merriam supporters always are depicted as the more worth-while element of the community, as popular favorites or as substantial business men. Sinclair supporters are invariably pictured as the riff-raff. Low paid "bit" players are said to take the leading roles in most of these "newsreels," particularly where dialogue is required. People conversant with movie personnel claim to have recognized in them certain aspirants to stardom.

★ ★ ★

But even cleverness has faltered at times in the ruthlessness of the anti-Sinclair campaign. A leading newspaper of Los Angeles is reported to have called upon one of the studios for a "still" picture of bums entering the State in response to Sinclair's invitation to the unemployed of the whole country. The picture was quickly furnished and published. The publicity department of another studio immediately recognized the photograph as a scene from a recent cinema. The recognition was made simple because the leading juvenile star on the feature was sitting stop the box car.

The studio managers have stopped at nothing to insure a full vote of their employes for Merriam. They have told them not to put too much stock in the writing genius of the man. "Out of forty-seven books he has written, not one has ever been filmed," an official is said to have told some of his employes the other day.

At another studio an official called in his scenario writers to give them a bit of "advice" on how to vote. "After all," he is reputed to have told his writers, "what does Sinclair know about anything? He's just a writer."

Stories of this kind can be picked up at every studio provided the teller, who invariably is a "Merriam" man, can be assured he will not be quoted and provided, too, that he can relate it out of any possible hearing of his associates.

A fun-making film news writer for an Eastern newspaper strolled into the commissary on the Metro-Goldwyn-Mayer lot a few days ago and began distributing Sinclair literature which he had purchased downtown, just to see what would happen. When the high-powered Metro publicity men, to whom he handed the leaflets, saw what they were, they crumpled them up and dropped them as if they were hot. They did not know whether to cram them in their pockets or what to do with them. They pleaded in all seriousness for the news writer not to play such a prank, which might be disastrous to their jobs.

These stories sound fantastic, but they are no more so than the very nature of the class war which is called the Sinclair campaign. It is a humorless, grim affair, made comical by its very lack of humor.

Source 5:   *Upton Sinclair Assesses His Loss* (1934)

In I, Candidate for Governor: And How I Got Licked, *Sinclair analyzes the reasons for the election outcome, including the role played by Louis B. Mayer. Was Sinclair correct in attributing his loss to the threat that EPIC posed to the moneyed class? Do you think the assertions in this source regarding the power of the "picture business" in politics have proven true?*

Source: I, CANDIDATE FOR GOVERNOR: AND HOW I GOT LICKED by Upton Sinclair, (Berkeley: University of California Press, 1994; originally published in 1934).

This is the story of the EPIC movement and the campaign to End Poverty in California; an "inside" story of events about which there has been much guessing. It is a revelation of what money can do in American politics; what it will do when its privileges are threatened. When I was a boy, the President of Harvard University wrote about "the scholar in politics." Here is set forth how a scholar went into politics, and what happened to him.

I am beginning this story three days after the election. Having known for a month what was coming, I had time to practice smiling. I write now in a mood of cheerful aloofness. To the gentlemen of great wealth who control the State of California I would not pay the compliment of grieving about anything they could do to me.

I grieve for the people. But the people have suffered for ages, and I have no way to help it. Whoever made this universe ordained it that people learn by suffering, and in no other way. The people of California have much to learn.

For the past fourteen months I have traveled up and down the State, addressing some two hundred meetings and facing half a million men and women. I spoke a score of times over the radio, so that practically every one in the State heard my voice. The substance of my message was this:

"All my life I have believed and preached democracy, in the broad sense of that word; the right and power of the people to govern their own affairs. I am proposing now that the people shall vote to End Poverty in California. I am willing to abide by the people's decision. If you have not suffered enough, it is your God-given right to suffer some more. All you have to do is to elect Governor Merriam, and he will see that you do it."...

While I was in New York some reporter asked: "What are you going to do with the unemployed motion picture actors?" I answered: "Why should not the State of California rent one of the idle studios and let the unemployed actors make a few pictures of their own?" That word was flashed to Hollywood, and the war was on.

Louis B. Mayer, president of Metro-Goldwyn-Mayer, was vacationing in Europe when he got this dreadful news, and he dropped everything and came home to take charge of the campaign to "stop Sinclair". You see, he is chairman of the State Committee of the Republican party, so he had a double responsibility....

... [T]hey started in making newsreels.... They invented a character called "the Inquiring Reporter". He was supposed to be traveling around California, interviewing people on the campaign. They were supposed to be real people, but of course they were actors....

Hitherto the movies have maintained that they could not do any kind of "educational" work; their audiences demanded entertainment, and they could have nothing to do with "propaganda." But now, you see, that pretense has been cast aside. They have made propaganda, and they have won a great victory with it, and are tremendously swelled up about it. You may be sure that never again will there be an election in California in which the great "Louie Bee" will not make his power felt.... [S]o will you see the "Inquiring Reporter" arriving in Minnesota, Mississippi, Washington, or wherever big business desires to ridicule the efforts of the disinherited to help themselves at the ballot-box.

Listen to the lords of the screen world vaunting themselves: The front page of the "Hollywood Reporter" eleven days prior to the election.

"When the picture business gets aroused, it becomes AROUSED, and, boy, how they go to it!

"This campaign against Upton Sinclair has been and is DYNAMITE. It is the most effective piece of political humdingery that has ever been effected, and this is said in full recognition of the antics of that master-machine that used to be Tammany. Politicians in every part of this land (and they are all vitally interested in the California election) are standing by in amazement as a result of the bombast that has been set off under the rocking chair of Mr. Sinclair.

"Never before in the history of the picture business has the screen been used in direct support of a candidate. Maybe an isolated exhibitor here and there has run a slide or two, favoring a friend, but never has there been a concerted action on the part of all theatres in a community to defeat a nominee.

"And this activity may reach much farther than the ultimate defeat of Mr. Sinclair. It will undoubtedly give the big wigs in Washington and politicians all over the country an idea of the real POWER that is in the hands of the picture industry.

QUESTIONS TO CONSIDER

1. Although Upton Sinclair's and Louis B. Mayer's politics were very different, in some ways, the two men were much alike. How would you compare Sinclair and Mayer? What are the most important factors in each man's life for understanding his public or political activities?

2. What do the rise and work of Mayer and MGM reveal about the forces that helped shape the motion-picture industry in the early twentieth century? How do the films that MGM produced in the early 1930s reflect those forces?

3. What were the goals of Sinclair's EPIC campaign? Given the circumstances in the 1930s, were they realistic?

4. Why did Sinclair lose the California governor's race in 1934? What do the actions of Mayer and the other opponents of Sinclair's campaign reveal about some of the forces that limited reform in the 1930s? Are the same forces at work in campaigns today?

5. Considering modern American politics and society as well as the issues in the 1934 California election, do you think Sinclair was correct in arguing that he and his supporters actually did win?

FOR FURTHER READING

Anthony Arthur, *Radical Innocent: Upton Sinclair* (New York: Random House, 2006), offers a recent biography of the author and political candidate.

Scott Eyman, *The Life and Legend of Louis B. Mayer* (New York: Simon and Schuster, 2005), provides a comprehensive account of Mayer's rise and fall.

Leon Harris, *Upton Sinclair: American Rebel* (New York: Thomas Y. Crowell Company, 1975), submits a sympathetic treatment of Sinclair that concentrates on his life through the 1934 campaign.

Greg Mitchell, *The Campaign of the Century: Upton Sinclair's Race for Governor of California and the Birth of Media Politics* (New York: Random House, 1992), offers a highly readable day-by-day account of the 1934 election, emphasizing the groundbreaking aspects of the anti-Sinclair campaign.

Robert Sklar, *Movie-Made America: A Cultural History of American Movies* (New York: Random House, 1994), explores motion pictures as a form of cultural expression related to important political, economic, and social developments.

Robert H. Stanley, *The Celluloid Empire: A History of the American Movie Industry* (New York: Hastings House, 1978), offers a brief overview of the development of moviemaking as a business dominated by large corporations.

8

Racism and Relocation During World War II: Harry Ueno and Dillon Myer

As Harry Ueno slept on the night of December 5, 1942, he was blissfully unaware that his life was about to take a turn for the worse. Ueno was one of the roughly one hundred twenty thousand Japanese and Japanese Americans confined in internment camps during World War II. He was awakened when three jeeps loaded with military police (MP) pulled up in front of his barracks at California's Manzanar Relocation Center. Startled by the MP's arrival, Ueno jumped from his bed when he heard a bang at the door and the demand that he get dressed. Earlier that evening, another Japanese-American internee had been beaten inside Manzanar by a group of masked men. It was no random act of violence. Home to more than ten thousand people of Japanese ancestry, Manzanar had been wracked by tensions among the internees. Many internees, including the assault victim, urged cooperation with the policy of internment. Other internees resented both the policy and its supporters. As Ueno approached his barracks door, he was about to become the focus of that division.

The MP took Ueno to the Manzanar police station, where he was interrogated about the beating for the next two hours. Then he was driven to the jail in nearby Independence, California, in handcuffs. The next afternoon, the Manzanar police chief drove Ueno back to the internment center, where he was thrown in jail with five or six other Japanese internees. As Ueno looked outside his jail window that evening, he noticed a large number of internees milling around. They had gathered to demand that camp authorities set Ueno free. The next day was the first anniversary of the Japanese attack on Pearl Harbor, and as the crowd grew bigger, he heard a sergeant exhort the MP to "remember Pearl Harbor!" Then he saw the MP put on gas masks and begin to throw tear gas canisters into the crowd. As smoke filled the air, Ueno heard five or six shots at

Hulton Archive/Getty Images

National Archives

Soldiers and civilians at the Manzanar
Internment Camp

Dillon Myer

close range. From farther away came the sound of machine gun fire. When the smoke cleared, he saw one man lying facedown on the ground.

The Manzanar Riot left two men dead and ten others wounded. It was the deadliest outbreak of violence in any of the nation's ten internment camps. It was also the kind of incident that Dillon Myer was determined to avoid. Myer was the head of the War Relocation Authority (WRA), the federal agency that administered the internment camps. A career bureaucrat in the federal government, he wanted no trouble in his facilities. Moreover, Myer was actually sympathetic to the Japanese Americans under the WRA's wartime control. He realized that camp disturbances like the one at Manzanar only reinforced anti-Japanese sentiment and the public perception that his agency needed to be tougher on the internees. Thus he had little use for "troublemakers."

Ueno seemed to be just that. He was accused of beating a fellow internee, and his arrest had sparked the deadly violence. In Myer's mind, Ueno needed to be dealt with swiftly. Although Ueno was never charged with any crime, he would be hauled off to isolation centers in Utah and Arizona. Later, he would be confined to another such center holding thousands of allegedly disloyal Japanese and Japanese Americans. Seeking release from criminal confinement, Ueno met resistance at every turn. In the minds of Myer and many Japanese-American internees, he was a dangerous agitator who threatened the future of all Japanese Americans.

"ONCE A JAP, ALWAYS A JAP"

Harry Ueno was a very unlikely troublemaker. Before the war, he had lived quietly in Los Angeles with his wife and three children. Never one to shy away from hard work, he had labored diligently at a variety of jobs in the fruit and vegetable business. For a time, he had run a small fruit stand near Hollywood frequented by movie stars and even studio boss Louis B. Mayer (see Chapter 7). Ueno had quickly learned that Mayer and the other movie people were hard to please, so he had tried to have a variety of produce in stock even when it was out of season. Always he had been careful to mind his own business.

Few Japanese and Japanese Americans in California had such an opportunity to brush up against Hollywood producers and movie stars. But in another way, Ueno was typical of many West Coast Japanese and Japanese Americans before World War II. As did many of the roughly forty-seven thousand Issei* and seventy-nine thousand Nisei* in the United States, Ueno had a lot of experience growing or marketing agricultural produce. Up and down the West Coast's fertile valleys, Japanese immigrants had begun to succeed as small farmers in the early twentieth century. Although many of them had originally come to Hawaii and the mainland as farm laborers in the late nineteenth century, they had always aspired to farm their own land. Frequently, they had worked modest plots of marginal land and managed to produce bountiful harvests. In 1920, people of Japanese descent represented only 2 percent of California's population, but they produced 92 percent of the state's strawberries, 80 percent of its celery, and 66 percent of its tomatoes.

Like many Japanese-American families, the Uenos got their start in agriculture. Harry Ueno's parents had moved from Hiroshima to the island of Hawaii around 1897 to work as agricultural laborers. When Harry was born in 1907, the second of three sons, his parents were working on a sugar plantation. Within a few years, however, his father was leasing land to grow his own sugarcane and watermelons. Achieving a measure of prosperity, he sent eight-year-old Harry back to Hiroshima to be educated. The boy lived with his grandparents for seven years until his father and mother also returned to Japan. By then, Harry felt alienated from his parents, and he moved to Tokyo, where he delivered morning and evening newspapers and attended school during the day. After earning only food and shelter for six months, he moved back home. "I was thinking," Ueno later recalled, " 'What to do? I must do something for myself.' " Two months after enrolling in a course to become a member of the merchant marine, he was on a ship bound for the United States.

By the time the freighter arrived in the Pacific Northwest in 1923, Ueno had decided that he was not cut out to be a sailor. At Tacoma, Washington, the last American port of call, he jumped ship and went to work in a sawmill. He was surprised by the large number of Japanese workers in the mill's labor camp. He discovered that many of them were illegal aliens and that their biggest fear was a raid by immigration officials. His camp quarters even had a trapdoor, and a couple of times he found himself escaping under the house to avoid arrest. Still only sixteen, he did not realize that being born in Hawaii had automatically made him an American citizen.

Ueno worked for three years at the sawmill before heading east to join his brother in Milwaukee. After working in Milwaukee for a time, the brothers moved to Chicago. As a Kibei—American born but educated in Japan—Ueno spoke little English. By contrast, his brother had been educated in the United States and spoke little Japanese. After a few years, Ueno split with his brother and headed back to the West Coast. At first, he

---

*Issei: First-generation immigrants from Japan who were not citizens of the United States and were referred to as Japanese.

*Nisei: Second-generation Japanese who had been born in the United States, were American citizens, and were referred to as Japanese Americans.

worked with a cousin on a farm in Stockton, California, and then he returned to Washington State. Once again, he found work in a sawmill, which employed about 150 other Japanese. Ueno worked ten hours a day, six days a week. At the onset of the Depression, when white workers started to unionize, Japanese workers were not allowed to join the union and were shut out of the mills. So Ueno went back to California. In San Francisco, he met Yaso Taguchi, a young woman whose family had emigrated from Japan in 1923. They were married in 1930.

The Uenos moved to Los Angeles, settled down, and had three sons. Harry Ueno quickly found work in the produce business. After running his own business for a couple of years, he worked for a market in the Hollywood area, and then as a buyer and manager for a market in Beverly Hills. Unlike many other Japanese-American families, the Uenos did not live in the Little Tokyo section of Los Angeles, but in another area close to downtown that was restricted to whites by a zoning ordinance. The Uenos were allowed to live there only because their landlady went to court three times to get them exempted from the zoning law. Although Ueno had contacts in Little Tokyo and went there occasionally to shop, he did not "mix in with any politics." Nor was he a member of the Japanese American Citizens League (JACL), the most prominent Japanese-American organization. Although his family was Buddhist, Ueno never went to the Buddhist temple in Los Angeles, and he sent his children to a Catholic school. He did not even belong to a *kenjinkai*, an association based on members' ties to their ancestral homes.

As a Kibei, Ueno had little in common with the Nisei, even though they were of the same generation. "The Kibei kind of withdrew," he later recalled. "They couldn't communicate good enough." Thus, even though most Japanese were forced by restrictive real-estate covenants and zoning laws to live in enclaves apart from white society, Ueno was doubly alienated, by both his Japanese ancestry and his Japanese education. As he later put it, "I just lived mostly by myself."

Whether Issei, Nisei, or Kibei, of course, the Japanese experienced isolation in American society because of deep-seated anti-Asian racism. Immigrants from across the Pacific had long been the targets of both periodic vigilante violence and discriminatory laws. In 1882, Congress had barred the Chinese from further immigration into the country, a ban extended to the Japanese in 1924. Since the late nineteenth century, American law had prevented Asians from becoming naturalized citizens. On the West Coast, long a hotbed of anti-Asian racism, immigrants from China, Japan, Korea, and the Philippines were frequently the targets of discrimination. California slapped these unwelcome immigrants with exclusion and restrictive zoning laws, as well as laws preventing land ownership by aliens. Fired by fears of cheap foreign labor, many Americans in the early twentieth century viewed the Japanese as a menace. Although they remained a minuscule portion of California's population, their growing numbers seemed evidence to many whites of a Japanese plot to take over the West Coast. Meanwhile, the very success of Issei farmers left them vulnerable to baseless accusations that they were driving white farmers off the land.

Pearl Harbor quickly brought anti-Japanese prejudice to a boil in the Golden State and elsewhere. In the days after the attack, many West Coast residents expressed doubts about the loyalty of the Japanese and Japanese Americans in their midst. Race set the Japanese apart in a way that it did not differentiate Americans of German or Italian extraction. Thus suspicions about disloyalty among those of German or Italian ancestry were dealt with on more of an individual basis. By contrast, people of Japanese descent were condemned as a group. As the *Los Angeles Times* put it shortly after Pearl Harbor, a "Japanese American born of Japanese parents ... grows up to be a Japanese, and not an American."

Such assumptions led to a rising anti-Japanese hysteria. It was fed by newspaper editors, politicians, and some military leaders. California governor Culbert Olson, for instance, claimed in a statewide radio address shortly after Pearl Harbor that Japanese residents were preparing to aid the enemy. About the same time, an influential columnist wrote that "the Pacific Coast is in imminent danger of a combined attack from within and without." False rumors fanned fears of sabotage and espionage. One report maintained that Japanese Americans in Hawaii had aided the attack on Pearl Harbor. Another story spread in the press and on radio claimed that class rings from American colleges had been found on some of the Japanese pilots shot down at Pearl Harbor. Speaking in Seattle less than two months after the attack, one journalist said that if the city were bombed, "you will be able to look up and see some University of Washington sweaters on the boys doing the bombing!" The absence of any evidence of sabotage or spying by longtime Issei, Nisei, or Kibei did not matter. In fact, to some observers, it only confirmed the danger that the Japanese posed. In defiance of logic, lack of sabotage seemed proof of a conspiracy to commit it.

By early 1942, numerous civilian and military officials were calling for the evacuation of the Japanese from the West Coast. "We cannot run the risk," the mayor of Los Angeles announced in early February 1942, "of another Pearl Harbor episode in Southern California." Members of Congress quickly agreed. One California congressman warned that the Japanese represented a "national threat." A congressman from Mississippi declared, "Once a Jap, always a Jap." In the middle of February, the entire West Coast congressional delegation sent President Franklin Roosevelt a unanimous recommendation to "evacuate all persons of Japanese lineage" from California, Washington, and Oregon. In the face of the mounting hysteria, few in the Roosevelt administration questioned the legality or morality of removing American citizens from their homes and placing them in relocation camps. Responding to the growing calls for evacuation, Roosevelt signed Executive Order 9066 on February 19, 1942. The order allowed the secretary of war to establish military zones along the West Coast and exclude any citizen or alien from them. In other words, it permitted the evacuation of the entire Japanese population. On the same day that FDR signed the evacuation order, army intelligence reported that "mass evacuation [was] unnecessary." Although some members of the armed forces supported evacuation, the decision for internment had clearly been driven by politics, not military necessity.

The next month, FDR signed another executive order creating the WRA, an independent government agency responsible for running the internment centers. Starting that spring, Japanese and Japanese Americans were ordered by the War Department to assembly centers—facilities along the West Coast that could accommodate large crowds. From there, they were moved to internment centers, which were scattered from eastern California to Arkansas. There, behind barbed wire and under the constant observation of armed guards, Harry Ueno, his family, and most of the other evacuees would live for nearly four years. Like Ueno, two-thirds of them were American citizens.

For Ueno, the months after the attack on Pearl Harbor were embittering. Like many other Japanese Americans, he "could see [hatred] in people's eyes." He also learned how quickly hatred could turn into doubts about loyalty. A few days after the Japanese attack on Pearl Harbor, a neighbor told Ueno that the "Japs" were cruel and inhuman. He replied that "this country is the same way too." Then he told the woman that a Japanese doctor in the Los Angeles area who had recently been taken in for questioning by the Federal Bureau of Investigation (FBI) had later been found dead in his jail cell. The doctor, he declared, had been killed by the FBI. Within hours, two FBI agents appeared at Ueno's door wanting to know the source of his information. Then they took him downtown for questioning. The harassment by the FBI continued right up to the night before Ueno's evacuation, when agents told him that he would go to jail unless he gave them a name.

At the same time, Ueno was annoyed by the response of the JACL to the growing anti-Japanese sentiment. Founded in 1929, the JACL was the largest and most powerful Japanese-American organization. What would now be called a civil rights organization, the Nisei-dominated JACL promoted the assimilation of Japanese immigrants into American society. After the attack on Pearl Harbor, it went out of its way to demonstrate Japanese-American loyalty to the United States. For instance, it put up a large banner outside a Los Angeles drugstore declaring it to be the headquarters of the Anti-Axis Committee.* Such actions dismayed Ueno, who wondered what the JACL was trying to prove. Later, when two JACL witnesses testified that a small group of Issei fishermen were spies for the Japanese navy, he was incensed. The JACL's leaders, Ueno said later, should have defended these "innocent victims of war."

In May 1942, the Ueno family left Los Angeles on a bus for Manzanar on the eastern slope of the Sierra Nevada. They were told to take whatever they could carry, except food and cooking utensils. The family departed their home with three or four suitcases. Originally scheduled to go to the Santa Anita Assembly Center (a racetrack near Los Angeles), they were instead transported by bus directly to Manzanar, a trip of some two hundred miles across southern California's Mojave Desert. Years later, Ueno recalled feeling that "it was open season for Jap hunting'" and that the camp would provide protection for them. Even though he found the conditions there austere, he later said, "We tried to make the best of the situation."

"KIND OF DIRTY WORK"

If Harry Ueno lived much of his life estranged from his environment, Dillon Myer could not have fit more perfectly into his. Myer was raised on what he called "a typical corn-belt farm of 135 acres in central Ohio." Like the Myer family itself, his childhood experiences were firmly fixed in the rural Midwest. When he was born in 1891, the farm had already been in the family for nearly sixty years, and the Myers had established themselves as one of the leading families in the small community of Hebron. Dillon's grandfather, of German extraction, had purchased the land after migrating from Maryland. An only child, Dillon's father stayed on the farm and married a woman of Scots-Irish descent. The second of the couple's four children, Dillon experienced a remarkably conventional rural upbringing filled with "plenty of food and many homey pleasures." Farm chores were punctuated by fishing in the summer, rabbit and quail hunting, and family gatherings around the fire in the winter. Later, as a teenager, Dillon would attend dances at a lakeside park.

Like almost everyone else they knew, the Myers were churchgoing people. The family attended the local Methodist Episcopal church, where Dillon's father served as an officer. Every day at home, Dillon later recalled, his father "sat at the head of the table and always gave the blessing." He also disapproved of Sunday baseball games and did not hesitate to give a tardy Dillon his first switching when he was only five. At the same age, Dillon was assigned his first farm chore, collecting eggs. Later, he took on milking and

---

Anti-Axis Committee: The Axis was the alliance formed by Germany, Italy, and Japan in 1940. The JACL was obviously trying to prove its loyalty to the United States.

wood-splitting duties. Meanwhile, his mother drummed into him the importance of correct spelling and good posture. Along with his brother and younger sisters, he walked more than a mile to a one-room country school. And like countless children in the late nineteenth century, he learned to read from William Holmes McGuffey's school readers, whose lessons were laced with Protestant morality. In short, Dillon Myer's childhood world was narrow, strict, and provincial. Yet he was never alienated from it. He demonstrated little youthful rebelliousness or inclination to challenge authority. In fact, classmates kidded him about being "the good little boy."

If Myer rebelled at all as a youth, it was by rejecting his father's wish that he become a Methodist minister. As a high school freshman, he was impressed by the salary and free living quarters provided to the manager of a nearby farm. So in 1910, he enrolled in the College of Agriculture at Ohio State. During his senior year, he was offered a job as an agronomy instructor at the University of Kentucky. Disgusted after he was twice denied a raise, he left for Evansville, Indiana, in 1916 to become a county agricultural agent. It was Myer's first step into a growing agricultural bureaucracy. Part of the national Cooperative Extension Service established by Congress in 1914, county agents shared the latest agricultural techniques and information with farmers. It was a perfect training ground for young Myer. Reporting to the county school board and township trustees, he learned the importance of making the right contacts. After another brief stint as a county extension agent in Ohio, he became a district supervisor. While in that position, he met another county agent, named Jenness Wirt, a clothing and interior decorating specialist in the extension service, and they were married in 1924.

In the coming years, Myer worked his way up in the government bureaucracy. Even the onset of hard times in the early 1930s did not slow his rise. In 1933, Ohio's extension director asked Myer to supervise the New Deal's Agricultural Adjustment Administration (AAA) programs in the state. Created in 1933, the AAA sought to lift farm prices by cutting agricultural output. Myer proved an energetic and effective administrator and was soon promoted to work at AAA headquarters in Washington, D.C. When the Supreme Court found the AAA unconstitutional in 1936, he moved to the Soil Conservation Service (SCS), established in response to the spread of the Dust Bowl. The SCS was part of the Department of Agriculture, headed by Henry A. Wallace (see Chapter 9). Myer quickly gained Wallace's attention and was promoted to assistant chief of the SCS. As Myer put it later, much of his work "had to do with the tough problems that nobody else wanted to handle." It was, he admitted, "kind of dirty work," but the farm boy turned bureaucrat proved very adept at it. Besides, it paid well. For a man who was able to recall decades later exactly how much he made in his various government positions, that was an important consideration. In fact, he had taken the SCS position only after threatening to quit if his salary was not increased to $6,500—an amount exceeding that earned by more than 97 percent of all Americans in 1935.

Myer was asked to take on another kind of "dirty work" when he was appointed director of the new WRA in June 1942. Since its creation by FDR's executive order earlier that year, the WRA had been headed by future president Dwight Eisenhower's younger brother, Milton Eisenhower, who happened to have been Myer's boss at the SCS. Eisenhower was deeply troubled by the injustice of Japanese relocation, as were many others in the Agriculture Department who had developed close contacts with West Coast Japanese farmers. Unable to carry out his WRA assignment in good conscience, Eisenhower had taken a job in the Office of War Information. During a dinner party, he told Myer that he should accept the WRA assignment only if he could "sleep and still carry on the job." Myer took the job, he later said, "with an open mind." With the exception of "two boys" in his class at Ohio State, he explained, he "didn't know any Japanese."

When Myer took over the WRA, relocation was largely accomplished. He had nothing to do with the decision to uproot the Japanese and Japanese Americans from their homes and place them in internment camps. Rather, he was charged with merely maintaining the policy. Nearly two decades later, he would claim to have believed that only selective Japanese evacuation was justified. He also would confess that he had "little information" about the Japanese on the West Coast and little knowledge about the reasons for the evacuation. Very soon, though, he had found out that "most of the reasons were phony." Yet in testifying before a subcommittee of the House Un-American Activities Committee (HUAC) in 1943, Myer defended mass evacuation. **[See Source 1.]** And unlike Milton Eisenhower, the new WRA head apparently slept quite soundly. Long after he accepted the appointment, Myer said, "[I am never] bothered when it comes to carrying on a job that I feel I am responsible for."

"TO LIVE ... IN A FREE AND EQUAL SOCIETY"

About the same time that Myer was taking over the WRA, the Uenos were settling into their new home at Manzanar. Arriving at night, they were handed sackcloth and told to stuff it with hay to make a mattress. Then they were assigned to a room with three other families. The families were separated by a sheet hung as a partition. Bathrooms were communal, and meals were taken in a mess hall. Ueno joined a work detail cutting sagebrush to make room for camp expansion. He was later transferred to a mess hall, where he found many other Kibei. Educated in Japanese preparatory schools, Kibei had "no special skill," Ueno recalled, "just basic training for college." Thus they were often assigned to work in the camp kitchens. In the mess, Ueno heard widespread complaints about shortages of meat and sugar, a vital wartime commodity. He and the other internees attributed the problem to embezzlement by white camp administrators. He told the mess steward and the assistant director of the camp that he would report them to the FBI if they did not follow up on his complaints. That fall, he decided to organize a union so that the internees' grievances could be heard. The Mess Hall Workers' Union gained the approval of camp authorities, including the director, Ralph Merritt. Ueno also won the backing of many internees, more than twelve hundred of whom signed a petition supporting the union.

Ueno later contended that his union was concerned only with improving conditions in the mess halls, yet his sudden activism also seemed related to Japanese–American politics. Not all of the internees at Manzanar welcomed Ueno's efforts. That was especially true of certain members of the JACL—Nisei who sought to cooperate with camp administrators. Some of them had already formed the Fair Employment Practices Committee, headed by an internee named Fred Tayama. Ueno was convinced that it was nothing more than a front for Manzanar's administrators. At the same time, Nisei internees had formed a JACL-dominated commission to help govern the camp. One of its members was Joe Masaoka, whose brother was the JACL's national secretary. Another was Togo Tanaka, a leader of the JACL in Los Angeles who had urged cooperation with authorities during the evacuation from southern California. Ueno believed that these internees "were not for the people in the camp but more for the benefit of the administration."

The Mess Hall Workers' Union was short-lived. On December 5, 1942, a small group of masked men beat Fred Tayama, who accused Ueno of having participated in the attack. Although Ueno claimed that he had been at a Parent Teacher Association meeting that night, Manzanar authorities picked him up and hustled him off to jail. The next evening, as Ueno looked on from the Manzanar jail, several thousand internees gathered to hear about his fate. Suddenly, the crowd got out of control. As Ueno looked on, MPs dispersed the crowd, but not before twelve people had been shot, two fatally. **[See Source 2.]** The Manzanar Riot brought an end to the Mess Hall Workers' Union, which was quickly disbanded. It was also the beginning of a long ordeal for Ueno.

Along with seven other internees, including five other members of his union, Ueno was transported later that night to the jail in Bishop, California. After four days, they were taken to the jail in Lone Pine, sixty miles to the south. Unable to talk or write to his wife, Ueno was held there for a month before he received a notice from Dillon Myer. According to Ueno, it said, "We're going to move you to someplace with a little more open space, and we're going to have a quick hearing for your case." Shortly after, Ueno and the others were taken to a depot, where they were placed on a train bound for Moab, Utah. There they were held in an old Civilian Conservation Corps* camp. Later, they were joined by internees from other centers who were also considered "undesirables." At Moab, the WRA routinely censored the letters that Ueno sent to his family and friends at Manzanar. **[See Source 3.]** Meanwhile, Ueno demanded to know when Myer was going to have a hearing. He also complained about his treatment. After a heated argument with the camp director over censorship of the mail, his lack of a hearing, and the "harsh regulations," Ueno was ready to renounce his American citizenship and return to Japan with his family. "I thought that the only way I could get all my freedom and happy living was in Japan," he declared. "Also, I wanted my children to live and grow in a free and equal society."

It would be a long time before Ueno got his freedom. Myer never arranged for a hearing. When Ueno requested a transfer to an alien internment camp, the WRA chief turned him down, claiming that U.S. citizens could not be transferred to such facilities. Instead, Ueno and five other prisoners were sent to the Leupp Isolation Center near Winslow, Arizona, where there were about eighty Japanese prisoners and 150 guards. By the time Ueno arrived, he had given up hope for a hearing. When the Leupp Isolation Center closed at the end of 1943, Ueno was moved once again. Still charged with no crime, he found himself at the Tule Lake Segregation Center in northeastern California, where several pro-Japanese and radical groups were interred. Determined to keep quiet and keep to himself, Ueno was accused by other internees of being both pro-Axis and procommunist. As he later put it, he was "getting it from both ends."

"CHAMPION OF HUMAN RIGHTS"

Dillon Myer felt that he was getting it from both ends, too. Committed to "carrying on" the job for which he was now responsible, Myer preferred what he once called "a middle-ground approach" to dealing with the Japanese and Japanese Americans. Thus he defended the mass evacuation while shielding the WRA from critics who believed that it did not go far enough. As a seasoned administrator, he knew that harsh treatment of "troublemakers and agitators" such as Harry Ueno could play an important role in defending his agency from assault.

Civilian Conservation Corps: A program created in 1933 as part of the New Deal to employ young, out-of-work men on conservation projects.

Myer's "middle ground," however, was not just the policy of a cautious bureaucrat. It also reflected his view that America's "Japanese problem" could be solved only by their complete assimilation into what he called America's "melting pot." The easiest way to achieve that, Myer believed, was to break down the Japanese community through dispersion. **[See Source 4.]** Shortly after taking over the WRA, therefore, he began relocating Nisei internees outside the internment camps to communities across the country. Although Ueno and other Kibei were excluded from the program, it eventually placed thirty-six thousand internees in communities as far away as the East Coast. Their first steps toward assimilation were to fill out a detailed questionnaire and then submit to an interview by WRA staff. **[See Source 5.]** A man who had little understanding or appreciation of Japanese culture, Myer wished to see any remnants of it eradicated as quickly as possible. Perhaps that explains his reaction to the vegetable and flower gardens planted by internees at the Poston Relocation Center in Arizona. According to one government official, they were "gardens of ancient Japanese beauty," but to Myer they were "the worst thing I have come on in all my inspections of the camps."

Myer's views dovetailed perfectly with those of the JACL, which had fought to assimilate the Nisei into American society by eradicating any trace of Japanese culture among them. Before the war, it had called on its members to eliminate "those mannerisms and thoughts which mark us apart, aside from our physical characteristics." Once relocation began, the JACL called it a "humane and democratic resettlement." Naturally, the WRA director felt comfortable working with the JACL. He conferred often with Mike Masaoka, the organization's national secretary and brother of Ueno's rival at Manzanar, Joe Masaoka.

Myer's policy of "leniency" toward the Nisei alarmed the WRA's critics. Their worst fears about the Japanese had been confirmed by the Manzanar Riot. Many of them believed that Myer's agency was, in the words of one California congressman, "coddling" the internees. Their suspicions were heightened when agents of the HUAC raided the JACL's national headquarters and seized papers revealing Masaoka's contacts with Myer. By 1943, the WRA had become the target of separate HUAC and military affairs subcommittee investigations. Under growing assault, Myer skillfully fended off his critics by cracking down on "bad" Japanese internees. In 1943, the WRA began segregating internees deemed dangerous, disloyal, or "potentially disloyal." The new policy reflected a belief shared by Myer and many other Americans that "unassimilated" Japanese posed a fundamental threat to American security. Kibei like Harry Ueno, who had spent part of their lives in Japan, were its prime targets. A WRA memorandum in 1942 had already identified the Kibei as "the potentially most dangerous" of the Japanese Americans. Despite the "protection afforded them by the Bill of Rights," the memo concluded, many Kibei should be placed in "custodial detention."

That, of course, is exactly where the WRA had put Harry Ueno after the Manzanar Riot. By early 1943, Myer longed to put more "hardboiled boys" in the "same place." He realized, however, that moving Japanese and Japanese Americans into internment camps was one thing but placing American citizens in jail only because they had lived for a time in Japan was quite another. He also knew that no law made greater allegiance to Japan than to the United States a crime. The courts were unlikely to accept a WRA policy of putting Kibei in prison and holding them there indefinitely. The key was finding a way to prove their "disloyalty" and then hope that the courts went along. In fact, Myer was correctly anticipating the Supreme Court's thinking on internment. In 1944, in *Korematsu* v. *United States*, the Court would uphold the right of the federal government to order the mass evacuation of Japanese Americans from the West Coast during a military emergency. Later that same year, however, in *Ex parte Endo*, the Court would rule that the WRA did not have the authority to hold "loyal" citizens indefinitely.

Myer soon got an opportunity to weed out "disloyal" internees from the camps and hold them for the duration of the war. It came when Secretary of War Henry Stimson moved in 1943 to create a segregated Nisei combat unit, later known as the 442nd Regimental Combat Team. All draft-age Nisei males had to register for the draft and be administered a loyalty oath. As Myer realized, that oath could be given to all internees and used to screen out "disloyal or potentially disloyal individuals." Myer's plan eventually netted about twelve thousand internees. As a WRA press release put it, "It is believed to be the first time that any group in the country has been sorted and segregated on the basis of National loyalty." By removing the "bad apples" from the camps, Myer countered criticism about WRA "coddling" of "pro-Japanese" internees. At the same time, he reassured a concerned public that their communities would not be endangered by his program to disperse and assimilate "loyal" internees around the country. The segregation program, however, came at a price. The "disloyals" were sent to the Tule Lake Segregation Center for the duration of the war. Unfortunately, the Tule Lake camp had been built to accommodate thousands fewer internees than the WRA sent there. In 1943, internees went on strike to protest their conditions, including cramped quarters and inadequate food and fuel. Violence surrounding the protest left one internee dead and resulted in the imposition of martial law.

One of the "incorrigible troublemakers" sent to Tule Lake was Harry Ueno. He did not realize that he and many other Kibei were pawns in Myer's effort to carry out a "middle-ground approach" to internment. Sent to Tule Lake after the riot there, he had learned enough to keep a low profile in his new home. Nonetheless, he was one of the last internees to leave the last WRA camp to close after the war. Unlike more than forty-seven hundred other internees, nearly two thousand of them American citizens, Ueno was not repatriated to Japan because he had never formally renounced his citizenship. And by the time he was released in March 1946 from Tule Lake, he had heard enough discouraging reports about conditions in Japan to change his mind about returning there.

Ueno found himself starting life all over again. Yaso Ueno, released from Manzanar only a month before, had already moved to San Jose, where Harry joined her. Together, they began to rebuild their lives. It was not easy. Altogether, internees had lost perhaps as much as $2 billion in homes and property. After the war, prejudice against the Japanese remained strong. Even returning Japanese-American veterans frequently encountered derision and discrimination. Like many other former internees, though, Ueno never complained publicly about his treatment. As he had before the war, he quietly went about his business. The family moved to the central California coast, where they worked for several years "about twenty-nine days out of thirty" and saved as much as they could. Then they returned to San Jose, where they grew strawberries. "When you are working for someone else," Ueno told his children, "you never get a chance to make yourself any headway."

By that time, Dillon Myer had come to be revered by many Japanese Americans. They had not forgotten how he had worked to shield Nisei internees from harsher treatment. Like most other Americans, they shared his ideal of assimilation. With his resettlement program, Myer had worked to fulfill both the JACL's and his own visions of Americanization through the elimination of native culture. In 1946, the organization presented Myer with a citation at a banquet held in New York City. "TO DILLON S. MYER," the citation read, "American and champion of human rights and common decency."

Later, Myer brought the same assimilationist assumptions to his job as head of the Bureau of Indian Affairs (BIA). As BIA chief in the early 1950s, Myer sought to break down the Indians' attachment to their traditional culture. He stressed the importance of sending Indian children away to school "in order to get them off the reservation complex and milieu." Indian reservations proved to be far more difficult to manage, however, than internment camps. Myer's attempt in 1952 to gain increased police power over reservation of Indians was met with quick protests, and he had no organization comparable to the JACL to come to his defense. The next year, he was terminated as BIA chief.

Myer held other government posts until he retired in 1964. About the same time, his assumption about the need to "Americanize" nonwhite minorities would come under mounting assault. By the late 1960s, the civil rights, Indian rights, and Chicano rights movements forced many Americans to reassess long-standing attitudes about race and culture. The decision to intern Japanese and Japanese Americans during World War II also came under growing attack. Six years after Myer died and forty-six years after Americans of Japanese ancestry were uprooted from their homes simply for having been born Japanese, Congress finally moved to right the wrong. In 1988, it formally apologized for the "grave injustice" of internment and gave each survivor of the camps, including Harry Ueno, $20,000.

•PRIMARY SOURCES•

Source 1: Dillon Myer, *"Constitutional Principles Involved in the Relocation Program"* (1943)

In July 1943, Dillon Myer presented this statement on Japanese exclusion from the West Coast to a subcommittee of the HUAC. On what grounds does he justify evacuation?

We believe, in the first place, that the evacuation was within the constitutional power of the National Government. The concentration of the Japanese-Americans along the West Coast, the danger of invasion of that Coast by Japan, the possibility that an unknown and unrecognizable minority of them might have greater allegiance to Japan than to the United States, the fact that the Japanese-Americans were not wholly assimilated in the general life of communities on the West Coast, and the danger of civil disturbance due to fear and misunderstanding—all these facts, and related facts, created a situation which the National Government could, we believe, deal with by extraordinary measures in the interest of military security. The need for speed created the unfortunate necessity for evacuating the whole group instead of attempting to determine who were dangerous among them, so that only those might be evacuated. That same need made it impossible to hold adequate investigations or to grant hearings to the evacuees before evacuation.

SOURCE: Reprinted in Richard Drinnon, KEEPER OF CONCENTRATION CAMPS: VILLON S. MYER AND AMERICAN RACISM (Berkeley: University of California Press, 1987), p. 38; originally from "Japanese American Evacuation and Resettlement Study," 67/14, T1.02, Bancroft Library, University of California, Berkeley.

Source 2: "Rifles Cow Manzanar Japs After Fatal Riots" (1942)

This front-page story from the Los Angeles Times *two days after the Manzanar Riot provides an account of the disturbance that left two Japanese internees dead. What attitudes does it reveal about Japanese Americans?*

MANZANAR, Dec. 7. — Cowed by the ready guns of the Army's military police after a riot yesterday during which one Japanese was killed and nine[1] other pro-Axis residents of the camp bent on "banzai-ing" the first anniversary of the Nipponese sneak attack on Pearl Harbor were wounded, the 10,000 occupants of this huge reception center were quiet today under martial law enforced by augmented troops.

Other would-be celebrants of the grim event which hurled America into war reposed in an Owens Valley community jail, while still others were reported under arrest in barracks within the center six miles south of Independence....

According to Ralph R Merritt, manager of the center, the disturbance was precipitated Saturday night by Japanese inmates who wished to celebrate the anniversary of the Pearl Harbor attack.

Shouting "Pearl Harbor, banzai, banzai!" an estimated 1000 pro-Axis Japanese, many of whom are Kibei, or natives of Japan, demonstrated in a firebreak and hooted down Japanese-American Nisei (second-generation Nipponese) who protested their antics.

Remonstrator Beaten

Fred Toyama [sic], secretary of the Los Angeles Japanese-American Citizens League, who attempted to dissuade the demonstrators from their wild celebration, was beaten so severely he was hospitalized outside the inter[n]ee area because irate Kibei attempted to wrest him from the doctors ministering to his serious wounds.

Harry Ueno, said to be an Axis-sympathizer, who was jailed following the Saturday-night disturbance, was removed to the Inyo County Jail at Independence....

Mob Numbers 4000

When authorities refused to free Ueno, a mob estimated at 4000 demonstrated wildly.

Then, when a large portion of the crowd moved menacingly toward the troops, the soldiers tossed tear-gas bombs. This proved of little effect because of a wind which wafted the fumes away, and the mob resumed its forward surge. Stones, clubs and other missiles were hurled at the troops.

Capt. Martin Hall, in command of the police, ordered the mob to halt. After several commands were ignored and the barrage of missiles threatened to maim the police, Capt. Hall reluctantly gave the order to fire.

Ten Rioters Fall

Ten rioters collapsed under the volley and the remainder retired to their quarters under the officer's orders.

---

1. The final toll was two dead and ten wounded.

Merritt said that about 4000 inmates were Japan-born, and 400 others, although born in this country, were pro-Axis, having been educated in Japan and indoctrinated with Japanese militarism....

Manzanar Blooming

Manzanar is a model community of neat prefabricated wooden barracks, a 150-bed hospital, mess halls, laundries, recreation halls and administration buildings. It occupies a 5800-acre site on the west side of the valley and, under labor by thousands of occupants, has begun to [appear as] a pleasant, blooming area of trees, gardens and flowers.

The riot here followed by two weeks a similar flare-up by Poston Relocation Center evacuees near Parker, Ariz., when the camp administration was overthrown and authority defied. At Poston, as here, loyal Japanese-Americans attempted to prevent disloyal outbreaks.

Source 3:   *Censored Letters of Harry Ueno* (1943)

While incarcerated at the Moab Isolation Center in Utah, Ueno wrote letters to his wife and friends at Manzanar. What do these letters, censored by the WRA, reveal about Ueno's general state of mind? What do they reveal about his feelings toward the United States?

Among the letters received from subject UYENO [*sic*] were several containing matters of [relevant] information.... There are being set forth hereinafter excerpts from these letters written by UYENO to his wife, YASOKO UYENO, who still resides at the Manzanar Relocation Center. In one letter UYENO states:

"A few detainees might be released from here and returned to Manzanar but I can't trust them except for one or two persons, and as I have mentioned in my last letter, 'The honest person will not be able to be released from this camp.' ...

"... Only one way we can see the future is wait till the end of war. It might solve itself. We understand the American democracy by Lieutenant Colonel's inquiry. I told him that I'm very glad to be a Japanese. Asked the question 'Do you have a desire to go out if there is a good job?' I answered him that no matter how much money is piled on me, I will not participate to the war effort and am thinking of the Japanese. I wish you have the same intention like I have."

In a letter dated March 29, 1943 to his wife, UYENO [stated:]

"Today I received your letter of March 27, 1943. I have learned that you did not receive No. 6 and No. 7 as yet. I may safely say that the government dares to do so. It is outrageous to confiscate or detain our legal mail on which the letters have stamps on them. This action which we are seeing before our eyes is called the democracy. The democracy is what they are praising is as different as light and darkness. This is what we call a thief that has some truth in him. Remember this, YASOKO.

"We have asked so many times, why are we segregated from the others and detained in jail for such a long time? But they cannot give us an exact answer for our question. They tortured us because we have a citizenship. If we tried to expatriate our

SOURCE: From the Department of Special Collections, Charles E. Young Research Library, University of California, Los Angeles.

citizenship, they insist that we cannot do such actions while we are staying in the motherland. I think this problem can be solved in the past war because we know who is translating our letters.

"Our victory is approaching day by day is the day we are able to settle and solve our problems. I will wait till then…. The victims who gave their lives on December 6th gave us a chance to observe the democracy of the United States of America.

"I realize that I am a happy fellow to be a Japanese. I tried to sign up on repatriation application, but they do not have such a form in here. I asked to have them bring those forms here so I might be able to sign up as soon as it comes. If you have a chance to do so you do it. I would like to renounce the children's citizenship too."

In his letter of April 8, 1943, UYENO stated:

"Non-suffering life will not know a pleasure of life. When I think of the expeditioned soldiers' families, our existing circumstances are the heaven. How hardship it is, I think we should bear. I believe you have sufficiently determined about your mind…."

In a letter dated April 9, 1943, UYENO states:

"Yesterday two fellows and today two fellows were compulsory transferred from our room to the others where the moderate party stay in. The remainder are those who expatriated a citizenship of American to the authority. I suppose you do understand our spirit. We became the pure Japanese and living with Japanese spirit. We are entirely different than those who praise Japanese victory and thinking of Japanese and doubtfully wondering their citizenship with worrying that America might win the war. I believe the man should have their faith and should die with their faith then that what we will call them as a true man….

"I hope to let the Manzanarians see our daily life and situation of ours. It is an easy thing to be born as a Japanese but it is a[s] hard to live as a real Japanese.

Source 4: *Dillon Myer on Japanese Resettlement* (1943)

In 1943, Dillon Myer was questioned by Senator Edwin C. Johnson of the Senate Military Affairs Subcommittee on War Relocation Centers. What assumptions does Myer reveal about his program to resettle Japanese-American internees outside the camps? How does his position here compare to that expressed in Source 1?

SENATOR JOHNSON: Is it your underlying idea that the Jap, no matter how long he is here, will finally merge with our citizenship the same as any white man?

MR. MYER: My underlying idea is that since these people are going to continue to be American citizens, they will have to merge into our economy and be accepted as part of it, otherwise we are always going to have a racial problem.

SOURCE: Reprinted in Richard Drinnon, KEEPER OF CONCENTRATION CAMPS: DILLON S. MYER AND AMERICAN RACISM (Berkeley: University of California Press, 1987), pp. 56–57; originally from Senate Military Affairs Subcommittee, 20 January 1943, 78th Cong.

SENATOR JOHNSON: Of course, you know that no Pacific States allow intermarriage. They are always going to be brown men. Do you think they will finally merge and just be accepted in every way like a white man?

MR. MYER: Well, I can't predict that. I can say this, that there are a good many hundreds of the youngsters of college age and many who have gone to college in the past who have been accepted in the professions and otherwise. Now, I think that you will find, other than color, that after about four or five generations these people will be living under the same standards as any other American citizens. They won't know anything else. I don't know what the ancestry of all the people around this room is. I know what my own is. We have been a melting pot of the nations here and we have accepted these people.

Source 5: *War Relocation Authority Questions for Resettlement Applicants* (1943)

When the WRA began Dillon Myer's program to resettle internees in 1943, it subjected those who wished to live and work outside the camps to a rigorous screening process. What do the questions asked of applicants reveal about administrators' cultural and racial assumptions? How do these questions compare to the sentiment expressed by Myer in Source 4?

Before questioning you any further, we would like to ask if you have any objection to signing a Pledge of Allegiance to the United States.

Will you assist in the general resettlement program by staying away from large groups of Japanese?

Will you try to develop such American habits which will cause you to be accepted readily into American social groups?

Are you willing to give information to the proper authorities regarding any subversive activity ... both in the relocation centers and in the communities in which you are resettling?

Would you consider an informer of this nature an "Inu"? (Stool-pigeon)

Will you conform to the customs and dress of your new home?

Have you been associated with any radical groups, clubs, or gangs which have been accused of anti-social conduct within the center?

Can you furnish any proof that you have always been loyal to the United States?

SOURCE: Reprinted in Richard Drinnon, KEEPER OF CONCENTRATION CAMPS: DILLON S. MYER AND AMERICAN RACISM (Berkeley: University of California Press, 1987), pp. 56–57; originally from Senate Military Affairs Subcommittee, 20 January 1943, 78th Cong, 1st session.

QUESTIONS TO CONSIDER

...apanese internment during World War II? What role did racism
: of Japanese Americans during the war?

...ound was different from that of many Japanese Americans.
...reveal about internment? About the Japanese-American com-
...eno's background shape his response to internment? How did
his internment experience affect his actions afterwards?

3. Dillon Myer claimed many years after World War II that he did "the best possible job under difficult circumstances." What were the circumstances or factors that led Myer to impose such strict measures against Ueno and other "troublemakers" in the internment camps? To understand Ueno's fate, is it necessary to understand Myer's own history?

4. How would you characterize Myer's policies as head of the WRA? Do you agree with the JACL's description of Myer at the end of the war?

FOR FURTHER READING

Roger Daniels, *Prisoners Without Trial: Japanese Americans in World War II* (New York: Hill and Wang, 1993), provides a concise overview of the decision to evacuate Japanese Americans and their experiences in the internment camps.

Richard Drinnon, *Keeper of Concentration Camps: Dillon S. Myer and American Racism* (Berkeley: University of California Press, 1987), offers a critical treatment of Myer as director of the WRA and later the BIA.

Kunitomi Embrey, Arthur A. Hansen, and Betty Kulberg Mitson, *Manzanar Martyr: An Interview with Harry Y. Ueno* (Fullerton: Oral History Program, California State University, 1986), offers an account of Ueno's early life and his experiences as an internee.

Alice Yang Murray, *Historical Memories of the Japanese American Internment and the Struggle for Redress* (Stanford: Stanford University Press, 2008), provides an insightful discussion of internment, and the memories and interpretations of it.

Dillon Myer, *Autobiography* (Berkeley: University of California, 1970), presents an oral history detailing Myer's life and career, including his experiences as director of the WRA.

John Tateishi, *And Justice for All: An Oral History of the Japanese American Detention Camps* (New York: Random House, 1984), offers brief oral histories of numerous Japanese-American internees, including Harry Ueno.

Confrontation and Compromise in the Cold War: James Byrnes and Henry A. Wallace

As Henry A. Wallace looked out at his audience in New York City's Madison Square Garden in September 1946, he feared for the future. The vice president under Franklin Roosevelt and now Harry Truman's secretary of commerce, Wallace was convinced that the United States and the Soviet Union were on the brink of war. The partners in World War II now faced off across a divided Europe. Their relationship, once cooperative, was engulfed in suspicion. Wallace was convinced that war between the two nations could be avoided, but that could happen only if the Truman administration rejected the dangerous policy of confrontation with the Soviets, advocated by Secretary of State James Byrnes.

A wily political infighter, Byrnes was sure that Wallace was a dreamer. The former South Carolina senator saw himself as a hardheaded realist. He was convinced that the Soviet Union would have to be dealt with forcefully. And, he feared, the commerce secretary's ideas were dangerous. Thrown together as allies against Nazi Germany, the United States and the Soviet Union had entered into a marriage of convenience. But now that Germany was defeated, Byrnes believed that the Soviets loomed as the new threat. Headed by dictator Joseph Stalin, the Soviet Union was a communist—and officially atheistic—state. It proclaimed the doctrine of worldwide communist revolution. Already it had established several communist states in Eastern Europe. The United States, Byrnes insisted, had to follow a "get tough" policy that met Soviet expansion with diplomatic and military force. Using the threat of war might force cooperation from the Soviets, but caving in to them would surely lead to war itself.

Wallace was equally convinced that he was the realist. Thus, as the commerce secretary launched into his Madison Square Garden address, he told his audience that the

James Byrnes

Henry Wallace

United States had to pay a "just price" for peace. If it took a belligerent stance against the Soviets, they would respond in a similar fashion. As each side became increasingly suspicious of the other, a war worse than the previous one would inevitably follow. The only way to build a lasting peace was to unite the nations of the world. American policy toward the Soviet Union should be based on trade agreements and economic aid, not diplomatic bluster, military threats, and atomic bombs. "He who trusts in the atom bomb," he declared, "will sooner or later perish by the atom bomb." By the time he sat down, Wallace had delivered the most important speech of his career. And although he did not realize it, he had set off a firestorm. Within days, Byrnes and Wallace were engaged in a dramatic showdown. In the balance, both believed, was the peace of the world.

"THIS MUST NOT BE"

Henry A. Wallace would not have denied that he was idealistic. Yet he would certainly have protested against any accusation that he was impractical. He was, after all, a midwestern farmer, born in Iowa in 1888. As a result, his political views were shaped by agricultural concerns. In 1895, his father and grandfather (both named Henry Wallace) began publishing a farm journal that came to be called *Wallaces' Farmer*. The journal advocated pro-farm political issues and discussed the latest scientific and mechanical advances in farming. It also provided the Wallace family with prosperity and a solid reputation among the farmers of the Midwest. Both staunch Republicans, Henry's grandfather worked in Theodore Roosevelt's administration, and his father served as secretary of agriculture under Warren Harding and Calvin Coolidge. After graduating from Iowa State

College in 1910 with a degree in animal husbandry, young Henry went to work on *Wallaces' Farmer*. He married and had three children. When his father left Iowa to work in Washington, D.C., in 1921, Henry took over as editor of the journal.

The young Wallace became a leading voice for farmers in the 1920s. Years before the onset of the Depression, agriculture was in a severe slump. Wallace used his position to protest the low prices for agricultural products. He called for government action to raise farm prices and promoted efficiency on the farm to enable farmers to help themselves. He also founded the first hybrid-corn company in the country. Hybrid crops were designed to increase yields, and Wallace was sure the application of science to agriculture would result in greater production. Eventually, his call for government intervention on behalf of farmers led to his break with the Republican Party. In 1928, he became a Democrat. Four years later, he supported Franklin Roosevelt for president and was rewarded for his help when FDR named him secretary of agriculture.

During the Great Depression, Wallace became the national leader of pro-farm politics. He promoted government programs that would revolutionize American agriculture by increasing the federal government's role in farming, including control over production and prices. This meant centralized planning, which to conservatives smacked of socialism. His actions, especially the move to slaughter millions of farm animals and limit crop acreage when many Americans were going hungry, made him one of the most controversial figures of the New Deal. Before the Depression was over, he even rejected the capitalist free-market economy of his grandfather and father in favor of a planned economy.

By the end of the 1930s, Wallace was a leader of the Democratic Party's liberal wing, which promoted more federal regulation and more governmental control of the economy. He wanted government regulations to establish better conditions for factory workers, which made him a hero to organized labor. As a prominent New Dealer and a prolific writer who had published many books, he also appealed to intellectuals. Because of his popularity with these groups, he was the clear choice for vice president when Roosevelt ran for a third term in 1940. The conservative southern wing of the Democratic Party opposed Wallace, arguing that he was a socialist. Roosevelt, however, fought hard for his nomination, and when FDR won the election, Wallace became vice president of the United States.

When World War II started, Wallace began to speak out more about his vision for America's role in the world. After the United States defeated Germany and Japan, he believed, it should work to set up an international organization that would regulate trade, raise living standards, and prevent future wars. Someday, he was sure, the world would have one government, and the common man would be free and prosperous. Indeed, he believed that the United States was about to embark on what he called the "Century of the Common Man."

Wallace's international views convinced James Byrnes and other conservative Democrats that he was a dreamer. If given the chance, they believed, he would destroy capitalism at home and abroad, weaken the American military, threaten national sovereignty, and destroy the Democratic Party. As another presidential election approached in 1944 and Roosevelt's health declined, conservative Democrats feared that Wallace might soon become president. Determined to prevent that, they pushed Byrnes as an alternative to Wallace. Although labor leaders and the influential first lady, Eleanor Roosevelt, continued to support Wallace, Roosevelt's reelection was not as certain as it had been in 1940. Hence he did not want to alienate the conservatives in his own party. Northern liberals, however, strenuously objected to the southerner Byrnes. When conservatives compromised by suggesting Harry Truman, a more moderate senator from

Missouri, Wallace's fate was sealed. After FDR won his fourth term in 1944 with Truman as his running mate, Wallace became secretary of commerce.

Wallace lost the vice presidency at a crucial time. When FDR died a few months after his inauguration in early 1945, Truman became president. The war in Europe was virtually over, and it would be left to Truman to conclude the war in the Pacific. It would also be Truman's job to deal with the Soviet Union after the war's end.

Since 1941, the Soviets had been allies of the United States in World War II, but it was not an easy relationship. Earlier in the war, while the Soviets were suffering enormous losses on the eastern front, the British and Americans had repeatedly postponed an invasion of France, which would have greatly relieved the Soviet position. A naturally suspicious Stalin feared that his Western partners were deliberately stalling until Germany and the Soviet Union wore each other down. Nonetheless, Roosevelt remained convinced that he could get along with Stalin, and he was hopeful that the two nations would continue to cooperate after the war. In fact, that hope was reinforced early in 1945 when Roosevelt, Stalin, and British prime minister Winston Churchill met at Yalta in the Soviet Union. At the Yalta Conference, the "Big Three" made plans for an international organization called the United Nations, which would work to maintain peace through collective security. Stalin also promised to enter the war against Japan three months after the war in Europe was over, and Allied leaders pledged to establish governments in liberated Europe responsible to the will of the people through "free elections."

Under Truman, FDR's personal diplomacy was quickly replaced by confrontation. When Truman became president, the Soviets had already "liberated" much of Nazi-occupied Eastern Europe. They also had established a Soviet puppet government in Poland. The United States and Great Britain had earlier excluded the Russians from a role in forming a new government in Italy—the first country in Europe to be liberated from enemy hands. FDR understood that the language of the Yalta agreements was vague and that it actually gave Stalin great latitude in Eastern Europe. But Roosevelt was gone, and some of Truman's advisers believed that the Soviets' quick move to establish communist regimes in Eastern Europe was evidence that Stalin had gone back on his word.

Henry Wallace also was alarmed. Just before Germany surrendered in May 1945, Wallace noted in his diary that "more and more it begins to look like the psychology is favorable toward our getting into war with Russia.* This must not be." Wallace knew he had to speak out. It was highly unusual for a commerce secretary to express his view on foreign policy publicly, but he was convinced that he, not Truman, should have succeeded Roosevelt. Furthermore, as secretary of commerce, he believed that he had a legitimate voice in foreign affairs. After all, economics was the key to diplomacy, and trade relations could be the means of preventing another war. That was especially true now because the Soviet Union had been economically devastated by the war, and the United States could use economic aid to assist its World War II ally. The more Wallace spoke out, though, the more it was apparent that many of his criticisms were directed at the man charged with overseeing foreign policy for the president—the new secretary of state, James Byrnes.

Russia: Technically, one of the fifteen republics that made up the Soviet Union. The names *Russia* and *Soviet Union* had been used interchangeably since the creation of the Soviet state after the Russian Revolution of 1917.

"GIVE IT TO THEM WITH BOTH BARRELS"

James "Jimmy" Byrnes was a superb politician. A pragmatic dealmaker who always put what was achievable ahead of what was desirable, he won a reputation as a man who could get things done. He skillfully used his humble origins to appeal to the common man, but rather than rock the boat, he pursued conservative policies on economics and race. Born in 1882 in Charleston, South Carolina, James F. Byrnes was the son of a clerk and a seamstress. The family's difficult financial situation was made much worse by the death of Jimmy's father before Jimmy was born. His mother would somehow provide for her own invalid mother as well as a sister, niece, daughter, and young son. By the time Jimmy was fourteen, the family's difficult financial circumstances forced him to drop out of school and go to work as a messenger for a law firm. He continued his education informally and then decided to become a lawyer himself. He passed the bar in 1903 and settled down to practice in Aiken, South Carolina, where he married and became increasingly interested in politics.

Byrnes's own political career began in 1908 when he won election to the office of public prosecutor. In 1910, he was elected to the U.S. House of Representatives, where he served for more than a decade. There he quickly established his reputation as a practical politician who was willing to compromise to help pass legislation. He also made powerful friends, including Franklin Roosevelt, who was then serving as assistant secretary of the navy. A white supremacist, Byrnes shared the racial attitudes of the early twentieth-century white South. Although he supported segregation, he denounced the Ku Klux Klan when it reemerged after World War I. In the 1920s, the Klan was not only antiblack but also anti-Catholic and anti-immigrant. Although Byrnes had converted to the Episcopalian faith, his family was Irish Catholic. He refused to have anything to do with anti-Catholic politics, which helped lead to his defeat in his overwhelmingly Protestant congressional district in 1924. Byrnes then returned to the practice of law, but six years later, he ran for the U.S. Senate. By then, the Klan's popularity had collapsed and the Depression had set in, and Byrnes was elected.

Byrnes quickly became an influential member of the Senate. His election had been partly due to the financial backing of Bernard M. Baruch, a fellow South Carolinian who had made a fortune in stock speculation on Wall Street. After Baruch and Byrnes became friends in the early 1930s, the financier put Byrnes in control of his vast campaign contributions to fellow Democrats. As Byrnes doled out these funds, his own influence increased. Meanwhile, during the Depression, his power in the Senate grew as he carefully balanced fiscal conservatism with the growing need for individual relief. In the process, he became a leader of the conservative wing of the Democratic Party in the Senate. Often southerners, these men defended racial segregation in the South, favored less government regulation of business, and distrusted the growth of federal power at the expense of the states. This position often pitted Byrnes against his old friend FDR, whose New Deal called for federal controls on the economy and a vast expansion of federal power. Yet Byrnes, ever the pragmatist, insisted that governing was "really a matter of policy not principle," and he never lost FDR's trust and support. Indeed, Byrnes was a fiscal conservative when federal money was spent in other states, but he became much more liberal when South Carolina was involved.

After the outbreak of World War II in 1939, Roosevelt and Byrnes became staunch allies. In fact, Byrnes was Roosevelt's man in the Senate, especially when it came to battling strong opposition to American involvement in the war. In 1940, Byrnes even set aside his own unfavorable ideas about the liberal Wallace to help persuade conservative delegates at the 1940 Democratic convention to accept the agriculture secretary as FDR's running mate. For his loyalty, Roosevelt rewarded Byrnes with an appointment to the Supreme Court in 1941. He served on the Court for a year, then resigned to accept Roosevelt's offer to head the Office of Economic Stabilization and, later, the Office of War Mobilization (OWM), agencies designed to boost production and oversee the distribution of war materiel. Although these agencies carried out the very centralized economic planning that Byrnes opposed, he agreed to lead them in the name of winning the war. His actions as OWM director soon earned him the nickname "Assistant President"; so pervasive were the agency's controls over the nation's economy.

By 1944, Byrnes was in a powerful position to challenge Henry Wallace for the privilege of being FDR's running mate. Given his dedicated service, Byrnes had reason to believe that the president would choose him. Like other Democratic conservatives, he disdained Wallace's politics. He also believed that the next vice president would eventually be president, either by winning the office in 1948 or by inheriting it if Roosevelt died. Roosevelt wanted to keep the southern base of his party happy, but he feared that Byrnes would be unpopular with organized labor and that his segregationist views would cost the Democrats African-American votes in the North. Byrnes also had another political liability: his Catholic background. In the end, of course, FDR compromised, ousting Wallace in favor of Truman, who seemed palatable to both liberal and conservative factions of the party.

Just as FDR did not forget the ousted Wallace, he did not forget Byrnes. In early 1945, Byrnes traveled with the president to meet Churchill and Stalin at the Yalta Conference. In fact, Byrnes's presence at Yalta helped make him a player in American foreign policy. When Roosevelt died that April, Truman named Byrnes secretary of state. "He'd been to Yalta," Truman said later, explaining his choice. Yet Truman, who had virtually no experience in foreign affairs, had another reason for asking Byrnes to take the job. As the new president wrote in his diary, he wanted someone who was "hard hitting," not "smart boys in the State Department," to advise him on foreign policy. Byrnes would not hesitate to speak his mind.

Byrnes's advice started with the atomic bomb. Roosevelt had told him all about the top-secret Manhattan Project to develop an atomic bomb, and it was Byrnes who informed Truman of the details of the program shortly after Truman became president. Throughout World War II, Byrnes had urged Roosevelt to pursue a "hard war" policy that used all the resources the United States could muster to inflict the maximum amount of damage and win the war quickly. Now he pushed Truman to use the atomic bomb, arguing that since it had cost about $2 billion to build, the public would want it to be used. Further, he was convinced that using the bomb would hasten the end of the war, make an invasion of Japan unnecessary, and save countless American lives. He also knew that using the bomb had another advantage. As he told Truman, it would put the United States "in a position to dictate our own terms at the end of the war." In other words, it would send a clear message to the Soviet Union that the United States was willing to use whatever force it took to win. Byrnes knew, of course, that the Soviets were set to come into the war against Japan in early August, but he was alarmed by the way the Soviets were exerting their authority in Eastern Europe. He believed that using the bomb would give the United States tremendous leverage in diplomatic relations with them.

Truman agreed with Byrnes. But even after the United States used two bombs to end the war with Japan, the Soviets did not seem any more willing to accede to American demands. Meeting with the Soviet foreign minister V. M. Molotov shortly after Japan surrendered, Byrnes protested the tightening of Soviet control over the governments of the Eastern European nations of Romania and Bulgaria. He insisted that the Soviets' actions violated the agreement at Yalta to conduct "free elections" in liberated nations. Yet Molotov was unmoved. He pointed out, for instance, that the Americans had excluded the Soviet Union from participating in the postwar occupation of Japan. When Byrnes got home, he reported that the Soviets were "welching" on the Yalta agreements. The United States, he went on, was facing a "new Russia, totally different than the Russia we dealt with a year ago."

The Truman administration seemed divided on Soviet actions in Eastern Europe and on what to do about them. Secretary of the Navy James Forrestal and Truman's Chief of Staff William D. Leahy, for instance, believed that Stalin's actions in Eastern Europe were driven by a desire for expansion and that the Soviets could not be trusted. Others, including Truman, believed that difficulties with the Soviets could be overcome and that the two powers might reach some accommodation. Differences were "inevitable," Truman said in October 1945, but he hoped that they could be worked out "if we [give] ourselves time." Byrnes agreed. In Congress, he had gotten things done by being flexible, and he had not given up on working with the Soviets. Thus, when he met with Stalin in Moscow at the end of 1945, Byrnes was willing to compromise. In exchange for Byrnes's promise of access to American atomic research in the future, the Soviets promised to support a proposed United Nations commission that would inspect all nations' nuclear facilities. Byrnes also got the Soviets to place a few non-communists in the Romanian and Bulgarian governments in exchange for American diplomatic recognition of those regimes and a token Soviet role in the postwar occupation of Japan. This agreement did nothing to weaken Soviet control in Eastern Europe, but the secretary of state was elated. He believed that it signaled the continuation of cordial relations between the United States and the Soviet Union. The conference in Moscow, he later said, had helped "restore 'peace on earth'."

When Byrnes returned from Moscow, he came under heavy fire from Republicans in Congress and administration officials who wanted no compromises at all with the Soviets. They believed that Byrnes, as one of them put it, had "given far too much away to the Russians." By early 1946, Truman agreed. The president was very close to Leahy who had argued for no concessions to Soviet demands and who had sharply criticized Byrnes after the Moscow meeting. Truman also had an eye on the opinion polls, which demonstrated that just in months, the public's willingness to trust the Soviets had dropped dramatically. In addition, Truman was miffed that Byrnes had announced the Moscow agreement without informing him. Later, he told his secretary of state that he "would not tolerate a repetition of such conduct."

Another Soviet action further hardened Truman's views about the Soviets. During World War II, Great Britain and the Soviet Union had moved troops into Iran to make sure that that country's rich oil fields did not fall into enemy hands. Each nation had promised to remove its forces six months after the end of the war. By early March 1946, however, Soviet forces had not yet withdrawn. The continued occupation, Truman told Byrnes, was "an outrage." Like many Americans, the president had drawn a lesson from the diplomacy leading up to World War II. Diplomatic efforts to prevent war by caving in to Germany's demand for territory in neighboring Czechoslovakia in 1938 had failed to head off war. Now Soviet actions in Eastern Europe and Iran had led Truman to conclude that appeasing the Soviets would not work either. "Unless Russia is faced with an iron fist and strong language," he informed Byrnes, "another war is in the making." He added, "I'm tired of babying the Soviets."

At the same time, Truman had another justification for a hard-line policy against the Soviets. It came from an American diplomat named George F. Kennan. While stationed in Moscow, Kennan sent the State Department a long diplomatic telegram arguing that Soviet conduct in the world was driven not by a desire to achieve harmonious relations with the rest of the world but by the Soviet system of government. Rejecting the idea that Soviet actions in Eastern Europe stemmed from legitimate concerns for security, Kennan argued that the Soviets had a "neurotic view of world affairs" created by the need to prop up their ruthless regime at home. In other words, the Soviets were building an empire in Eastern Europe to ensure that the Soviet Union remained united and to keep those at the top in power. The implications were clear: Soviet expansionism had to be contained. **[See Source 1.]** Kennan's analysis was widely read in the administration, and it also struck a chord with the president and his advisers who had been skeptical of Soviet actions in Eastern Europe all along. It provided the administration with the intellectual framework to justify an uncompromising stance toward the Soviets. From now on, the Soviets were not a shaky ally but the enemy.

Byrnes quickly reflected the emerging administration consensus regarding the Soviets. With Soviet forces continuing to occupy northern Iran, Byrnes believed that the Soviets were preparing to launch an invasion of the country. Referring to both diplomatic and military force, he said, "We'll give it to them with both barrels." As American officials devised a plan to encircle the Soviet Union with a permanent ring of military bases, Byrnes made it clear in a series of speeches that the United States would consider using military force to defend Iran. Then he took the matter to the United Nations, which sparked a Soviet walkout. A week later, however, the Soviets agreed to pull their troops out of Iran.

For the United States—and for Byrnes—the Iran crisis was a turning point. Combined with earlier developments in Eastern Europe and Kennan's analysis, events in Iran made it increasingly difficult for Byrnes, Truman, and most other administration officials to believe that Soviet actions were driven by legitimate security needs. When it came to the Soviet Union, Byrnes remarked shortly after the Iranian crisis, "American opinion was no longer disposed to make concessions on important questions." From now on, those would have to come from the Soviets. Nowhere would that be clearer than in Germany. Occupied by the United States, the Soviet Union, Great Britain, and France, Germany remained divided in late 1946. Unable to come to terms with the Soviet Union on the reunification of the country, Byrnes announced a new policy in September. If Germany could not be entirely reunified, he said in a speech in Stuttgart, the United States would move to reunify the western zones. Under no circumstances would the United States allow Germany to fall under Soviet influence. "As long as there is an occupation army in Germany," he told his German audience, "American forces will be part of that occupation army." The United States was now prepared to accept a divided Germany—and a divided world. **[See Source 2.]**

"THE TOUGHER WE GET"

Henry Wallace watched with alarm the hardening relations between the United States and the Soviet Union. He was not alone. Many officials, often with ties to the Roosevelt administration, were dismayed at the Truman administration's harsh rhetoric and uncompromising stance toward the Soviets. They had witnessed FDR's diplomacy with Stalin and hoped that some accommodation could be reached, preserving the "Grand Alliance" after the war. Former ambassador to the Soviet Union Joseph E. Davies called the breakdown in relations "tragic." Senator Claude Pepper of Florida said that Soviet actions were the result of their fears of growing British and American hostility toward them. Even FDR's son James Roosevelt said that the Truman administration had not fairly informed the American people of the Soviet views on foreign relations. No one, however, was more outspoken than Henry A. Wallace. The Soviets, he believed, had legitimate security concerns in Eastern Europe. He opposed any increase in the military power of the United States in response to the Soviet occupation of the area. Such military muscle flexing would only provoke Soviet fears. In the spring of 1946, he sent two long letters to Truman arguing that the Soviets had reasonable grounds to fear the United States and calling on the president to take steps to promote trade between the two nations. He also began speaking out publicly, warning Americans of the dangers of an atomic arms race.

These pronouncements made Jimmy Byrnes irate. By March 1946, the secretary of commerce was the lone holdover from Roosevelt's cabinet in the Truman administration. Wallace had the support of farmers, organized labor, and intellectuals. Many members of these groups disliked the more conservative Truman, and the president knew it. He needed Wallace, at least through the November elections. Thus he could afford to ignore Wallace's policy recommendations, but he could not afford to muzzle him. In fact, he wanted Wallace to campaign for the Democrats. Ironically, although Wallace had less and less influence in the administration, his position remained secure, and he was free to influence administration policy by swaying public opinion.

Wallace delivered his first major campaign address at Madison Square Garden in September only six days after Byrnes's Stuttgart speech. Wallace declared that the United States had "no more business in the *political* affairs of Eastern Europe than Russia [had] in the *political* affairs of Latin America, Western Europe and the United States." In a jab at Byrnes's intervention in the Iranian crisis, he said that American foreign policy was "purchasing oil in the Near East with the lives of American soldiers." Instead of military posturing, he called for a diplomatic policy that addressed Soviet fears—one emphasizing trade and economic assistance. A hard line, he insisted, was no way to build peace. Getting tough never worked, "whether for schoolyard bullies or businessmen or world powers." "The tougher we get," he predicted, "the tougher the Russians will get." **[See Source 3.]**

When he read about Wallace's address several days later, Byrnes was livid. He was especially incensed by Wallace's remark that Truman had reviewed the commerce secretary's Madison Square Garden address two days before and had agreed with it. Two days after the speech, however, the president said, in the face of a growing controversy about the administration's foreign policy, that he had approved only Wallace's right to deliver the speech, not the content. Several days later, when Wallace said that he intended to give more speeches on foreign policy, Byrnes sent Truman an ultimatum in which he threatened to resign if Wallace was not muzzled. Truman now had to choose between his link to the liberals in the Democratic Party and the spokesman for the administration's hard-line foreign policy. Letting Byrnes go could open up Truman to the charge that he was soft on communism only two months before the congressional elections. And, of course, it meant repudiating the very policy he had endorsed and believed to be correct. Several days later, he fired Wallace.

Byrnes had his victory, but he did not enjoy it for long. Never popular with organized labor, the secretary of state soon came under attack from the powerful Congress of Industrial Organizations (CIO). The CIO had become a force in the late 1930s by successfully targeting millions of workers in the automobile, steel, and tire and rubber industries. Its support was crucial to the political success of Truman and the Democrats. Two days after Wallace's speech, Truman received a telegram from the CIO's leadership condemning Byrnes as an enemy of democracy abroad and calling for his resignation. At the same time, liberals began to attack Byrnes for his views on segregation.

These attacks, however, were not as damaging as those from Republican and administration hard-liners, who criticized Byrnes for being soft on communism. In 1945, Byrnes had defended a State Department employee named John Service who had been accused of passing secret documents to a magazine critical of U.S. foreign policy. Service and several others involved in the case had been exonerated by a grand jury, and the charges against them had been dropped. Nonetheless, without realizing it, Byrnes had opened himself up to the charge of not being sufficiently vigilant in protecting the State Department from subversives. As the United States entered into a worldwide struggle against communism, it was tempting for politicians to exploit the issue of communist subversion at home for political gain. That was especially true by 1946, in the wake of the publicity surrounding the Service case and several other cases of alleged spying. Indeed, Republicans would make significant gains in the congressional elections that year by accusing the Democrats of not doing enough to root out subversives in the United States (see Chapter 10). Suddenly Byrnes was a political liability to Truman.

At the same time, Truman had come to depend on new men in the administration. Presidential aide Clark Clifford, Undersecretary of State Dean Acheson, and Chief of Staff William Leahy supported an even more confrontational approach toward the Soviets than Byrnes now pursued. Clifford, for instance, advised Truman in a confidential report in September 1946 that the United States had to be prepared "to wage atomic and biological warfare, if necessary" against the Soviet Union. Earlier, Clifford had joined Byrnes in calling for Wallace's head, and now he was working to turn the president against Byrnes. He even implied that the secretary of state was appeasing the Soviets beneath the surface of his "get tough" policy. In poor health and aware that he was being forced out, Byrnes resigned his cabinet post in early 1947.

As Byrnes's career demonstrates, both Republicans and Democrats had learned how explosive charges about being soft on communism could be. In addition, virtually anyone was now open to suspicion. That would be especially clear within two months after Byrnes's departure, when the president announced the Truman Doctrine in a dramatic speech before Congress. It was the first expression of what came to be known as the containment policy—a sweeping American commitment to contain the expansion of communism on a global scale. The Truman Doctrine committed the United States to assisting any nation resisting Soviet-backed aggression and would serve as the foundation for American foreign policy for the next four decades of Cold War with the Soviet Union. **[See Source 4.]** As it happened, the initial drafts of Truman's address quoted Byrnes's statement during the Iranian crisis that the United States would not let "coercion or pressure" on other nations go unchallenged. At Clifford's insistence, Byrnes's name and remarks were excised from the speech. Thus his name would not be associated with the policy he had helped devise.

"IS THIS AMERICA?"

Once Wallace and Byrnes left the Truman administration, they would become thorns in the president's side. In 1948, Wallace abandoned the Democratic Party and ran as the Progressive Party's candidate for president. He advocated his long-held plans for an international government and called for domestic reform that would curb the excesses of capitalism and bring prosperity to all Americans—and the rest of the world as well. Most of all, he attacked Truman's foreign policy of containment. This policy, he said, went against the American principles of liberty, equality, and self-government. A creation of big business and the military, the policy represented American imperialism. **[See Source 5.]** By appealing to liberals, organized labor, farmers, and even radicals, Wallace threatened to draw enough votes from Truman to swing the election to Republican candidate Thomas Dewey. But Truman campaigned vigorously, ferociously attacking Wallace for his communist ties. Labor leaders, worried about communist influence in their unions, refused to support Wallace and began expelling radicals from their organizations. Meanwhile, the Democrats created an anticommunist organization called Americans for Democratic Action, which attacked Wallace and accused him of being a front for the communist movement. Wallace's political fortunes took another blow when he traveled in the South and called for civil rights for African Americans. He was soon the target of angry crowds, which sometimes pelted him with rotten fruits and vegetables. At one point, surrounded by a shouting mob, Wallace turned to a bystander and asked, "Are you an American? Is this America?"

By 1948, the rising political star of the 1930s had become a pariah. In November, Wallace received only 2.4 percent of the vote, while Truman scored a dramatic come-from-behind victory over Dewey. After the election, Wallace continued to oppose Truman's Cold War policies, but his career as an office seeker was over. He contented himself with a private life devoted to reading, writing, and agricultural science. Meanwhile, his hybrid-corn company thrived, and, ironically, he became a wealthy capitalist. Until his death in 1965, he enjoyed a comfortable retirement on his farm in New York.

Jimmy Byrnes also became a harsh critic of the Truman administration after leaving the cabinet. His attacks came from the other end of the political spectrum. After his resignation, Byrnes returned to South Carolina, where he served as governor from 1951 to 1955. Still a supporter of segregation, he attacked the Truman administration on another front: the growing battle over civil rights. In 1948, Truman had run for reelection on a civil rights platform, after moving to desegregate the armed forces. Byrnes also blasted Truman's support of national health insurance, increased unemployment benefits, and greater federal subsidies for public housing, measures Byrnes associated with a "welfare state." Eventually, he abandoned the Democratic Party, and in 1960, he endorsed Republican Richard Nixon for president. By the time he died in 1972, Byrnes had become an important figure in the Republican Party by helping it break the traditional Democratic hold on the South.

Henry Wallace and Jimmy Byrnes shared strangely similar fates. They had both narrowly missed making it to the presidency, and each believed that he would have made a better president than Truman. In addition, both had been let go by Truman. Yet they were very different men. Wallace was a visionary whose idealistic views about international cooperation led him to put principles above compromise. Byrnes was a realist, a pragmatic wheeler-dealer willing to give in for the sake of agreement. The two men had very different views of and plans for the post–World War II world and U.S. relations with the Soviet Union. Wallace believed that if the United States addressed legitimate Soviet security concerns, the two nations could continue to cooperate. Byrnes believed that the United States had to use force against the Soviet Union to prevent the spread of communism, protect American interests, and make the Soviets more cooperative. In his view, a practical Cold War policy involved a balance of military and diplomatic threats. Yet as the United States began a worldwide crusade against communism, neither man's approach was acceptable. Neither Wallace's idealism nor Byrnes's willingness to compromise fit with the growing American consensus about Soviet motives. In the Cold War mindset already fixed by the late 1940s, the ability to demonstrate ideological purity was more important than skill at fashioning political compromises. Thus, in their own ways, Wallace and Byrnes were two of the early victims of the long Cold War.

•PRIMARY SOURCES•

Source 1:   George F. Kennan, *"The Long Telegram"* (1946)

As an attaché at the American embassy in Moscow, George F. Kennan cabled his "long telegram" to the State Department in Washington, D.C., in February 1946. His analysis of the Soviet government and its behavior in foreign affairs was widely read in the Truman administration and did a great deal to shape the administration's foreign policy toward the Soviets. What are Kennan's views of the Soviets? What are the implications for American policy? Which of Kennan's points would Wallace and Byrnes agree or disagree with?

[W]e have here [in the Soviet Union] a political force committed fanatically to the belief that with U.S. there can be no permanent *modus Vivendi** that it is desirable and necessary that the internal harmony of our society be disrupted, our traditional way of life be destroyed, the international authority of our state be broken, if Soviet power is to be secure. This political force has complete power of disposition over energies of one of world's greatest peoples and resources of world's richest national territory, and is borne along by deep and powerful currents of Russian nationalism. In addition, it has an elaborate and far flung apparatus for exertion of its influence in other countries, an apparatus of amazing flexibility and versatility, managed by people whose experience and skill in underground methods are presumably without parallel in history. Finally, it is seemingly inaccessible to considerations of reality in its basic reactions. For it, the vast fund of objective fact about human society is not, as with us, the measure against which outlook is constantly being tested and re-formed, but a grab bag from which individual items are selected arbitrarily and tendenciously to bolster an outlook already preconceived. This is admittedly not a pleasant picture. Problem of how to cope with this force [is] undoubtedly greatest task our diplomacy has ever faced and probably greatest it will ever have to face. It should be point of departure from which our political general staff work at present juncture should proceed. It should be approached with same thoroughness and care as solution of major strategic problem in war, and if necessary, with no smaller outlay in planning effort. I cannot attempt to suggest all answers here. But I would like to record my conviction that problem is within our power to solve—and that without recourse to any general military conflict. And in support of this conviction there are certain observations of a more encouraging nature I should like to make:

1. Soviet power, unlike that of Hitlerite Germany, is neither schematic nor adventuristic. It does not work by fixed plans. It does not take unnecessary risks. Impervious

SOURCE: Reprinted in Thomas H. Etzold and John Lewis Gaddis, CONTAINMENT: DOCUMENTS ON AMERICAN POLICY AND STRATEGY, 1945–1950 (New York: Columbia University Press, 1978), pp. 61–62; originally from "Foreign Relations of the United States: 1946" (Washington, D.C.: Government Printing Office, 1946), VI, 696–709.

Modus vivendi: Manner of getting along.

to logic of reason, and it is highly sensitive to logic of force. For this reason it can easily withdraw—and usually does—when strong resistance is encountered at any point. Thus, if the adversary has sufficient force and makes clear his readiness to use it, he rarely has to do so. If situations are properly handled there need be no prestige-engaging showdowns.

2. Gauged against Western World as a whole, Soviets are still by far the weaker force. Thus, their success will really depend on degree of cohesion, firmness, and vigor, which Western World can muster. And this is factor which it is within our power to influence.

Source 2: *James Byrnes Restates American Policy Toward Germany* (1946)

James Byrnes laid out his views regarding a still-divided Germany in a major speech in Stuttgart, Germany, in September 1946. Notice that Byrnes does not make any direct accusations against the Soviets but alludes to certain problems that have arisen under the joint-occupation arrangement. What are they? How does he justify the American action to create a partially reunified Germany? How does the new American policy for Germany reflect a firmer approach toward the Soviets? What points would Wallace have agreed or disagreed with?

I have come to Germany to learn at first hand the problems involved in the reconstruction of Germany and to discuss with our representatives the views of the United States Government as to some of the problems confronting us.

We in the United States have given considerable time and attention to these problems because upon their proper solution will depend not only the future well-being of Germany but the future well-being of Europe....

The carrying out of the Potsdam Agreement* has ... been obstructed by the failure of the Allied Control Council* to take the necessary steps to enable the German economy to function as an economic unit. Essential central German administrative departments have not been established, although they are expressly required by the Potsdam Agreement.

The equitable distribution of essential commodities between the several zones so as to produce a balanced economy throughout Germany and reduce the need for imports has not been arranged, although that too is expressly required by the Potsdam Agreement.

The working out of a balanced economy throughout Germany to provide the necessary means to pay for approved imports has not been accomplished, although that too is expressly required by the Potsdam Agreement.

SOURCE: James F. Byrnes, "Restatement of D.S. Policy," Department of State Bulletin, September 15, 1946, pp. 496, 497–498, 499, 500.

Potsdam Agreement: The agreement reached at a meeting of Stalin, Churchill, and Truman in Potsdam, Germany, in the summer of 1945. A major issue dividing the participants at the Potsdam Conference was postwar reparations—that is, the right of the Allies to remove assets from their German zones of occupation to pay for war damages. The agreement allowed the Western Allies to ship German industrial equipment from their zones to the Soviets. In return, the Soviets agreed to ship food from their heavily agricultural zone in the east to the western zones of occupation.

Allied Control Council: A council composed of representatives from the United States, Britain, France, and the Soviet Union to control postwar Germany. In reality, the military commanders in the four nations' zones of occupation had more power than the council.

The United States is firmly of the belief that Germany should be administered as an economic unit and that zonal barriers should be completely obliterated so far as the economic life and activity in Germany are concerned.

The conditions which now exist in Germany make it impossible for industrial production to reach the levels which the occupying powers agreed were essential for a minimum German peacetime economy. Obviously, if the agreed levels of industry are to be reached, we cannot continue to restrict the free exchange of commodities, persons, and ideas throughout Germany. The barriers between the four zones of Germany are far more difficult to surmount than those between normal independent states.

The time has come when the zonal boundaries should be regarded as defining only the areas to be occupied for security purposes by the armed forces of the occupying powers and not as self-contained economic or political units.

That was the course of development envisaged by the Potsdam Agreement, and that is the course of development which the American Government intends to follow to the full limit of its authority. It has formally announced that it is its intention to unify the economy of its own zone with any or all of the other zones willing to participate in the unification....

We favor the economic unification of Germany. If complete unification cannot be secured, we shall do everything in our power to secure the maximum possible unification....

From now on the thoughtful people of the world will judge Allied action in Germany not by Allied promises but by Allied performances. The American Government has supported and will continue to support the necessary measures to de-Nazify and demilitarize Germany, but it does not believe that large armies of foreign soldiers or alien bureaucrats, however well motivated and disciplined, are in the long run the most reliable guardians of another country's democracy....

Security forces will probably have to remain in Germany for a long period. I want no misunderstanding. We will not shirk our duty. We are not withdrawing. We are staying here. As long as there is an occupation army in Germany, American armed forces will be part of that occupation army....

While we shall insist that Germany observe the principles of peace, good-neighborliness, and humanity, we do not want Germany to become the satellite of any power or powers or to live under a dictatorship, foreign or domestic. The American people hope to see peaceful, democratic Germans become and remain free and independent.

Source 3:   Henry A. Wallace, *"The Way to Peace"* (1946)

Henry Wallace's Madison Square Garden speech in September 1946 marked a break with the Truman administration's foreign policy and led to his resignation from the cabinet. How does Wallace challenge the policies of Truman and Byrnes? How does he propose to deal with the Soviets? Why do you think this speech caused such anger on the part of Byrnes and caused Truman to remove Wallace?

During the past year or so, the significance of peace has been increased immeasurably by the atom bomb, guided missiles and airplanes which soon will travel as fast as sound. Make no mistake about it—another war would hurt the United States many times as

SOURCE: Henry A. Wallace, "The Way to Peace," VITAL SPEECHES OF THE DAY, October 1, 1946, pp. 738–741.

much as the last war. We cannot rest in the assurance that we invented the atom bomb—and therefore that this agent of destruction will work best for us. He who trusts in the atom bomb will sooner or later perish by the atom bomb—or something worse....

[W]e are reckoning with a force which cannot be handled successfully by a "Get tough with Russia" policy. "Getting tough" never brought anything real and lasting— whether for schoolyard bullies or businessmen or world powers. The tougher we get, the tougher the Russians will get.

We must not let our Russian policy be guided or influenced by those inside or outside the United States who want war with Russia. This does not mean appeasement.

We most earnestly want peace with Russia—but we want to be met half way. We want cooperation. And I believe that we can get cooperation once Russia understands that our primary objective is neither saving the British Empire nor purchasing oil in the Near East with the lives of American soldiers. We cannot allow national oil rivalries to force us into war. All of the nations producing oil, whether inside or outside of their own boundaries, must fulfill the provisions of the United Nations Charter and encourage the development of world petroleum reserves so as to make the maximum amount of oil available to all nations of the world on an equitable peaceful basis—and not on the basis of fighting the next war.

For her part, Russia can retain our respect by cooperating with the United Nations in a spirit of openminded and flexible give-and-take.

The real peace treaty we now need is between the United States and Russia. On our part, we should recognize that we have no more business in the *political* affairs of Eastern Europe than Russia has in the *political* affairs of Latin America, Western Europe and the United States. We may not like what Russia does in Eastern Europe. Her type of land reform, industrial expropriation, and suppression of basic liberties offends the great majority of the people of the United States. But whether we like it or not the Russians will try to socialize their sphere of influence just as we try to democratize our sphere of influence. This applies also to Germany and Japan. We are striving to democratize Japan and our area of control in Germany, while Russia strives to socialize eastern Germany....

Under friendly peaceful competition the Russian world and the American world will gradually become more alike. The Russians will be forced to grant more and more of the personal freedoms; and we shall become more and more absorbed with the problems of social-economic justice.

Russia must be convinced that we are not planning for war against her and we must be certain that Russia is not carrying on territorial expansion or world domination through native communists faithfully following every twist and turn in the Moscow party line. But in this competition, we must insist on an open door for trade throughout the world. There will always be an ideological conflict—but that is no reason why diplomats cannot work out a basis for both systems to live safely in the world side by side....

In the United States an informed public opinion will be all-powerful. Our people are peace-minded. But they often express themselves too late—for events today move much faster than public opinion. The people here, as everywhere in the world, must be convinced that another war is not inevitable. And through mass meetings such as this, and through persistent pamphleteering, the people can be organized for peace—even though a large segment of our press is propagandizing our people for war in the hope of scaring Russia. And we who look on this war-with-Russia talk as criminal foolishness must carry our message direct to the people—even though we may be called communists because we dare to speak out.

I believe that peace—the kind of peace I have outlined tonight—is the basic issue, both in the Congressional campaign this fall and right on through the Presidential election in 1948. How we meet this issue will determine whether we live not in "one world" or "two worlds"—but whether we live at all.

Source 4:   Harry S. Truman, *The Truman Doctrine* (1947)

Harry Truman chose to follow a forceful policy toward the Soviet Union, a policy that included the concept of containment. He outlined this policy in what came to be known as the Truman Doctrine. How does he define the challenge facing the United States? What are the implications for the United States? Do you see the influence of Wallace or Byrnes in this policy?

The gravity of the situation which confronts the world today necessitates my appearance before a joint session of the Congress.

The foreign policy and the national security of this country are involved.

One of the primary objectives of the foreign policy of the United States is the creation of conditions in which we and other nations will be able to work out a way of life free from coercion. This was a fundamental issue in the war with Germany and Japan. Our victory was won over countries which sought to impose their will and their way of life, upon other nations.

To ensure the peaceful development of nations, free from coercion, the United States has taken a leading part in establishing the United Nations. The United Nations is designed to make possible lasting freedom and independence for all its members. We shall not realize our objectives, however, unless we are willing to help free peoples to maintain their free institutions and their national integrity against aggressive movements that seek to impose upon them totalitarian regimes. This is no more than a frank recognition that totalitarian regimes, imposed upon free peoples, by direct or indirect aggression, undermine the foundations of international peace and hence the security of the United States.

The peoples of a number of countries of the world have recently had totalitarian regimes forced upon them against their will. The Government of the United States has made frequent protests against coercion and intimidation, in violation of the Yalta agreement, in Poland, Rumania, and Bulgaria. I must also state that in a number of other countries there have been similar developments.

At the present moment in world history nearly every nation must choose between alternative ways of life. The choice is too often not a free one.

One way of life is based upon the will of the majority, and is distinguished by free institutions, representative government, free elections, guarantees of individual liberty, freedom of speech and religion, and freedom from political oppression.

The second way of life is based upon the will of a minority forcibly imposed upon the majority. It relies upon terror and oppression, a controlled press and radio, fixed elections, and the suppression of personal freedoms.

I believe that it must be the policy of the United States to support free peoples who are resisting attempted subjugation by armed minorities or by outside pressures.

I believe that we must assist free peoples to work out their own destinies in their own way.

Source: "Public Papers of the Presidents of the United States: Harry S. Truman, 1947" (Washington, D.C.: Government Printing Office, 1963), pp. 176–180.

I believe that our help should be primarily through economic and financial aid which is essential to economic stability and orderly political processes....

The free peoples of the world look to us for support in maintaining their freedoms.

If we falter in our leadership, we may endanger the peace of the world—and we shall surely endanger the welfare of this Nation.

Great responsibilities have been placed upon us by the swift movement of events. I am confident that the Congress will face these responsibilities squarely.

Source 5:   Henry A. Wallace, *"The Path to Peace with Russia"* (1946)

Henry Wallace expressed his dissatisfaction with the Truman administration's foreign policy in speeches and articles, including this article published in the liberal New Republic in 1946. How does Wallace challenge James Byrnes's policies? What alternatives does he propose?

How do American actions since V-J Day[*] appear to other nations? I mean by actions the concrete things like $13 billion for the War and Navy Departments, the Bikini [Island] tests of the atomic bomb and continued production of bombs, the plan to arm Latin America with our weapons, production of B-29's and planned production of B-36's, and the effort to secure air bases spread over half the globe from which the other half of the globe can be bombed. I cannot but feel that these actions must make it look to the rest of the world as if we were only paying lip-service to peace at the conference table. These facts rather make it appear either (1) that we are preparing ourselves to win the war which we regard as inevitable or (2) that we are trying to build up a predominance of force to intimidate the rest of mankind. How would it look to us if Russia had the atomic bomb and we did not, if Russia had 10,000-mile bombers and air bases within a thousand miles of our coast lines and we did not?

Some of the military men and self-styled "realists" are saying:

"What's wrong with trying to build up a predominance of force? The only way to preserve peace is for this country to be so well armed that no one will dare attack us. We know that America will never start a war."

The flaw in this policy is simply that it will not work. In a world of atomic bombs and other revolutionary new weapons, such as radioactive poison gases and biological warfare, a peace maintained by a predominance of force is no longer possible....

Insistence on our part that the game must be played our way will only lead to a deadlock. The Russians will redouble their efforts to manufacture bombs, and they may also decide to expand their "security zone" in a serious way. Up to now, despite all our outcries against it, their efforts to develop a security zone in Eastern Europe and in the Middle East are small change from the point of view of military power as compared with our air bases in Greenland, Okinawa and many other places thousands of miles from our

SOURCE: Henry A. Wallace, "The Path to Peace with Russia," NEW REPUBLIC, September 30, 1946, pp. 401–402, 103, 404–405. Reprinted by permission.

---

[*]*V-J Day:* August 15, 1945, the day that fighting between the United States and Japan in World War II officially ended.

shores. We may feel very self-righteous if we refuse to budge on our plan and the Russians refuse to accept it, but that means only one thing—the atomic-armament race is on in deadly earnest....

Why Russia Distrusts the West

I should list the factors which make for Russian distrust of the United States and of the Western world as follows: The first is Russian history, which we must take into account because it is the setting in which Russians see all actions and policies of the rest of the world. Russian history for over a thousand years has been a succession of attempts, often unsuccessful, to resist invasion and conquest—by the Mongols, the Turks, the Swedes, the Germans and the Poles. The scant thirty years of the existence of the Soviet government has in Russian eyes been a continuation of their historical struggle for national existence....Then, in 1941, the Soviet state was almost conquered by the Germans after a period during which the Western European powers had apparently acquiesced in the rearming of Germany in the belief that the Nazis would seek to expand eastward rather than westward. The Russians, therefore, obviously see themselves as fighting for their existence in a hostile world....

Our interest in establishing democracy in Eastern Europe, where democracy by and large has never existed, seems to her an attempt to reestablish the encirclement of unfriendly neighbors which was created after the last war and which might serve as a springboard of still another effort to destroy her.

If this analysis is correct, and there is ample evidence to support it, the action to improve the situation is clearly indicated. The fundamental objective of such action should be to allay any reasonable Russian grounds for fear, suspicions and distrust. We must recognize that the world has changed and that today there can be no "one world" unless the United States and Russia can find some way of living together....

Two-way Trade

It is of greatest importance that we should discuss with the Russians in a friendly way their long-range economic problems and the future of our cooperation in matters of trade. The reconstruction program of the USSR and the plans for the full development of the Soviet Union offer tremendous opportunities for American goods and American technicians....

Many of the problems relating to the countries bordering on Russia could more readily be solved once an atmosphere of mutual trust and confidence is established and some form of economic arrangements is worked out with Russia.

QUESTIONS TO CONSIDER

1. Citing specific sources, how would you compare the foreign policy positions of Henry Wallace and James Byrnes? In what ways did each man's views about foreign policy after World War II reflect his experiences or views about other issues prior to that time? Given the circumstances at the end of the war, whose position was more realistic?

2. Very shortly after World War II, the Truman administration develope
    ment policy that was directed against the Soviet Union. What was that
    circumstances or ideas shaped it? What was Byrnes's role in its develo

3. Although Wallace and Byrnes had very different views about how the United States
    should deal with the Soviet Union after World War II, both met similar fates in the
    Truman administration. What does the career of each man reveal about the various
    influences on postwar foreign policy? To what extent did domestic political consid-
    erations influence American foreign policy in the early stages of the Cold War?
    What do the fates of Wallace and Byrnes reveal about the impact of foreign policy
    on American politics at the beginning of the Cold War?

4. Do you think relations between the United States and the Soviet Union would
    have turned out differently if Wallace or Byrnes had been chosen as Franklin
    Roosevelt's running mate in 1944? How so?

FOR FURTHER READING

John C. Culver and John Hyde, *American Dreamer: A Life of Henry A. Wallace* (New York: W. W. Norton & Company, 2000), provide a recent and engaging biography of Wallace.

John Lewis Gaddis, *Now We Know: Rethinking Cold War History* (Oxford: Oxford University Press, 1997), offers a post–Cold War evaluation of the long conflict between the United States and the Soviet Union.

Melvyn Leffler, *A Preponderance of Power: National Security, the Truman Administration, and the Cold War* (Stanford: Stanford University Press, 1992), submits a comprehensive treatment of the origins of the Cold War.

David Robertson, *Sly and Able: A Political Biography of James F. Byrnes* (New York: W. W. Norton & Company, 1994), offers a thorough examination of Byrnes's life and political career.

10

Politics and Principle in the Second Red Scare: Joseph McCarthy and Margaret Chase Smith

Margaret Chase Smith trembled as she stood to speak on the floor of the U.S. Senate. Part of her doubted that she should do this. As a freshman senator, she knew that she was expected to keep quiet. Of ninety-six senators in 1950, she was the only female. Worse, she was about to criticize the actions of a colleague. In the past several months, fellow Republican Joseph McCarthy had gained nationwide attention with shocking charges about communist subversives working in the federal government. At first, Smith took the Wisconsin senator's allegations very seriously. Like most Americans, she feared the specter of worldwide communism—and the dangers of communist spies in the government. But the more she listened to McCarthy, the more she doubted him. Meanwhile, people's reputations were being ruined, and none of her colleagues had condemned McCarthy's actions on the senate floor. In the end, she believed she had to do it.

As Smith glanced around the chamber, she spotted a glaring McCarthy directly behind her. She knew he would not like what she was about to say and would find some way to punish her. But she was determined not to let him intimidate her. Nervously, she began: "I speak as a Republican. I speak as a woman. I speak as a United States Senator. I speak as an American." Then she went on to observe that some "of us who shout the loudest about Americanism" ignore "some of the basic principles of Americanism," including the rights to criticize, protest, and hold unpopular ideas.

Smith's address stirred many observers, but it did nothing to silence McCarthy. In fact, he was only at the beginning of a spectacular senate career. In coming years, Americans

Joseph McCarthy   Margaret Chase Smith

heard many more alarming charges from him about communist subversion. By the time his career was over, so were those of many other Americans—individuals accused of communist sympathies or associations. And by then, his name had become synonymous with the post–World War II anticommunist hysteria.

McCarthy, of course, did not start the postwar anticommunist hysteria that came to be known as McCarthyism. In fact, ever since the Red Scare of 1919, the threat of communist subversion had periodically provoked deep fears in Americans. During the Great Depression, the American Communist Party and the various front organizations that it sponsored drew thousands of members, and communists became active in labor unions supported by the New Deal. Prodded by conservative and antiunion groups, Congress established the House Un-American Activities Committee (HUAC) in 1938 to respond to charges that communists had infiltrated the federal government. HUAC investigations fought the New Deal by focusing on communist influence in unions and federal agencies, but concerns about subversion subsided when the United States entered into a wartime Grand Alliance with the Soviet Union. As World War II gave way to the Cold War, however, anticommunism moved to the center stage of American politics. Through the late 1940s, the issue stayed there as young congressman Richard Nixon and members of HUAC investigated alleged communist influence, from Washington, D.C., to Hollywood. Those investigations and the publicity that Federal Bureau of Investigation (FBI) director J. Edgar Hoover gave to the alleged threat of communist subversion played a large role in promoting a second red scare. They also set the stage for McCarthy, the most vocal anticommunist politician by the early 1950s, to exploit it.

If McCarthy did not start the post–World War II anticommunist hysteria, Smith was not alone in attacking him. For a time, though, she was perhaps the most prominent politician in the nation to speak up against him. In so doing, she too played a unique role in this red scare and, like McCarthy, highlighted important aspects of it. Together, these two colleagues and adversaries illustrate factors that fostered this scare, kept it alive, and finally led to its demise.

TAIL-GUNNER JOE

The man who sat glowering behind Margaret Chase Smith started life in circumstances that made it unlikely he would land in the U.S. Senate only thirty-nine years later. Joseph R. McCarthy was born in the tiny settlement of Grand Chute in central Wisconsin, the grandson of a poor Irish immigrant and son of a farmer. On their modest farm, McCarthy's parents raised a small herd of cows and five sons and two daughters. By the time Joseph was born in 1908, the McCarthys had moved from a log cabin to a white clapboard house without electricity or plumbing. Although stories abound regarding Joe's childhood, little is known for sure. Also of Irish descent, his mother was a devout Catholic and apparently uneducated. By all accounts, his no-nonsense father worked incessantly. Neighbors remember young Joe as strong, energetic, and extroverted. Like his father, he was a hard worker. He was also an excellent student. He attended a one-room school, where his teacher was impressed by his sharp mind and keen memory, and let him sit in on the older students' lessons.

McCarthy's native intelligence seemed matched only by his energy and ambition. Dropping out of school at fourteen to help out his father, young Joe soon grew tired of farm work. His mother constantly encouraged her youngest son to be somebody, and by age sixteen, he was ready to strike out on his own. Renting an acre from his father, he raised chickens and within a year had a thriving business. Although it eventually failed when he was laid low by flu, the determined McCarthy rebounded quickly. After talking his way into a job as a grocery store manager in a nearby town, he introduced aggressive marketing and soon racked up the biggest sales in the chain. When not at work, he found time to attend high school. Twenty years old when he enrolled, he worked at an accelerated pace and finished in a year. Now consumed by the desire for an education, he headed off in 1930 to attend Catholic Marquette University in Milwaukee.

The ambitious McCarthy thrived at Marquette. Outgoing and friendly, he was elected senior class president. Few of his classmates seemed as devoted to the Catholic faith. Few, too, could match his energy. To earn money, he worked numerous jobs, from cook to service station manager. He also made money gambling. He played poker without fear, aggressively raising the stakes even on poor hands until his opponents folded. McCarthy even arm wrestled for money. When not gambling, he boxed. In all these extracurricular activities, he seemed to demonstrate a trait that many who knew him later would recognize: what one biographer called "exaggerated masculinity."

McCarthy left Marquette with a law degree five years after he entered. With little time to study, he had succeeded with dogged determination. And he was motivated by his new plan: He would enter politics. Heading to Waupaca, a small county seat near his hometown, he set up a one-man law practice in 1935. He was friendly and aggressive in both pursuing clients and handling their cases. The next year, he ran unsuccessfully for district attorney as a staunch New Deal Democrat. When he ran for a nonpartisan judgeship for the Appleton district three years later, though, the outcome was different. McCarthy outpolled the incumbent by outhustling him. By election day, he had talked to practically every eligible voter. He won many of them over with informal, neighborly charm. He also put out advertisements that deliberately misstated his opponent's age and deceived voters about his pay. At twenty-nine, McCarthy took a seat on the bench.

When the United States entered World War II, McCarthy realized that a war record would help him win higher office, so he enlisted in the Marines in 1942 and shipped off to the South Pacific to serve as an intelligence officer. For nearly three years, he debriefed pilots after they returned from bombing runs. By 1943, however, Wisconsin newspapers began to carry stories about McCarthy's exploits as a tail gunner who flew on dangerous missions. According to one report, he fired off more bullets on a single mission than any other Marine in history. In reality, McCarthy and many other Marines often went along on routine flights to relieve their boredom. On one such trip, eager to break the record for most ammunition used on a flight, McCarthy had fired numerous rounds into coconut trees. When he returned, the public relations officer wrote up a press release about his record for newspapers back home. On another mission, McCarthy falsely claimed, he was wounded by enemy fire. He actually broke his foot in a hazing incident on board one flight. When a *Milwaukee Journal* reporter later uncovered the real story of McCarthy's war "wound," McCarthy called the paper "pro-Communist." By then, however, his war record did not matter. The legend of Tail-Gunner Joe was embedded in the minds of Dairy State voters.

McCarthy came home to a hero's welcome in 1945. Having switched parties years before, he ran for the Republican nomination for the Senate in 1946. After winning the backing of wealthy conservatives who saw an opportunity to defeat the liberal incumbent, McCarthy entered the primary with a large campaign war chest. Some of the money was used to produce campaign literature emphasizing the candidate's combat experience. "Yes, folks," declared one advertisement, "CONGRESS NEEDS A TAIL-GUNNER." Meanwhile, McCarthy campaigned in his usual dogged style. When the votes were tallied, he had won.

McCarthy sounded a new theme in the general election. With the backing of ultra-conservative *Chicago Tribune* publisher Colonel Robert McCormick, McCarthy emphasized the "disloyalty" of the Democratic Party and attacked his Democratic rival as "Communistically inclined." At one campaign rally, he pledged to remove "the vast number of Communists from the public payroll." Like other Republicans running for office in 1946, McCarthy tapped into some voters' repugnance for the New Deal, which conservatives like McCormick equated with communism. At the same time, many Americans were frustrated by the onset of the Cold War and the seeming inability of the Truman administration to deal with what appeared to be a growing Soviet threat in Europe. In 1946, Republicans made large gains in Congress. One of the party's new senators was Tail-Gunner Joe, who had gotten his first lesson in anticommunism's potency as a political issue.

For the next three years, though, Wisconsin's new senator was just another anti-New Deal Republican. His voting record reflected those views—as well as his ties to powerful corporate interests. He took up the cause of the real-estate lobby. He also championed the decontrol of sugar prices and received financial backing from Pepsi-Cola, a company in desperate need of sugar after the war. Before long, he had a new nickname on Capitol Hill: the Pepsi-Cola Kid.

At the same time, McCarthy began to strike colleagues as rude and disrespectful of the Senate's procedures and customs. Many observers noted his often disheveled appearance and his rumpled, ill-fitting clothes. He gambled, drank heavily, and developed a reputation as a womanizer. He also struck many acquaintances as boorish. "He is ignorant, crude, boastful," said one, "unaware of either intellectual or social refinements." It was an image McCarthy went out of his way to cultivate now that he mixed with people from a different world. In his elevated circumstances, the self-made former boxer and ex-Marine relished his lowbrow, tough-talking masculine image. In the minds of voters, he knew, it set him apart from opponents he routinely characterized as soft and unmanly.

If McCarthy's colleagues dismissed the brash senator as inconsequential, that assessment soon changed. Halfway through his term, he faced sagging support in Wisconsin. Searching for an issue to boost his popularity in late 1949, he turned to one he had used before: communism. Speaking in Madison, he said the city's liberal *Capital Times* newspaper was spreading "the Communist Party-line propaganda." Later, he told Republican gatherings that the State Department was "honeycombed and run by communists" and that "Christian nations" were losing the war with communism. At the time, such charges made perfect political sense. Democrats made a remarkable comeback in 1948 with the Truman administration's anti-Soviet containment policy and attacks on Republican economic and social policies. Republicans now had only one obvious response: stepped-up attacks on Democrats as soft on communism at home. Many of McCarthy's fellow Republicans may have been skeptical about his charges regarding subversion in the government, but they were not about to muzzle him. As one Republican senator told him, "Joe, you're a real SOB. But sometimes it's useful to have SOBs around to do the dirty work."

It mattered little that the threat of communist subversion was enormously exaggerated by 1950. Although many Americans were attracted to the Communist Party or its numerous front organizations during the Depression, the party's membership and appeal had diminished considerably by 1946. And even though some communists stole secrets, they had never been in a position to influence American foreign policy or undermine the nation's ability to defend itself. In fact, most of the suspected communists in the government had been fired or quit their jobs after the passage in 1939 of the Hatch Act, which barred communists from government jobs.

In the face of American setbacks in the Cold War and several well-publicized spy cases, however, the dangers of communist subversion seemed real enough. Americans had only recently watched half of Europe fall behind the Iron Curtain. Frustrated and fearful, they took seriously the notion that the United States was losing the Cold War because it had not done enough to root out communists at home. A frightening train of events bolstered that idea. In 1945, accusations regarding stolen classified documents led to the arrest of several journalists and a prominent State Department official. Responding to growing concern about subversives in the government and the effective Republican accusation in the 1946 elections that Democrats were soft on communism, the Truman administration created a loyalty program the next year. This massive internal security effort to screen government employees found little evidence of spying. Yet it seemed to confirm the fears of many Americans that communist subversion posed a serious threat to the nation. Spy charges leveled in 1948 against a former State Department official named Alger Hiss, who had attended the Yalta Conference[*] in 1945 as an aide to Franklin Roosevelt, only reinforced these fears. The fall of China to communists in 1949 and the Soviet detonation of an atomic bomb the same year raised them even further. Then, in early 1950, Hiss's conviction seemed to seal the case. As many Americans asked how the United States could have "lost" Eastern Europe and China to the communists, this and other spy cases suggested a ready answer: communist subversion at the highest levels of the government was responsible.

---

[*]*Yalta Conference:* A meeting in 1945 between Franklin Roosevelt, British prime minister Winston Churchill, and Soviet leader Josef Stalin to discuss the fate of postwar Europe.

Against this backdrop, Joe McCarthy stepped forward with shocking revelations and hit political pay dirt. Only three weeks after Hiss's conviction, he delivered a speech in Wheeling, West Virginia, that warned of the dangers of espionage facing the nation. Borrowing freely from a recent address of Richard Nixon, he went on to attack the Truman administration and its secretary of state, Dean Acheson. Then he added something new and stunning. He claimed to have "here in my hand" a list of 205 names of known communists working in the State Department. In coming days, McCarthy made a similar claim in speeches across the country. **[See Source 1.]** He also warned that the failure of the Truman administration to open the department's loyalty files immediately "will label the Democratic Party as being the bedfellow of international Communism." By the time he returned to Washington, D.C., McCarthy's shocking charges had made headlines. A U.S. senator claimed to have hard evidence that a communist underground had burrowed into the government and the Truman administration was covering it up. Tail-Gunner Joe did not realize it yet, but he was about to become the leading actor in a growing red scare.

"PARALYZED WITH FEAR"

Margaret Chase Smith had much in common with Joe McCarthy. Both were relative newcomers to the Senate, sat on the Republican side of the aisle, hailed from small towns, and rose from meager circumstances. In the club-like atmosphere of the Senate, both considered themselves outsiders. Yet Smith also differed from her Wisconsin colleague in fundamental ways. The product of a small-town New England upbringing, Smith was raised in Skowhegan, Maine. She never considered the woolen and textile mill center on the Kennebec River anything but home. Like Mainers in general, most of the town's five thousand residents could easily list the personal qualities they valued most: frugality, honesty, practicality, common sense, and independence. In a long public career, this daughter of Skowhegan seemed the very embodiment of these simple Yankee virtues. They firmly rooted Smith in her hometown throughout her life, even as they carried her far from her humble beginnings there.

Smith was born in 1897, the oldest of George and Carrie Chase's four children. George made only a sporadic living as a barber, and Carrie was forced to work as a waitress, store clerk, and stitcher at a shoe factory. She even took in laundry and ironing for neighbors. As the oldest child, Margaret helped out by waiting tables, performing temporary domestic work, and clerking at a store. In the process, she learned the value of thrift and hard work. She knew that her grandfather faithfully saved fifty cents of his weekly pay and died with $10,000 in the bank and holding the deed to the Chase family home. She also imbibed the lessons about work and money from her grandfather's set of Horatio Alger[*] stories, which became her favorite books. She learned, too, that she wanted a better life, a desire that kept her in school. Like many girls, she studied commercial subjects such as shorthand and typing, a practical choice given the increasing demand for female office workers in the early twentieth century.

Although college was the obvious way to rise in life, family finances prevented it. In a way easily recognized by Horatio Alger's readers, however, pluck and luck soon offered another path for Margaret to better her circumstances. For several years, she worked

---

[*]*Horatio Alger.* The author of a series of children's tales in the nineteenth century whose youthful male protagonists begin life in humble circumstances and rise up with "pluck and luck": hard work, thrift, and perseverance combined with good fortune.

part-time as a telephone operator. One night she took a call from a Clyde Smith. The two supposedly talked for some time, and that one call turned into many more. Recently divorced, Smith was a prominent businessman, Skowhegan town selectman, and Maine State senator. Carrie Chase reminded her daughter that Smith was old enough to be her own husband. Margaret also knew that he had a reputation for liking the girls, especially younger ones. Before long, though, Smith was seeing Margaret and her family a lot. He also offered her a temporary job in the assessor's office. Then, after a brief stint as a schoolteacher and two more years at the phone company, Margaret landed a job as general office assistant at a newspaper. All the while, Smith (himself a partner at the newspaper) hovered nearby.

At the same time, Margaret found another avenue for advancement. She helped organize a local branch of the Maine Federation of Business and Professional Women's Clubs (BPW). With few professional or business opportunities for women in the 1920s, the club offered important support for ambitious working women. It provided Margaret opportunities for public speaking and to hone her office and organizational skills. With abundant energy and a sharp eye for details, she blossomed in the BPW. In a few years, she was president of the local branch and, by 1925, president of the Maine State Federation. As she traveled, spoke, and organized on the BPWs behalf, Chase broadened her horizons and gained self-confidence. Since the BPW often lobbied the legislature, it also offered her a political education—and an opportunity to become involved in the Republican Party. By 1930, she was elected a Maine State Republican Committeewoman.

The same year, Chase's life changed dramatically when she married Clyde Smith and moved into his thirty-two-room mansion. She insisted that she be known as Margaret Chase Smith to retain her own identity. She would need it, for her marriage was far from perfect. Clyde expected a well-managed household. As Margaret put it later, he wanted "his soup on the table when he came in." And he never lost his eye for women. Her one consolation was the opportunity her marriage offered to further her political education. As Smith worked his way from the state senate to the governor's executive council and then to the House of Representatives, Margaret was with him at every step. She brought along her organizational and political skills. Campaigning with him, she kept track of names, typed letters, and mixed with local politicians. After he won his seat in Congress, Margaret served as his chief aide and office assistant. When poor health limited his trips back to Maine, she often went in his place to make speeches, visit party officials, and meet constituents.

Margaret also took note of her husband's strategy for political success. Maine was a rock-ribbed Republican state. The major political division was between the party's moderates and conservatives. Clyde Smith was a moderate Republican who supported workmen's compensation, limits on child labor, and a state old-age pension program. Proud of their own self-reliance, Mainers were not fond of New Deal social welfare programs. When he ran for Congress in 1936 in the midst of the Depression, though, Smith bet they would support someone who demonstrated compassion for the down and out. He was right. Margaret did not realize it, but this moderate stance would work for her, too. By late 1939, Clyde Smith's health had deteriorated, and doctors confirmed that he was suffering from late-stage syphilis. Before he died in 1940, he urged Margaret to run for his seat, and that spring, she won a special election to fill his unexpired term.

If Clyde Smith's political career taught Margaret important lessons, she learned another at the very outset of her own. German forces had rolled over most of Europe by 1940, and Maine's new representative talked up the importance of national defense. When she ran for reelection later that year, she prevailed in part because her strong support for preparedness helped blunt gender-oriented attacks from her male Republican primary challenger, who declared that the coming of war required a "militant" representative in Congress and that "a flick of the wrist and a smile won't do it." Smith never wavered from her strong support for the military and national defense. Within two years, she won a spot on the House Committee on Naval Affairs, where she gained a reputation for expertise in military affairs. When World War II gave way to the Cold War, she endorsed the Truman Doctrine* announced in 1947 and the Marshall Plan* proposed in 1948, the two pillars of the Truman administration's Cold War containment policy. From the beginning, Smith neutralized concerns about her gender among conservative Maine voters. No one would ever attack *her* as weak on national defense or the Cold War.

As only one of seven female representatives in 1940, Smith entered a masculine world on Capitol Hill. She decided to ignore discrimination and worked to be taken seriously by her colleagues. She never tried to be one of the boys and always wore conservative attire topped off by a fresh rose in her lapel—her fashion trademark. With her frank honesty and deeply ingrained sense of integrity, she also took advantage of the long-standing assumption that women were more moral than men. Besides her independence, and plainspoken honesty, Mainers loved her frugality. She sold her late-husband's mansion and moved into an unadorned wood frame house. Meanwhile, she faithfully minded constituents' concerns, making sure she answered every letter the same day it arrived. She also knew that her image of integrity permitted her to defy her party. A moderate on social issues, she frequently broke Republican ranks on labor, education, and social welfare legislation. As the *New York Times* later put it, "If she had been born in any other state except Maine she'd be a Democrat."

With wide support among Maine voters, Smith won three more terms in the House and then captured a Senate seat in 1948. At age fifty-one, she was the first female Republican senator and the only woman in the chamber. Denied a position on the powerful Armed Services Committee, she was assigned to the Expenditures Committee. There, she turned to the ranking Republican on the committee for a spot on its investigations subcommittee. Joe McCarthy agreed to give it to her. She found her Wisconsin colleague pleasant, but was disturbed to learn that he had talked to reporters about supposedly confidential deliberations among several members of the subcommittee. Nonetheless, when McCarthy began speaking out about subversion in the State Department in early 1950, she took his charges seriously enough to go to the senate floor to listen.

Like millions of other Americans, Smith believed the problem of domestic spying was real. In fact, she initially believed that McCarthy was "on to something disturbing and frightening." But her fear soon turned to dismay and disgust. When he handed her copies of the evidence he waved around in the Senate chambers, she noted that the information the documents contained was not relevant to the cases at hand. As she said later, "I began to wonder whether I was as stupid as I thought." In fact, McCarthy's charges about communists in the State Department were based on old files that had been thoroughly investigated. McCarthy did not know that many of the subjects had already been fired and that communists had been lumped together in these investigations with such "security risks" as homosexuals and alcoholics.

Listening to the tough-talking Tail-Gunner, Smith began to hear a loudmouth. As one of the few women in Congress, she had learned that decorum and respect for rules

---

Truman Doctrine: A policy that the United States would assist any nation facing the threat of communist takeover from the outside or within.
Marshall Plan: A massive economic relief program for Western European nations intended to lessen the appeal of communism.

paid off. Clearly, McCarthy had not. Above all, though, she was disturbed by his methods. Smith had suffered smears during her own Senate campaign in 1948, including the accusation that she was soft on communism. She understood how reckless charges could destroy people's reputations. She was especially concerned after McCarthy pointed to his first "security risk," a woman who was an acquaintance of Smith. McCarthy charged that this former member of a UN committee on women belonged to twenty-eight "Communist front organizations." Smith did not believe the charges, and, in fact, they quickly fell apart—as did his charges against several prominent Foreign Service officers—but not until after the accusations had destroyed their reputations and careers.

Smith had no interest stoking public fears for political gain. As a congresswoman, she voted against making HUAC a permanent House committee because she saw how its members could destroy people for their own political benefit. Congressional investigating committees like HUAC generated enormous publicity for their members, who were not bound by the courts' procedures guaranteeing due process and were free to denounce witnesses and ruin their lives. Such behavior was common during HUAC's investigations of alleged communist influence in Hollywood in the late 1940s. By the time anticommunist investigators were done there, more than two hundred actors, producers, screenwriters, and other studio employees had lost their jobs and were blacklisted, which prevented them from seeking employment elsewhere in the motion-picture industry. Meanwhile, many more government employees, and those in the radio, television, and other industries nationwide, experienced a similar fate. Smith knew that under such lax procedures, it was easy for anyone who held dissenting views to become a target. Expressing unconventional ideas could easily become synonymous with treason. **[See Source 2.]**

Smith was not alone in perceiving dangers in McCarthy's charges. Democrats in Congress saw political peril in them as well. Shortly after McCarthy spoke out, the Senate's Democratic majority created a special committee headed by conservative Maryland Democrat Millard Tydings to look into his accusations. Meanwhile, some editorial writers and others also questioned McCarthy's tactics and findings. But no one really seemed prepared to stop him. In a couple of months, he had gone from an obscure senator to a national figure whose face graced the covers of major news magazines. Public opinion polls showed widespread support for him. McCarthy could confidently proclaim that nothing would prevent him from exposing the "egg-sucking phony liberals" or the "Communists and queers" in the State Department. Just as confidently, he could dismiss the Tydings Committee as a Democratic Party's effort to whitewash the Truman administration's wrongdoings.

Now appalled by McCarthy's dirty work, Smith was dismayed that none of her Republican colleagues had spoken up on the Senate floor to denounce his tactics. Believing that he had the Senate "paralyzed with fear," she decided to do it. After drafting a statement, she quietly rounded up six other moderate Republican senators to sign it. Then she strode into the Senate chamber to read her "Declaration of Conscience." Without mentioning McCarthy by name, she declared that the Senate had been debased to a "forum of hate" and individual reputations had been sacrificed "for selfish political gain." **[See Source 3.]**

"HAVE YOU NO SENSE OF DECENCY?"

Fifteen minutes after Smith started, she sat down. She fully expected that McCarthy would stand to offer a rebuttal. Instead, he sat through her speech white-faced and then left the Senate floor without saying a word. Smith quickly heard from many other people, though. After her Declaration was picked up by the press, letters of praise flooded her office. One newspaper declared that her speech had the "ring of Lexington, of Valley Forge, of the Gettysburg address." *Newsweek* magazine even put her on its cover. "Senator Smith: A Woman Vice President?" read the accompanying caption. But not all the reaction was favorable. One Massachusetts paper, for instance, condemned Smith for failing to see that McCarthy was responsible for bringing attention to "this Communist issue." And the day after her speech, Smith heard from McCarthy on the Senate floor. The fight against those who "are attempting to betray this country shall not stop," he declared, "regardless of what any individual or group in this Senate ... may say or do." Later, he labeled Smith and her cosigners "Snow White and her Six Dwarfs."

McCarthy had good reason to go on the offensive. Smith's Declaration may have stirred positive editorial comment, but it had little impact on her colleagues. Smith hoped that her statement would elicit wide support in the Senate. McCarthy, though, was too valuable to Republicans, and five of Smith's six cosigners soon abandoned her. Meanwhile, few Democrats wanted to be charged with being soft on communism. And timing was again on McCarthy's side. Only weeks after Smith denounced McCarthy's behavior, communist North Korean forces launched a massive invasion of South Korea. Under the auspices of the United Nations, Truman quickly committed American troops to the conflict. But the communists were again on the march in Asia. Three weeks later, the Tydings Committee released its report, which concluded that McCarthy's allegations were a "fraud and a hoax." Only three days after that, however, another espionage bombshell exploded. Julius Rosenberg, who had earlier worked on the Manhattan Project to develop the atomic bomb, was arrested for spying. Gains made by Republicans in the elections later in 1950 strengthened McCarthy's hand even more. One of the Senate Democrats who lost that year was Millard Tydings, who went down to defeat after a vicious campaign supported by the Wisconsin senator. By then, the Korean War was descending into stalemate. After American commander Douglas MacArthur publicly criticized Truman for not seeking victory by attacking China, the president, who feared such a move would provoke an even bigger war, fired MacArthur for publicly criticizing the commander-in-chief. In early 1951, MacArthur came home a hero to millions of Americans who believed that limited war against communism represented appeasement.

With the momentum of events shifting his way, McCarthy began to play for bigger stakes. He called Truman a son of a bitch for firing MacArthur and declared that he should be impeached. Then he launched a renewed attack on the State Department, which he said was the root cause of the country's Cold War setbacks. His first target was Secretary of State Dean Acheson. Like the convicted Alger Hiss, Acheson was well-bred and highly educated. He spoke with an English accent and exuded an air of refinement. The secretary and "his lace handkerchief crowd" made inviting targets for McCarthy, who sensed that such attacks played well with folks back home. McCarthy now charged that Acheson had "betrayed us." Then he moved on, declaring that former secretary of state George Marshall was involved in an "immense" conspiracy. Marshall was a hero of World War II and architect of the Marshall Plan to rebuild Western Europe to prevent communist expansion after the war, but McCarthy declared that he bore responsibility for the loss of Eastern Europe and for the "sellout" of China under Truman. Marshall, he declared, was a "willing instrument of the Hisses and the Achesons, ... the misguided men who let American boys die to make America safe for Communism."

When he was criticized for such charges, the former boxer punched back. He compared critical newspapers to the *Daily Worker*, the American Communist Party publication. He defended his "brass-knuckle" methods by reminding audiences that the fight against the Reds required such tactics. And he could always charge that Democrats who criticized him were only attempting to whitewash the failure of the Truman administration to root out communists from the government.

McCarthy—and his allies—could also enlist assumptions about gender, which associated masculinity with toughness and women with the home, to undermine critics. McCarthy frequently cited his Marine training, declaring, "We weren't taught to wear lace panties and fight with lace hankies." In 1952, Smith herself was the target of a gender-based McCarthyite attack with the publication of a book titled *U.S.A. Confidential*, written by two best-selling authors. Their sensationalist account of the "shockingly corrupt under-life of America" declared that lesbianism was the result of "Marxist teaching" and the State Department was "more than thirty percent faggot." In one chapter titled "Reds in Clover," the authors called Smith one of the nation's "left-wing apologists," a consort of pro-communists, and "a lesson why women should not be in politics." **[See Source 4.]**

Smith promptly filed a libel suit and later trial testimony established that one of the authors talked with McCarthy and that Smith was included in the book because of her Declaration. Yet McCarthy and his allies knew what they were doing. Given the hold of the postwar era's domestic ideology, which defined women's proper place in the home, it was easy to imply that those who defied traditional gender roles were, if not communists themselves, subversive of the status quo. It mattered little that Smith's anticommunist rhetoric was often as strident as McCarthy's, as when she advocated dropping the atomic bomb on North Korea to "stop the Red murderers." Such heated rhetoric was no match for McCarthy's clever use of masculinity. It was a useful political weapon, he knew, in his battle against alleged communists—or his lone female colleague in the Senate.

As Margaret Chase Smith also learned, McCarthy also knew how to defend himself by wielding senatorial power. After reading her declaration, Smith got a lesson about his growing clout when Republican Senate leaders stripped two of her committee assignments. At the same time, McCarthy bumped Smith from his investigations subcommittee and replaced her with Richard Nixon, who had earlier gained nationwide fame as a member of HUAC and now sat in the Senate. McCarthy bored in on Smith again in 1951 when she served as a member of a committee looking into his role in the campaign against Millard Tydings in Maryland. When the committee's final report characterized McCarthy's behavior as dishonest, he retaliated by calling Smith a "puny" politician and accusing her of launching "one of the most vigorous attacks … upon my exposure of Communists."

Nonetheless, Smith continued to stand up to McCarthy. She declared on the Senate floor that opposition to communism was not his "exclusive possession" and that differing with him on tactics did not make one a communist. "I shall not permit intimidation," she announced, "to keep me from expressing my honest convictions." McCarthy responded to these attacks by supporting another Republican candidate when Smith ran for reelection in 1954. Backed by Texas oil millionaires close to McCarthy, Smith's primary challenger called Smith too "weak-willed" to fight the "ominous clouds of atheistic, international Communism." In fact, he sounded so much like the Wisconsin senator on the stump that reporters called him "Junior McCarthy." The contest gained nationwide attention as the first election in 1954 to show, as one magazine put it, "how the voters feel about 'McCarthyism.'" When their votes were counted, Mainers demonstrated that they resented McCarthy's interference and still valued Smith's independence. She won by a five-to-one margin.

It was a sign of things to come. After winning his own landslide reelection in 1952, McCarthy seemed invincible. Yet for all his charges, he had not uncovered a single subversive. And with Republican Dwight Eisenhower as president and Republicans in control of Congress by 1953, McCarthy's political usefulness had suddenly diminished. Most Republicans had little interest in continued charges about communist subversion with their party now running the government. McCarthy, however, was not about to give up on the issue that had catapulted him to national prominence.

Instead, he launched his last crusade to root out the communists. As the new chairman of the Senate Committee on Government Operations, McCarthy turned first to the Government Printing Office in 1953. The subversion there, he suggested, was "worse than the Hiss case." He investigated the Voice of America, an arm of the State Department that beamed radio broadcasts on four continents to counter communist propaganda. Then he went on to the department's Overseas Library Program, charging that books written by "Communist authors" sat on its shelves in overseas nations. By the time these investigations were over, more people had lost their jobs, at least one had committed suicide, and books were pulled from libraries and many of them burned. **[See Source 5.]**

Then McCarthy made two big mistakes. First, he insinuated in early 1954 that the popular veteran CBS newsman Edward R. Murrow had supported an exchange program in the 1930s allegedly used by the Soviet Union to train people to teach in American schools. Murrow, whose *See It Now* program was a pioneer in the use of television to cover the news, had already countered McCarthy's allegations on the air. Now he responded by devoting the entire program to the senator. Most of it showed McCarthy delivering speeches and interrogating witnesses as Murrow offered pointed rebuttals. At the end, however, Murrow delivered a closing commentary, a blistering attack on McCarthy and his methods. "This is no time for men who oppose Senator McCarthy's methods," he declared, "to keep silent." **[See Source 6.]** McCarthy's second—and bigger—mistake was his decision to take on the U.S. Army. After investigating allegations of spying at an army base in New Jersey, he charged that the army was unable to counter "the deliberate Communist infiltration of our Armed Forces." In doing so, he incurred the wrath of military brass and Eisenhower, a former army general. And in early 1954, McCarthy handed them a weapon to use against him. Army officials knew that a member of his legal staff named Roy Cohn had intervened repeatedly on behalf of a friend and former McCarthy staff consultant to get him preferential treatment in the army. When McCarthy refused to fire Cohn, the army released a report accusing McCarthy of also intervening numerous times on behalf of Cohn's friend. Now McCarthy would become the victim of his own weapon: a Senate investigation conducted by his own Government Operations Committee.

The televised Army–McCarthy Hearings started in April 1954. Before they ended, millions of Americans had tuned in. On their TV screens, they saw McCarthy bully witnesses at first hand. Toward the end of the hearings, McCarthy rashly accused a young assistant of Joseph Welch, the army's chief counsel at the hearings, of communist leanings. It was clear he had gone too far, and Welch cut into him: "Little did I dream you could be so reckless and so cruel," Welch declared. "Have you no sense of decency?" After the hearings, much of McCarthy's public support evaporated. Before the end of the year, the Senate voted on a resolution to censure McCarthy for "unbecoming" conduct, a reprimand one step short of removal. The vote was sixty-seven to twenty-two. One of the Republicans who voted for censure, of course, was Margaret Chase Smith.

By late 1954, McCarthy's four years in the national spotlight were over. Although he continued his attacks in speeches, he was now largely ignored by the press and shunned in the Senate. Just the year before, McCarthy had married a member of his Senate staff, abandoning his erratic bachelor's life. But he still drank heavily despite deteriorating health, and in 1957 died of cirrhosis of the liver. By then, McCarthyism had mostly died out too. In its wake lay thousands of victims: those in government, business, academia, and Hollywood who lost jobs or reputations. McCarthy had never been alone in exploiting communism, and he did not start the episode that came to bear his name, but he could claim a fair number of those victims.

One of them was Smith, although the price she paid was not very steep compared to many others. In fact, she would go on to enjoy a career as long and steady as McCarthy's was short and volatile. Sitting in the Senate until 1972, Smith won a seat on the powerful Armed Services Committee and became one of the Senate's most ardent Cold Warriors. At the same time, she continued to be lauded for her honesty and integrity. Smith never remarried, and until she died in 1995, she never lost her reputation for independence.

All the while, though, she never examined basic Cold War assumptions. Protesting only McCarthy's methods, not his goals, she never doubted the threat of internal subversion. The American Communist Party, she declared in 1953, was "a subversive organization working to place us under domination of Communist Russia." Ignoring the First Amendment, she even introduced a bill to prevent the distribution of "Communistic propaganda." Likewise, she never doubted the logic of the American Cold War containment policy. As that war continued long after McCarthyism ended, Smith never questioned the need for American military intervention abroad in the name of containing communism. She was unwavering, for instance, in her support for the American commitment to Vietnam. As she declared in 1968, "We are in Vietnam to stop the Communists from conquering the world." Many Mainers would come to disagree with that assessment, and in 1972, she lost her seat in the Senate to an antiwar Democrat, partly for that reason. Unlike Joe McCarthy, Smith never exploited the fear of communism. But she never asked if it was realistic either. And for that, her political career finally came to an end.

•PRIMARY SOURCES•

Source 1: *McCarthy Assaults the State Department* (1950)

No copy exists of the speech that Joseph McCarthy delivered in Wheeling, West Virginia, in which he asserted that he had 205 names of subversives working in the State Department. In another speech only days later, McCarthy claimed to have fewer names. He put that version of his speech into the Congressional Record. *How does McCarthy characterize his targets in this speech? What emotions do you think he stirred in those who listened to it? What does it reveal about the basis of his appeal?*

At war's end we were physically the strongest nation on earth and, at least potentially, the most powerful intellectually and morally. Ours could have been the honor of being a beacon in the desert of destruction, a shining living proof that civilization was not yet

SOURCE: Senator Joseph McCarthy, speech, Congressional Record, Senate, 81st Cong., 2nd sess., February 20, 1950, pp. 1954, 1957.

ready to destroy itself. Unfortunately we have failed miserably and tragically to arise to the opportunity.

The reason why we find ourselves in a position of impotency is not because our only powerful potential enemy has sent men to invade our shores, but rather because of traitorous actions of those who have been treated so well by this Nation. It has not been the less fortunate or members of minority groups who have been selling this Nation out, but rather those who have had all the benefits that the wealthiest nation on earth has had to offer—the finest homes, the finest college education, and the finest jobs in Government we can give.

This is glaringly true in the State Department. There the bright young men who are born with silver spoons in their mouths are the ones who have been worst....

I have in my hand 57 cases of individuals who would appear to be either card carrying members or certainly loyal to the Communist Party, but who nevertheless are still helping to shape our foreign policy.

One thing to remember in discussing the Communists in our Government is that we are not dealing with spies who get 30 pieces of silver to steal the blueprints of a new weapon. We are dealing with a far more sinister type of activity because it permits the enemy to guide and shape our policy....

This brings us down to the case of one Alger Hiss who is important not as an individual any more, but rather because he is so representative of a group in the State Department. It is unnecessary to go over the sordid events showing how he sold out the Nation which had given him so much. Those are rather fresh in all of our minds....

If time permitted, it might be well to go into detail about the fact that Hiss was Roosevelt's chief adviser at Yalta when Roosevelt was admittedly in ill health and tired physically and mentally....

Of the results of this conference, Arthur Bliss Lane of the State Department had this to say: "As I glanced over the document, I could not believe my eyes. To me, almost every line spoke of a surrender to Stalin."

As you hear this story of high treason, I know that you are saying to yourself, "Well, why doesn't the Congress do something about it?" Actually, ladies and gentlemen, one of the important reasons for the graft, the corruption, the dishonesty, the disloyalty, the treason in high Government positions—one of the most important reasons why this continues is a lack of moral uprising on the part of the 140,000,000 American people. In the light of history, however, this is not hard to explain....

As you know, very recently the Secretary of State proclaimed his loyalty to a man guilty of what has always been considered as the most abominable of all crimes—of being a traitor to the people who gave him a position of great trust. The Secretary of State in attempting to justify his continued devotion to the man who sold out the Christian world to the atheistic world, referred to Christ's Sermon on the Mount as a justification and reason therefor, and the reaction of the American people to this would have made the heart of Abraham Lincoln happy.

When this pompous diplomat in striped pants, with a phony British accent, proclaimed to the American people that Christ on the Mount endorsed communism, high treason, and betrayal of a sacred trust, the blasphemy was so great that it awakened the dormant indignation of the American people.

He has lighted the spark which is resulting in a moral uprising and will end only when the whole sorry mess of twisted, warped thinkers are swept from the national scene so that we may have a new birth of national honesty and decency in Government.

Source 2: HUAC Investigates Subversion in Hollywood (1947)

In 1946, the HUAC turned its attention to communist influence in Hollywood movie studios. Many of the witnesses, including actor Ronald Reagan, were friendly. Ten of them, however, were not. All of the so-called Hollywood Ten, including screenwriter Ring Lardner, were on the political left and some of them were or had been communists. All of them would be sent to jail for contempt of Congress. All were also blacklisted and lost their jobs. What does this testimony reveal about HUAC's methods? What does it reveal about the attitude of this unfriendly witness?

STRIPLING:*   Mr. Lardner, the charge has been made before this committee that the Screen Writers Guild which, according to the record, you are a member of, whether you admit it or not, has a number of individuals in it who are members of the Communist Party. This committee is seeking to determine the extent of Communist infiltration in the Screen Writers Guild and in other guilds within the motion-picture industry.

LARDNER: Yes.

STRIPLING: And certainly the question of whether or not you are a member of the Communist Party is very pertinent. Now, are you a member or have you ever been a member of the Communist Party?

LARDNER: It seems to me you are trying to discredit the Screen Writers Guild through me and the motion-picture industry through the Screen Writers Guild and our whole practice of freedom of expression.

STRIPLING: If you and others are members of the Communist Party you are the ones who are discrediting the Screen Writers Guild.

LARDNER: I am trying to answer the question by stating first what I feel about the purpose of the question which, as I say, is to discredit the whole motion-picture industry.

CHAIRMAN: You won't say anything first. You are refusing to answer this question.

LARDNER: I am saying my understanding is as an American resident—

CHAIRMAN: Never mind your understanding. There is a question: Are you or have you ever been a member of the Communist Party?

LARDNER: I could answer exactly the way you want, Mr. Chairman—

CHAIRMAN: No—

LARDNER: (continuing). But I think that is a—

CHAIRMAN: It is not a question of our wanting you to answer that. It is a very simple question. Anybody would be proud to answer it—any real American would be proud to answer the question, "Are you or have you ever been a member of the Communist Party"—any real American.

SOURCE: Ring Lardner Jr., testimony, "House Committee on Un-American Activities, Hearings regarding Communist Infiltration of the Hollywood Motion Picture Industry," 80th Cong., 1st sess., October 30, 1947.

---

*Robert Stripling, the committee's chief counsel.

LARDNER: It depends on the circumstances. I could answer it, but if I did I would hate myself in the morning.

CHAIRMAN: Leave the witness chair.

LARDNER: It was a question that would—

CHAIRMAN: Leave the witness chair.

LARDNER: Because it is a question—

CHAIRMAN: (pounding gavel). Leave the witness chair.

LARDNER: I think I am leaving by force.

CHAIRMAN: Sergeant, take the witness away.
                (Applause.)

Source 3:   Margaret Chase Smith, *"Declaration of Conscience"* (1950)

In June 1950, Margaret Chase Smith stood on the Senate floor and read her condemnation of McCarthy. What is the basis of her attack on him? What is her own view about subversives in the government? Why do you think McCarthy left the Senate chamber rather than respond to her?

I speak as briefly as possible because too much harm has already been done with irresponsible words of bitterness and selfish political opportunism. I speak as simply as possible because the issue is too great to be obscured by eloquence. I speak simply and briefly in the hope that my words will be taken to heart.

I speak as a Republican. I speak as a woman. I speak as a United States Senator. I speak as an American.

The United States Senate has long enjoyed worldwide respect as the greatest deliberative body in the world. But recently that deliberative character has too often been debased to the level of a forum of hate and character assassination sheltered by the shield of congressional immunity.

It is ironical that we Senators can in debate in the Senate directly or indirectly by any form of words, impute to any American who is not a Senator any conduct or motive unworthy or unbecoming an American—and without that non-Senator American having any legal redress against us—yet if we say the same thing in the Senate about our colleagues we can be stopped on the grounds of being out of order.

It is strange that we can verbally attack anyone else without restraint and with full protection and yet we hold ourselves above the same type of criticism here on the Senate Floor. Surely the United States Senate is big enough to take self-criticism and self-appraisal. Surely we should be able to take the same kind of character attacks that we "dish out" to outsiders.

SOURCE: William C. Lewis Jr., ed., DECLARATION OF CONSCIENCE: MARGARET CHASE SMITH (Garden City, New York: Doubleday & Company, Inc., 1972).

I think that it is high time for the United States Senate and its members to do some soul-searching—for us to weigh our consciences—on the manner in which we are performing our duty to the people of America—on the manner in which we are using or abusing our individual powers and privileges.

I think that it is high time that we remembered that we have sworn to uphold and defend the Constitution. I think that it is high time that we remembered that the Constitution, as amended, speaks not only of the freedom of speech but also of trial by jury instead of trial by accusation.

Whether it be a criminal prosecution in court or a character prosecution in the Senate, there is little practical distinction when the life of a person has been ruined....

The Democratic Administration has greatly lost the confidence of the American people by its complacency to the threat of communism here at home and the leak of vital secrets to Russia through key officials of the Democratic Administration. There are enough proved cases to make this point without diluting our criticism with unproved charges.

Surely these are sufficient reasons to make it clear to the American people that it is time for a change and that a Republican victory is necessary to the security of this country....

Source 4:   *Margaret Chase Smith Feels McCarthy's Sting* (1952)

In their exposé U.S.A. Confidential, *two pro-McCarthy journalists attacked numerous people, including leading politicians. One of them was Margaret Chase Smith, who would eventually win a retraction and a cash settlement from the publisher. What does this excerpt reveal about the way attitudes toward gender and such reforms as the New Deal intersected with anticommunism in the early 1950s?*

There are cliques and factions and wings and blocs among the Reds, as there are among Democrats, Republicans, unions and Wall Street trusts. Some are orthodox Stalinists. Others are Trotskyites.* Some are nationalists. Like Tito,* they practice communism but do not want it directed from an outside source. These "native" Communists are the most insidious. They preach against Russia but work for a revolution they will run themselves. All these forms are closer to each other than they are to us, as honest Republicans and Democrats are for the American way despite policy differences.

Holding up the rear, like a huge infantry, are the millions of "intellectual" Socialists and welfare-stators, the Americans for Democratic Action, the Fair Dealers, the liberals and progressives, etc. Among them are shrewd and ambitious politicians like Hubert Humphrey, Warren Magnuson, Wayne Morse and F. D. Roosevelt, Jr., as well as stunted visionaries like Margaret Chase Smith....

SOURCE: U.S.A. CONFIDENTIAL (New York: Crown Publishers, Inc., © 1952).

---

*Followers of Russian communist leader Leon Trotsky, who opposed Josef Stalin after the death of Soviet leader Vladimir Lenin and was later exiled and assassinated.
*Marshall Josip Broz Tito was the communist leader of Yugoslavia after World War II.

The last time we were in Washington she was making one of her typical boneheaded speeches. A Senate doorman couldn't stand it any longer. When she reached the high point of her peroration, he sniffed and remarked about the lone female, "There's too many women in the Senate!" She is a lesson in why women should not be in politics. When men argue matters of high policy they usually forget their grudges at the door. She takes every opposing speech as a personal affront and lies awake nights scheming how to "get even." She is sincere —but a dame—and she reacts to all situations as a woman scorned, not as a representative of the people. She is under the influence of the coterie of left-wing writers and reporters who dominate Washington and they praise her so assiduously she believes it.

Maggie is pals with Esther Brunauer* and made a trip to Europe with her, fare paid by the State Department. Mrs. Brunauer is now under suspension from the department as a security risk. Her husband was suspended by the Navy on the same grounds. Maggie traveled with her after the original charges were presented to the Tydings whitewash committee.

Source 5:   *McCarthy Investigates Overseas Libraries* (1953)

As the chairman of a Senate Government Operations Subcommittee on Investigations, Joseph McCarthy accused the State Department's Information Program of stocking its overseas libraries with books written by communist authors. After State Department official Theodore Kaghan criticized McCarthy's probe, Kaghan was called before McCarthy's committee and later fired. How does McCarthy attack Kaghan in this excerpt from the hearings? How would you compare this exchange with the one in Source 2? How do you account for the differences?

THE CHAIRMAN: So that we have this picture completely clear, I assume it is agreed that the public affairs officer, a man in your position, should have available the works of Communists, so that you can tell what they are doing, what they are thinking, and can have enough knowledge so that you can fight communism. And we are speaking about these books on the shelves. We are speaking about books not on the shelves of some private library for the public affairs officers, but books for the general public of Germany. Is that right?

MR. KAGHAN: That is right.

THE CHAIRMAN: So these Communists books are not books merely for your benefit or something for men allegedly fighting communism. They were available for the German people in our libraries with our approval.

MR. KAGHAN: Yes, they were.

SOURCE: U.S. Senate, 83rd Congress, 1st sess., Permanent Subcommittee on, Investigations of the Committee on Government Operations, Hearings, pp. 190, 199–200.

*Esther Brunauer was a State Department official who lost her job for her alleged communist affiliations. McCarthy charged that she and Smith had traveled together to a United Nations conference in Italy, shared a hotel room, and discussed Brunauer's communist sympathies. In fact, Smith met Brunauer only briefly at the conference and barely knew her.

THE CHAIRMAN: And you say you have taken the works of how many authors off the shelves?

MR. KAGHAN: When I left there were 4 or 5 authors off. They may be more now. Possibly half a dozen before I left. When I directed someone to take them off, that order would go to the man in charge of the American Houses, who was in charge of the libraries, and he would remove the books....

THE CHAIRMAN: Let me ask you: Did you write a play Beyond Exile?

MR. KAGHAN: The name is familiar; yes.

THE CHAIRMAN: Does this play consist largely of a series of conversations between a father and son?

MR. KAGHAN: Sir, I don't remember what that play was about.

THE CHAIRMAN: Well, I will refresh your recollection, then, if I may. Here is one of the speeches made by the son to the father. And this consists largely of a running argument, the father trying to convince the son he should not be a Communist, the son trying to convince the father that he should be a Communist. Let us take the finale of this play. The son says:

Well, that's a fine how-do-you-do. It isn't enough that my father has to be a capitalist, but he's got to come out openly and betray his employees, just like all the other dirty capitalists. Do I have to come here and tell my own father that he is a slavedriver, an exploiter of labor, an enemy to civilization?

And the father, finally, in the close, has this to say. He says:

Peter, Peter, for God's sake listen to me, Peter. You were right, do you hear, you were right! I have been all wrong, Peter.

Would you say that that would make good anti-Communist propaganda?

MR. KAGHAN: No, sir. It sounds pretty corny, now.

THE CHAIRMAN: Is it merely corny? Is not that the Communist Party line right down to the last period?

MR. KAGHAN: One of those statements would be the Communist Party line, yes. One of the characters that said that, apparently—

THE CHAIRMAN: What part of this would not be the Communist line? The son arguing with the father that he should be a Communist, pointing out that the father is a dirty capitalist, an exploiter of labor, and the father ending by saying: "You were right, do you hear, you were right! I have been all wrong, Peter."

Is that not Communist propaganda?

MR. KAGHAN: That would be Communist propaganda if that is what the whole play ends up with and is about. I don't recall what the play is about.

THE CHAIRMAN: Would you like to review that play and give me your view of it?

MR. KAGHAN: If you wish; yes, sir.

THE CHAIRMAN: Yes; I would like to have you do it.

I think this is what we will let you do. We will be going over your plays. Just so there will be no claim that we have taken the material out of context, I believe you should review these plays of yours and come back here tomorrow morning, and tell us which ones you consider are Communist-line plays and which ones are not; whether you think we have been unfair to you in reading the excerpts that we have.

Now let me ask you this question. If you today felt the same as you felt in 1939, would you think that you were a proper man to head this information program?

MR. KAGHAN: No, sir....

Source 6:   *Edward R. Murrow Attacks McCarthy* (1954)

During a See It Now *program devoted to McCarthy, Edward R. Murrow offered viewers a closing commentary aimed at the Wisconsin senator. How do you compare Murrow's message with that of Margaret Chase Smith's "Declaration of Conscience" in 1950?*

No one familiar with the history of this country can deny that congressional committees are useful. It is necessary to investigate before legislating. But the line between investigation and persecuting is a very fine one, and the junior senator from Wisconsin has stepped over it repeatedly. His primary achievement has been in confusing the public mind between the internal and the external threat of Communism. We must not confuse dissent with disloyalty. We must remember always that accusation is not proof and that conviction depends upon evidence and due process of law. We will not walk in fear, one of another. We will not be driven by fear into an age of unreason if we dig deep in our history and our doctrine and remember that we are not descended from fearful men, not from men who feared to write, to speak, to associate, and to defend causes which were for the moment unpopular.

This is no time for men who oppose Senator McCarthy's methods to keep silent, *or* for those who approve. We can deny our heritage and our history, but we cannot escape responsibility for the result. As a nation we have come into our full inheritance at a tender age. We proclaim ourselves, as indeed we are, defenders of freedom— what's left of it—but we cannot defend freedom abroad by deserting it at home. The actions of the junior senator from Wisconsin have caused alarm and dismay amongst our allies abroad and given considerable aid and comfort to our enemies. And whose fault is that? Not really his; he didn't create this situation of fear, he merely exploited it and rather successfully. Cassius was right. "The fault, dear Brutus, is not in our stars, but in ourselves." Good night, and good luck.

QUESTIONS TO CONSIDER

1. What do the essay and primary sources in this chapter reveal about the factors that led to the rise of a red scare in the late 1940s and early 1950s? What do they reveal about its impact?

2. What was Joseph McCarthy's role in this red scare? Why did he have the impact that he did? Is "McCarthyism" an accurate label for this episode?

3. What does this chapter reveal about McCarthy's motives and methods? What does it reveal about the sources of his appeal?

4. How would you explain why Margaret Chase Smith was the lone Republican to speak out on the Senate floor against McCarthy in 1950? What did her background and political situation have to do with it? What do Smith and McCarthy reveal about the role of gender in the second red scare?

5. What was Margaret Chase Smith's criticism of McCarthy? Was it valid? Did it go far enough? Why was it not effective in 1950? What changed by 1954 to make his censure possible?

FOR FURTHER READING

Richard M. Fried, *Nightmare in Red: The McCarthy Era in Perspective* (New York: Oxford University Press, 1990), provides a useful overview of the anticommunist crusade after World War II.

Elaine Tyler May, *Homeward Bound: American Families in the Cold War Era* (New York: Basic Books, 1988), explores the Cold War's impact on family life and the role of women.

David M. Oshinsky, *A Conspiracy So Immense: The World of Joe McCarthy* (New York: The Free Press, 1983), offers a detailed and engaging account of McCarthy's rise, methods, and downfall.

Ellen Schrecker, *Many Are the Crimes: McCarthyism in America* (Princeton: Princeton University Press, 1998), presents a critical assessment of McCarthyism and its impact.

Janann Sherman, *No Place for a Woman: A Life of Senator Margaret Chase Smith* (New Brunswick, New Jersey: Rutgers University Press, 2000), provides one of several recent biographies of the Maine senator.

Stephen J. Whitfield, *The Culture of the Cold War* (Baltimore: Johns Hopkins University Press, 1996), provides a useful and often entertaining overview of anticommunism's impact on popular culture after World War II.

From Black Protest to Black Power: Roy Wilkins and Fannie Lou Hamer

The very thought of Fannie Lou Hamer made Roy Wilkins furious. As executive secretary of the National Association for the Advancement of Colored People (NAACP), Wilkins led the largest civil rights organization in the United States. He possessed power and influence and even had the ear of President Lyndon Johnson. In August 1964, Wilkins had come to the Democratic National Convention in Atlantic City to celebrate Johnson's nomination as the Democrats' candidate for president. The NAACP leader believed that nothing should tarnish the event—or diminish the president's chances in the fall election. He certainly was not going to let an uneducated daughter of a Mississippi sharecropper bring down the president of the United States.

That, Wilkins feared, was exactly what Hamer and others in the Mississippi Freedom Democratic Party (MFDP) might end up doing. Along with other southern civil rights activists, Hamer had organized the MFDP only months earlier. They hoped to seat its delegates at the Atlantic City convention as a protest against the exclusion of blacks from primary elections by Mississippi's regular Democratic Party. Like the other MFDP delegates in Atlantic City, Hamer had grown tired of the conditions that African Americans faced in Mississippi. She had been denied the right to vote because of the color of her skin and been beaten for her involvement in civil rights organizing. Now she believed that the Democratic convention should acknowledge that Mississippi's Democratic Party delegates represented only the state's white voters. Wilkins, however, was convinced that such a move would drive southern delegates right out of the convention and into the arms of the Republicans. That would be a stunning setback for the civil rights movement and the position of blacks in American society. Wilkins was no stranger

LBJ Library photo by Yoichi Okamoto

AP Images

Roy Wilkins   Fannie Lou Hamer

to racial discrimination, and while working for the NAACP, he had fought numerous civil rights battles. He was well aware of the conditions in

Mississippi. During a demonstration in Jackson in 1963, Wilkins had been arrested along with NAACP field secretary Medgar Evers. Less than two weeks later, Evers had been gunned down outside his home. Still, Wilkins was distrustful of the direct-action techniques of some of the younger civil rights activists. He put his faith in legal and political action as the best way to achieve gains for African Americans. That approach, he realized, often involved compromise.

Hamer and the other MFDP delegates saw things differently. They had challenged the South's racial caste system and suffered greatly for it. As one MFDP delegate put it, "We have been treated like beasts in Mississippi. They shot us down like animals." Thus, when Lyndon Johnson offered the MFDP delegation only two seats at the convention as a compromise, Hamer was incensed. "We didn't come all this way for no two seats," she announced. It was not the response Wilkins wanted to hear. "You don't know anything, you're ignorant, you don't know anything about politics," he said as he confronted Hamer on the convention floor. "You people have put your point across, now why don't you pack up and go home?" Hamer and the other MFDP delegates, though, were not going anywhere.

"NEVER ... TURN YOUR BACK ON A CRUMB"

Roy Wilkins was not about to apologize to the MFDP delegates for the power he wielded by 1964. Nor would he listen for long to lectures about Mississippi's virulent racism. In fact, he had only to look to his own father to see its crippling effects. Born in St. Louis, Missouri, in 1901, Wilkins was the son of a college-educated porter who had fled Mississippi after hitting a white man who had called him a "nigger." Fearful that he would be lynched, William Wilkins and his wife, Mayfield, had taken the train north to St. Louis that very night. William soon found work at a brick kiln, and the couple moved into a flat in a black neighborhood, where Roy was born a year later. St. Louis was not Mississippi, but Jim Crow* was enforced in the city's schools, restaurants, and theaters. When he was old enough, Roy began his education at a segregated school. By then, William and Mayfield had had two more children, a boy and a girl, but they had found little happiness. William was soured by his dirty, low-paying job, and Mayfield soon died of tuberculosis. Realizing that William could not raise his three children alone, Roy's aunt and uncle took six-year-old Roy and his younger brother and sister to live with them in St. Paul, Minnesota.

In the home of Sam and Elizabeth Williams, Roy found a very different environment from the one he had known in St. Louis. Sam was the chief steward on the Great Northern Pacific Railroad president's private car. The Williamses owned a home in an integrated neighborhood, and they shared the middle-class outlook of their Scandinavian and German immigrant neighbors. They also instilled in the Wilkins children the value of thrift and hard work. From Sam, Roy learned "that the world was not the universally hostile place my own father had taken it to be." At the same time, Sam Williams had no illusions about the position of blacks in American society. Like many other members of the small but growing black middle class, he joined the NAACP, which W. E. B. Du Bois and a number of white progressives founded in 1909 to fight racial discrimination. Du Bois's magazine, the *Crisis*, came into the Williams home every month. In it, Du Bois called on an educated black elite—the "talented tenth"—to take the lead in improving the status of African Americans. Not surprisingly, Sam Williams drilled into the Wilkins children the importance of education. "You should go to school," he told Roy, "and be the best."

Wilkins's grammar school and high school in St. Paul were integrated, and he got along easily with white classmates. Originally intent on becoming an engineer, he fell in love with books in high school. He was editor of the school's literary magazine, president of the literary society, and editor of the yearbook. After graduating in 1919, he headed to the nearby University of Minnesota still relatively innocent about race. His innocence was shattered the next year when sixteen black roustabouts attached to a traveling circus were accused of raping a young white woman in Duluth. The day after they were arrested, a mob of five thousand whites descended on the jail, smashed through a thick brick wall with a battering ram, seized three of the suspects, and lynched them on nearby light poles as they pleaded for their lives. No evidence linked any of the roustabouts to the rape. The cases against eleven of them were dismissed, and one was found innocent. The remaining man, found guilty and sentenced to thirty years in prison, was freed after several years of legal work by the NAACP. For the first time in his life, Wilkins found himself thinking of black people "as a very vulnerable *us*—and white people as an unpredictable *them*." A little later, he joined Du Bois's organization.

At about the same time, Wilkins decided on a career in journalism. He worked on the college paper as its first black reporter and later became editor of a local black weekly, where he denounced black separatist Marcus Garvey's Universal Negro

---

Jim Crow: The South's rigid system of legal racial segregation of public facilities. Extending from railroad cars to drinking fountains, Jim Crow had been established in the late nineteenth century and upheld by the Supreme Court in *Plessy* v. *Ferguson* in 1896.

Improvement Association and even Du Bois's growing interest in pan-Africanism.*
Du Bois, he observed, should "use his time and talents" fighting the "evils" of lynching,
disfranchisement, and segregation rather than waste them on promoting the unity of
American blacks and Africans. Wilkins had already developed a deep hostility not only
toward segregation but also toward self-segregation. Thinking back to his old St. Paul
neighborhood, he later said, "For me, integration is not an abstraction."

Segregation, on the other hand, was an abstraction for Wilkins, although that
quickly changed after his graduation in 1923. Taking a job as managing editor of the
Kansas City Call, another black weekly, Wilkins got his first full introduction to Jim
Crow. Kansas City was, as he later put it, "a Jim Crow town right down to its
bootstraps." Neighborhoods, schools, hospitals, theaters, and even the stands in the Kansas City Blues baseball stadium were racially divided. For years, the city's major daily
newspaper refused to run any pictures of African Americans. To attend a vaudeville
show, Wilkins had to use an alley entrance and climb the stairs leading to the Jim
Crow roost—the last row of seats in the highest gallery of the theater. He found such
indignities "infuriating." For the next eight years in the pages of the *Call*, he denounced
police brutality, neighborhood "improvement" associations that prevented blacks from
moving into white areas, a school district that provided dilapidated schools for African-
American students, and Jim Crow stores and restaurants.

When not agitating against Kansas City's color line, Wilkins wooed a social worker
named Aminda "Minnie" Badeau. She had come to Kansas City in 1928 to work for the
local chapter of the National Urban League. Influenced by the self-help philosophy of
Booker T. Washington,* the Urban League was dominated by more prosperous
middle-class blacks who wished to assist their fellow African-American city dwellers.
Badeau was from an old St. Louis family, and, like Sam and Elizabeth Williams, her parents owned a home in an integrated neighborhood. Wilkins found her not only beautiful
but also well informed and intelligent. The two hit it off immediately and were married
in 1929.

By then, Wilkins was more interested in fighting "Jim Crow's hard knocks" than in
reporting about them. He also had grown weary of Kansas City's racial atmosphere. His
opportunity to leave came in 1931, when the new executive secretary of the New York
City-based NAACP asked Wilkins to be his assistant. Walter White had met Wilkins on
a trip to Missouri and was impressed by the young editor's campaign against Jim Crow.
Under White, Wilkins did "a little bit of everything": lectured, organized new branches,
raised money for the organization's "Depression-dry" treasury, and even worked on the
NAACP's legal cases. One of them, the 1931 Scottsboro case, involved nine young black
men who were convicted of raping two white women on a train near Scottsboro, Alabama. Even though the evidence against them was questionable, eight of the men were
sentenced to death, and the ninth was given a life sentence. The case gave Wilkins his
first taste of white justice in the South.

Meanwhile, the NAACP's investigation of black workers employed by the U.S.
Army Corps of Engineers provided Wilkins's first exposure to the economic oppression
of southern blacks. In the early 1930s, Wilkins discovered that blacks employed on a le-
vee construction in Mississippi were paid as little as ten cents an hour for a twelve-hour

---

Pan-Africanism: Cultural or political unity or cooperation among African states or people
of African descent.
Booker T. Washington: A black leader who preached self-help, counseled blacks to
temporarily accept second-class citizenship, and helped found the Tuskegee Institute, a
vocational school for blacks, in the late nineteenth century.

shift. As a result of the investigation, the Corps of Engineers raised black workers' pay by as much as a dime an hour. It was not much, but it doubled what some of the men were earning. The investigation also proved to Wilkins that pressure on the government could result in changes, even if small.

In the 1930s and 1940s, in the face of continued white vigilante action against blacks in the South, the NAACP fought unsuccessfully to get the Roosevelt administration to support antilynching legislation. During World War II, Wilkins pressed the administration without success to desegregate the armed services. Yet he remained convinced that working "from on high in the Congress and Supreme Court" would eventually bring an end to discrimination and Jim Crow. In 1954, the year before he was named NAACP executive secretary, the civil rights organization won a huge legal victory. In *Brown* v. *Board of Education*, the Supreme Court ruled that segregation in public schools was unconstitutional and that states must move to end it "with all deliberate speed." The case, initiated by the NAACP and argued before the Court by Thurgood Marshall, confirmed Wilkins's faith in working "from on high."

Many blacks, however, were becoming increasingly impatient with the slow progress of civil rights. As whites moved to block desegregation, the Eisenhower administration did little to stop them. At the same time, Congress seemed unwilling to move on civil rights. In 1957, for instance, it gutted a civil rights bill pushed by the NAACP by removing a provision that would have allowed the Justice Department to sue in school desegregation and other civil rights cases. In the face of such resistance, some blacks embraced a new tactic: direct action. In 1955, an NAACP secretary named Rosa Parks was arrested for refusing to give up her seat to a white passenger on a bus in Montgomery, Alabama. Her action sparked a nearly yearlong boycott of the city's segregated buses by black riders. Several years later, members of an NAACP youth council sat down at a number of Oklahoma City segregated lunch counters and demanded to be served. By 1960, college students in Greensboro, North Carolina, and other southern cities also were "sitting in."

Initially, Wilkins supported this kind of direct action. The Montgomery bus boycott's roots had been in black churches, and the boycott had been led by Martin Luther King Jr. and other black ministers, but the NAACP had provided legal assistance. Later, Wilkins directed local NAACP branches to support the sit-ins. All the while, Wilkins preferred to work quietly behind the scenes. Influence in the corridors of power was more important, he believed, than action in the streets. Thus legal battles had to be the NAACP's main focus. Inevitably, he knew, there would be many disappointing compromises. In 1957, for example, as Wilkins had deliberated whether to accept a watered-down version of the civil rights bill, Senator Hubert Humphrey of Minnesota had helped him make up his mind. "Roy," he had said, "if there's one thing I've learned in politics, it's never to turn your back on a crumb." Wilkins had supported the bill. Later, he said, "If I had spurned [the bill], we might have been waiting outside the bakery for a much longer time." In the 1960s, however, Wilkins realized that many blacks were no longer willing to accept mere "crumbs."

"NOW WE'RE TIRED OF WAITIN'"

In 1960, Fannie Lou Hamer knew nothing about Roy Wilkins, the NAACP, or their patient legal work. She was, however, painfully aware of the conditions she faced in Sunflower County, Mississippi. Hamer was born in the hill country of central Mississippi in 1917, the youngest of Jim and Lou Ella Townsend's twenty children. When she was two, her parents moved to a plantation in Sunflower County about twenty-five miles from the Mississippi River. Like most of the other poor blacks in the Mississippi Delta, they picked cotton. Six-year-old Fannie Lou started working in the fields when a plantation owner asked her if she would like to pick cotton so she could buy treats. That week, she picked thirty pounds of cotton. Only later did she realize that she had been trapped. "I never did get out of his debt again," she recalled later. After sixth grade, she left school to work full time in the fields. She walked between the rows of cotton with a limp, probably from a broken leg that had not been set properly when she was a baby. She would drag a cotton sack behind her for much of her life.

Even with the children's help, the Townsends never got ahead. As sharecroppers, they owed the white landowner half of their crop, plus whatever provisions they had borrowed. The family lived in a wooden shack without heat, electricity, running water, or indoor plumbing. Like other black sharecroppers, they lacked the education to know when the owner had cheated them. As Fannie Lou grew up, Mississippi consistently spent less on educating blacks than any other state. In 1950, Sunflower County did not have one black high school.

As bad as the family's circumstances were, the Townsends' lives differed little from those of other poor blacks in Mississippi. In this notorious stronghold of white supremacy, most blacks worked for low wages in the fields and homes of white people. Meanwhile, they were denied justice in the courts and the right to vote. If need be, they were kept in their place with violence. The year Fannie Lou was born, more than eighty blacks were lynched in Mississippi. Things had changed little by 1955, when the badly beaten body of Emmett Till, an African-American teenager from Chicago who was visiting relatives in Mississippi, was found in the Tallahatchie River. Till had supposedly made a pass at a white woman, and the two men who had abducted him were acquitted.

In 1944, Fannie Lou married a sharecropper named Perry Hamer. The couple moved to a plantation in Ruleville, where they lived in a small house with running water and a broken toilet. Fannie Lou considered the house "decent," until one day, when she was cleaning the boss's house, she saw that the family dog had its own bathroom. "I just couldn't get over that dog having a bathroom," she recalled, "when [the owner] wouldn't even have the toilet fixed for us." Despite their poverty, the Hamers took in two girls to raise as their own.

Fannie Lou Hamer's deep religious faith helped her endure the poverty and racial hatred all around her, as well as the trauma resulting from what she called "a knot on my stomach." Hamer entered a hospital in 1961 for an operation to remove a uterine tumor and discovered later that doctors had also performed a hysterectomy without her permission. When she asked for an explanation, the doctor "didn't have to say nothing—and he didn't." A decade later, the sterilization of poor black women in the South would be taken up in the courts, but in the early 1960s, legal action was unthinkable. "I would have been taking my hands and screwing tacks in my own casket," Hamer said. The experience left her feeling helpless, angry, and bitter.

When civil rights organizers associated with the Student Nonviolent Coordinating Committee (SNCC, pronounced "snick") arrived in Sunflower County the next year, Hamer was ready to join their crusade. SNCC had been founded in 1960 by students involved in the early sit-ins in North Carolina and elsewhere in the South. They rejected the policies of Martin Luther King, Jr. and other black ministers who had formed the Southern Christian Leadership Conference (SCLC) in 1957 after the Montgomery bus boycott. Instead, SNCC's young activists encouraged local black people to act on their own. By 1962, much of SNCC's grassroots organizing was devoted to a voter registration drive in Mississippi. The Voter Education Project brought together representatives from a reluctant NAACP and the Congress of Racial Equality (CORE), which had earlier launched the Freedom Rides to desegregate the South's interstate bus system. It also brought civil rights organizers into a state previously overlooked by the NAACP and other civil rights organizations.

One of the Voter Education Project's targets was Sunflower County, which had a reputation as one of the most antiblack counties in the state. In 1962, virtually all of the county's roughly fifteen thousand voting-age blacks were excluded from the voting booth, and whites there were not about to let them in. When civil rights workers showed up in the delta, the mayor of Ruleville declared that anyone attending a voter registration school "would be given a one-way ticket out of town." If that did not stop potential voters, local authorities "would use whatever [means] they had available." Such threats did not faze the SNCC organizers. SNCC leader James Forman told blacks that they could vote people out of office and get rid of bad police officers if they would only register to vote. As Hamer listened to Forman speak at a meeting in the Williams Chapel Baptist Church in Ruleville, she remembered that one of Ruleville's cops was the brother of a man suspected of killing Emmett Till seven years before. When the SNCC representatives asked who would be willing to register to vote, she raised her hand.

Four days later, Hamer was on a rented bus with seventeen other people headed to the county courthouse. When they arrived, they were greeted by a crowd of gun-toting whites. Inside, Hamer was required to take a literacy test based on the Mississippi Constitution. She flunked. "I knowed as much about [it] as a horse knows about Christmas Day," she said later. When she returned home, the owner of the plantation where she worked told her to take her name off the registration forms if she wanted to stay there. "I didn't go down there to register for you," she replied. "I went down to register for myself." Evicted from the plantation, Hamer packed her bags and headed to town with her two girls, leaving her husband behind. She stayed with friends for several days, and then, fearful that she might be killed, moved in with relatives in Tallahatchie County.

By the time she returned to Ruleville later that fall, a black municipal employee had been fired because his wife had attended voter registration classes, the Williams Chapel Baptist Church had lost its tax-exempt status, two black-owned laundries had been shut down, shots had been fired into the house where Hamer had stayed before leaving town, and her husband had been evicted from the plantation. Hamer had already heard about the sit-ins elsewhere in the South, and she knew that black and white Freedom Riders had been met with firebombs and mob violence. She was ready to join SNCC. Voter Education Project director Robert Moses was impressed by Hamer's personal sacrifice and realized that she was exactly the kind of person who could help carry on SNCC's campaign long after its student volunteers had left the community.

Living on a ten-dollar monthly stipend, Hamer served as a SNCC field secretary, worked on voter registration, and taught citizenship classes. After spending long hours studying the Mississippi Constitution, she finally passed the literacy test. Meanwhile, the harassment of Hamer and other civil rights workers continued. After attending a civil rights workshop in 1963, she and six other participants were arrested in Winona, Mississippi, for going into the "whites only" section of a bus terminal. Thrown into jail for four days, Hamer was brutally beaten by two black prisoners who were threatened by the white guards. Bruised and swollen, she left the jail with a permanent loss of feeling in her arms and an even greater desire to fight the oppression of African Americans.

Increasing numbers of African Americans now shared her determination. By 1963, a growing civil rights movement was sweeping the South. Earlier, the Kennedy administration had intervened with force to protect black protesters from violence. About the same time Hamer was released from jail, President John Kennedy called on Congress to pass a sweeping civil rights bill that would end segregation in public accommodations and discrimination in employment. Two months later, Martin Luther King Jr. delivered his famous "I Have a Dream" speech during the March on Washington. These events led to a growing awareness of the civil rights movement, but conditions in Mississippi remained unchanged. By the end of 1963, SNCC's voter education campaign had little to show for its efforts. Given the state's brutal record, Roy Wilkins and many other civil rights leaders believed that SNCC's focus on Mississippi was folly. In 1964, however, Hamer and SNCC would turn the spotlight on the state.

First, Robert Moses and other SNCC members launched Mississippi Freedom Summer, which called for recruiting a thousand white college students to work on voter registration in the state. Violence directed against affluent white civil rights workers, they reasoned, would capture the attention of a nation that had generally ignored atrocities committed against blacks. Despite a death threat against her, Hamer served as a Freedom Summer organizer, and in the end, the program had exactly the effect that SNCC organizers had anticipated: The press began to pay more attention to conditions in Mississippi, especially after the murders of three civil rights workers, two of whom were white.

Meanwhile, Hamer and other SNCC activists had already made plans to get the nation's attention in another way. Earlier in 1964, they had formed the MFDP to challenge the state's white Democratic Party. Hamer was among its first political candidates. Running for Congress against an incumbent, she was determined to demonstrate that blacks could participate in politics. "We've been waiting all our lives, and still gettin' killed, still gettin' hung, still gettin' beat to death," she told a reporter in June. "Now we're tired of waitin'." Although she and the other MFDP candidates were trounced in the Democratic primary, she and other party organizers had already set their sights on another goal: unseating the segregationist Democratic Party delegates at the party's national convention later that summer in Atlantic City. Doing so would force the nation to acknowledge the horrible conditions in Mississippi.

" 'CAUSE THEY'RE NOT LEADING US"

When Roy Wilkins arrived in Atlantic City in late August 1964, he knew that the election of Lyndon Johnson later that fall represented the best hope for achieving progress in civil rights. Despite being a Texan with a long segregationist voting record, Johnson had quickly taken up the cause of civil rights after the assassination of President Kennedy in late 1963. LBJ, who had succeeded Kennedy, had called on Congress to pass the sweeping civil rights act proposed by the late president. While Wilkins had lobbied on Capitol Hill, Johnson had cajoled and threatened enough reluctant members of Congress into passing the Civil Rights Act of 1964 just weeks before the Democratic National Convention. Calling for an end to discrimination in employment and public accommodations, the act was a huge blow to Jim Crow. An elated Wilkins called it the "Magna Carta for the race." Meanwhile, the Republicans had already nominated Barry Goldwater as their presidential candidate. An outspoken conservative, Goldwater opposed the Civil Rights Act. He was also in favor of states' rights, the very position that white southerners battling desegregation had embraced to prevent federal action on civil rights. For the first time since the end of Reconstruction, a Republican presidential candidate threatened to steal the Democratic Party's base in the South. By appealing to pro-segregation voters, he might even win the election. In 1964, the NAACP broke a long tradition of nonpartisanship by opposing Goldwater. For Wilkins, the decision to endorse LBJ was easy. Deciding what to do about the MFDP's challenge to Mississippi's regular Democrats was much more difficult. The regular Mississippi Democratic delegation represented everything that his organization opposed. The state's blacks had no hand in choosing any of its delegates, and it was led by a governor who described the NAACP as "niggers, alligators, apes, coons, and possums." At the same time, a floor fight over the seating of MFDP delegates at the convention would embarrass the party and LBJ. It would also drive southern Democrats right into Goldwater's arms. Yet, an outright rejection of the MFDP was politically risky. Race riots had recently erupted in several cities, and demonstrators from nearby Philadelphia and New York, angry over the treatment of the MFDP at the convention, could embarrass Johnson and fuel a white backlash against civil rights.

Wilkins was in a difficult spot. How could he reconcile the MFDP's moral high ground with the practical necessities of politics? The situation called for a moderate course, one that would appease both sides. Wilkins would offer his support to the MFDP before the Democratic National Committee's Credentials Committee, which certified the legitimacy of the convention's delegates. At the same time, he would work for a compromise with the MFDP over the seating of their sixty-eight delegates. He hoped that would keep peace on the convention floor and in the streets.

Wilkins's calculations did not account for the influence of Fannie Lou Hamer. Also called to testify before the Credentials Committee, Hamer was the star witness. Sitting at a table in front of more than a hundred committee members, reporters, and television cameras that carried her message nationwide, Hamer told an electrifying tale of beatings and oppression. **[See Source 1.]** Johnson's forces finally offered the MFDP two at-large seats* and the rest of the biracial delegation the status of nonvoting honorary guests. Wilkins and Martin Luther King, Jr. told the delegates to accept the offer, but Hamer was unyielding. Some of the delegates agreed with Wilkins and King, arguing that they should take the offer and claim a "moral victory." In response to those calling for compromise, Hamer retorted, "What do you mean, moral victory? We ain't got nothin'." One of the two delegates who had been offered an at-large seat suggested that the delegates listen to leaders who knew more about politics than Hamer. "Tell me what leaders you talking about," she demanded. " ... But now don't go telling me about somebody that ain't been in Mississippi for two weeks...'cause they're not leading us."

Hamer "carried the delegation," and the MFDP delegates voted to reject the compromise. As Wilkins had hoped, the white Mississippi delegation was officially seated, and the Democrats avoided a nasty fight on the convention floor. Yet, that did not prevent most of the state's regular delegation from walking out of the convention anyway. Nor did it prevent LBJ from losing Mississippi and six other Deep South states in the November election—a development that marked the beginning of the end of the solidly Democratic South. The fight over the MFDP at the convention had other long-lasting consequences as well. By the time Hamer and some of the other MFDP delegates left Atlantic City, they were thoroughly disillusioned with the traditional black leaders who seemed so eager to accept compromises. Hamer referred to them as "tom* teachers and chicken-eating ministers." She was particularly disgusted with Wilkins and the NAACP.

At-large seats: Seats not connected to a particular state, district, or delegation. By offering at-large seats, Johnson refused to acknowledge the MFDP's claims that its delegates were legitimate representatives of the state party.

Tom: A reference to a patient and humble slave named Tom, the main character in Harriet Beecher Stowe's antislavery novel *Uncle Tom's Cabin* (1852).

"There ain't nothing I respect less than the NAACP," she declared. After the Democratic convention, Hamer took a brief trip to West Africa that was sponsored by the black entertainer Harry Belafonte. In Africa, she saw blacks running their own businesses and even their own countries. When she returned to Mississippi, she began to talk less about civil rights and more about the need to build institutions at the local level to help blacks help themselves.

Hamer's new attitude paralleled that of many civil rights workers. SNCC members were especially disillusioned with the slow pace of economic and social change for blacks, and they were embittered by political compromises. Despite the passage of major civil rights legislation, most African Americans continued to live in poverty and suffer from discrimination. Rejecting appeals to the goodwill of whites as the best way to gain civil rights, they began to call for black control of their own institutions. In 1966, a disillusioned MFDP member and SNCC activist named Stokely Carmichael gave this new approach a name. "We been saying freedom for six years and we ain't got nothin'," he declared. "What we gonna start saying now is 'Black Power!' "

"Black Power" meant different things to different people. For many blacks, it clearly involved the rejection of Lyndon Johnson, the liberal white allies of the civil rights movement, and traditional civil rights leaders such as Roy Wilkins and Martin Luther King, Jr. Both Hamer and Carmichael accused Wilkins of selling out blacks. For a growing number of increasingly militant blacks, however, Black Power involved a rejection of nonviolence. **[See Source 2.]** That idea had special appeal in northern ghettos, where many residents also began to demand community control of neighborhoods and businesses in the late 1960s. The growing frustration with peaceful protests and police brutality helps explain the appeal of organizations such as the Black Panthers. Founded in Oakland, California, in 1966 by two college-educated activists named Huey Newton and Bobby Seale, the Black Panthers symbolized growing black militance in the minds of many whites. Conspicuously displaying their weapons, Seale and Newton spoke frequently about the need for armed revolt.

Though no Black Panther, Fannie Lou Hamer had been converted to the cause of Black Power even before Carmichael had coined the term. After the 1964 Democratic National Convention, she was thoroughly disillusioned with the white-dominated power structure. In 1966, she began to express support for Carmichael and speak at rallies that promoted black separatism. She was never able to go as far as Robert Moses, however, who declared that he would not have anything to do with white people again. Nor did she agree with SNCC when it decided in 1968 to kick whites out of the organization. Although she agreed with Black Power advocates about the need for black self-determination, she did not believe that separating themselves from whites was the best way for blacks to achieve a larger voice in government. African-American communities needed to control their own educational, economic, and political institutions. Appealing to whites in positions of power to help blacks did not work. **[See Source 3.]**

For Hamer, Black Power was a practical guide for action in her own community. As the civil rights movement fragmented in the face of growing black militance, Hamer was promoting alternative institutions that would further black economic self-reliance. By 1965, she was devoting much of her energy to the Mississippi Freedom Labor Union (MFLU). A union of domestic workers, truck drivers, and laborers, the MFLU promoted black ownership of homes, businesses, and land before falling victim to internal squabbling and shaky finances in 1966. Several years later, she helped found the Freedom Farm Cooperative to provide poor blacks and whites in Sunflower County with food and homes. The cooperative lasted for only five years, but during that time, it purchased nearly seven hundred acres and built seventy low-cost homes.

As Hamer's focus narrowed on helping what she called the "everyday" people of her county, her political concerns broadened. While Roy Wilkins and many other civil rights leaders continued to defend LBJ's policies in the Vietnam War, she criticized the war, in which blacks were fighting and dying in numbers disproportionate to those for whites. She also began to address the plight of black women. In 1971, she joined National Organization for Women founder Betty Friedan and feminist Gloria Steinem in establishing the National Women's Political Caucus (see Chapter 13). All the while, she continued to work on voter registration, building the MFDP, and getting blacks elected to office. Despite her harsh words for the NAACP, in 1968 she joined with it and other liberal, pro-integration groups to challenge the regular Mississippi Democrats once again. This time, the insurgents were successful. When Hamer addressed the Democratic National Convention in 1968, she was greeted with a standing ovation. She also continued to speak around the country on her understanding of Black Power. "I am not fighting for an all black world," she told a Seattle audience in 1969, "just like I am not going to tolerate an all white world." Two years later, she ran for a seat in the Mississippi state senate on a platform that reflected her concern about black poverty as well as fair voting procedures. Although she lost the election, Hamer lived long enough to see more black elected officials in Mississippi than in any other state in the South and nearly 60 percent of eligible blacks registered to vote. She died in 1977.

" 'BLACK POWER' ... MEAN[S] ... BLACK DEATH"

If the 1964 Democratic convention was a turning point for Fannie Lou Hamer, it was a preview of difficult times ahead for Roy Wilkins. To be sure, his loyalty to LBJ was vindicated again in 1965, when the president signed the Voting Rights Act, which provided new guarantees and protections for black voters. Only days later, however, Wilkins watched helplessly as the Watts section of Los Angeles erupted in a race riot that lasted for six days and claimed thirty-four lives. The race riots in Watts and other cities in the late 1960s were an indication that desegregating the South was not the only civil rights battle. Millions of blacks still faced inadequate housing, low incomes, and poor job opportunities—problems unlikely to be solved by getting rid of Jim Crow and opening up the voting booth. "Suddenly," Wilkins said, "we found ourselves in the middle of a two-front war."

Wilkins would confront the war on this second "front" for the rest of his career. Unfortunately, he was not adequately prepared to fight it. As race riots and Martin Luther King, Jr.'s assassination in 1968 brought an end to the civil rights era, the NAACP's program seemed to offer little hope to poor blacks. Caught off guard, Wilkins confessed that "no one was really prepared with a strategy or workable program" for dealing with the dire economic and social conditions among the nation's blacks. **[See Source 4.]** Nor was he prepared for the challenge to his leadership posed by many young blacks impatient with the slow progress of achieving equality. By 1966, Wilkins's main battle was not with white segregationists but with blacks who were increasingly alienated from the NAACP. Attacked as an "Uncle Tom," Wilkins was convinced that "Black Power" was an empty, dangerous slogan that would provoke a white backlash against civil rights. The "rhetorical excesses of the black power people," he charged, had made it easier for Congress to kill additional civil rights legislation. " 'Black power'," he said in an address at the NAACP's annual convention in 1966, "can mean in the end only black death." **[See Source 5.]**

After the speech, Wilkins was a marked man. In 1967, members of a small group called the Revolutionary Action Movement were arrested for plotting to assassinate him. The following year, a faction of younger NAACP members revolted against his leadership, charging that he was out of touch with the concerns of most African Americans. When they called for the organization to come out against the Vietnam War, Wilkins countered that "mingling" the civil rights and antiwar movements would only weaken the cause. Although he faced numerous challenges, in the end he won the battle and held on to his position for another decade. Until he stepped down in 1979, he continued to wage his "two-front war." One front was against growing white opposition to desegregation; the other was against Black Power advocates who promoted what he called "reverse Jim Crow." He never lost faith in the NAACP's goal of integration and legal equality for blacks, and after his retirement he noted with pride, "The NAACP is still with us." The same could not be said of some of the other civil rights organizations. Nor did Wilkins ever lose faith in the American legal system. "We have believed in our Constitution," he wrote in his autobiography, completed just before his death in 1981. "We have believed that the Declaration of Independence meant what it said."

• PRIMARY SOURCES •

Source 1:   Testimony of Fannie Lou Hamer Before the Credentials Committee of the Democratic National Convention (1964)

As part of the Mississippi Freedom Democratic Party's effort to get recognition at the Democratic National Convention in 1964, Fannie Lou Hamer offered the Credentials Committee moving testimony based on her experience in Mississippi. As LBJ watched Hamer on television, according to one witness, he "went right up the wall." Then he hastily called a news conference that preempted the live broadcast of her testimony. What does Hamer's testimony reveal about conditions in Mississippi? About the reasons for her influence in the MFDP?

It was the 31st of August in 1962 that 18 of us traveled 26 miles to the county courthouse in Indianola to try to register to try to became first-class citizens. We was met in Indianola by Mississippi men, Highway Patrolmen and they allowed two of us in to take the literacy test at the time. After we had taken the test and started back to Ruleville, we was held up by the City Police and the State Highway Patrolmen and carried back to Indianola where the bus driver was charged that day with driving a bus the wrong color.

After we paid the fine among us, we continued on to Ruleville near…, where I had worked as a time-keeper and sharecropper for 18 years. I was met there by my children, who told me the plantation owner was angry because I had gone down to try to register.

After they told me, my husband came, and said the plantation owner was raising cain because I had tried to register and before he quit talking the plantation owner

Source: Reprinted in Peter B. Levy, ed., *Documentary History of the Modern Civil Rights Movement* (New York: Greenwood Press, 1992), pp. 139–141.

came, and said, Fannie Lou, do you know—did Pap[*] ell you what said And said, Yes, sir. He said, "I mean that....If you don't go down and withdraw ... well—you might have to go because we are not ready for that."...

And I addressed him and told him and said, "I didn't try to register for you. I tried to register for myself."

I had to leave that same night.

On the 10th of September, 1962, 16 bullets was fired into the home of Mr. and Mrs. Robert Tucker for me....

And in June, the 9th, 1963, I had attended a voter registration workshop, was returning back to Mississippi. Ten of us was traveling by the Continental Trailways bus. When we got to Winona, Mississippi..., four of the people got off to use the washroom.... I stepped off the bus to see what was happening and somebody screamed from the car that four workers was in and said, "Get that one there," and when I went to get in the car, when the man told me I was under arrest, he kicked me.

I was carried to the county jail and put in the holding room. They left some of the people in the booking room and began to place us in cells....

I was carried out of that cell into another cell where they had two Negro prisoners. The State Highway patrolmen ordered the first Negro to take the blackjack. The first Negro prisoner ordered me, by orders from the State Highway Patrolmen, for me to lay down on a bunk bed on my face, and I laid on my face.

...After the first Negro had beat until he was exhausted the state Highway Patrolman ordered the second Negro to take the blackjack.... I began to scream and one white man got up and began to beat me in my head and tell me to hush....

All of this on account we want to register, to become first-class citizens...

Source 2:   Stokely Carmichael, "What We Want" (1966)

In this widely quoted essay, SNCC leader Stokely Carmichael expresses impatience with slow pace of racial change in American society. How does Carmichael define "Black Power"? What lessons does he draw from the experience of SNCC organizers in the South?

Black Power can be clearly defined for those who do not attach the fears of white America to their question about it. We should begin with the basic fact that black Americans have two problems: they are poor and they are black. All other problems arise from this two-sided reality: lack of education, the so-called apathy of black men. Any program to end racism must address itself to that double reality.

Almost from its beginning, SNCC sought to address itself to both conditions with a program aimed at winning political power for impoverished Southern blacks. We had to begin with politics because black Americans are a propertyless people in a country where property is valued above all. We had to work for power, because this country does not function by morality, love, and nonviolence, but by power. Thus we determined to win political power, with the idea of moving on from there into activity that would have

SOURCE: Originally published in *The New York Review of Books*, 1966.

---

[*]Pap: Hamer's husband, Perry.

economic effects. With power, the masses could *make or participate in making* the decisions which govern their destinies, and thus create basic change in their day-to-day lives.

But if political power seemed to be the key to self-determination, it was also obvious that the key had been thrown down a deep well many years earlier.... The right to vote had to be won, and SNCC workers devoted their energies to this from 1961 to 1965....

SNCC had already gone to Atlantic City for recognition of the Mississippi Freedom Democratic Party by the Democratic convention and been rejected; it had gone with the MFDP to Washington for recognition by Congress and been rejected. In Arkansas, SNCC helped thirty Negroes to run for School Board elections; all but one were defeated, and there was evidence of fraud and intimidation sufficient to cause their defeat. In Atlanta, Julian Bond ran for the state legislature and was elected—twice—and unseated— twice. In several states, black farmers ran in elections for agricultural committees which make crucial decisions concerning land use, loans, etc. Although they won places on a number of committees, they never gained the majorities needed to control them.

In Alabama, the opportunity came to see how blacks could be organized on an independent party basis.... On May 3, five new county "freedom organizations" convened and nominated candidates for the offices of sheriff, tax assessor, members of the school boards. These men and women are up for election in November—if they live until then. Their ballot symbol is the black panther: a bold, beautiful animal, representing the strength and dignity of black demands today. A man needs a black panther on his side when he and his family must endure—as hundreds of Alabamians have endured—loss of job, eviction, starvation, and sometimes death, for political activity. He may also need a gun and SNCC reaffirms the right of black men everywhere to defend themselves when threatened or attacked. As for initiating the use of violence, we hope that such programs as ours will make that unnecessary; but it is not for us to tell black communities whether they can or cannot use any particular form of action to resolve their problems. Responsibility for the use of violence by black men, whether in self defense or initiated by them, lies with the white community....

ULTIMATELY, the economic foundations of this country must be shaken if black people are to control their lives. The colonies of the United States—and this includes the black ghettoes within its borders, north and south—must be liberated....

This is what the white society does not wish to face; this is why that society prefers to talk about integration. But integration speaks not at all to the problem of poverty, only to the problem of blackness.

Source 3:   *Fannie Lou Hamer on the Lessons of the Democratic National Convention* (1967)

In her autobiography, Fannie Lou Hamer discusses what she learned from her experiences at the Democratic National Convention in 1964. How do her conclusions put her at odds with Roy Wilkins and the approach of the NAACP in achieving civil rights?

In 1964 we registered 63,000 black people from Mississippi into the Freedom Democratic Party. We formed our own party because the whites wouldn't even let us register.

SOURCE: Reprinted in Clayborne Carson et al., THE EYES ON THE PRIZE CIVIL RIGHTS READER: DOCUMENTS, SPEECHES, and FIRSTHAND ACCOUNTS FROM THE BLACK FREEDOM STRUGGLE, 1954/ 1990 (New York: Viking Press, 1991), pp. 178–179; originally from TO PRAISE OUR BRIDGES: AN AUTOBIOGRAPHY OF MRS. Fanny [*sic*] LOU HAMER (Jackson, Miss.: KIPCO, 1967).

We decided to challenge the white Mississippi Democratic Party at the National Convention. We followed all the laws that the white people themselves made. We tried to attend the precinct meetings and they locked the doors on us or moved the meetings and that's against the laws they made for their ownselves. So we were the ones that held the real precinct meetings. At all these meetings across the state we elected our representatives to go to the National Democratic Convention in Atlantic City. But we learned the hard way that even though we had all the law and all the righteousness on our side— that white man is not going to give up his power to us.

We have to build our own power. We have to win every single political office we can, where we have a majority of black people....

The question for black people is not, when is the white man going to give us our rights, or when is he going to give us good education for our children, or when is he going to give us jobs—if the white man gives you anything—just remember when he gets ready he will take it right back. We have to take for ourselves.

Source 4: *Poverty Rates, by Race and Family Relationship, 1959–1999*

Poverty rates for blacks, compared to those for whites, remained high in the late twentieth century. The graph below shows the percentage of each group living in poverty. What does this graph suggest about the traditional civil rights movement's impact on what Stokely Carmichael called the problem of black poverty? Does it suggest why the message of Hamer and Carmichael was popular with many blacks by the mid-1960s?

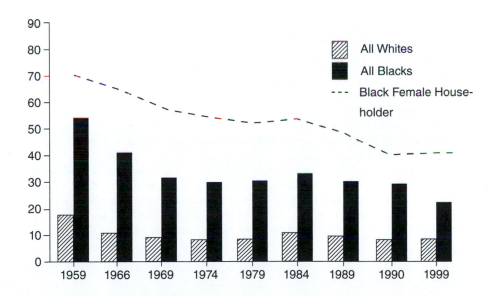

SOURCE: 1959–1989 from Peter B. Levy, ed., DOCUMENTARY HISTORY OF THE MODERN CIVIL RIGHTS MOVEMENT (New York: Greenwood Press, 1992), p. 249; 1990 and 1999 from "Historical Statistics of the U.S.; Statistical Abstract of the U.S." (Washington, D.C.: Government Printing Office, 2000), p. 43.

Source 5:   Roy Wilkins, *"Sail Our N.A.A.C.P. Ship 'Steady as She Goes'"* (1966)

In 1966, Roy Wilkins denounced "Black Power" in his keynote address to the NAACP's annual convention. In this excerpt, on what grounds does he judge it to be dangerous and misguided?

No matter how endlessly they try to explain it, the term "black power" means anti-white power. In a racially pluralistic society the concept, the formation and the exercise of an ethnically-tagged power, means opposition to other ethnic powers, just as the term, "white supremacy" means subjection of all non-white people. In the black-white relationship, it has to mean that every other ethnic power is the rival and the antagonist of "black power." It has to mean "going-it-alone." It has to mean separatism.

Now separatism, whether on the rarefied debate level of "black power" or on the wishful level of a secessionist Freedom City in Watts, offers a disadvantaged minority little except the chance to shrivel and die.

The only possible dividend of "black power" is embodied in its offer to millions of frustrated and deprived and persecuted black people of a solace,... quite apart from its political and economic implications.

Ideologically it dictates "up with black and down with white." In precisely the same fashion that South Africa reverses that slogan.

It is a reverse Mississippi, a reverse Hitler, a reverse Ku Klux Klan.

If these were evil in our judgment, what virtue can be claimed for black over white? If, as some proponents claim, this concept instills pride of race, cannot this pride be taught without preaching hatred or supremacy based upon race?

Though it be clarified and clarified again, "black power" in the quick, uncritical and highly emotional adoption it has received from some segments of a beleaguered people can mean in the end only black death. Even if, through some miracle, it should be enthroned briefly in an isolated area, the human spirit, which knows no color or geography or time, would die a little, leaving for wiser and stronger and more compassionate men the painful beating back to the upward trail.

We of the N.A.A.C.P. will have none of this. We have fought it too long. It is the ranging of race against race on the irrelevant basis of skin color. It is the father of hatred and the mother of violence.

It is the wicked fanaticism which has swelled our tears, broken our bodies, squeezed our hearts and taken the blood of our black and white loved ones. It shall not now poison our forward march.

We seek, therefore, as we have sought these many years, the inclusion of Negro Americans in the nation's life, not their exclusion. This is our land, as much as it is any American's—every square foot of every city and town and village. The task of winning our share is not the easy one of disengagement and flight, but the hard one of work, of short as well as long jumps, of disappointments and of sweet successes.

SOURCE: From Keynote Address given by Roy Wilkins in 1966 at NAACP Convention. Reprinted in Sondra Kathryn Wilson, ed., IN SEARCH OF DEMOCRACY: THE NAACP WRITINGS OF JAMES WELDON JOHNSON, WALTER WHITE, AND ROY WILKINS (1920–1977) (New York: Oxford University Press, 1999), p. 424.

QUESTIONS TO CONSIDER

1. How would you compare Roy Wilkins's and Fannie Lou Hamer's approaches to achieving civil rights for blacks? In what ways did their methods and goals reflect their backgrounds and experiences?

2. By the middle of the 1960s, Hamer and other advocates of Black Power had denounced the moderation and compromises of Wilkins and the NAACP. Years later, however, Wilkins could declare that the NAACP "is still with us." What were the achievements and limitations of Hamer's and Wilkins's methods? Which leader do you think was more effective? Why?

3. If you had been a member of the Credentials Committee at the Democratic National Convention in 1964, what would your position have been regarding the seating of the Mississippi Freedom Democratic Party delegation at the convention? If you had been a MFDP delegate, what would your position have been regarding Lyndon Johnson's offer of only two at-large seats at the convention? Was Wilkins right in encouraging the delegates to accept the offer, or was Hamer right in urging them to reject it?

4. What do this chapter's essay and sources reveal about the reasons for the popularity of Black Power among many African Americans by the late 1960s? How do you think Hamer would have responded to Wilkins's assertion that Black Power was merely a slogan rather than a program? Do you agree with Wilkins?

5. If Wilkins and Hamer had the opportunity to examine American society and race relations today, do you think either of them would feel vindicated? What circumstances or problems do you think each would point to as signs of progress or failure?

FOR FURTHER READING

Chana Kai Lee, *For Freedom's Sake: The Life of Fannie Lou Hamer* (Urbana: University of Illinois Press, 1999), submits an overview of Hamer's life and a useful discussion of her local organizing efforts after the 1964 Democratic convention.

Kay Mills, *This Little Light of Mine: The Life of Fannie Lou Hamer* (New York: Penguin Books, 1993), provides a gripping account of the conditions that Hamer confronted in her battle for black equality in Mississippi.

Charles M. Payne, *I've Got the Light of Freedom: The Organizing Tradition and the Mississippi Freedom Struggle* (Berkeley: University of California Press, 1995), examines the fight for black equality in Mississippi by focusing on the role of Fannie Lou Hamer and other grassroots organizers.

John A. Salmond, *"My Mind Set on Freedom": A History of the Civil Rights Movement, 1954–1968* (Chicago: Ivan R. Dee, 1997), offers a concise treatment of the civil rights struggle from the *Brown* v. *Board of Education* decision to the assassination of Martin Luther King, Jr.

Bruce Watson, *Freedom Summer: The Savage Season That Made Mississippi Burn and Made America a Democracy* (New York: Viking, 2010), presents an engaging account of the effort to challenge the racial status quo in Mississippi in the summer of 1964.

Roy Wilkins, *Standing Fast: The Autobiography of Roy Wilkins* (New York: Viking Press, 1982), details Wilkins's rise as the leader of the nation's largest civil rights organization and offers a defense of his policies.

The Battles of Vietnam: Robert McNamara and Jan Barry

Robert McNamara was livid. By late 1967, the secretary of defense was no stranger to protests against the war in Vietnam. But one protest launched in November caught his eye and raised his ire like few others. It took the form of a full-page advertisement in the *New York Times*. Headlined "Vietnam Veterans Speak Out," it declared that the nation's military involvement in Vietnam was "unjustifiable and contrary to the principle of self-determination on which this nation was founded." Antiwar demonstrations had been growing steadily in the last two years, including one that drew fifty thousand people right outside McNamara's Pentagon office window. But the defense secretary realized that this protest was especially dangerous. By virtue of their military service, the sixty-five veterans who signed the advertisement threatened to give the antiwar movement legitimacy in the minds of many Americans. That very day, McNamara called the Federal Bureau of Investigation (FBI) and demanded an investigation of those responsible for it.

The advertisement was the work of a small outfit called Vietnam Veterans Against the War (VVAW). Founded only a month earlier by a twenty-four-year-old named Jan Barry, the fledgling organization sought to end the war in Southeast Asia by educating the public about it. After starting the VVAW in his New York City living room, Barry had worked hard to round up signatures and collect money for the ad. Driven by convictions based on his own experience in Vietnam, he believed that veterans of the war there, once organized, could be its most effective opponents.

When Barry entered the service, few Americans challenged their nation's commitment in Vietnam or the assumptions behind it. John Kennedy was president, and the United States was engaged in a global struggle against communism whose roots dated to Harry Truman's containment policy in 1947. By the early 1960s, that Cold War struggle had entered a new and dangerous phase, characterized by a growing nuclear arms race with the Soviet Union and rising unrest in the Third World, the nations in

Robert McNamara   Jan Barry

Latin America, Africa, and Asia. At the outset of his presidency, Kennedy urged Americans to "bear any burden" in the defense of freedom around the world. Convinced that the Third World represented the new Cold War battleground, it was easy for Kennedy and advisers to see the small conflict between the government of South Vietnam and communist insurgents as a case of expansionism by the Soviets or their Chinese communist surrogates, which required an American response.

The result was one of the longest wars in American history. As secretary of defense for seven years, Robert McNamara was one of its principal planners. In fact, the Vietnam War became so closely identified with him that it was often referred to as "McNamara's war." A man of legendary mental abilities and managerial skills, he often left those around him awestruck. McNamara applied his impressive talents to managing a small conflict in far-off Vietnam, which few Americans knew or cared about. The central goal of his efforts was to make sure that it stayed a relatively little war and minor concern for Americans. Under McNamara's management, though, the conflict in Vietnam turned into a very large war. By 1967, thousands of Americans and tens of thousands of Vietnamese lay dead, and the war had come home to the United States. As the growing protests at home demonstrated, Vietnam was no longer a minor concern.

Jan Barry's tour of duty ended before McNamara guided the Johnson administration's massive escalation of American forces in the mid-1960s. It also ended before many of the American forces there came to be made up primarily of working-class, often nonwhite, draftees. In coming years, though, Barry's conclusions about the war would be shared by many of these veterans, even as his organization came to mirror social divisions among them. Although Jan Barry never met Robert McNamara, few veterans offered an earlier critique of the war that McNamara did so much to shape. And few did more to help erode public support for it. If McNamara reveals much about why and how the United States fought there, Barry reveals much of what McNamara missed about Vietnam. Together, their stories illuminate what went wrong in Vietnam—and why the war there came home to the United States.

"WE'RE WINNING THIS WAR"

People marveled at Robert McNamara's remarkable mind. They often marveled more that he arose from such unremarkable circumstances. McNamara was born in San Francisco in 1916 and grew up across the bay in Oakland in a struggling middle-class household. His father, the son of a poor, Irish Catholic immigrant, was a man of iron self-discipline and obsessive frugality. As a manager for a San Francisco wholesale shoe company, his chief concern was providing for his family, especially during the hard times of the Depression. McNamara's mother was the daughter of a more prosperous Presbyterian family, and she raised her son and daughter in her faith. Convinced her son was special, she also instilled in him a strong sense of purpose and a burning ambition to succeed.

McNamara took his first step in that direction in 1933 when he headed off to the nearby University of California at Berkeley. With a love for numbers and logic, he considered majoring in mathematics, but wanted to study something more practical. Economics was the answer, and he excelled at it. By his senior year, he was elected to an elite academic society, traveled in the school's top social circles, and came to know the university's president. When he graduated in 1937, he turned down the option of graduate school and instead chose a more lucrative way to exercise his knack for numbers. He went east to attend Harvard Business School.

At Harvard, McNamara specialized in statistical control, an academic field that fit him perfectly. It had been developed several decades earlier to provide data that allowed managers to measure their company's performance and make financial projections. Statistical control saved companies money by eliminating even the smallest inefficiencies. Above all, it gave them the means to centralize control over far-flung and diverse operations. The flaw was its assumption that only managers at the top, not the rank-and-file workers, had enough information to make decisions. But running a company by the numbers represented rational business management in the 1950s.

Mastery of statistical control propelled McNamara to the top of powerful organizations in business and government. After a brief stint with a San Francisco accounting firm and an equally brief courtship of an old Berkeley acquaintance named Margy Craig, McNamara—twenty-four and married to Craig—returned to Harvard to teach accounting. He did not stay long. With the United States in World War II, the Army Air Corps came calling in 1942. It wanted McNamara and other faculty to devise a statistical control system to track the massive amount of materiel needed to fight an air war. It was a huge task, and again McNamara excelled, demonstrating an enormous appetite for work and an ability to get things done. McNamara's wartime experience left him with a key lesson: Statistical data was power. Using statistical analysis, for instance, military planners analyzed the combat experience of B-17s and B-24s, found the B-17 more successful, and altered production of the bombers accordingly. One could derive important truths from numbers, even the best way to fight a war.

After the war, McNamara used his mastery of numbers to control an entire organization. Faced with the unhappy prospect of supporting a growing family on a professor's salary, he joined a group of former army statistical control men who sold their services to the struggling automobile manufacturer Ford. The company had suffered for years under the dictatorial control of its founder Henry Ford, but had just been taken over by grandson Henry Ford II. McNamara and the others modernized Ford's management, devising detailed inventory and financial control systems. Before long, people were talking about the company's "Whiz Kids"—the young managers who had used tools of modern finance to save an American business icon. The most ambitious of the Whiz Kids, McNamara quickly rose through the company ranks to comptroller, division vice president, and then president.

McNamara was president of Ford for a month. John Kennedy, elected president of the United States in 1960, was impressed by McNamara's obvious talents and asked him to be his secretary of defense. Kennedy was eager to attract the "best and brightest" people in the country to his administration, and McNamara was just as eager for public service. Detroit provided him a nice living, but never a home for his intellect and ambition. He wanted more out of life than debates about the size of tail fins and bumpers. When Kennedy summoned the nation to commit itself to higher purposes, he heard the call.

McNamara immediately set out to strengthen the nation's defense by applying rational management techniques. Planning and accounting systems replaced the whims of military brass. Resources were allocated only after the military determined its missions and assessed the best means to carry them out. Forceful, decisive, self-assured, and always in command of the facts, McNamara shouldered aside generals and brought to the tradition-encrusted Pentagon a managerial revolution that attracted wide attention in the press. McNamara, concluded *Business Week*, was a "prize specimen" of a new breed of business manager who could move easily from one area into another.

One area was foreign policy. McNamara had no experience in this field, but as the new administration turned to the battle against communism in the Third World, the hard-charging secretary of defense emerged as one of its most powerful members. His role in one Third World hot spot sped his rise. In 1959, communist Fidel Castro came to power in Cuba. In 1961, the Kennedy administration tried to overthrow Castro by launching an invasion at the Bay of Pigs of Cuba by Central Intelligence Agency–trained Cuban refugees. The next year, the Soviet Union installed medium-range nuclear missiles on the island, intending to counter a massive, McNamara-initiated buildup of American long-range missiles. In the resulting face-off with the Soviets, known as the Cuban Missile Crisis, McNamara was a forceful advocate for a carefully controlled American response, including the enforcement of a naval blockade around Cuba. That show of force got the Soviets to remove the weapons in exchange for an American pledge not to invade the island again. McNamara had helped stand down the Soviets, giving rise to his reputation as a brilliant crisis manager. Meanwhile, he took a lasting lesson from the experience: The thoughtful application of force elicited a favorable reaction from the other side. Future Cold War crises could be resolved with carefully modulated responses. In a perilous world of nuclear arms, such rational crisis management was far less dangerous than solutions often advanced by liberals, who were too reluctant to use any force, and Pentagon brass, who were too eager to use excessive force. It was a lesson that McNamara would apply to another Cold War crisis halfway around the world in Vietnam.

Compared to Cuba, the problem in Vietnam seemed insignificant at first. Snaking along the South China Sea, the country had been a French colony until 1954, when France was defeated by a Vietnamese independence movement led by communist Ho Chi Minh. Under the peace settlement, Vietnam was temporarily divided, with nationwide elections to be held within two years. Ho then set up a communist government in North Vietnam with its capital at Hanoi. With American help, a non-communist but hardly democratic government arose in South Vietnam under Ngo Dinh Diem, backed by the United States as a bulwark against the spread of communism. By 1961, however, the corrupt and unpopular Diem regime confronted a growing insurgency launched by the Vietcong (South Vietnamese communists) in the countryside. The Vietcong posed a small threat at first, but Diem's military was unable to counter it.

Faced with the prospect of Diem's fall, Kennedy acted. The president and his advisers had not forgotten the devastating attacks on Democrats launched by Joseph McCarthy and other Republicans in the early 1950s for "losing" China to the communists (see Chapter 10), and they were determined to avoid similar charges now over Vietnam. Nor did they question the domino theory, the idea advanced in the early 1950s by Dwight Eisenhower, who likened Vietnam to the first of a row of dominos. If it fell to communism, according to this theory, a chain reaction of falling countries would ensue. It was a simple— some would later say simplistic—image that elevated Vietnam's strategic significance in the minds of American leaders. In 1961, the United States stepped up American assistance to Diem, including military equipment and advisers. With his forces doing the actual fighting, Vietnam would be a model of counterinsurgency war. It would show how the United States could fight against communist "wars of liberation" in the Third World.

When the Kennedy administration entered this military partnership with Diem, McNamara began to play a decisive role in Vietnam. Volunteering to look after the guerrilla war there, he made his first trip to the country in 1962. McNamara showed little interest in the political, social, or economic conditions of the Vietnamese or their history or culture. He put his faith in the power of numbers to yield objective information. He came away impressed by the progress Diem's forces were making against the Vietcong, even though the trip lasted only forty-eight hours. When asked later if staying longer might have changed his outlook, he replied, "Absolutely not."

Although followed by many others, that first trip demonstrated some of the flaws in McNamara's optimistic and arrogant approach to the war. Before he left for Vietnam, he sent a list of detailed questions he wanted answered. After he arrived, American military leaders at every stop told him what he wanted to hear. He learned that thirteen hundred strategic hamlets—villages designed to be safe from the Vietcong guerrillas—had been built by the Diem government with American assistance. In fact, only a handful were built, often through the forced relocation of villagers from ancestral homes. At one briefing, he saw maps—altered for his visit—indicating that communist-controlled areas in the country had shrunk. He heard that Diem had one hundred seventy thousand troops facing only twenty thousand insurgents, numbers that did not explain why Diem's forces were having such difficulties subduing the Vietcong. The body count—the ratio of dead friendly to unfriendly soldiers—seemed encouraging too. This statistic came to be associated with McNamara's handling of the war, but also called for skepticism. With American aid and individual promotions on the line, it was too tempting for South Vietnamese and American military personnel to fudge the numbers. Some counterinsurgency experts in Vietnam realized that the challenge there was to capture the "hearts and minds" of the peasants, a mostly nonmilitary task that was impossible to quantify. Smitten with statistics, McNamara counted enemy bodies and saw only progress. "Every quantitative measurement we have," he declared, "shows that we're winning this war."

Yet it was not so. As the Vietcong insurgency continued to grow, so did the American military commitment. By the fall of 1963, the United States had fifteen thousand advisers in Vietnam. There only to train the South Vietnamese to fight, some of them were killed on patrols against the guerrillas. McNamara would report in 1963 that "the corner has definitely been turned toward victory," but away from his statistics, there was little real evidence of that. By the end of the year, Kennedy realized that the political situation in Vietnam would make victory unlikely. Only weeks before his assassination in late 1963, he approved a coup against the unpopular and corrupt Diem regime in which the South Vietnamese leader was killed. But changing the government did not improve the political situation. In coming years, South Vietnam would be governed by a string of rulers who were no more able than Diem to gain popular support.

Meanwhile, McNamara continued as defense secretary under Lyndon B. Johnson. Kennedy's successor had little experience in foreign affairs and was primarily interested in getting his Great Society[*] enacted. Like other Americans, he had learned from World War II that appeasement only invited further aggression. Infatuated with his defense secretary's abilities, LBJ placed him in charge of Vietnam. In fact, McNamara had already turned pessimistic about South Vietnam's progress against the Vietcong. Rather than reassess his basic assumptions about the war, however, he now concluded that deeper American military commitment was necessary. Instead of assessing the commitment of the Vietnamese on both sides, asking whether Ho was only doing the Soviet Union's or China's bidding or had more compelling motives, and examining whether the United States could win militarily, McNamara would serve LBJ by trying to carefully manage the war's escalation so as to create few political ripples at home. **[See Source 1.]**

The opportunity to escalate was not long in coming. In August 1964, the military reported that two American naval vessels cruising in the Gulf of Tonkin off the coast of North Vietnam had been fired on by North Vietnamese patrol boats. LBJ quickly persuaded an outraged Congress to pass the Tonkin Gulf resolution, which gave the president a free hand to wage undeclared war in Vietnam. Only later did Americans learn that the resolution was based on faulty intelligence that a publicly unwavering McNamara actually doubted. Soon, the United States began a bombing campaign against North Vietnam, a move intended to encourage Ho to stop supplying the growing insurgency in the south. Johnson and McNamara picked the targets at weekly luncheons. Guided by the lesson of the Cuban Missile Crisis, McNamara wanted controlled escalation, not the massive use of force favored by the military. *Limited* force would move Ho to cut back military assistance to the Vietcong without provoking Chinese intervention and a wider war. Instead, McNamara got a much bigger war. The bombing campaign never led to Chinese intervention, but it failed to deter the North Vietnamese, who responded by sending their own ground forces into the south. That made the commitment of American combat troops imperative. They began arriving in the spring of 1965. By the end of the year, the United States had nearly one hundred eighty-five thousand ground troops in Vietnam. Still thinking quantitatively, McNamara supported the military's strategy of simply grinding down the enemy. To expedite a war of attrition, he backed a massive bombing campaign, in which huge B-52 bombers rained fifty powerful conventional bombs at a time on "suspected enemy concentrations." He approved the use of napalm firebombs and herbicides that stripped bare jungle vegetation to remove the guerrillas' cover. He seemed unconcerned about the effects of these weapons on civilians. Banking on superior numbers and technology to turn the tide, he never considered the war's impact on the hearts and minds of the Vietnamese.

---

[*]*Great Society:* The sweeping domestic program launched in 1964 that resulted in new civil rights laws and numerous social welfare programs, including job training, child care, and medical assistance for the elderly and poor.

"DEVASTATING THE SHIT OUT
OF THESE ... PEOPLE"

The experience of many Americans in Vietnam demonstrated the limits of McNamara's approach to war and the flawed assumptions of American policymakers. One of those Americans was a nineteen-year-old army enlistee named Jan Barry.* The son of an automobile mechanic, Barry was born in Ithaca, New York, in 1943. Shortly afterward, the family moved to the nearby town of Interlaken. Reflecting later on his childhood, Barry said he was a "stereotypical kid in a rural area." He joined the Boy Scouts, delivered newspapers, and worked at gas stations, on farms, and at a veterinarian's office. In high school, he played sports, participated in class plays and in band, and did well academically. "I grew up in a society," he said later, "in which I didn't realize that there were any limitations."

Later, Barry realized the limits imposed on his childhood environment. "Even the movies of the 1950s," he declared, "can't do justice to the deadening effect of the culture of this country." When he graduated from high school in 1961, "we had no idea you could question anything. No matter what the government did, there wasn't even the thought that you could question whatever it was." Military service, on the other hand, seemed fascinating. World War II was fresh in the minds of most Americans, including Barry's father, who had served in the navy during the war. Barry grew up hearing "all the World War II stories of my family ... plus those of the society at large." He was especially intrigued by *The Long Gray Line*, a television program in the 1950s about life at the West Point military academy. All this left him with a "romantic fixation" on a military career. Failing to get an appointment to West Point, he enlisted in the army in 1962.

Barry arrived in Vietnam on Christmas Eve that year. After completing radio school at Fort Benning, Georgia, he had opted for service in Vietnam when a friend told him that between combat pay and overseas pay he could "really clean up." Looking for "an adventure in Asia," Barry knew very little about Vietnam. When he went to the library before deployment there, he found only references to French Indochina. Nor did he learn anything about it in his army training, which was focused on war with the Soviet Union. That turned out to be a blessing. As Barry later put it, in 1962 "people ... had to find out for themselves what was going on." He would do just that.

Barry was assigned to a small, crude base camp at Nha Trang, a former French resort on the coast of the South China Sea. There he helped maintain the planes that flew supplies to outposts of the Special Forces, the counterguerrilla forces that the Kennedy administration deployed to train the South Vietnamese Army to fight the Vietcong. The United States had only about eleven thousand advisory and support troops in Vietnam and, as Barry later observed, "there probably weren't more than five hundred in any one place." When he arrived at Nha Trang, he quickly got the impression that the Americans were not taking the war seriously. He was met by a drunken commander of quarters who promptly took him to town to bar hop. After Barry made his way back to the base camp, he woke the next morning in a room filled with drunken soldiers.

Barry would see a lot more that left him unimpressed with the American involvement in Vietnam. He became convinced that most of the Americans he met had no clue

---

Jan Barry: Barry was born Jan Barry Crumb, but later took the pen name Jan Barry. He is known by that name in published works on the antiwar movement.

as to why they were in Vietnam and could not have located it on a map. Worse still, they knew little about its history or culture and had little respect for its people. Most of the Americans referred to the Vietnamese by derogatory terms such as "slopes" or "gooks." Barry, however, began to realize that he had "more of an affinity with the Vietnamese people than with Americans." He came to know the servants who worked at the base camp. He made friends with students who were aware of the repressive nature of the South Vietnamese government. He went into the homes of Vietnamese friends and met their families. He learned that many of them were "scared to death of the Saigon government" and feared for their own lives. Warned that some South Vietnamese soldiers would just as soon shoot American military personnel, he also saw little to respect in the "nasty" allies of the United States in the South Vietnamese Army. Then in 1963, Barry witnessed an antigovernment demonstration, the first of several in Nha Trang. And he watched as South Vietnamese soldiers "turn[ed] loose tanks and machine guns." As he observed later, "This was supposed to be our arsenal of democracy."

At the same time, he developed a growing respect for the Vietcong as resourceful and dedicated fighters that, like the war, the Americans were not taking seriously enough. Early one morning, Barry and the other men at the base camp were "blown out of bed" after Vietcong guerrillas sneaked through the barbed wire and blew up the airplanes. Although the guards began shooting with "no idea what they were shooting at," Barry and the other men at the base camp could not get to their weapons because they were locked up and the soldier with the key was "downtown shacked up with his girlfriend."

Talks with seasoned veterans also shaped Barry's views about the enemy and the American mission in Vietnam. Many of them, he learned, came back from the field disillusioned and convinced that the Vietcong had legitimate grievances against the government. As one of them put it to him, "We're supporting the wrong side." In Barry's mind, the rationale for American involvement in Vietnam gradually gave way. As he declared later, "We were devastating the shit out of these little people, and for what purpose?" **[See Source 2.]**

Although Barry left Vietnam in the fall of 1963 with the feeling that he was "being had," he was not ready to leave the military. In fact, he was still intent on getting into West Point, and the following spring he was accepted. He was the first student there who had been in Vietnam. His experiences in the war, however, eventually led him to question his commitment to the military. He envisioned returning to "an impossible situation" in Vietnam as a platoon leader. He also thought about spending "another thirty years of my life involved in things where we can't tell the public the truth." When he heard about the alleged attack on American warships in the Tonkin Gulf in August 1964, he did not believe that it had actually happened. As Barry's doubts about a war that "made no sense whatsoever" kept building, he finally realized that he "was in the wrong place." In 1965, he dropped out of West Point.

Barry thought little about protesting the war, though. To finish his enlistment, he had to serve with an infantry unit in Alabama, training for helicopter assaults in Vietnam. The Johnson administration was deploying the first regular combat troops to Vietnam, but Barry quickly found out that fellow infantrymen did not "want to hear about anything." Discharged in 1965, Barry headed home, moved to Manhattan the next year, and got a job at the New York Public Library. Still deeply troubled by the war, he continued to read widely about it and, as he had in Vietnam, talked to a lot of people, including reporters who had interviewed returning veterans. They told him that these vets were "more bitter than you are." Already, the antiwar movement had expanded dramatically. Beginning with teach-ins at colleges across the nation in 1965 in response to the draft and the Johnson administration's escalation of the war, the movement had grown to include a wide mix of men and women. In 1967, antiwar demonstrations in New York, Washington, D.C., and other cities drew thousands of participants.

Barry was not yet one of them. He could not imagine marching in the streets "making a fool of myself." But that would change in the spring of 1967 when antiwar activists launched a massive Spring Mobilization to protest the war with rallies across the nation. In New York City, some three hundred thousand people marched from Central Park to the United Nations, where they listened to antiwar speeches, including one delivered by Martin Luther King Jr. That demonstration drew hundreds of veterans, mostly from World War II and the Korean War, who were members of a group called Veterans for Peace in Vietnam. At the time, few Vietnam veterans had spoken out against the war. Most of them still supported it, and those who did not usually kept quiet. Seeking to meet other veterans opposed to the war, Barry went to the rally and found himself walking with a small group of other Vietnam vets under a banner that proclaimed "VIETNAM VETERANS AGAINST THE WAR!"

Marching that day, Barry felt the little group's impact. Hostile bystanders who yelled at the protesters were often silenced by the sight of Vietnam veterans protesting the very war in which they had fought. "You heard this sea change in the crowd," Barry recalled. He was now ready to do more, but he had no idea who his fellow Vietnam vets were when they disbanded at the end of the march. After several frustrating weeks making phone calls and writing letters, Barry rounded up five of them and founded the VVAW. The others then elected him president.

Barry and the other VVAW members were animated by a strong sense of purpose. They were convinced that as people learned more about the war they would turn against it. "You change the public attitude in this country things change," Barry later declared. "It wasn't any grander than that." And as McNamara approved the Pentagon's ever-larger troop requests, the organization had an ever-expanding pool of potential members. In early 1967, American forces in Vietnam jumped to three hundred eighty thousand. By the end of the year, they numbered more than a half million.

Yet Barry and the VVAW faced daunting obstacles. Overshadowed by more flamboyant and radical antiwar student protesters, VVAW members were ignored by the media. Contacting Vietnam veterans also proved frustrating. When the organization did locate them, they were often reluctant to join. As one early recruit declared, "A veteran, after two years of organization, doesn't want to be part of any organization again." Others, Barry discovered, were doubtful that collective action against the war would do any good. All the while, members of the VVAW were in an unenviable position. Like other war protesters, antiwar veterans were frequently attacked as traitors. At the same time, they were sometimes scorned by other antiwar Americans as "baby killers" for fighting in an "unjust" war against innocent civilians. When Barry attended one peace group meeting, for instance, a woman asked him, "And how many babies did you kill?"

The appearance of the *New York Times* advertisement in late 1967 was a turning point for the VVAW. Letters and calls from interested veterans flooded the organization's New York office. Newspapers and radio and television stations contacted it. And it got the attention of officials in the government. One was Senator Ernest Gruening, one of only two senators to vote against the Tonkin Gulf Resolution, who offered to meet with Barry and other VVAW leaders to help persuade the Senate Foreign Relations Committee to conduct hearings on the war.

Other officials, including FBI director J. Edgar Hoover and, of course, McNamara, were far less pleased. A rabid anti-communist, Hoover believed that communist agents had targeted the antiwar movement, and his bureau was already busy monitoring and infiltrating it. In fact, when McNamara requested an investigation of the VVAW after the publication of its *New York Times* ad, the FBI had already conducted a two-month investigation of the group and concluded that its leaders had no known ties to communist groups. Meanwhile, McNamara's concern about the VVAW had less to do with a fear of communist subversion than his own growing doubts about the war itself.

"OVER 335,000 OF OUR BUDDIES HAVE BEEN KILLED OR WOUNDED"

To many Americans opposed to the war, Robert McNamara represented an alliance of Pentagon "warmongers" and war-profiteering corporations. He seemed the very symbol of a technological war waged by a military-industrial establishment run by men with perfectly combed hair. Despite his continued upbeat pronouncements about the war, though, he knew by the fall of 1967 that he had guided the United States into a hopeless swamp. For a while, he held out hope for an acceptable diplomatic settlement, but now he did not even believe that was possible. He realized the North Vietnamese, unlike the Soviets in the Cuban Missile Crisis, were not going to respond in a "rational" way to the increased application of American force. In October, McNamara proposed an end to the escalation of American troops and the fruitless bombing of North Vietnam. The time had come, he concluded, to turn more of the fighting over to South Vietnamese forces and find a way out. Unfortunately, he also believed that the antiwar movement would only erode American morale and steel the enemy's resolve and thus make *any* diplomatic settlement impossible. And it did not help that Vietnam veterans had now organized against the war. As he declared to LBJ, the war's unpopularity "generates patience in Hanoi." **[See Source 3.]**

McNamara never informed the public, however, of his belief that the war could not be won. Nor did he level with his troops that the sacrifice asked of them would not lead to victory. In fact, McNamara never seriously considered the war's impact on his own troops. For years, he had received feedback in statistics generated by the military: body counts, kill ratios, and bomb tonnages. Armed with these numbers, the stat control Whiz Kid–turned war manager believed that he understood a technological war of attrition better than the soldiers slogging through Vietnamese villages, rice paddies, and jungles. He had little idea of the corrosive impact on young troops of a guerrilla war against an elusive enemy who easily blended into the civilian population. Those asked to fight in "McNamara's war" found themselves engaged in a seemingly endless succession of patrols, ambushes, and firefights. In the words of one veteran, Vietnam was "an exhausting, indecisive war of attrition in which we fought for no cause other than our own survival." **[See Source 4.]**

Nor did McNamara consider the military draft's impact on the composition of American forces or the morale of the troops. Because mostly white college students were exempt from the draft, the ranks of American soldiers by the late 1960s were filled disproportionately with working-class and poor draftees, often black or Hispanic. The civil rights movement, racial violence at home, and outspoken opposition to the war by such prominent black figures as Muhammad Ali, who refused to serve in the armed forces, and Martin Luther King, Jr. spilled over to Vietnam in growing racial consciousness and rising racial tensions among American troops. As morale sank, drug abuse among draftees rose. They also became more willing to defy their commanding officers, often white and college-educated. By 1968, cases of desertion, insubordination, and even fragging—draftees killing their own officers with fragmentation grenades—increased dramatically. The nation's social divisions and racial tensions, in short, had come to the battlefield. **[See Source 5.]**

At the same time, a growing division over the war among Americans brought the conflict in Vietnam home to the United States. In 1968, communist forces launched a massive military campaign known as the Tet Offensive. A well-coordinated North Vietnamese and Vietcong attack during the Tet (Vietnamese New Year's) holiday, it was aimed at Saigon and numerous provincial capitals in South Vietnam. American forces eventually repelled the offensive and inflicted heavy casualties on the communist forces, but the enemy had demonstrated enormous offensive power. In just a few weeks, the heavy fighting undermined McNamara's and Johnson's optimistic predictions about the war and led many Americans to conclude that McNamara, Johnson, and military leaders had deliberately misled them. With the death toll rising and victory nowhere in sight, many more Americans now saw their nation's involvement in Vietnam as a terrible mistake. A month after the communist offensive and after rejecting disengagement, Johnson relieved McNamara of his duties.

After Tet, the antiwar movement exploded, sparking more protests, increasing violence, and political turmoil. Faced with rising opposition to the war, LBJ announced shortly after McNamara's departure that he would not seek reelection in 1968. That June, antiwar Democratic presidential candidate Robert Kennedy was gunned down in Los Angeles after winning the California primary. Later that summer, police launched a bloody assault on antiwar demonstrators at the Democratic Convention in Chicago, watched live by millions of shocked television viewers. That fall, Republican Richard Nixon, appealing to growing disillusionment with the war and widespread unease at rising violence at home, narrowly defeated Johnson's vice president, Hubert Humphrey, in the presidential race with a promise to end the war and restore "law and order."

For the next four years, Nixon worked to achieve what he called "peace with honor." His strategy called for "Vietnamizing" the war by gradually withdrawing American forces, turning over more of the fighting to the South Vietnamese, and negotiating with the North Vietnamese. The goal was to secure a "decent interval" between complete American withdrawal and South Vietnam's inevitable fall—a period long enough for people not to associate one with the other. But this interval would be created only if the North Vietnamese allowed South Vietnamese military forces to stand for a time against the Vietcong. To achieve that, the enemy had to be convinced that Americans retained the will to carry on the fight. Like McNamara, Nixon and his top aides feared that the antiwar movement only boosted the enemy's patience.

Yet Nixon's moves to achieve a "decent interval" only stoked antiwar sentiment further. To persuade the North Vietnamese to withdraw their own troops from the south, Nixon stepped up McNamara's massive bombing of North Vietnam. To root out alleged communist sanctuaries in Cambodia, he ordered an American invasion of that country in the spring of 1970. Meanwhile, revelations in 1971 that American soldiers had massacred civilians at the village of My Lai in South Vietnam in 1968 turned more Americans against the war. So did the publication in 1971 of the *Pentagon Papers*, a secret Defense Department study ordered by McNamara in 1967 that revealed the deception by American leaders regarding the war.

After these events, Barry's organization moved to the forefront of the antiwar movement. In late 1970, the VVAW began numerous meetings around the country in which veterans testified about atrocities committed in Vietnam. These gatherings brought new recruits to the organization. So did a VVAW advertisement in *Playboy* magazine in late 1970 that boldly proclaimed, "Over 335,000 of Our Buddies Have Been Killed or

Wounded." By early 1971, the VVAW had nearly ten thousand members and chapters in every state.

Yet Barry and other leaders were frustrated. The organization's atrocity investigations had drawn only limited media attention, and Nixon's Vietnamizarion policy had convinced many Americans that the war was ending. After the widespread protests against the invasion of Cambodia in the spring of 1970, the antiwar protests on campus and elsewhere began to subside, even though more than three hundred thirty thousand American troops still fought in Vietnam in early 1971. At one meeting, Barry recalled, VVAW members were "hollering and screaming" at one another as they debated what to do when a recent VVAW recruit named John Kerry suggested that the group's members march on Washington to take their case to Congress. That April, twenty-three hundred of them, some in wheelchairs, gathered at the Capitol to launch what the VVAW called "a limited incursion into the country of Congress." During the week-long protest, many of the veterans threw away their war medals and ribbons, and Kerry himself spoke before the Senate Foreign Relations Committee against what he called a "barbaric" war. Carried live to a nationwide television audience, that testimony was the culmination of a long effort to bring Vietnam vets before the committee that had started when Barry met with Senator Ernest Gruening after the publication of the VVAW's *New York Times* ad in 1967.

The VVAW's "incursion" into Washington, D.C., Kerry's testimony, and the massive antiwar rally that brought perhaps a half million protesters to the Capitol Mall a few days later finally put the media spotlight on Barry's organization. Nightly television newscasts led with the veterans' protest. Because veterans were at the center of this protest, press commentary was overwhelmingly favorable. Afterward, membership soared.

At the same time, the VVAW became a high-profile target for the Nixon administration. In fact, no antiwar group caused more concern in Nixon and his top aides, who knew that its members, unlike student antiwar protesters, could not be labeled draft dodgers. As McNamara had earlier, Nixon and his aides turned to the FBI, which infiltrated and harassed the VVAW. By 1972, that infiltration led to the indictment of several VVAW members for allegedly conspiring to disrupt the Republican Convention that summer.

In the end, though, divisions among veterans themselves were a bigger threat to the VVAW than was government harassment. By the early 1970s, the organization's membership reflected the growing numbers of draftees from poor and working-class backgrounds. As the VVAW grew, it attracted more working-class recruits, who resented the participation of former officers. Disgusted by in-fighting in the organization, Barry insisted that members set aside their differences and focus on educating the public as "moral witnesses" against the war, but many militant new recruits disagreed. As one VVAW member put it, Barry's "moral witness [approach] was completely out of sync with the gritty, blue-collar temper of the antiwar veteran." By 1971, many veterans were far more angry than Barry and other VVAW organizers had been in 1967. That year, more than twenty-five thousand military personnel were dishonorably discharged. According to one army survey, nearly half of all troops were engaged in illegal drug use. Many of them would have little patience with educating Americans one by one about the war.

Race and gender divisions also worked against the VVAW, which never recruited more than 1 percent of all Vietnam veterans. When the group's membership peaked at roughly twenty-five thousand in late 1971, half of its members were white males from blue-collar backgrounds. Although Latinos and blacks joined the VVAW and several became leaders in it, the organization recruited relatively few nonwhites and very few women. Many Hispanic veterans were caught up in issues affecting their own community particularly the long strike by Cesar Chavez's United Farm Workers' Union against the growers in California. Many antiwar black veterans were drawn to the Black Panther Party while others perceived that the VVAW ignored racial issues. As one black veteran told a VVAW gathering, "You ain't got no black people behind you, because you forgot about racism, man." Many of the roughly eleven thousand female veterans who served in Vietnam often felt unwelcome as well. When one army nurse came to a VVAW meeting to help plan a march on the White House, she was told that she could not participate in the protest because she was not a vet. When she countered that she served in Vietnam, a VVAW member told her that she "didn't look like a vet" and that Nixon and the media would accuse the group of "swelling the ranks with non-vets." She left the meeting and never joined the organization.

Frustrated by the VVAW's internal politics, Barry stepped down as the group's president in 1971. When the Nixon administration officially ended American involvement in the war in 1973 with the signing of the Paris Peace Accords,* he left the organization he had founded seven years earlier. The VVAW would live on until the end of the century fighting for veterans' rights, but he was convinced that its usefulness had ended. Barry, who pursued a career in journalism and later became an antinuclear activist, could leave with some satisfaction. By then, fifty-eight thousand Americans and maybe a million Vietnamese lay dead. Perhaps more than any other antiwar group, however, the VVAW had helped erode public support for the war, making it more difficult for American leaders to prolong the fighting and exact an even higher toll.

When South Vietnam fell to communist forces just two years after the peace agreement, Robert McNamara was serving as president of the World Bank, the international bank established by the United States and other nations to extend loans to developing countries. Appointed by Lyndon Johnson when he stepped down as defense secretary, McNamara served there until 1981, as the bank became controversial for its role in saddling poor countries with high debt. He rarely spoke about the Vietnam War. In his memoir published in 1995, though, he wrote that American leaders were "terribly wrong" and had gotten involved in a country they knew nothing about, a confession condemned by many angry critics. McNamara, they insisted, had waited far too long to speak out.

•PRIMARY SOURCES•

Source 1:   *Robert McNamara Assesses the Situation in Vietnam* (1964)

Robert McNamara's memorandum to Lyndon Johnson in March 1964 summarized the situation in Vietnam and recommended specific actions to assist the government of South Vietnam in its growing conflict with Vietcong guerrillas. What does this excerpt from that memo reveal about McNamara's

SOURCE: John P. Glennon, ed., FOREIGN RELATIONS OF THE UNITED STATES, 1964–1968 (Washington, D.C.: United States Government Printing Office, 1992), I, pp. 154, 155, 159.

Paris Peace Accords: The agreement signed by representatives of the United States, North Vietnam, and South Vietnam that provided for an end to American military involvement in Vietnam, but did not require North Vietnamese troops to withdraw from the south.

assumptions regarding the stakes in Vietnam? What actions does he recommend if the situation there should deteriorate further?

We seek an independent non-communist South Vietnam. We do not require that it serve as a Western base or as a member of a Western Alliance. South Vietnam must be free, however, to accept outside assistance as required to maintain its security. This assistance should be able to take the form not only of economic and social measures but also police and military help to root out and control insurgent elements.

Unless we can achieve this objective in South Vietnam, almost all of Southeast Asia will probably fall under communist dominance (all of Vietnam, Laos, and Cambodia), accommodate to communism so as to remove effective U.S. and anti-communist influence (Burma), or fall under the domination of forces not now explicitly communist but likely then to become so (Indonesia taking over Malaysia). Thailand might hold for a period with our help, but would be under grave pressure. Even the Philippines would become shaky, and the threat to India to the west, Australia and New Zealand to the south, and Taiwan, Korea, and Japan to the north and east would be greatly increased.

All of these consequences would probably have been true even if the U.S. had not since 1954, and especially since 1961, become so heavily engaged in South Vietnam. However, that fact accentuates the impact of a communist South Vietnam not only in Asia, but in the rest of the world, where the South Vietnam conflict is regarded as a test case of U.S. capacity to help a nation meet a communist "war of liberation." ...

We are now trying to help South Vietnam defeat the Viet Cong, supported from the North, by means short of the unqualified use of U.S. combat forces. We are not acting against North Vietnam except by a very modest "covert" program operated by South Vietnamese (and a few Chinese Nationalists)—a program so limited that it is unlikely to have any significant effect....

The key elements in the present situation are as follows:

A. The military tools and concepts of the GVN*/US effort are generally sound and adequate. Substantially more can be done in the effective employment of military forces and in the economic and civic action areas. These improvements may require some selective increases in the U.S. presence, but it does not appear likely that major equipment replacement and additions in U.S. personnel are indicated under current policy.

B. The U.S. policy of reducing existing personnel where South Vietnamese are in a position to assume the functions is still sound.... However, the U.S. should continue to reiterate that it will provide all the assistance and advice required to do the job regardless of how long it takes....

We have given serious thought to all the implications and ways of carrying out direct military action against North Vietnam in order to supplement the counterinsurgency program in South Vietnam....

This program would go beyond reacting on a tit-for-tat basis. It would include air attacks against military and possibly industrial targets.... Before this program could be implemented it would be necessary to provide some additional air defense for South Vietnam and to ready U.S. forces in the Pacific for possible escalation.

The analysis of the more serious of these military actions ... revealed the extremely delicate nature of such operations, both from the military and political standpoints. There

---

*GVN: Government of South Vietnam.

would be the problem of marshalling the case to justify such action, the problem of communist escalation, and the problem of dealing with the pressures for premature or "stacked" negotiations. We would have to calculate the effect of such military actions against a specified political objective. That objective, while being cast in terms of eliminating North Vietnamese control and direction of the insurgency, would in practical terms be directed toward collapsing the morale and the self-assurance of the Viet Cong cadres now operating in South Vietnam.

Source 2: *Jan Barry Assesses the Situation in Vietnam* (1997)

In an oral history of the VVAW, Jan Barry discussed what led him to question the American rationale for fighting in South Vietnam. What does the following excerpt reveal about factors regarding the war that were overlooked by Robert McNamara in the early 1960s?

I spent an awful lot of time talking to officers and sergeants about the military. Here I am with people who were through some of the worst shit in World War II and Korea. The top professionals the military's got to send out to this end of the world are shaking and scratching their heads. This was crazy. This did not make any sense compared to their previous experience.

The ones who were the real gung-ho professionals, who were out there pressing it, came back very disillusioned. They kept saying, "We're backing the wrong side. The other side is raising the right issues on behalf of the people here, and the side we're backing is a dictatorship." One day, I was speaking to a Special Forces sergeant, and he said, "I been out there; we're supporting the wrong side." He said, "These [NLF forces] out there, who are from the south, that didn't come from anyplace else, are responding to these legitimate grievances that these people have against the Saigon government." He explained the whole thing to me. He put the pieces together. He says, "When you go out there, these villagers' only protection is the NLF against this police state in Saigon. What we're here for is the palace guard of a police state." He did not like to be a protector of a police state, which was the first time anybody ever said that in so many words. I had enough understanding of things to understand that part of it, and you could see for yourself that in essence, we were supporting this rotten dictatorship.

It became very clear that what was being claimed in Washington and out of Saigon headquarters had nothing to do with what we could see for ourselves. McNamara [Robert McNamara, secretary of defense] and various other VIPs would come through, and there were warnings that no one was to tell these people what was really going on. I had also heard from people who had been stationed in South Korea, Turkey, and other places that this was not unusual, that we had two different agendas: one for the public and what the real agenda was.

Slowly, one by one by one, everything was undermined as to the presumed reasons we were there. We were devastating the shit out of these little people, for what purpose? After some of them became your friends, you had to think about what was your purpose. We weren't in any way helping these people.

SOURCE: Richard Stacewicz, WINTER SOLDIERS: AN ORAL HISTORY OF THE VIETNAM VETERANS AGAINST THE WAR (New York: Twayne Publishers, 1997), pp. 90–91.

Source 3:   *McNamara Offers a Bleak Assessment* (1967)

In May 1967, McNamara wrote another memorandum for Johnson that revealed his growing doubts about a positive outcome from American military actions in Vietnam. On what basis does he draw his conclusions? How do they compare to the assessment in Source 1?

The Vietnam war is unpopular in this country. It is becoming increasingly unpopular as it escalates—causing more American casualties, more fear of its growing into a wider war, more privation of the domestic sector, and more distress at the amount of suffering being visited on the non-combatants in Vietnam, South and North. Most Americans do not know how we got where we are, and most, without knowing why, but taking advantage of hindsight, are convinced that somehow we should not have gotten this deeply in. All want the war ended and expect their President to end it. Successfully. Or else.

This state of mind in the U.S. generates impatience in the political structure of the United States. It unfortunately also generates patience in Hanoi....

The "big war" in the South between the U.S. and the North Vietnamese military units (NVA) is going well. We staved off military defeat in 1965; we gained the military initiative in 1966; and since then we have been hurting the enemy badly spoiling some of his ability to strike. "In the final analysis," General Westmoreland said, "we are fighting a war of attrition." In that connection, the enemy has been losing between 1500 and 2000 killed-in-action a week, while we and the South Vietnamese have been losing 175 and 250 respectively....

Regrettably, the "other war" against the VC is still not going well. Corruption is widespread. Real government control is confined to enclaves. There is rot in the fabric. Our efforts to enliven the moribund political infrastructure have been matched by VC efforts—more now through coercion than was formerly the case. So the VC are hurting badly too....

Hanoi's attitude towards negotiations has never been soft nor open-minded. Any concession on their part would involve an enormous loss of face.... They seem uninterested in a political settlement and determined to match U.S. military expansion of the conflict.... Hanoi appears to have concluded that she cannot secure her objectives at the conference table and has reaffirmed her strategy of seeking to erode our ability to remain in the South. The Hanoi leadership has apparently decided that it has no choice but to submit to the increased bombing. There continues to be no sign that the bombing has reduced Hanoi's will to resist or her ability to ship the necessary supplies south. Hanoi shows no signs of ending the large war and advising the VC to melt into the jungles. The North Vietnamese believe they are right; they consider the Ky regime to be puppets; they believe the world is with them and that the American public will not have staying power against them....

The war in Vietnam is acquiring a momentum of its own that must be stopped. Dramatic increases in U.S. troop deployments, in attacks on the North, or in ground actions in Laos or Cambodia are not necessary and are not the answer. The enemy can absorb them or counter them, bogging us down further and risking even more serious escalation of the war.

Source: John P. Glennon, ed., FOREIGN RELATIONS OF THE UNITED STATES, 1964–1968 (Washington, D.C.: United States Government Printing Office, 1992), V, pp. 424, 425, 426, 437.

Source 4:   *A Marine Describes a Technological War of Attrition* (1977)

Philip Caputo was a Marine lieutenant in Vietnam in 1965. His memoir, A Rumor of War, *describes his experiences there. What does this source reveal about the impact of the American counterguerrilla strategy in Vietnam on the soldiers fighting there? What does it reveal about aspects of the war that McNamara missed?*

Everything rotted and corroded quickly over there: bodies, boot leather, canvas, metal, morals. Scorched by the sun, wracked by the wind and rain of the monsoon, fighting in alien swamps and jungles, our humanity rubbed off of us as the protective bluing rubbed off the barrels of our rifles. We were fighting in the cruelest kind of conflict, a people's war. It was no orderly campaign, as in Europe, but a war for survival waged in a wilderness without rules or laws; a war in which each soldier fought for his own life and the lives of the men beside him, not caring who he killed in that personal cause or how many or in what manner and feeling only contempt for those who sought to impose on his savage struggle the mincing distinctions of civilized warfare—that code of battlefield ethics that attempted to humanize an essentially inhuman war. According to those "rules of engagement," it was morally right to shoot an unarmed Vietnamese who was running, but wrong to shoot one who was standing or walking; it was wrong to shoot an enemy prisoner at close range, but right for a sniper at long range to kill an enemy soldier who was no more able than a prisoner to defend himself; it was wrong for infantrymen to destroy a village with white-phosphorus grenades, but right for a fighter pilot to drop napalm on it. Ethics seemed to be a matter of distance and technology. You could never go wrong if you killed people at long range with sophisticated weapons. And then there was that inspiring order issued by General Greene: kill VC. In the patriotic fever of the Kennedy years, we had asked, "What can we do for our country?" and our country answered, "Kill VC." That was the strategy, the best our best military minds could come up with: organized butchery. But organized or not, butchery was butchery, so who was to speak of rules and ethics in a war that had none?

Source 5:   *A Black Soldier Sees Another Enemy* (1984)

Richard Ford III served in South Vietnam in 1967 and 1968. After volunteering for reconnaissance patrols, the army sent him to a Special Forces school at Nha Trang, Jan Barry's former base. There, Ford and six other African-American soldiers trained together. In the following excerpt from an oral history about black soldiers in Vietnam, he recalls their experience at Nha Trang. What does his account reveal about racial tensions among American troops in Vietnam? How would you compare the effects of the war revealed here with those revealed in Source 4?

Source 4: Philip Caputo, A RUMOR OF WAR, (New York: Henry Holt and Company, Inc., 1977).

Source 5: From BLOODS: AN ORAL HISTORY OF THE VIETNAM WAR BY BLACK VETERANS by Wallace Terry, copyright © 1984 by Wallace Terry. Used by permission of Random House, Inc.

I didn't believe Nha Trang was still part of Vietnam, because they had barracks, hot water, had mess halls with three hot meals and air conditioning. Nha Trang was like a beach, a resort. They was ridin' around on paved streets. They be playing football and basketball. Nobody walked around with weapons. They were white. And that's what really freaked me out. All these white guys in the rear.

They told us we had to take our weapons to the armory and lock 'em up. We said naw. So they decided to let us keep our weapons till we went to this show.

It was a big club. Looked like 80 or 90 guys. Almost everybody is white. They had girls dancing and groups singin'. They reacted like we was some kind of animals, like we these guys from the boonies. They a little off. I don't know if I was paranoid or what. But they stare at you when you first come in. All of us got drunk and carryin' on. I didn't get drunk, 'cause I didn't drink. And we started firin' the weapons at the ceiling. Telling everybody to get out. "Y'all not in the war." We was frustrated because all these whites were in the back having a big show. And they were clerks. Next thing I know, about a hundred MPs all around the club. Well, they took our weapons. That was all....

In the field most of the guys stayed high. Lot of them couldn't face it. In a sense, if you was high, it seemed like a game you was in. You didn't take it serious. It stopped a lot of nervous breakdown....

We had a medic that give us a shot of morphine anytime you want one. I'm not talkin' about for wounded. I'm talkin' about when you want to just get high. So you can face it.

In the rear sometimes we get a grenade, dump the gunpowder out, break the firing pin. Then you'll go inside one of them little bourgeois clubs. Or go in the barracks where the supply guys are, sitting around playing bid whist and doing nothing. We act real crazy. Yell out, "Kill all y'all motherfuckers." Pull the pin and throw the grenade. And everybody would haul ass and get out. It would make a little pop sound. And we would laugh. You didn't see anybody jumpin' on them grenades.

One time in the field, though, I saw a white boy jump on a grenade. But I believe he was pushed. It ain't kill him. He lost both his legs.

The racial incidents didn't happen in the field. Just when we went to the back. It wasn't so much that they were against us. It was just that we felt that we were being taken advantage of, 'cause it seemed like more blacks in the field than in the rear.

In the rear we saw a bunch of rebel flags. They didn't mean nothing by the rebel flag. It was just saying we for the South. It didn't mean that they hated blacks. But after you in the field, you took the flags very personally.

One time we saw these flags in Nha Trang on the MP barracks. They was playing hillbilly music. Had their shoes off dancing. Had nice, pretty bunks. Mosquito nets over top the bunks. And had the nerve to have this camouflaged covers. Air conditioning. Cement floors. We just came out the jungles. We dirty, we smelly, hadn't shaved. We just went off. Said, "Y'all the real enemy. We stayin' here." We turned the bunks over, started tearing up the stereo. They just ran out. Next morning, they shipped us back up....

Right after Tet, the mail chopper got shot down. We moved to Tam Ky. We didn't have any mail in about three weeks. Then this lady by the name of Hanoi Helen come on the radio. She had a letter belong to Sir Drawers. From the chopper that was shot down. She read the letter from his wife about how she miss him. But that didn't unsettle the brothers as much as when she got on the air after Martin Luther King died, and they was rioting back home. She was saying, "Soul brothers, go home. Whitey raping your mothers and your daughters, burning down your homes. What you over here for? This is not your war. The war is a trick of the Capitalist empire to get rid of the blacks." I really thought—I really started believing it, because it was too many blacks than there should be in infantry....

I remember February 20. Twentieth of February. We went to this village outside Duc Pho. Search and destroy. It was suppose to have been VC sympathizers. They sent fliers to the people telling them to get out. Anybody else there, you have to consider them as a VC.

It was a little straw-hut village. Had a little church at the end with this big Buddha. We didn't see anybody in the village. But I heard movement in the rear of this hut. I just opened up the machine gun. You ain't wanna open the door, and then you get blown away. Or maybe they booby-trapped.

Anyway, this little girl screamed. I went inside the door. I'd done already shot her, and she was on top of the old man. She was trying to shield the old man. He looked like he could have been about eighty years old. She was about seven. Both of them was dead. I killed an old man and a little girl in the hut by accident.

I started feeling funny. I wanted to explain to someone. But everybody was there, justifying my actions, saying, "It ain't your fault. They had no business there." But I just—I ain't wanna hear it. I wanted to go home then.

It bothers me now. But so many things happened after that, you really couldn't lay on one thing. You had to keep going.

The flame throwers came in, and we burnt the hamlet. Burnt up everything. They had a lot of rice. We opened the bags, just throw it all over the street. Look for tunnels. Killing animals. Killing all the livestock. Guys would carry chemicals that they would put in the well. Poison the water so they couldn't use it. So they wouldn't come back to use it, right? And it was trifling.

They killed some more people there. Maybe 12 or 14 more. Old people and little kids that wouldn't leave. I guess their grandparents. See, people that were old in Vietnam couldn't leave their village. It was like a ritual. They figured that this'll pass. We'll come and move on....

We had a lot of new guys in the company that had never seen a dead NVA. And the officer was telling them to get in line. If they didn't do anything, he wanted them to go past and look at him anyway.

That's how you do this game Guts.

So they took the NVA's clothes off and tied him to a tree. Everybody in the unit got in line. At least 200 guys.

The first guy took a bayonet and plucked his eye out. Put the bayonet at the corner of the eye and popped it. And I was amazed how large your eyeball was.

Then he sliced his ear off. And he hit him in the mouth with his .45. Loosened the teeth, pulled them out.

Then they sliced his tongue. They cut him all over. And we put that insect repellent all over him. It would just irritate his body, and his skin would turn white.

Then he finally passed out.

Some guys be laughing and playing around. But a lotta guys, maybe 30, would get sick, just vomit and nauseated and passed out.

The officer be yelling, "That could be your best friend on that tree. That could be you. You ever get captured, this could be you."

I don't know when he died. But most of the time he was alive. He was hollering and cursing. They put water on him and shaking him and bringin' him back. Finally they tortured him to death. Then we had to bury him. Bury both him and the lieutenant.

A couple of days later we found three guys from the 101st that was hung up on a tree, that had been tortured. Hands was tied. Feet was tied. Blood was everywhere. All you saw was a big, bloody body. Just butchered up. That's how they left GIs for us to see.

QUESTIONS TO CONSIDER

1. What do the biographical essay and primary sources in this chapter reveal about why the United States fought in Vietnam? What do they reveal about why American forces fought as they did?

2. How would you characterize Robert McNamara's approach to the war in Vietnam? How did his training and background influence that approach? Were antiwar protesters correct to see him as a fitting symbol for that war and the way the United States fought it?

3. What were Jan Barry's and the VVAW's criticisms of the American involvement in Vietnam? To what extent did they reflect his experiences there?

4. What do the experiences of Jan Barry and other American personnel who served in Vietnam reveal about the problems involved in fighting there? What do they reveal about why the war turned out as it did?

5. What do the essay and sources in this chapter reveal about why the Vietnam War and antiwar movement were—and remain—so controversial?

FOR FURTHER READING

Christian G. Appy, *Working-Class War: American Combat Soldiers and Vietnam* (Chapel Hill: University of North Carolina Press, 1993), examines the experiences of working-class soldiers, who came to make up the majority of the American troops in Vietnam.

David Barrett, *Uncertain Warriors: Lyndon Johnson and His Vietnam Advisers* (Lawrence: University of Kansas Press, 1993), provides a concise analysis of the Johnson administration's decision-making regarding Vietnam.

David Halberstam, *The Best and the Brightest* (New York: Random House, 1972), offers one of the most engaging treatments of McNamara and the other advisers around John Kennedy and Lyndon Johnson.

George Herring, *America's Longest War: The United States in Vietnam, 1950–1975,* rev. ed. (Boston: McGraw-Hill, Inc., 2002), offers a useful overview of the war and its impact.

Andrew E. Hunt, *The Turning: A History of Vietnam Veterans Against the War* (New York: New York University Press, 1999), provides a brief look at one of the most important antiwar groups.

Deborah Shapley, *Promise and Power: The Life and Times of Robert McNamara* (Boston: Little, Brown and Company, 1993), submits a thorough and illuminating examination of McNamara and his role as secretary of defense.

13

From Mystique to Militance: Betty Friedan and Gloria Steinem

When Betty Friedan strode into the packed New York hotel conference room, she needed no introduction. Friedan was the founder of the National Organization for Women (NOW) and the author of *The Feminine Mystique*, the 1963 best seller that analyzed the widespread discontent of American housewives. In fact, the waiting reporters had often called her the mother of the modern women's movement. All that, though, was in the past. On this day in July 1972, the press was interested only in what Friedan had to say about feminist Gloria Steinem, who had just published the first regular issue of *Ms.* magazine and spoken at the Democratic National Convention. For several years, Friedan had listened to Steinem's attacks on the family, on men, and on women who wanted to make husbands equal partners in marriage. Now she was fed up. Women were not "forever wronged by men," Friedan declared. Feminists like Steinem who insisted otherwise were "female chauvinist boors" who threatened to corrupt the women's movement and create a backlash against it.

As she looked out at the crush of reporters, Friedan knew how many of them would interpret this attack. The often-abrasive Friedan, they would say, was jealous because Steinem had grabbed the media spotlight from her. Young, chic, and glamorous, Steinem had once worked as a Playboy Bunny to write an exposé of the Playboy Club's treatment of female employees. In just the past year, her smiling face had appeared on the covers of *Newsweek* and *New Woman*. She had even pushed aside the movie stars and models who frequently graced *McCall's* cover. Steinem was "the most visible of the activists," the magazine had announced in early 1972 as it named her its "Woman of the Year." She looked, *McCall's* proclaimed, "like a life-size, counterculture Barbie Doll." Friedan knew she never could have landed a job as a Playboy Bunny. Yet she also

AP Images

Betty Friedan

Bettmann/Corbis

Gloria Steinem

knew that her most important differences with Steinem were ideological, not personal. Steinem and many younger feminists focused too much on fighting private injuries committed by men against women. Instead, Friedan believed, the women's movement had to focus on changing women's public lives in politics and the workplace. Its top priority had to be an end to legal gender discrimination. Women's personal lives would improve after the battle for legal equality was won, and that would never happen if Steinem and other feminists focused on their personal grievances and alienated men with antimale rhetoric. Friedan also knew that the soft-spoken Steinem would not respond to her accusations. Confrontation was not Steinem's style. Claiming to have laryngitis, Steinem merely issued a press release. "Having been falsely accused … of liking men too much," it declared, "I am now being falsely accused … of not liking them enough." Steinem could remain silent, but that was not Friedan's style. The women's movement, she believed, was at a crossroads. And she was not going to stand by quietly as Steinem and other feminists destroyed what she had worked so hard to build.

"THE PROBLEM THAT HAS NO NAME"

Betty Friedan had never been without strong opinions or a willingness to express them. Born in 1921, the daughter of a Peoria, Illinois, jewelry store owner, Betty grew up in comfortable but challenging circumstances. Her father, Harry Goldstein, was a Jewish immigrant from Russia who made sure that family dinners were occupied with serious discussions. He also demanded that Betty respond thoughtfully to his questions. Meanwhile, Betty and her mother fought constantly. Pretty and proper, Miriam Goldstein saw her daughter as unattractive, and the two frequently clashed over her appearance and dress. As a child, Betty also witnessed her parents' bitter fights, often provoked by her mother's outbursts. The daughter of a prominent physician, Miriam was a college graduate who had written for a newspaper society page until her marriage. She was also used to a certain lifestyle. The Goldsteins lived in an eight-room house in an upper-middle-class area of Peoria. After Betty and her younger sister and brother were born, Miriam devoted her time to golf, bridge, and shopping. She continued to spend even as business turned down during the Depression. Looking back much later on her parents' stormy relationship, Friedan observed that her own feminism "began in my mother's discontent." After Miriam quit her job at her husband's insistence, Friedan concluded, she had too much power inside her home and too little outside it. Her mother had "a typical female disorder"—that is, "impotent rage," which was often directed at her husband.

Isolation compounded Betty's unhappiness at home. In high school, her grade school friends joined sororities that excluded blacks and Jews. Feeling alone, Goldstein immersed herself in books. In fact, she read so much that her parents worried that there was something wrong and took her to a therapist. "It doesn't look nice for a girl to be so bookish," her father told her. Schoolwork, however, was her escape. She vowed that if her fellow students did not like her, they would at least respect her. The precocious child became a star student, skipped one grade, and wound up as one of the class valedictorians.

Betty Goldstein found college liberating. In 1938, she entered Smith, a women's college in Massachusetts. Many of Smith's professors were women. At a time when most women were expected to become housewives and mothers, they encouraged their female students' professional and intellectual ambitions. At Smith, Goldstein grew more interested in social and political issues. She also excelled academically. She became editor of the *Smith College Monthly* and the campus newspaper. Her first love, however, was psychology, and she was known on campus as "the psychology brain." Her last year, she submitted a thesis that one Smith administrator said "could stand for a Ph.D."

Her future seemed certain. After graduating summa cum laude in 1942, Goldstein headed to the University of California at Berkeley for graduate study in psychology. She won a scholarship that would have supported her until she finished her doctorate, but she turned it down. Later, in *The Feminine Mystique*, Friedan revealed that she had fallen in love with a jealous physics graduate student who told her she had to choose between the scholarship and him. As she related, she was in the grip of the "feminine mystique"—the widespread belief that women could find happiness only as wives and mothers. Her decision to leave graduate school may have been more complicated, however. As a senior at Smith, Goldstein had already said that a career as an academic no longer interested her. Furthermore, when she left Berkeley, she left academia *and* her boyfriend.

Soon, however, Goldstein was following the well-trod postwar path into marriage, motherhood, and suburban life. Fleeing Berkeley for New York City, she went to work for a radical labor newspaper. In 1946, she met Carl Friedan, who had only recently returned from the war in Europe. They were married within a year, and two years after that, their first child was born. Betty continued to work, writing for another labor publication. When she got pregnant again several years later, she was fired—not an uncommon experience for women at the time. By then, she had already found a new career as a housewife. The Friedans moved into an apartment in Queens and then to Rockland County, north of New York City. There Betty busied herself restoring the couple's old Victorian house on the Hudson River. Like millions of other postwar mothers, she diligently read *Baby and Child Care*, Dr. Benjamin Spock's guide to child rearing, which advised mothers of small children not to work outside the home. She even took classes at a local maternity center and at a cooking school.

Still, Betty Friedan never fell completely under the spell of the "feminine mystique" or the middle-class, suburban conformity that she later described in her book. For one thing, her reporting on workers' struggles stood in stark contrast to the flood of articles in postwar popular magazines promoting the joys of motherhood. And although the Friedans were part of the massive postwar migration of new parents to the suburbs, in many ways their experience was not typical. In Rockland County, they lived in a village of less than four hundred residents, many of whom were artists and writers. Betty pursued a successful freelance career writing for popular publications such as *Cosmopolitan*, *Harper's Magazine*, and *Mademoiselle*, which helped teach the legions of mostly white, middle-class, suburban women how to live. To millions of women who had taken wartime jobs, these magazines preached that they could find happiness as wives, mothers, and consumers in the home. In *The Feminine Mystique*, Friedan wrote that her articles had helped create an "almost childlike" picture of the modern housewife who was "gaily content in a world of bedroom and kitchen, sex, babies and home." Often, however, Friedan's pieces challenged conformity to domestic ideals or profiled independent women who had succeeded in careers.

Friedan's own marriage fell far short of the images of domestic contentment projected by the mass media. In fact, her union was just as stormy as her parents' had been. Betty was dissatisfied with the inadequate income of Carl's one-man advertising and public relations firm and felt that he did not support her career aspirations, an intellectually stimulating life, or equality in their marriage. According to friends, Carl complained that when he came home from work, Betty had been too busy writing to prepare dinner.

Friedan discovered the connection between her life and the lives of other women when she returned to Smith College for her fifteenth reunion in 1957. She realized that she was going back not as a successful psychologist but as a housewife. "It rankled me," she confessed, "because I hadn't lived up to my brilliant possibilities." Smith had already asked Friedan to put together a questionnaire about her classmates' lives and attitudes for the reunion. In their responses, she found a consistent theme: Her classmates had frequently written of a strange sense of emptiness and uncertainty about who they were. She later labeled this "The Problem That Has No Name." On the basis of the questionnaire results, Friedan wrote an article for *McCall's* criticizing women's role as homemakers and the monotony of housekeeping. When the magazine rejected the article, she submitted it to the *Ladies' Home Journal*. The editors there rewrote it to emphasize how education made women maladjusted as wives and mothers. Refusing the magazine permission to publish the article, she turned to *Redbook*. "Only the most neurotic housewife could agree with this," the editor informed Friedan's agent. Shortly after that, Friedan contacted a book editor. Six years later, *The Feminine Mystique* was published.

Friedan's book presented a picture of conformity to a "mystique" that trapped millions of middle-class housewives. They had accepted the message of advertisers, psychologists, and educators that happiness was to be found only as homemakers. Left with unfulfilled lives, she argued, they could find emancipation only outside the home. Friedan, of course, ignored the fact that most working women had not returned to domesticity after World War II and that millions of American women had to work to make ends meet. By focusing on the white middle class, *The Feminine Mystique* overlooked the experiences of white working-class and minority women. Nor did she offer any concrete solutions to the problem, besides insisting that women had to take responsibility for their lives. **[See Source 1.]**

Even with these shortcomings, Friedan's book had a tremendous impact. As sales climbed, letters poured in from female readers. They expressed gratitude to Friedan for having put into words their feelings that the promise of domestic bliss had proved empty. Meanwhile, Friedan began speaking around the country, preaching that women needed the same opportunities as men for meaningful work outside the home. The timing was right. Many women had found that the postwar domestic ideal poorly reflected their own experiences as wives and mothers. In addition, the millions of women who did enter the workforce in the 1950s often found limited opportunities and pervasive discrimination. Between 1940 and 1960, the proportion of women who worked outside the home doubled from 15 to 30 percent. At the same time, the proportion of married working mothers jumped 400 percent. Yet in 1960, nearly two-thirds of all female workers still labored in occupations categorized as "women's work." In fact, newspaper help-wanted advertisements routinely specified whether jobs were for men or women. As a result, most women never had the same opportunities available to men. Few women served in professions such as medicine and law, and fewer still were corporate executives. Only a handful sat in Congress or on the bench. None sat on the Supreme Court. Even when women performed the same work as men, they received far less pay. In 1960, women were paid only 61 percent as much as male workers, a *drop* of 3 percent since 1955. Other issues plagued working women as well. Organized childcare was practically nonexistent. Many women also were subject to various forms of sexual harassment at a time when the term itself did not even exist, much less have legal standing. At the same time, a chorus of social scientists, psychologists, doctors, and other "experts" broadcast the message that working women were unfulfilled, unhappy, and even un–American.

When *The Feminine Mystique* was published, women were already stirring to action. In 1961, President John Kennedy had appointed the President's Commission on the Status of Women. Chaired by Eleanor Roosevelt, it had documented the inequalities women confronted in the workplace and had recommended the establishment of federal and state commissions to help women overcome them. About the same time, the civil rights movement was encouraging many women to confront their own inequality. Just as many nineteenth-century women's rights advocates had had their roots in the abolitionist movement, some modern women had participated in the fight for civil rights. Televised images of black protests against discrimination presented many other women with a powerful example of a movement for social change. Nowhere was the connection between the civil rights and women's movements more evident than in the Civil Rights Act of 1964. As a result of pressure from a handful of female activists, Title VII of the act made it illegal for employers to discriminate on the basis of sex as well as race.

As Friedan spoke to women around the country, she heard of more and more examples of gender discrimination. And as women began to flood the Equal Employment Opportunity Commission* with complaints, she came to realize that the federal government had no serious interest in enforcing Title VII. To get the civil rights law enforced, she concluded, women had to create a pressure group similar to the National Association for the Advancement of Colored People. In a Washington, D.C., hotel in 1966, Friedan and a handful of other women attending a conference of state women's commissions met to do just that. Writing on a napkin, Friedan defined the purpose of the new organization: "to take the actions needed to bring women into the mainstream of American

---

Equal Employment Opportunity Commission: The federal body established to enforce Title VII of the Civil Rights Act of 1964.

society." She also scribbled a name for the organization: National Organization for Women (NOW). Then the women anted up and elected a president. When they were finished, NOW had $135 in its treasury and Betty Friedan as its leader. **[See Source 2.]**

"SHE DIDN'T HAVE TO"

The Beach Book hit the bookstores the same year as *The Feminine Mystique*. As the title suggests, it was very light summer reading. In fact, it contained little more than excerpts from other books about beaches and author Gloria Steinem's sunbathing fantasies. "What a tan will do is make you look good," Steinem wrote, "and that justifies everything." In 1963, the twenty-nine-year-old magazine writer knew all about looking good—and having a great time. After all, Steinem was one of New York's "beautiful people," the young professionals in the early 1960s who turned their backs on suburban domesticity for a glamorous—and single—life in the big city. It was a life far removed from Betty Friedan's world of barbecues, station wagons, and Parent–Teacher Association meetings.

It was also a long way from the life Steinem had known as a child. The daughter of a ne'er-do-well father and a mentally ill mother, Steinem grew up in a rat-infested house in Toledo, Ohio. Her father, Leo, was the son of a Jewish immigrant who had made a tidy fortune in real estate. Leo's mother was an early Ohio suffragette. Leo had inherited neither his father's business acumen nor his mother's concern for women's rights. Instead, the amiable college dropout took jobs and chased moneymaking schemes that never worked out. Gloria's mother, the daughter of a locomotive engineer, had come from far more modest circumstances. Like Betty Friedan's mother, Ruth Steinem was a newspaper society-page reporter who was forced to give up her job after her marriage. Unlike Miriam Goldstein, however, Ruth had a great fear of financial insecurity. In 1930, five years after the birth of the Steinems' first daughter, she suffered a nervous breakdown. By the time Gloria was born four years later, the Steinems had moved to Michigan, where Leo was developing a resort. As Leo pursued his latest dream, Ruth slipped into mental illness.

Gloria Steinem's childhood was defined by her father's declining financial circumstances and her mother's deteriorating mental state. When she was a girl, the family lived at the Michigan resort during the summer and traveled to California or Florida during the rest of the year, while Leo plied his second trade as an itinerant antiques dealer. Wartime rationing eventually sank Leo's resort, and conflicts about money between Leo and Ruth finally led to their divorce in 1945. By then, Gloria's sister, Susanne, had gone off to Smith College, and eleven-year-old Gloria was left to care for her mother. After they moved into a rundown house that Ruth's family owned in Toledo, Gloria grew up fast. While other girls were playing, she kept house and prepared meals. The experience left her independent and detached. Escape finally came in 1951, when Gloria spent her senior year in high school in Washington, D.C., where Susanne now worked. At her sister's urging, Gloria also applied to Smith and was accepted. The next fall, a decade after Betty Friedan had graduated, Gloria Steinem entered Smith's ivy-covered walls. With the help of money that her mother had managed to save for her college education, she thrived in her new environment. Making the dean's list three years in a row, she graduated in 1956 magna cum laude.

"Socially precocious," as one classmate put it, Steinem also had little difficulty attracting men. In her senior year, she fell in love with one and accepted his proposal of marriage. Then suddenly, she changed her mind. Having taken care of her mother for so long, she saw marriage as a loss of freedom and control. Unlike many of her college friends who sought security in marriage, she was terrified at the prospect. After graduation, while in London awaiting a visa to study in India, Steinem discovered that she was pregnant as the result of a final fling with her former fiancé. Overcome with panic, she even contemplated suicide. After finding a doctor who would perform an abortion, a procedure that was illegal in the United States, she felt a sense of responsibility for having taken control of her life.

After a year and a half abroad, Steinem returned to the United States, determined to land a job as a reporter in New York City. Gradually, she began to find writing assignments. In 1963, she spent three weeks working as a Playboy Bunny at the Playboy Club to gather information for an article for the entertainment magazine *Show*. The result, "A Bunny's Tale," caused a sensation. It also opened doors. Gradually, Steinem began to write celebrity profiles and articles on fashion for publications such as the *Ladies' Home Journal, Glamour*, and the *New York Times Magazine*. Steinem made her mark, however, with pieces that offered advice for single women.

Her timing was excellent. By the early 1960s, increasing numbers of young people, growing affluence, more leisure time, and the invention of the birth control pill had conspired to spark a "sexual revolution." Many young professionals had been attracted to the single life in New York and other large cities. Some of them had no doubt been inspired by Helen Gurley Brown's best seller *Sex and the Single Girl*, which touted a single and sexually active life as an alternative to marriage. The chic Steinem epitomized this "swinging singles" lifestyle. She was an attractive, well-educated, professional, unattached woman. In the vanguard of the sexual revolution, Steinem was well positioned to offer advice to young women who had rejected the "feminine mystique" but were unsure about the sexual revolution's new rules. By 1965, she commanded $3,000 per article and made $30,000 a year—more than five times the median income for men. She also had become something of a celebrity. In 1965, with only seven years' experience as a freelance writer, she was profiled in *Newsweek*.

Soon Steinem's involvement in numerous causes made her even more visible. She was active in the antiwar movement, organized peace demonstrations in New York, and worked on the unsuccessful presidential campaigns of Democratic candidates Eugene McCarthy and George McGovern. She helped raise funds in New York for the United Farm Workers, organized in 1966 by Cesar Chavez to unionize migrant farmworkers. She even marched in California with Chavez in support of the union's boycott of table grapes. To some observers, she personified "radical chic," a term coined by writer Tom Wolfe to describe the desire of affluent liberals to associate with causes such as Black Power and the unionization of farm workers. Steinem countered that label by saying that she identified with "out" groups because she belonged to one.

Compared to many other feminist leaders, Steinem had come relatively late to the women's movement. She had read *The Feminine Mystique* but thought it pertained mostly to white, middle-class, suburban women, with whom she had little interest in associating. She had not joined the rapidly growing NOW because she did not want to identify with women who were asking men for things. Thus she refused to join Friedan and other NOW members in 1969 when they attempted to change the policy of an exclusive restaurant in New York that barred women at lunchtime. Shortly after that, however, she attended a meeting on abortion held by a feminist organization called Redstockings. There she experienced a feminist awakening, just as Friedan had at her college reunion.

Formed by writers Shulamith Firestone and Ellen Willis, Redstockings was one of a growing number of radical feminist organizations. The members of these groups had often encountered widespread sexual exploitation in civil rights and antiwar organizations.

For them, the comment by Student Nonviolent Coordinating Committee (SNCC) leader Stokely Carmichael that the "position of women in SNCC is prone" summed up their problem. These activists rejected as far too limited NOW's primary goal of gaining equal access for women. They attributed women's problems to class oppression rather than discrimination and believed that women needed not rights but liberation from a male-dominated society. At the Redstockings meeting, Steinem listened to the tales of women who had had illegal abortions or had tried unsuccessfully to get abortions. She began to realize that these women's experiences, like her own years before, were a reflection of women's subordinate position in society. No one at the meeting used the phrase "the personal is political," but that idea, soon popular with many feminists, was beginning to dawn on Steinem.

Steinem's awakening led her to a different view of women's struggle for equality than Friedan's. While Friedan and NOW worked to end gender discrimination, Steinem called for a fundamental restructuring of institutions to do away with the nuclear family and what she called "patriarchal society." Securing laws ending discrimination against women was not enough, she said. Instead, women needed to concentrate on sexual issues and a broad range of relationships between men and women. A growing number of younger women shared these views by the early 1970s. In fact, thousands of these women were coming together in numerous small groups that made up a grassroots "women's liberation" movement. Many of these women rejected more than the makeup and feminine clothing worn by older women's rights advocates. They also spurned NOW as too stuffy, respectable, and conservative. They concentrated on creating numerous alternative institutions and services, from support groups to rape crisis centers to women's shelters. They also focused on the "hidden injuries" suffered by women as a class. In "consciousness-raising" sessions, small groups of women gathered to discuss their concerns regarding work, health, sex, family, and marriage. Attacking the everyday practices that seemed to degrade women, these feminists concluded that problems in their personal relationships reflected the organization of society. In thousands of protests, marches, and rallies, they called for sweeping changes in everything from college courses to childcare.

Steinem's career reflected these broader concerns. As a journalist, she focused on women's "capitulation to the small humiliations." In 1971, she founded *Ms.*, the first feminist mass-circulation magazine. By targeting housewives and other women who never read feminist publications or alternative newspapers, Steinem sought to bring the concerns surrounding "women's liberation" to a wider audience. *Ms.* concentrated on traditional women's rights issues such as the Equal Rights Amendment (ERA)* and job discrimination, and it also took up the more "radical" issues of abortion rights, lesbianism, sexuality, pornography, women's health, and gender roles. **[See Source 3.]** Later issues of *Ms.* contained a "No Comment" page to which readers could submit advertisements that debased women. Steinem also emphasized the need for "sisterhood." **[See Source 4.]** *Ms.* began to receive a flood of letters from readers who for the first time felt that they were not alone. Within a year, the magazine had a circulation of three hundred fifty thousand and an estimated readership of 1.4 million.

Once again, Steinem's timing was perfect. When the national media finally discovered the women's movement in the early 1970s, they thrust Steinem into the spotlight. To many journalists, Steinem had little competition: She was photogenic and quick-witted, and she made good copy. She also refuted the widespread assumption that feminists were

---

*Equal Rights Amendment (ERA): First proposed in 1923, the amendment called for equal rights for women under the law. It was taken up by NOW in the late 1960s and generally embraced by the women's movement in the early 1970s.

either lesbians or, as *Newsweek* put it, "losers who couldn't play the game according to conventional rules." The newsmagazine observed, "What gets nearly everyone about Steinem as Liberationist is that She Didn't Have To."

"THANK GOD FOR GLORIA STEINEM"

After NOW's founding in 1966, Betty Friedan spent countless hours laboring in the fields, planting seeds of local NOW chapters all over the country. For Friedan, divorced in 1969, the struggle on behalf of women's equality involved endless picketing, petitioning, writing, speaking, and marching. Slowly, though, all that work began to pay off. By 1973, NOW claimed more than twenty thousand members. The growing women's movement also started to see concrete gains in the workplace and the law. NOW successfully challenged gender discrimination in newspaper help-wanted ads and secured gender as a category in affirmative action guidelines. Its efforts ended the widespread airline policy of dismissing flight attendants when they married or turned thirty-five. It also filed a successful complaint against thirteen hundred corporations, forcing them to give underpaid female workers back pay.

Friedan now believed that the biggest threat to further progress lay within the movement's own ranks. And in her mind, Gloria Steinem was the most obvious symbol of that growing threat. True, the lines separating Friedan and Steinem were often blurred. Friedan had come out shortly after NOW's founding in support of abortion rights, driving some women from the organization. Likewise, both Steinem and Friedan supported the passage of the ERA and lobbied Congress to secure its passage. In addition, Steinem was hardly the most radical of feminists. Kate Millett, the author of *Sexual Politics* (1970), and Shulamith Firestone, the socialist author of *The Dialectics of Sex* (1970) and cofounder of Redstockings, were only two of the many visible and far more radical feminists. Firestone, for example, argued that gender was the root of women's oppression and that women needed to be freed as soon as possible from the obligatory tasks of bearing and rearing children. In fact, after *Ms.* began publication, radical feminists often attacked it for accepting advertisements that frequently depicted women as thin and rich. Still, Friedan did not appreciate the telegenic Steinem's increasing visibility in the movement and the media. A lot of unglamorous effort had gone into building NOW, and it was galling to watch Steinem steal the spotlight.

Friedan's growing bitterness toward Steinem was about more than jealousy, however. The NOW founder was convinced that sexual matters were private. The more antimale, antimarriage feminists discussed them, the more middle-class people would be alienated from the women's movement. Few feminists seemed more antimarriage than Steinem, who remained single and once declared that "a woman without a husband is like a fish without a bicycle." Younger feminists like Steinem, Friedan insisted in 1969, had to understand that the "gut issues" of this revolution were employment and education, not "sexual fantasy." Later, she said, "I didn't think ... it mattered who was in the missionary position—if unequal power positions in real life weren't changed."

Friedan was especially worried about the potentially divisive and alienating issue of lesbianism. Opposed to shows of solidarity with lesbians in the movement, she characterized the lesbian issue as a "lavender menace." She also had little use for feminist consciousness-raising sessions, which often involved frank discussions of sex. Friedan and many older women's rights advocates were repulsed by what they considered a self-indulgent activity. Politics, she believed, involved hard work and discipline, not self-absorbed talk. Thus transforming one's personal life—or one's consciousness—was not a political act. As she put it, the women's movement could not "afford the mental masturbation" that such sessions represented.

In 1970, Friedan announced that NOW's primary "thrust" would be "political." Unlike some other feminists, Steinem actually agreed with Friedan about the importance of taking the feminist cause into the political arena. In 1971, several hundred women, including Friedan, Steinem, and Fannie Lou Hamer (see Chapter 11), formed the National Women's Political Caucus (NWPC). The idea was Friedan's. The NWPC's goal was to get more women elected to office. At the time, women held only 1.6 percent of the top jobs in government, including only one U.S. Senate seat and twelve seats in the House of Representatives. They held no governorships and no seats on the Supreme Court. Friedan and Steinem split immediately over the NWPC's membership. Friedan envisioned a mainstream organization in which even conservative Republican women were welcome. Allied with New York congresswoman Bella Abzug, Steinem wanted to open membership only to women who agreed on important issues. In her view, the NWPC's membership should be limited to those who wanted "to humanize society." In the end, Steinem and Abzug were able to define the guidelines by which female candidates would be evaluated. They included support for withdrawal from the Vietnam War, the ERA, and the repeal of abortion and contraception laws. The division surfaced at the Democratic National Convention in 1972 when Steinem, not Friedan, was chosen as the NWPC's spokeswoman at the convention. After watching the takeover of the NWPC by Steinem and Abzug, Friedan had had enough. At a press conference called by *McCall's* magazine shortly after the convention, Friedan revealed why she was blasting Steinem and her approach to the women's movement in the magazine's next issue. "If we make men the enemy they will surely lash back at us," she observed. **[See Source 5.]**

Friedan's press conference generated much attention. The fight between Friedan and Steinem seemed to symbolize the split in the women's movement between "moderates," who fought primarily for equality under the law, and "radicals," who believed in the abolition of gender roles. Only later was it clear that the press conference actually marked Friedan's declining influence in an increasingly fragmented women's movement. As the movement spread, the women involved in it were splintering into thousands of organizations and groups. Meanwhile, Friedan had no organizational base from which to operate. No longer the head of NOW and eclipsed in the media by Steinem as the symbol of feminism, her visibility rapidly began to fade. When nearly five thousand women attended the National Women's Conference[*] in 1977, Friedan had no official position and her presence drew little fanfare.

By then, however, the movement that Friedan had helped spark had triumphed in many ways. Women's issues had become largely institutionalized in American society. Under assault by administrative, legislative, and court decisions, many barriers blocking women's access to institutions and equal treatment were finally falling. Beginning in 1971, Congress passed a flood of gender equity laws. They ranged from penalties for unequal funding of male and female school sports programs to a ban on discrimination in lending based on gender or marital status. Meanwhile, the courts began to overturn gender-labeled jobs and upheld the principle of equal pay for equal work. And in 1973, the Supreme Court upheld a woman's right to have an abortion in *Roe* v. *Wade*.

The impact of these triumphs would be particularly evident in education and employment. By the mid-1970s, schools had begun to eliminate gender-segregated classes, all-male colleges had opened their doors to women, and publishers were working to rid textbooks of sexist stereotypes. In the 1970s, the number of female college students rose

---

[*]*National Women's Conference:* A conference held in Houston, Texas, in 1977. Originally proposed in 1975 during the United Nations' International Women's Year, it was funded by Congress to promote "equality between men and women."

by more than 60 percent. By the decade's end, more women than men were enrolled in college. At the same time, the ranks of women workers continued to swell. Aided by numerous class-action suits and sex discrimination charges, millions of them worked in jobs that had once been classified as men's work. Meanwhile, Americans' attitudes about women and gender also were changing. In 1971, a minority of women in one poll approved of "efforts to strengthen and change women's status in society." Four years later, 63 percent approved of such efforts. As attitudes changed, so did sexist language— a major target of feminists. *Ms.*, for instance, came to replace *Miss* or *Mrs.* as a common form of address for women—a change that Steinem's magazine helped bring about.

Another measure of the movement's success by the mid-1970s was the growing assault on it. The antifeminist backlash was ignited by the landmark *Roe* v. *Wade* ruling on abortion. It was stoked further by the fight over the ERA. Prohibiting discrimination based on gender, the ERA was passed by Congress and submitted to the states for ratification in 1972. Conservative antifeminists such as Phyllis Schlafly, however, argued that the ERA would erase differences between men and women and undermine the family. Schlafly, the founder of Stop ERA, asserted that feminism was a movement led by a "cosmopolitan elite" out of touch with the values of "traditional" families**. [See Source 6.]** In the late 1970s, as many Americans grew more conservative in a stagnant economy, Schlafly and other antifeminists found a larger audience. At the same time, many younger women began to reject the label "feminist" even though they actually accepted the movement's goals. Increasingly unaware of the struggles waged by women since the early 1960s, many of them simply took the gains of the women's movement for granted. By the time Ronald Reagan was elected president in 1980, the increasingly fragmented women's movement had lost its momentum and the ERA was a dead issue. The deadline for its adoption passed in 1982 without its ratification.

Even as the women's movement dissipated in the wake of its successes, Friedan and Steinem carried on their personal fight. Concerned about the growing conservative attack on the women's movement, Friedan continued her long struggle to disassociate it from "radical" feminists. In the mid-1970s, she blamed the ERA's defeat by various state legislatures on "extremist groups" such as *Ms.* magazine. Later, in *The Second Stage* (1981), she argued that they were responsible for the rise of antifeminism and called for a new stage in the women's movement in which women would move beyond the desire to "do it all." Women were no longer oppressed by a feminine mystique, Friedan concluded, but by a "feminist mystique." Feminists had to stop "wallowing in the victim state" and accept the importance of families. Meanwhile, under Steinem's guidance, *Ms.* simply wrote Friedan and NOW out of women's history and rarely mentioned them at all. Steinem remained convinced that the "first stage" of feminism—battling the pervasive sexism in American society—was not over, despite the movement's impressive legal victories. As a speaker, a writer, and *Ms.* editor, she continued to call for changes in the everyday lives of women.

By the 1980s, Steinem and her magazine no longer commanded the attention they once had. Steinem's goal in founding *Ms.* had been to bring the women's movement into the mainstream of American society. Despite the conservative backlash against feminism, the magazine had helped the movement do just that. As the *New York Times* put it in 1984, "'Women's Issues' have become everyone's." To many Americans, there now seemed little need for a mainstream feminist magazine. In 1987, Steinem stepped down as editor of *Ms.* when an Australian publisher purchased it, but she remained fixed in the public's mind as the symbol of the women's movement. Thus, when Sally Ride blasted off in 1983 as the first American woman in space, Ride's mother paid tribute not to Friedan but to her long-time rival. "Thank God," Joyce Ride exclaimed, "for Gloria Steinem."

• P R I M A R Y   S O U R C E S •

Source 1:   Betty Friedan, *The Feminine Mystique* (1963)

In 1963, Betty Friedan attacked the postwar domestic ideal in her best-selling book, The Feminine Mystique. *How does Friedan define the problem confronting middle-class housewives? What
is her solution to it?*

The problem lay buried, unspoken, for many years in the minds of American women. It
was a strange stirring, a sense of dissatisfaction, a yearning that women suffered in the
middle of the twentieth century in the United States. Each suburban wife struggled
with it alone. As she made the beds, shopped for groceries, matched slipcover material,
ate peanut butter sandwiches with her children, chauffeured Cub Scouts and Brownies,
lay beside her husband at night—she was afraid to ask even of herself the silent
question—"Is this all?" …

The suburban housewife—she was the dream image of the young American women
and the envy, it was said, of women all over the world. The American housewife—freed
by science and labor-saving appliances from the drudgery, the dangers of childbirth and
the illnesses of her grandmother. She was healthy, beautiful, educated, concerned only
about her husband, her children, her home. She had found true feminine fulfillment.
As a housewife and mother, she was respected as a full and equal partner to man in his
world. She was free to choose automobiles, clothes, appliances, supermarkets; she had
everything that women ever dreamed of.

In the fifteen years after World War II, this mystique of feminine fulfillment became
the cherished and self-perpetuating core of contemporary American culture. Millions of
women lived their lives in the image of those pretty pictures of the American suburban
housewife, kissing their husbands goodbye in front of the picture window, depositing
their station-wagonsful of children at school, and smiling as they ran the new electric
waxer over the spotless kitchen floor.…

It would be quite wrong for me to offer any woman easy how-to answers to this
problem. There are no easy answers, in America today; it is difficult, painful, and takes
perhaps a long time for each woman to find her own answer. First, she must unequiv-
ocally say "no" to the housewife image. This does not mean, of course, that she must
divorce her husband, abandon her children, give up her home. She does not have to
choose between marriage and career; that was the mistaken choice of the feminine
mystique. In actual fact, it is not as difficult as the feminine mystique implies, to combine marriage and motherhood and even the kind of lifelong personal purpose that
once was called "career." It merely takes a new life plan—in terms of one's whole life
as a woman.

The first step in that plan is to see housework for what it is—not a career, but something that must be done as quickly and efficiently as possible.…

The second step … is to see marriage as it really is, brushing aside the veil of over-
glorification imposed by the feminine mystique. Many women I talked to felt strangely
discontented with their husbands, continually irritated with their children, when they

saw marriage and motherhood as the final fulfillment of their lives. But when they began to use their various abilities with a purpose of their own in society, they not only spoke of a new feeling of "aliveness" or "completeness" in themselves, but of a new, though hard to define, difference in the way they felt about their husbands and children....

The only way for a woman, as for a man, to find herself, to know herself as a person, is by creative work of her own. There is no other way. But a job, any job, is not the answer—in fact, it can be part of the trap. Women who do not look for jobs equal to their actual capacity, who do not let themselves develop the lifetime interests and goals which require serious education and training, who take a job at twenty or forty to "help out at home" or just to kill extra time, are walking, almost as surely as the ones who stay inside the housewife trap, to a nonexistent future.

Source 2:   *NOW's Statement of Purpose* (1966)

The National Organization for Women proclaimed its premises and goals after its formation in 1966. How do NOW's goals reflect Friedan's analysis of the problems facing women? Do its proposals to achieve equality pertain to problems confronting women in the "public" or "private" sphere of life?

The purpose of NOW is to take action to bring women into full participation in the mainstream of American society now, exercising all the privileges and responsibilities thereof in truly equal partnership with men....

NOW is dedicated to the proposition that women first and foremost are human beings, who, like all other people in our society, must have the chance to develop their fullest human potential. We believe that women can achieve such equality only by accepting to the full the challenges and responsibilities they share with all other people in our society, as part of the decision-making mainstream of American political, economic and social life.

We organize to initiate or support action, nationally or in any part of this nation, by individuals or organizations, to break through the silken curtain of prejudice and discrimination against women in government, industry, the professions, the churches, the political parties, the judiciary, the labor unions, in education, science, medicine, law, religion and every other field of importance in American society....

There is no civil rights movement to speak for women, as there has been for Negroes and other victims of discrimination. The National Organization for Women must therefore begin to speak.

WE BELIEVE that the power of American law, and the protection guaranteed by the U.S. Constitution to the civil rights of all individuals, must be effectively applied and enforced to isolate and remove patterns of sex discrimination, to ensure equality of opportunity in employment and education, and equality of civil and political rights and responsibilities on behalf of women, as well as for Negroes and other deprived groups....

WE REJECT the current assumptions that a man must carry the sole burden of supporting himself, his wife, his family, and that a woman is automatically entitled to lifelong support by a man upon her marriage, or that marriage, home and family are primarily woman's world and responsibility—hers, to dominate, his to support. We believe that a true

SOURCE: From the National Organization for Women. This is a historical document and may not reflect the current language or priorities of the organization.

partnership between the sexes demands a different concept of marriage, an equitable sharing of the responsibilities of home and children and of the economic burdens of their support. We believe that proper recognition should be given to the economic and social value of home-making and child care. To these ends, we will seek to open a reexamination of laws and mores governing marriage and divorce, for we believe that the current state of "half-equality" between the sexes discriminates against both men and woman, and is the cause of much unnecessary hostility between the sexes.

Source 3:   *Ms. Cover* (1972)

Started in 1971 as a one-shot insert in New York *magazine,* Ms. *claimed to be a magazine for "female human beings." Early issues included articles such as "Raising Your Kids Without Sex Roles," "Women Tell the Truth about Their Abortions," and "Why I Want a Wife" (which detailed how wives created a lot of options for their husbands that wives themselves did not have). What does this cover from an early issue of* Ms. *reveal about its approach to the women's movement? What does it reflect about the ways Steinem's concerns differed from—or were similar to—those of Friedan and other members of NOW?*

SOURCE: Ronald W. Hogeland, ed., *Women and Womanhood in America* (Lexington: D.C. Heath and Company, 1973), p. 173; originally from *Ms.*

Source 4:   Gloria Steinem, *"Sisterhood"* (1972)

In this column from the preview issue of Ms. *magazine, Gloria Steinem discusses her feminist awakening. How does her analysis of this experience differ from Betty Friedan's in* The Feminine Mystique?

At first my discoveries seemed personal. In fact, they were the same ones so many millions of women have made and are continuing to make. Greatly simplified, they go like this: Women are human beings first, with minor differences from men that apply largely to the single act of reproduction. We share the dreams, capabilities, and weaknesses of all human beings, but our occasional pregnancies and other visible differences have been used—even more pervasively, if less brutally, than racial differences have been used—to create an "inferior" group and an elaborate division of labor. The division is continued for a clear if often unconscious reason: the economic and social profit of males as a group.

Once this feminist realization dawned, I reacted in what turned out to be predictable ways. First, I was amazed at the simplicity and obviousness of a realization that made sense, at last, of my life experience. I couldn't figure out why I hadn't seen it before. Second, I realized how far that new vision of life was from the system around us, and how tough it would be to explain this feminist realization at all, much less to get people (especially, though not only, men) to accept so drastic a change....

Occasionally, these efforts at explaining actually succeed. More often, I get the feeling that most women are speaking Urdu and most men are speaking Pali.*

Whether joyful or painful, both kinds of reaction to our discovery have a great reward. They give birth to sisterhood.

First, we share the exhilaration of growth and self-discovery, the sensation of having the scales fall from our eyes. Whether we are giving other women this new knowledge or receiving it from them, the pleasure for all concerned is enormous. And very moving.

In the second stage, when we're exhausted from dredging up facts and arguments for the men whom we had previously thought advanced and intelligent, we make another simple discovery: women understand. We may share experiences, make jokes, paint pictures, and describe humiliations that mean little to men, but *women understand*....

[Lack of self-esteem] is the most tragic punishment that society inflicts on any second-class group. Ultimately the brainwashing works, and we ourselves come to believe our group is inferior. Even if we achieve a little success in the world and think of ourselves as "different," we don't want to associate with our group. We want to identify up, not down (clearly my problem in not wanting to join women's groups). We want to be the only woman in the office, or the only black family on the block, or the only Jew in the club.

The pain of looking back at wasted, imitative years is enormous. Trying to write like men. Valuing myself and other women according to the degree of our acceptance by men—socially in politics, and in our professions. It's as painful as it is now to hear two grown-up female human beings competing with each other on the basis of their husband's status, like servants whose identity rests on the wealth or accomplishments of their employers.

SOURCE: Gloria Steinem, "Sisterhood," from OUTRAGEOUS ACTS AND EVERYDAY REBELLIONS (New York: Holt, Rinehart and Winston, 1983), pp. 113, 114, 116–117. © Gloria Steinem; originally from *Ms.* Magazine, December 1971 issue.

Urdu and Pali: Two languages spoken on the Indian subcontinent.

And this lack of esteem that makes us put each other down is still the major enemy of sisterhood. Women who are conforming to society's expectations view the nonconformists with justifiable alarm. *Those noisy, unfeminine women,* they say to themselves. *They will only make trouble for us all.* Women who are quietly nonconforming, hoping nobody will notice, are even more alarmed because they have more to lose. And that makes sense, too.

The status quo protects itself by punishing all challengers, especially women whose rebellion strikes at the most fundamental social organization: the sex roles that convince half the population that its identity depends on being first in work or in war, and the other half that it must serve as docile, unpaid, or underpaid labor.

In fact, there seems to be no punishment inside the white male club that quite equals the ridicule and personal viciousness reserved for women who rebel. Attractive or young women who act forcefully are assumed to be either unnatural or male-controlled. If they succeed, it could only have been sexually, through men. Old women or women considered unattractive by male standards are accused of acting out of bitterness, because they could not get a man. Any woman who chooses to behave like a full human being should be warned that the armies of the status quo will treat her as something of a dirty joke. That's their natural and first weapon. She will *need* sisterhood.

Source 5: Betty Friedan, *"Beyond Women's Liberation"* (1972)

In this column for McCall*'s magazine, Betty Friedan blasts Gloria Steinem and other feminists who think like Steinem. What is the basis of Friedan's disagreement with them?*

On a recent evening, over coffee in a sparsely furnished New York apartment, the forty-five-year-old male recipient of an act of female banishment talks of Gloria Steinem's proclamation of Sisterhood in the magazine *Ms.* In a tone of cold, measured outrage I find positively startling (previously he has identified completely with the women's movement), he says: "I think we have had just about enough of this." I reread the article, to find out why it makes him so murderous. Is it a certain tone implying that women are special and pure, forever wronged by men? "I get the feeling that we are speaking Urdu and the men are speaking Pali ..." the article says. "Women understand. We may share experiences, make jokes, paint pictures, and describe humiliations that mean nothing to men, but *women understand....* Any woman who chooses to behave like a full human being should be warned that the armies of the *status quo* will treat her as something of a dirty joke.... She will *need* sisterhood." ...

If I were a man, I would object strenuously to the assumption that women have any moral or spiritual superiority as a *class* or that men share some brute insensitivity as a *class*. This is male chauvinism in reverse; it is female sexism. It is, in fact, female chauvinism, and those who preach or practice it seem to me to be corrupting our movement for equality and inviting a backlash that endangers the very real gains we have won these past few years....

Female chauvinism denies us full humanity as women in another way, too, one that threatens backlash among women even more than men. Those who would make an *abstract ideology* out of sex, aping the old-fashioned rhetoric of class warfare or the separatist extremists of race warfare, paradoxically deny the concrete reality of women's sexuality, mundane or glorious, burden or pleasure, exaggerated or repressed, as it has been in the past. When Gloria Steinem dismisses marriage as "prostitution," in a speech to the League of Women Voters, the assumption is that no woman would ever want to go to bed with a man if she didn't need to sell her body for bread or a mink coat. Does this mean that any woman who admits tenderness or passion for her husband, or any man, has sold out to the enemy? …

I have always objected to rhetoric that treats the women's movement as class warfare against men—women oppressed, as a class, by men, the oppressors. I do not believe that the conditions we are trying to change are caused by a conspiracy for "the economic and social profit of men as a group," as Gloria Steinem sees it. The causes are more complex, and burden men as well as benefit them. My definition of feminism is simply that women are people, in the fullest sense of the word, who must be free to move in society with all the privileges and opportunities and responsibilities that are their human and American right.

Source 6: Phyllis Schlafly, "What's Wrong with 'Equal Rights' for Women" (1972)

Phyllis Schlafly, the chairwoman of STOP ERA, was a leading critic of the Equal Rights Amendment. On what grounds does she argue against equal rights for women? How do you think Friedan and Steinem would have responded to her argument? What does this source reveal about important factors limiting the success of the women's movement in the 1970s?

The Fraud of the Equal Rights Amendment

In the last couple of years, a noisy movement has sprung up agitating for "women's rights." Suddenly everywhere we are afflicted with aggressive females on television talk shows yapping about how mistreated American women are, suggesting that marriage has put us in some kind of "slavery," that housework is menial and degrading, and—perish the thought—that women are discriminated against. New "women's liberation" organizations are popping up, agitating and demonstrating, serving demands on public officials, getting wide press coverage always, and purporting to speak for some 100,000,000 American women.

It's time to set the record straight. The claim that American women are downtrodden and unfairly treated is the fraud of the century. The truth is that American women never had it so good. Why should we lower ourselves to "equal rights" when we already have the status of special privilege?

The proposed Equal Rights Amendment states: "Equality of rights under the law shall not be denied or abridged by the United States or by any state on account of sex." So what's wrong with that? Well, here are a few examples of what's wrong with it.

This amendment will absolutely and positively make women subject to the draft. Why any woman would support such a ridiculous and un-American proposal as this is beyond comprehension. Why any Congressman who had any regard for his wife, sister or daughter would support such a proposition is just as hard to understand. Foxholes are bad enough for men, but they certainly are not the place for women—and we should reject any proposal which would put them there in the name of equal right....

Another bad effect of the Equal Rights Amendment is that it will abolish women's right to child support and alimony, and substitute what the women's libbers think is a more "equal" policy, that "such decisions should be within the discretion of the court and should be made on the economic situation and need of the parties in the case."

Under present American laws, the man is *always* required to support his wife and each child he caused to be brought into the world. Why should women abandon these good laws—by trading them for something so nebulous arid uncertain as the "discretion of the Court"? ...

Women's Libbers Do NOT Speak for Us

The "women's lib" movement is not ah honest effort to secure better jobs for women who want or need to work outside the home. This is just the superficial sweet-talk to win broad support for a radical "movement." "Women's lib" is a total assault on the role of the American woman as wife and mother, and on the family as the basic unit of society.

Women's libbers are trying to make wives and mothers unhappy with their career, make them feel that they are "second class citizens" and "abject slaves." Women's libbers are promoting free sex instead of the "slavery" of marriage. They are promoting "Federal" day care-centers for babies instead of homes. They are promoting abortions instead of families....

Women's libbers do *not* speak for the majority of American women. American women do *not* want to be liberated from husbands and children....

QUESTIONS TO CONSIDER

1. Citing specific primary sources, compare Betty Friedan's and Gloria Steinem's views about feminism's tactics and goals. Was the conflict between them primarily one of style or substance?

2. How did Friedan's and Steinem's backgrounds and experiences influence their views about the women's movement? Do you think their disagreements were influenced more by the life experiences that were unique to each woman, the different times in which they matured, or other factors?

3. Based on the essay and primary sources in this chapter, how would you respond to the argument of one historian that Friedan left unchallenged the dividing line between public and private issues in seeking equality for women, whereas "radical" feminists wished to make "personal life itself into a political issue"? Did Steinem make the personal political?

4. What are the similarities and differences between the rise of the women's movement in the late 1960s and the rise of the earlier civil rights movement? What are the similarities and differences between the issues that divided Friedan and Steinem and those separating Roy Wilkins and Fannie Lou Hamer (see Chapter 11)?

5. Did Friedan or Steinem have a bigger impact on changing the status of women in American society in the 1960s and 1970s? Why do you think Steinem frequently received more public acclaim than Friedan?

FOR FURTHER READING

William H. Chafe, *The Paradox of Change: American Women in the 20th Century* (New York: Oxford University Press, 1991), submits a brief overview of the modern women's movement and the struggle for women's rights in the twentieth century.

Sara Evans, *Personal Politics: The Roots of Women's Liberation in the Civil Rights Movement and the New Left* (New York: Vintage Books, 1980), discusses the impact of the civil rights and student movements on the struggle for women's liberation.

Betty Friedan, *It Changed My Life: Writings on the Women's Movement* (New York: Random House, 1976), presents her views during the early stages of the movement.

Carolyn Heilbrun, *The Education of a Woman: The Life of Gloria Steinem* (New York: Dial Press, 1995), offers a positive account of Steinem's life and contributions to feminism.

Daniel Horowitz, *Betty Friedan and the Making of the Feminine Mystique: The American Left, the Cold War, and Modern Feminism* (Amherst: University of Massachusetts Press, 1998), presents a thorough examination of Friedan's life up to the publication of *The Feminine Mystique* that emphasizes the way she reinvented her life in the book.

Ruth Rosen, *The World Split Open: How the Modern Women's Movement Changed America* (New York: Viking Press, 2000), provides an engaging analysis of the women's movement and its impact on society.

Miriam Schneir, ed., *Feminism in Our Time: The Essential Writings, World War II to the Present* (New York: Vintage Books, 1994), provides selections from numerous women involved in the twentieth-century women's movement.

14

Individualism and the Environment in the 1980s: Edward Abbey and James Watt

The new bridge was a massive symbol of civilization's conquest of nature. Built on the Utah-Arizona border right next to the Glen Canyon Dam, it arched seven hundred feet over the Colorado River. As the governors of Utah and Arizona cut the ceremonial ribbons to mark the magnificent structure's opening, the assembled guests cheered. Then the fireworks began. The frightened spectators thought the pyrotechnics were part of the celebration, but they were wrong. The fireworks had been set off to clear the four-hundred-foot-long bridge of people. As the last person ran off the structure, a huge explosion ripped it in two. Within seconds, the bridge sat in the sandstone canyon below, the victim of the Monkey Wrench Gang. The gang's next target was the dam itself. Behind its seven hundred ninety-two thousand tons of concrete and steel lay Lake Powell, a reservoir that had inundated some of the most spectacular desert land on earth. To these ecoterrorists, the dam was a sacrilege—the ultimate symbol of humankind's rape of the wilderness.

The bombing of the bridge at Glen Canyon, of course, never happened. It is the opening scene in Edward Abbey's novel *The Monkey Wrench Gang*, published in 1975. A park ranger turned writer, Abbey was a self-proclaimed "voice crying in the wilderness." Introduced to the deserts of the American Southwest as a young man, he saw them as both beautiful and sacred. He also believed that they were under an "immoral" assault by corporate interests and government bureaucrats. For Abbey, how-ever, the destruction of the deserts was more than a crime against nature. Rather, it threatened Americans' very freedom, which depended on the existence of open, un-spoiled land. With his fictional band, Abbey hoped to stir people to take actions that he was too "cowardly" to perform himself. He did. In the 1980s, ecoterrorists claimed credit

Edward Abbey   James Watt

for acts of sabotage against developers, ski resorts, power and timber companies, and other private interests doing business on public lands. They were inspired, they said, by Abbey's writings.

Whether real or fictional, environmental saboteurs appeared frightening and dangerous to many people. James Watt, for one, had nothing but contempt for them. The secretary of the interior under Ronald Reagan, Watt shared Abbey's belief that freedom was associated with access to the vast areas of the American West. And like the creator of the Monkey Wrench Gang, he considered himself an individualist with a strong distrust of government. But unlike Abbey, Watt believed that the land was to be used for the economic benefit of the people who lived on it. Guided by flawed assumptions about people's proper relationship to nature, environmentalists had succeeded in setting aside far too many areas as wilderness. The time had come to restore the right to earn a living from the land. In the early 1980s, Watt stepped forward to lead that fight.

"KEEP IT LIKE IT WAS!"

Although Edward Abbey's roots were far removed from the desert, they were close to nature. Born in 1927, the first of Paul and Mildred Abbey's five children, Edward grew up on a small, run-down farm in the backwoods of Appalachia. For the Abbeys, contact with the natural environment was an integral part of their existence. The family's food and livelihood came directly from the land. When not tending crops, Paul Abbey took his sons hunting and trapping in the woods and meadows. The family gathered nuts from the land and tapped the numerous maple trees on the farm for syrup. While Mildred Abbey cultivated wildflowers for sale, Edward and his brothers and sister often explored a large tract of uncut forest near the farm.

The greatest influence on Edward was not the outdoors, however, but his father. Although Mildred was a churchgoing Presbyterian, Paul Revere Abbey was a radical who frequently railed against capitalism and religion. While Mildred played the family piano and taught the children good manners and proper English, Paul exposed them to unconventional ideas. At family gatherings, Paul often held forth on the virtues of social- ism. He also liked to recite passages from the work of the nineteenth-century poet Walt Whitman. One of his favorites, from the preface to *Leaves of Grass*, would stay with Edward his entire life. "This is what you shall do," Whitman wrote: "Love the earth and sun and the animals, despise riches, give alms to everyone that asks, stand up for the stupid and crazy, devote your income and labor to others, hate tyrants … have patience and in- dulgence toward the people, take off your hat to nothing known or unknown."

Years later, Edward Abbey wrote that his father was "cantankerous, ornery, short- tempered, and contentious.… He had strong opinions on everything and a neighborly view on almost nothing." The other Abbey children claimed that Edward bore a re- markable resemblance to their father. Indeed, Edward demonstrated a rebellious streak from a young age. At ten, he stormed out of Sunday school when the teacher told him that everything in the Bible was true. A couple of years later, Edward and his brother Howard were crossing the street when a car pulled into the crosswalk. Howard walked around the front of the car, but Edward went straight up over its hood, leaving a large dent in it.

Abbey admitted much later that he enjoyed "provoking people." At the same time, however, he had a thoughtful side. Finding farm chores disagreeable, he preferred to spend time reading and writing stories. Fascinated by his father's stories about his travels in the American West, Edward realized that there was "something else out there." A year before he graduated from high school, the seventeen-year-old got his first opportunity to travel west. He went by himself. When Howard asked Edward why he did not want him to go along, Edward answered, "Because frankly you bore me." As Edward left, his father told him that things would go better on the trip if he were not so arrogant.

Arrogant or not, things went well enough for Edward. He was thrown in jail only once— in Flagstaff, Arizona, for vagrancy. Hitchhiking and riding the rails, he traveled to Seattle, down the Pacific coast to California, and back across Arizona and New Mexico to the East. Although he saw the verdant Northwest, Yosemite National Park, and California's fragrant orange groves, it was the deserts of the Southwest that stole his heart. "It was love at first sight," he said later. When he got home, he was determined to return.

After high school and a two-year stint in the U.S. Army, which left him even more distrustful of regulations, Abbey enrolled at the University of New Mexico, where he studied on and off for the next decade. In college, he developed an interest in philoso- phy, anarchy, and exploring the desert in an old Chevrolet. He realized that anarchy was not about bombs but about opposition to coercion, especially by government. He also came to believe that anarchy was associated with open space. The West, he concluded, offered a place where free individuals could live without the constraints imposed by organizations. Unfortunately, the possibilities for freedom there were rapidly disappear- ing. The place was being "foreclosed, outmoded, fenced out, smothered under progress," he observed.

After earning a B.A. in 1951, Abbey studied in Scotland on a Fulbright scholarship and then enrolled in a master's program in philosophy at the University of New Mexico. Completed in 1956, his master's thesis was titled "Anarchy and the Morality of Violence," themes that figured prominently in all his writing. Starting with *Jonathan Troy*, a novel about a young anarchist published in 1954, Abbey began to explore the clash between civilization and freedom. With its appraisal of modern technology's destruction of nature, the book foreshadowed Abbey's later work. Two years later, he published *The Brave Cowboy*, a novel about another anarchist, named Jack Burns, who loses his freedom as barbed wire intrudes on the open range. Burns protests the invasion of powerful ranchers on public lands by cutting the barbed wire. As he flees the authorities, he is hit by a truck loaded with plumbing products. In the end, he lies bleeding by the side of the road on a Navajo rug. A remnant of the Old West, Abbey's hero does not fit into the New West.

Abbey's early novels brought him only modest success. *The Brave Cowboy* was made into the movie *Lonely Are the Brave* in 1962, starring Kirk Douglas, but Abbey was paid only $7,500 for the screen rights. The same year, he published *Fire on the Mountain*, a novel about a proud, independent rancher who loses his land. Meanwhile, Abbey faced the problem of making a living. He had been briefly married to a fellow student before he graduated from college. Then in 1952, he had married a fine artist named Rita Deanin. Unable to support himself by writing, he had taken a series of jobs with the U.S. Forest Service and the National Park Service, including stints in remote fire lookout towers on the North Rim of the Grand Canyon, at Glacier National Park, and at Organ Pipe Cactus National Monument. Abbey had quickly come to dislike the Department of the Interior's bureaucracy and regulations. The work and a series of affairs also ended his second marriage in 1965. Nonetheless, these jobs suited his temperament and gave him plenty of time to write. His first assignment for the Park Service took him to remote and seldom visited Arches National Monument in Utah. There he kept a journal, which became the basis for *Desert Solitaire*, a semiautobiographical series of essays about his time at Arches.

Published in 1968, *Desert Solitaire* came out amid growing environmental activism. By the mid-1960s, increasing concern about pollution and ecological destruction had contributed to rising ecological awareness and transformed an older *conservation* movement into a broader *environmental* movement. Conservationists in the first half of the twentieth century were chiefly concerned about the efficient use of resources. Environmentalists in the second half were primarily concerned about the health of the entire ecosystem. In 1949, Aldo Leopold published *A Sand County Almanac*, a call for a new ecological consciousness. Trained as a forester and wildlife manager, Leopold argued that an "ecological conscience" would change the role of *"Homo sapiens* from conqueror of the land-community to plain member and citizen of it." Thirteen years later, a former researcher for the U.S. Fish and Wildlife Service named Rachel Carson published *Silent Spring*, which awoke many Americans to the threat of chemical pollution. *Desert Solitaire* reflected this new ecological consciousness. It argued that a human-centered view of nature had to give way to a biocentric view in which all species had an equal standing. At the same time, it decried the way "industrial tourism" centered on the automobile threatened to destroy the national parks.

Desert Solitaire quickly became an underground environmental classic. Within four years, it had sold five hundred thousand copies and its author was an environmental cult figure. Thus Abbey already commanded a large audience as he responded to the signal event in his life as a wilderness defender: the building of the Glen Canyon Dam sixty miles north of Grand Canyon National Park. The dam created Lake Powell—the second-largest reservoir in the United States. Abbey and the few thousand other people who trekked into the sandstone wonderland eventually inundated by the lake found it to be of incomparable beauty. The Bureau of Reclamation, however, viewed the dam as a "cash cow." Completed in 1962, it would generate cheap electric power for the burgeoning cities of the Southwest. Sales of this power in turn provided funds for the bureau to finance other reclamation projects designed to provide low-cost water primarily to western farmers and ranchers. To Abbey, these water users were nothing more than "welfare parasites" who mouthed antigovernment rhetoric while relying on government assistance.

The decision to build the Glen Canyon Dam was part of a larger battle over the use of public lands that extended back to the beginning of the conservation movement. At the turn of the twentieth century, Sierra Club founder John Muir and other preservationists had argued that nature should be preserved for its own sake. At the same time, Gifford Pinchot, head of the U.S. Forest Service under Theodore Roosevelt, had insisted that natural resources should be used for the economic benefit of many. In the first decade of the twentieth century, Muir and Pinchot went head-to-head in a battle over a proposal to dam the Tuolumne River near Yosemite National Park in California. The dam would provide badly needed water for San Francisco, but it would also flood the magnificent Hetch Hetchy Valley that rivaled nearby Yosemite Valley. Arguing that preservation was an act "of worship," Muir fought to include the valley in the national park. Insisting that preservation should not override the "economic and moral aspects of the case," Pinchot fought for flooding the valley. In the end, Roosevelt sided with Pinchot. Like Glen Canyon half a century later, Hetch Hetchy was destroyed.

By the time the environmental movement emerged in the 1960s, Glen Canyon was already doomed. Even after the dam was finished, relatively few people cared about the canyon's destruction. For Edward Abbey, however, its loss symbolized the threat that modern, technological society posed to nature—and to the freedom that he associated with it. Like Muir, Abbey elevated his love of nature to a religion, and also like Muir, he was stirred to action by a dam's destruction of nature. The result was his best-known work of fiction, *The Monkey Wrench Gang*. Published thirteen years after the completion of the dam, the novel centered on a gang of ecoterrorists who do battle with the forces invading and exploiting the red rock canyons and plateaus of the Southwest. Their rallying cry is "Keep it like it was!" **[See Source 1.]** The novel and its sequel, *Hayduke Lives!* (published posthumously in 1990), turned Abbey into an internationally recognized writer. According to *Newsweek*, he had "invented a new fictional genre, the ecological caper." Many readers, however, were not amused. One Tucson newspaper reviewer, for instance, called *The Monkey Wrench Gang* "eco-pornography." In the *New York Times*, another reviewer expressed amazement that such a violent novel could be published with no consequences.

The Monkey Wrench Gang would no doubt have sparked an even larger controversy were it not for the growing acceptance of the ecological perspective. Environmental disasters such as the Santa Barbara oil spill in 1969 had already provoked widespread fears about the destruction of nature. The blowout of an offshore oil well platform had sent two hundred thirty-five thousand gallons of crude oil into the ocean and blackened beaches for thirty-five miles. The next year, Americans celebrated the first Earth Day, an indication of a growing ecological consciousness. As environmental awareness grew, so did the desire to preserve wilderness areas. The bitter three-year battle over a trans-Alaska oil pipeline, finally approved by Congress in 1973, only fed the sense of urgency regarding preservation. At the same time, the rise of a youth counterculture provided a further boost to wilderness appreciation. By the early 1970s, many young people were attempting to live on the land or seeking wilderness experiences as an escape from society.

Americans' growing concern for the environment was reflected in the scores of environmental groups that vied for the public's support. Like the civil rights and women's movements, environmentalism was split into numerous organizations representing a diverse array of views and tactics. The Natural Resources Defense Council, for instance, emphasized litigation in the courts. The Sierra Club, the Wilderness Society, and other groups often concentrated on political activity and had considerable experience lobbying in the halls of power. It was actually longtime Sierra Club leader David Brower, for instance, who had cut the political deal dooming Glen Canyon. Later, the Wilderness Society's Howard Zahniser would receive most of the credit for shepherding the Wilderness Act of 1964 through Congress. That act set aside large tracts of federal land as wilderness areas, where most economic activities and even motorized vehicles were barred. Meanwhile, groups such as Greenpeace, founded in 1971, and Earth First! turned to the direct-action approach of the earlier civil rights and antiwar demonstrators. The most radical group, Earth First! was founded in 1979, four years after the publication of *The Monkey Wrench Gang*. A relatively small group, Earth First! was organized by Dave Foreman and several other former Wilderness Society employees. Much like Fannie Lou Hamer and the Black Power advocates of the late 1960s (see Chapter 11), they had grown disgusted with the willingness of moderate organizations to compromise. Such an approach, Foreman believed, was doomed to fail.

Ironically, by 1979, mainstream environmental organizations could take credit for a growing body of environmental legislation. In 1969, the National Environmental Policy Act had ordered all federal agencies to develop environmental impact statements to assess "potential damage to the environment from any government action." Four years later, the Endangered Species Act had forced federal land managers to survey public lands and to prohibit uses that would endanger threatened wildlife. In 1974, Congress had created the Environmental Protection Agency, the first independent federal agency to assume responsibility for environmental regulation. And in 1976, the Federal Land Policy and Management Act and the National Forest Management Act had called for "scientific land-use planning"—that is, the development of long-range plans for federal lands based on ecological principles rather than economic use. By the end of the 1970s, roughly two-thirds of all public lands were still open for multiple uses, including mining, grazing, timber cutting, and motorized recreation. Nonetheless, ecological awareness and the desire to preserve wilderness were increasingly reflected in federal policy.

For many people, however, the environmental movement's success was precisely the problem. To many westerners, who traditionally had access to public lands and resources, it appeared that environmental "radicals" had succeeded in closing off access to anyone not wearing a backpack. When Ronald Reagan won the presidency in 1980 with the promise to "get the federal government off the backs of the people," James Watt believed the time had come to end the "privileged position of the select few" (that is, environmentalists) on public lands. Abbey and other environmentalists, of course, had a very different view of things. Yet that did not entirely explain their angry response to news of Watt's appointment as Reagan's secretary of the interior. As one environmental writer put it, the "real source of their objections [to Watt] springs from who he is."

"TRAMPLE THE WILDERNESS IN EXPENSIVE HIKING BOOTS"

James Watt traced his roots to the frontier West. Traveling from St. Louis in a covered wagon, one of Watt's grandparents had homesteaded in Sheridan County in north-central Wyoming. James was born in 1938, the second of William and Lois Watt's three children. Home for them was Lusk, Wyoming, a small ranching town where William practiced law. While growing up, James spent summers on the family ranch, performing chores such as mending fences and pumping water for the cattle. It was that experience, he later claimed, that gave him a love of the West "in the special way of those who have to grapple with its sometimes hostile environment."

Early on, James also developed a love of politics. When he was a child in Lusk, Lois organized the family into a club to play games and teach the children parliamentary rules. She recalled that James "liked to make speeches" at the club's meetings. In junior high school, he became interested in reading about current events. Later, he was active in a variety of high school clubs and varsity sports. He also was the natural choice as the local American Legion post's delegate to Boys State, where he was elected "governor" of Wyoming. By then, the family had moved to Wheatland, the county seat of Platte County in southeastern Wyoming. There William, a conservative Republican, continued to practice law and became active in local Republican Party politics. "Franklin Roosevelt was a cuss word in our house," recalled James, who eagerly absorbed his father's views.

After graduating from high school as valedictorian, Watt headed off to the University of Wyoming in Laramie. Sociable but serious, he won a number of honors. Naturally, he was involved in student government, winning election as student body business and finance manager. In his sophomore year, he married his high school sweetheart, Leilani Bomgardner, who had entered the university with him. A diligent student, he graduated with honors in 1960. By then, he also had completed his first year of law school. When he graduated two years later, after having served as editor of the *Wyoming Law Journal*, he was admitted to the Wyoming State Bar. Only twenty-four, Watt was already the father of a son and daughter. With the help of connections, he quickly found work.

In 1962, Watt worked as a volunteer in Wyoming Republican Milward Simpson's campaign for the U.S. Senate. Simpson happened to be a longtime Watt family acquaintance and the father of Watt's college friend and future U.S. senator Alan Simpson. Milward Simpson won the Senate seat, and after the election, Watt moved east to work as Simpson's legislative assistant and counsel. He did not realize it, but Washington would be his home for a long time to come. His love of politics had led him in the opposite direction from Abbey—away from his beloved West. Ironically, it also had landed him in the federal bureaucracy so despised by the Watt family.

Despite his political views, Watt's attraction to Washington was in many ways fitting. For much of their history, Americans have held a romantic view of the West as a place of limitless freedom for "rugged individualists." In the West, however, myth and reality have often been at odds. In fact, the federal government has long played a dominant role in the region's development, from the construction of the transcontinental railroads in the nineteenth century to the building of massive water projects in the twentieth. Even as Watt packed his bags for the nation's capital, the federal government continued to play a crucial role in the region's economy, pumping billions of dollars into water development, military bases, and roads. It also owned and administered most of the land in the West. **[See Source 2.]** In short, the region's well-being was tied to the federal government. Whatever their views about the government, therefore, westerners could not afford to ignore it. That was especially true of those whose livelihoods were tied directly to the land. Naturally, they were interested in making sure that federal agencies operated in a friendly manner—especially the Department of the Interior, charged with overseeing vast public rangelands, controlling numerous dams and water development projects, and administering the national parks and monuments.

In his new job, Watt was perfectly positioned to learn all about the Interior Department. Milward Simpson sat on the Senate Committee on Interior and Insular Affairs, which had control over public land policy and oversight over the Interior Department. As Congress passed a host of important environmental bills in the mid-1960s, the young staffer sat in on the committee's meetings, and he began to learn about land use issues.

About the same time, Watt had another experience that would influence his views about such issues. Shortly after moving to Washington, he had a religious awakening. After attending a gospel meeting for businessmen, he joined the fundamentalist* Assembly of God Church. As a born-again Christian fundamentalist, Watt took literally the declaration in the Book of Genesis that man had dominion over the earth and all its creatures. That reading of the Old Testament conformed perfectly to his belief that people in the West should have the freedom to use the land for their own economic benefit. Now Watt would fight for his land use views with a religious zeal.

Simpson retired four years after his election because of poor health, but Watt's work on the Committee on Interior and Insular Affairs had attracted the attention of the U.S. Chamber of Commerce, a pro-development organization that lobbied for the interests of businesses. Hired as a lobbyist, Watt was on the losing end of some major battles as Congress passed a wave of environmental bills in the late 1960s. His work as a pro-business lobbyist, however, caught the attention of the Nixon administration. Starting in 1969, he was named to a series of Interior Department posts and soon became the principal spokesman for the administration on recreation and conservation issues. In 1975, Nixon's successor, Gerald Ford, named Watt to the Federal Power Commission, the agency responsible for the development and oversight of federal energy projects such as hydroelectric dams.

The election of Democrat Jimmy Carter in 1976 halted Watt's steady rise as a federal administrator, but he would soon have another opportunity to fight for his views. After the conservative Colorado brewing heir Joseph Coors established the Denver-based Mountain States Legal Foundation (MSLF) to fight environmental legislation, Watt landed the job as the organization's first president. In his new role, he took on the Environmental Protection Agency, the Sierra Club, and even his old employer, the Interior Department. In his words, he was out to fight "those bureaucrats and no-growth advocates who challenge individual liberties and economic freedoms." With Watt at the helm, the MSLF filed nearly fifty legal cases reflecting its free-enterprise agenda. Frequently, the cases involved disputes over the use of public lands, such as the defense of ranchers' permits to graze their livestock on rangeland controlled by the Interior Department. By 1980, Watt had drawn the ire of environmentalists, but he also had gained the attention of the leaders of a resurgent conservative movement centered on the presidential campaign of Republican Ronald Reagan.

By the late 1970s, rising energy prices had sparked high inflation, an economic recession, and widespread fear about the erosion of America's power. At the same time, the Sagebrush Rebellion, led by disgruntled ranchers and other users of public lands, had erupted in many western states. Rebels called for the transfer of federal lands to the states and an end to policies that "protect endangered species to the detriment of human beings." By 1980, a number of western politicians had endorsed the Sagebrush Rebellion, including Reagan, who said that a handful of "environmental extremists" had succeeded in locking up the nation's public lands. Fulfilling the nation's energy needs, he asserted, could not be "thwarted by a tiny minority opposed to economic growth." By that time, many Americans were receptive to the argument that America's natural resources, especially energy resources on public lands, needed to be tapped more aggressively. Holding out the hope that the country would be able to

---

*Fundamentalist: Related to the twentieth-century Protestant movement based on the literal interpretation of everything in the Bible and on the belief that such a reading of the Scriptures is fundamental to faith and morals.

solve its energy and economic crises with little sacrifice, Reagan won a landslide victory over Carter.

Shortly after his election, Reagan named Watt secretary of the interior. Because of the Interior Department's large role in western affairs, it has traditionally been headed by someone from that region. Watt was the logical choice for that and other reasons. He believed that Reagan's election was an "opportunity to make [a] massive change" in the nation's environmental policies. He assumed that such a change was crucial to realizing the new president's vision of economic growth, abundant energy, and national security. Thus, he declared, his goal was to make more land available for "multiple uses" rather than just wilderness or recreation. Watt also appealed to Christian conservatives who supported Reagan. "My responsibility," he said, "is to follow the Scriptures, which call upon us to occupy the land until Jesus returns." And, as he announced after his appointment, he did not know "how many future generations we can count on before the Lord returns."

News of Watt's appointment elicited a wave of criticism from environmental organizations such as the Wilderness Society, whose director called Watt "a joke" and his appointment "disastrous." Nonetheless, he was easily confirmed by the Senate and took office in early 1981, moving quickly to carry out his program. **[See Source 3.]** In his first year in office, the new interior secretary opened nearly half of the offshore continental shelf surrounding the United States to oil drilling, a move that brought back memories of the Santa Barbara oil spill. He also ordered a halt to further federal land purchases and ended three major national park purchase programs. The next year, he announced plans to sell thirty-five million acres of wilderness to reduce the federal debt. He also called for a relaxation of "regulatory burdens" on coal exploration on federal lands and an easing of environmental rules. Ordering a rewrite of department management regulations, Watt was determined to make federal resources available even if existing laws prohibited the development of public lands. Meanwhile, in the national parks, Watt instituted a policy of road, campground, and latrine construction to provide "easy access" and "safe shelter" to park visitors. The "vast majority of Americans," the secretary observed, are not "rugged young backpackers." In frequent speeches around the country, Watt linked his department's resource policy to a "war" to protect "liberty and freedom." Environmentalism, he said in 1982, was "bad for the economy, bad for the environment, bad for freedom." At the same time, he continued to lash out at "radical environmentalists." These "elitists," he told a group in Reno, Nevada, wanted "to lock away the land so that it [could not] be used—except by those with the time, money and good health to trample the wilderness in expensive hiking boots."

"THE IDEOLOGY OF A CANCER CELL"

Long dismayed by what he called "our contemporary techno-industrial greed-and-power culture," Edward Abbey was not surprised by Watt's appointment. In fact, Reagan's secretary of the interior only confirmed his worst fears for the Southwest. Nonetheless, Abbey found outrageous Watt's assertion that environmentalists were "elitists." A journey into the wilderness, he countered, was "the freest, cheapest, most non-privileged of pleasures." All it took was two legs and a pair of $17.95 army surplus boots. In public appearances and rallies in opposition to Reagan administration policies, Abbey urged concerned citizens to become activists, admonishing one audience in 1983 not to be a "tick on a dog, ornamental but useless."

By 1982, Watt's policies had elicited widespread media and popular scrutiny. *Time* magazine's coverage was typical. Its August 23 cover story featured a picture of the secretary and the headline, "GOING, GOING …! Land Sale of the Century"—a reference to Watt's proposal to sell millions of acres of federal land. In the early 1980s, membership in environmental groups increased dramatically. For instance, between 1981 and 1983, membership in the Sierra Club and the Wilderness Society roughly doubled. The growth of environmental organizations was particularly impressive because it came during a period of economic recession. It reflected many Americans' rejection of Watt's premise that economic growth had to come at the expense of the environment. Even hunters and sportfishing enthusiasts were worried about the impact of Watt's policies on their ability to use public lands. Millions of Americans now considered themselves "environmentalists" even if they did not belong to an organized group.

The uproar over Watt's policies alarmed some conservatives. Watt, they now believed, alienated too many voters and threatened to strengthen the environmental movement. By playing right into his opponents' hands, he could jeopardize the entire "Reagan Revolution." Conservative columnist George Will, for instance, observed in 1982 that Watt was stimulating Edward Abbey's brand of environmental radicalism. As Will put it, Watt had only made more popular the type of environmentalism that wanted to put "sand in the gears of industrialism."

Under pressure from fellow Republicans, Watt began to take on a more conciliatory tone. In 1983, he announced that there would "not be a massive land sell-off" and in an effort to help the "eastern press corps" better understand him, he projected a less confrontational style in interviews. **[See Source 4.]** Yet Watt could not avoid bad publicity. After he insisted on auctioning off Interior Department coal leases, an eight-month investigation concluded that the leases had been disposed of at "fire sale" prices. He also continued to make remarks that environmentalists found outrageous. In a *Business Week* interview, for instance, he compared environmentalists to Nazis, declaring that each sought "centralized planning." Speaking to a meeting of U.S. Chamber of Commerce lobbyists in the fall of 1983, Watt made what *Newsweek* called his "last gaffe" when he described the members of a coal-lease commission as "a black … a woman, two Jews and a cripple." This "latest misfiring of his infamous mouth," as *Newsweek* put it, immediately brought calls for his resignation. Facing reelection the next year, Reagan and many Republicans realized that Watt was a political liability. Three weeks after his Chamber of Commerce speech, Watt resigned.

By the time Watt settled down to a law practice and relative obscurity, many mainstream environmentalists had developed remarkably similar concerns about Edward Abbey. As with Watt, many people who sympathized with Abbey's views came to believe that his extremism only played into the hands of their opponents. His endorsement of ecoterrorism as "illegal but ethically imperative" was especially troubling. The Sierra Club and other politically active environmental organizations had been working for years to broaden their movement and bring it into the mainstream of American life. To them, Abbey was an embarrassment and counterproductive to the cause.

Just as embarrassing were Abbey's views about numerous social issues, from gun control to the women's movement and immigration. No feminist, Abbey developed a reputation for treating women as little more than sexual objects. Frequently bored with his wives and lovers, he was married five times in all. His antifemale reputation was reinforced by the shallow treatment of women in his published works and by the run-ins he had with feminist leaders such as Gloria Steinem (see Chapter 13). Feminists, he believed, were fighting a "trivial" battle. Why would women "wish to fulfill their human potential in offices, boutiques, boardrooms, army tanks, or coal mines," he asked in a scathing review of Steinem's book *Outrageous Acts and Everyday Rebellions* (1983). Calling himself "Cactus Ed," he wrote a letter to *Ms.* magazine that began "Dear Sirs." "Out here a woman's place is in the kitchen, the barnyard and the bedroom in exactly that order," he wrote, "and we don't need no changes." Even if Abbey was just poking fun, many people did not appreciate his humor. Nor did they approve of his membership in the National Rifle Association or his opposition to gun control. Equally embarrassing were his attacks on immigration from Mexico. Open borders, he argued in a 1988 essay, were bringing an influx of "millions of hungry, ignorant, unskilled, and culturally-morally-generically impoverished people."

Aside from an ability to alienate their own allies, however, Abbey and Watt had something else in common. By associating individual freedom with the western land-scape, both reflected the romantic assumption that the West was the last domain of the unrestrained individual. Both also saw the land, and thus freedom, under assault. For Watt, defending the American faith meant doing battle with powerful outside forces that had the West in their grip. Abbey, too, feared such forces. In his mind, they threat-ened the liberty that he associated with access to the land. "Oppose the destruction of our homeland by those alien forces from Houston, Tokyo, Manhattan, D.C. and the Pentagon," he once urged at an Earth First! rally.

What Watt and Abbey disagreed on, of course, was the exact nature of the threat. Watt associated economic growth with personal freedom. For him, federal bureaucrats in league with "elitist" environmentalists were the danger. Because neither bureaucrats nor urban environmentalists had to wrest a living from the land, they did not understand the importance of individuals' freedom to use the resources of the West to their own advan-tage. By contrast, Abbey perceived the danger as emanating from those exercising such unfettered freedom: ranchers, farmers, miners, and corporations in league with their powerful allies in the government. Worse, all these "individualists" were riding an un-controlled technological wave. Engaged in a lifelong battle against unthinking growth, Abbey, unlike Watt, rejected the dominant American faith in technology and progress. The twenty books that Abbey wrote before his death in 1989 stand as an eloquent cry against this often unquestioned faith. Growth for growth's sake, he maintained, was "the ideology of a cancer cell." It threatened to rob individuals of a more important kind of freedom: from the very constraints of civilization. In the end, what separated these two environmental "extremists" was not their differing views of the land but the meaning that they assigned to freedom itself.

• PRIMARY SOURCES •

Source 1:   Edward Abbey, *The Monkey Wrench Gang* (1975)

The Monkey Wrench Gang remains Edward Abbey's best-selling novel. Based on certain real people, the little gang of ecoterrorists is led by Doc Sarvis, an Albuquerque physician. Other members are George Washington Hayduke, a mentally unstable former Green Beret; Bonnie Abbzug, a refugee from the Bronx; and Seldom Seen Smith, a polygamous Mormon river guide. Do you think Abbey's purpose was only to entertain his readers or also to challenge them? What is Doc Sarvis's message in this excerpt?

During the early morning, Hayduke and Bonnie had "borrowed" the front license plates from tourist automobiles from three different states and attached them (temporarily) to their own vehicles. Assuming, naturally, that the loss would not be noticed for hundreds of miles.

Bonnie driving, they went up the road to the rim of Black Mesa. From a vantage point near the road, armed with binoculars, they examined the layout of the coal transmission system.

To the east, beyond the rolling ridges on the mesa's surface, lay the evergrowing strip mines of the Peabody Coal Company. Four thousand acres, prime grazing land for sheep and cattle, had been eviscerated already; another forty thousand was under lease. (The lessor was the Navajo Nation, as represented by the Bureau of Indian Affairs under the jurisdiction of the U.S. Government.) The coal was being excavated by gigantic power shovels and dragline machines, the largest equipped with 3600-cubic-foot buckets. The coal was trucked a short distance to a processing depot, where it was sorted, washed and stored, some of it loaded into a slurry line for a power plant near Lake Mohave, Nevada, the rest onto a conveyor belt for transportation to storage towers at the railhead of the BM & LP railway, which in turn hauled the coal eighty miles to the Navajo Power Plant near the town of Page.

Smith and Hayduke, Abbzug and Sarvis were especially interested in the conveyor belt, which seemed to be the weakest link in the system. It ran for nineteen miles from mine to railhead. For most of this distance the conveyor was vulnerable, running close to the ground, half concealed by juniper and pinyon pine, unguarded. At the rim of the mesa it descended to the level of the highway, where it rose again, over the highway and into the top of the four storage silos. The belt ran on rollers, the entire apparatus powered electrically.

They sat and watched this mighty engine in motion, conveying coal at the rate of 50,000 tons per day across the mesa and down to the plain and up into the towers. Fifty thousand tons. Every day. For thirty-forty-fifty years. All to feed the power plant at Page.

"I think," said Doc, "these people are serious."

"It ain't people," said Smith. "It's a mechanical animal."

"Now you've got it," Doc agreed. "We're not dealing with human beings. We're up against the megamachine. A megalomaniacal megamachine."

"No sweat," Hayduke said. "It's all rigged up for us. We'll use that fucking conveyor to blow up the loading towers. Nothing could be prettier. Look—it's so goddamned simple it makes me nervous. We take our shit out in the woods there, close to the belt. We throw it on the belt, light the fuse, cover it up with a little coal, let it ride up over the road and into the tower. *Ka-blam!*" ...

The doctor was thinking: All this fantastic effort—giant machines, road networks, strip mines, conveyor belt, pipelines, slurry lines, loading towers, railway and electric train, hundred-million-dollar coal-burning power plant; ten thousand miles of high-tension towers and high-voltage power lines; the devastation of the landscape, the destruction of Indian homes and Indian grazing lands, Indian shrines and Indian burial grounds; the poisoning of the last big clean-air reservoir in the forty-eight contiguous United States, the exhaustion of precious water supplies—all that ball-breaking labor and all that backbreaking expense and a heartbreaking insult to land and sky and human heart, for what?

All that for what? Why, to light the lamps of Phoenix suburbs not yet built, to run the air conditioners of San Diego and Los Angeles, to illuminate shopping-center parking lots at two in the morning, to power aluminum plants, magnesium plants, vinyl-chloride factories and copper smelters, to charge the neon tubing that makes the meaning (all the meaning there is) of Las Vegas, Albuquerque, Tucson, Salt Lake City, the amalgamated *metropolis* of southern California, to keep alive that phosphorescent putrefying glory (all the glory there is left) called Down Town, Night Time, Wonderville, U.S.A.

Source 2:   *Map of Federal Lands* (1978)

In 1978, just three years before James Watt's appointment as secretary of the interior, the federal government controlled approximately 900 million acres of land, of which 516 million were controlled by the Department of the Interior. What does this map reveal about the likely response to Watt's message by many people in the West?

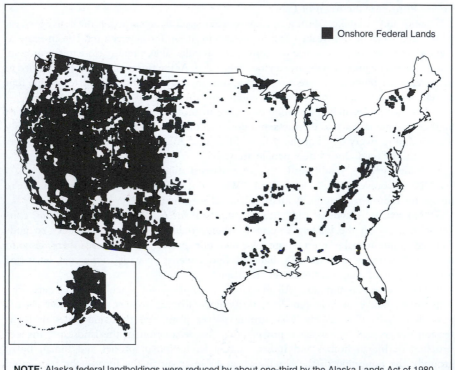

■ Onshore Federal Lands

NOTE: Alaska federal landholdings were reduced by about one-third by the Alaska Lands Act of 1980 (PL 96–487).

© Cengage Learning 2017

Source 3:   *James Watt Outlines His Program* (1981)

In this interview with U.S. News and World Report, *conducted shortly after his appointment as secretary of the interior, James Watt discusses his plans for opening public lands to greater development. How does he intend to accomplish this?*

Q: Mr. Secretary, people are afraid that you are going to push for greater development of natural resources at the expense of the environment. How do you respond?

A: With our technology, we can protect the environment and still bring on the development that is necessary for improving the quality of life and bolstering national defense. Environmental sensitivity requires a balance of economic development and environmental preservation.

   In the last 10 years, we have not had proper energy and mineral development in America. If a crisis comes because of shortages and the political scene dictates a crash development program, I fear that it will be done without regard to the ecology. That's what we must avoid....

Q: Why do we need more development of federal lands?

A: Because America needs more energy, more timber, more agricultural grazing. We have not had an oil-and-gas lease issued onshore Alaska since the mid-1960s. We have not had a major coal lease issued since the early 1970s. Applications have been pending for oil-and-gas leases in the overthrust belts of Wyoming, Montana and Idaho for 10 years. Our mining industry is in very bad shape. Yet we ask why there's an energy crisis....

Q: Why do you favor a moratorium on the creation of new national parks when so many are overcrowded?

A: There has been deterioration and degradation in almost every park because we have not been good stewards of what we have.

   The emphasis in recent years has been on acquiring more and more lands while at the same time refusing to take care of the park lands we have.

   We will reverse that. We have put a moratorium on the acquisition of additional lands until the economic situation changes. In the meantime, we have shifted substantial money to the National Park Service for restoration and improvement of these fragile lands.

Q: How can you make the most popular parks accessible to more people if you don't expand the parks?

A: We need to provide proper access and development of facilities to handle people in the areas where they want to be. For example, they want to see Old Faithful. It doesn't help people to see that geyser if we buy another 100,000 acres outside the present boundaries of that park. So we're clearing up transportation bottlenecks and improving accommodations near popular attractions....

Q: Are more restrictions needed on park use?

A: In recent years, there's been a movement in the National Park Service to make parks available only to the select few. Attention needs to be given to all Americans—backpackers and people who go rafting on the rivers—as well as those who roll up to the park on a bus tour. We want parks to be attractive and accessible to people of all economic levels and not just to people who have lots of time and money.

SOURCE: "James Watt Outlines His Program (1981)" excerpted from "Interview with James Watt" May 25, 1981. U.S. NEWS & WORLD REPORT. 1982.

Source 4:   James Watt, *"It's the People's Land"* (1983)

Increasingly under fire by 1983, James Watt tried to be more conciliatory in dealing with the media. How does his message in this interview differ from his message in Source 3?

On proper use of public lands: You enjoy these lands in many ways ... by picnicking, by looking at them and by grazing on them, by taking the trees from them to build cheaper houses, by using their energy, coal, oil, gas, uranium, etc. But you do that in a way that retains the value of those lands, so that when we—this generation—pass them on to the next generation, they will be in as good as or better condition than when we inherited them....

There will not be a massive land sell-off there was never intended to be a massive land sell-off Last year we sold 1,312 acres. This year we've offered [approximately] 5,500 acres for sale ... and sold 3,500 acres. People don't even want some of the land.... It's totally a political, partisan issue. How can a governor complain from Idaho when he sells about 18,000 acres in one year, and we sell, across the country, 1,312?

On the national parks: We need to acquire more parkland, and I'm hopeful that within the next year or so ... we'll be able to aggressively increase the amount of acreage required for national parks and refuges and wetlands. But right now we don't have economic strength in this country, and so we have to make the decision, where do you want your priorities? Do you want to take care of what you have, or do you want to acquire? The Carter administration ... made the same decisions we made that at this time of economic distress, America could not afford to continue purchasing land at, say, $300 or $400 million a year. I would like to, and I would hope that yet in my tenure we will be spending $300, $400, $500 million a year to acquire the needed parklands.

On wilderness areas: We're continuing to recommend more additions to the wilderness system.... How much is enough? I don't know. I can't put a figure on it.... We can't afford to lock it *all* up, but we do have sufficient numbers of real wilderness areas, and I mean it in the literal sense here, that we can afford to set aside millions of acres for just pure wilderness value.

QUESTIONS TO CONSIDER

1.   According to the essay, both Edward Abbey and James Watt feared that powerful external forces were assaulting the West and undermining individual freedom. Abbey and Watt, however, ended up on opposite sides of the environmental debate. Citing specific primary sources, compare Abbey's and Watt's views about the environment and the threat that these external forces posed to the West and to individual freedom. What did each see as the connection between the land and liberty?

2.   What were the most important factors in Abbey's and Watt's backgrounds in determining their views about the environment? What were the most important developments by the 1980s working to make their views popular?

SOURCE: From NEWSWEEK July 25, 1983. © 1983 Newsweek, Inc.

3. What does the battle over the environment in the early 1980s reveal about the extent to which an "ecological ethic" prevailed among Americans? What do the receptions given to Watt's program and Abbey's ideas reveal about the appeal of environmental radicalism in the late twentieth century? How do the issues raised by Watt and Abbey relate to the current environmental debate?

4. One critic said that Abbey's views were "childish"—and typically American—because they reflected a desire to "have everything," to revolt against authority and to escape from the responsibilities of civilization. Do you agree? Do you think that the same criticism could be leveled against Watt?

FOR FURTHER READING

Edward Abbey ed., *The Best of Edward Abbey* (San Francisco: Sierra Club Books, 1988), provides a useful introduction to Abbey's work, including selections from a number of his most popular books.

Ron Arnold, *At the Eye of the Storm: James Watt and the Environmentalists* (Chicago: Regnery Gateway, 1982), submits a sympathetic discussion of Watt's life prior to his appointment as secretary of the interior and the controversy over his policies during his first two years in office.

James Bishop Jr., *Epitaph for a Desert Anarchist: The Life and Legacy of Edward Abbey* (New York: Atheneum, 1994), gives a brief treatment of Abbey's life and reviews of his major works.

Marc Reisner, *Cadillac Desert: The American West and Its Disappearing Water* (New York: Viking Penguin, 1986), details Americans' efforts to irrigate the arid West by damming its rivers and the consequences of doing so.

Hal K. Rothman, *Saving the Planet: The American Response to the Environment in the Twentieth Century* (Chicago: Ivan R. Dee, 2000), offers a brief overview of the growth of environmental consciousness in the twentieth century.

C. Brant Short, *Ronald Reagan and the Public Lands: America's Conservation Debate, 1979–1984* (College Station: Texas A & M University Press, 1989), provides a brief overview of the controversies surrounding the Reagan administration's federal land policies during its first term.

15

Fighting a "War on Terror": Richard Clarke and John Yoo

When the first plane hit the North Tower of the World Trade Center in New York City at 8:46 a.m. on September 11, 2001, Richard Clarke was in a conference at the Ronald Reagan Building in Washington, D.C. Clarke, the Bush administration's National Coordinator for Counterterrorism, raced to his car and drove to the White House. When he arrived, he learned that the South Tower of the Trade Center had also been hit. Hurrying to Vice President Richard Cheney's office, he met with Cheney and National Security Advisor Condoleezza Rice. After a brief conversation about what to do in the event of another attack, Clarke moved to the White House Situation Room as most other White House personnel were evacuated. Put in charge by Rice, he immediately ordered the military be placed on high alert, the nation's borders closed, and all commercial flights grounded. Soon Clarke and others gathered there would learn that a third plane had hit the Pentagon, and that a fourth, also hijacked with the intent of attacking Washington, had crashed in rural Pennsylvania.

The same morning, John Yoo turned on the television in his office at the Robert F. Kennedy Building in Washington, D.C., in time to see the second plane hit the World Trade Center at 9:03 a.m. Yoo, who worked as deputy assistant attorney general in the Department of Justice's Office of Legal Counsel, would also stay behind with a few other staffers as his and other government buildings were evacuated. Immediately, Yoo set to work on the legal issues surrounding any American response to this attack. Arriving home late that night after driving past the still-burning Pentagon, he was unable to sleep. Telephone callers with questions about legal issues related to the attacks kept him up the remainder of the night.

Altogether, the attacks on September 11 would take nearly three thousand lives. In coming days, Americans began to learn more about al Qaeda, the militant Islamic network headed by the Saudi Arabian Osama bin Laden that was responsible for the

John Yoo   Richard A. Clarke

attacks, and President George W. Bush would declare that the nation was in a "war on terror." That war engaged Richard Clarke and John Yoo in very different ways. From his Justice Department office, John Yoo would frame and aggressively defend a controversial legal foundation for the Bush administration's prosecution of that war. As George Bush's onetime counterterrorism "czar," Richard Clarke would emerge as one of its most vocal and visible critics. Relatively obscure administration functionaries at the time of the attacks, Clarke and Yoo soon became very public figures who symbolized a sharp public divide over the Bush administration's approach to fighting terrorism at home and abroad.

"BUT MR. PRESIDENT, AL QAEDA DID THIS"

Despite several attacks by Islamic radicals on American installations, including a prior attempt to bomb the World Trade Center in 1993, many Americans had never heard of Osama bin Laden or his organization when the planes struck the World Trade Center. On September 11, Richard Clarke needed no introduction to the group. It had been obvious to him who was responsible for the attacks as soon as he pulled up to the White House gate that day and learned that the second tower had been hit. As President Bill Clinton's right-hand man for counterterrorism, he monitored al Qaeda for years and had continued to do so under Bush. With service in seven presidential administrations, he had become a sought-after adviser on national security. In fact, Clarke's entire career seemed to have prepared him to serve in that capacity after the September 11 attacks.

Clarke was born in 1951 in Dorchester, Massachusetts, the son of a factory worker and a nurse. Though his parents were divorced when he was growing up and he lived with his mother in Boston, Clarke was influenced by his father. The son of a Scottish immigrant who served in World War I, Clarke's father had fought in the Pacific during World War II and imparted to Richard a respect for the military. Whenever a nearby military base or navy ship had an open house, his family went. Already during high school he took a keen interest in the growing American military commitment to Vietnam. A senior when the Tet Offensive[*] occurred in early 1968, Clarke turned against the war. As he later put it, he came to believe that "we were hopelessly off track" in Vietnam. As a student at the University of Pennsylvania, he joined antiwar protests and after graduation in 1972 decided to work in government service, specifically in national security, out of a belief that the military had been misused in Vietnam. His motivation, he later wrote, was "a desire to contribute however I could to ensure that there would be 'no more Vietnams.'" Applying to work at the Pentagon, he landed a management trainee job and began to learn about budget and weapons systems. After taking time off in 1978 to earn a degree in management at the Massachusetts Institute of Technology, Clarke moved the next year to the State Department's Bureau of Political-Military Affairs, the "Little Pentagon." There he developed a never-implemented plan of psychological warfare to destabilize the regime of Muammar al-Qadhafi, the dictator of Libya and supporter of terrorist activities, and coordinated diplomatic efforts in support of the Persian Gulf War of 1990–1991.[*] The unmarried Clarke also developed a reputation as an obsessive and extremely focused worker. After accusations that he had ignored the Israeli transfer of American technology to China, Clarke left the State Department in 1992 and moved to the National Security Council, where he became the counterterrorism chief under the new Clinton administration.

Clarke's timing could not have been better. Although most Americans were not paying much attention to it, the threat posed to the United States by radical Islamists, particularly al Qaeda, was rising rapidly by the early 1990s. With roots in the decade-long fight against Soviet occupation of Afghanistan that ended in 1989, al Qaeda turned its anger on the United States by the 1990s. In 1992, it issued a call for a *jihad*—holy war—against Western "occupation" of Islamic nations and singled out the United States, what bin Laden called "the head of the snake," for attack. A string of attacks followed, some clearly connected to al Qaeda. When the United States deployed troops to Somalia in late 1992, bombs exploded at two hotels in Aden on the southern Arabian peninsula, where American troops often stopped on their way to Somalia. Al Qaeda also helped supply and train Somalian warlords battling American forces. Early the next year, a massive truck bomb exploded in a parking garage beneath the World Trade Center towers, ripping a hole seven stories high and killing six people. In 1996, another huge truck bomb exploded outside a complex in Saudi Arabia housing American military personnel, killing 19 Americans and wounding 372 more. Then two years later, bombs exploded simultaneously outside the American embassies in Kenya and Tanzania, leaving twelve Americans dead and more than five thousand people wounded.

In the face of a rising terrorist threat, Clarke assumed a more prominent position in the Clinton administration. The president turned increasingly to his counterterrorism aide for briefings. According to one national news magazine, Clinton "got his intelligence from

---

[*]*Tet Offensive:* The offensive launched inside South Vietnam in February 1968 by the Vietcong and North Vietnamese. It led to devastating losses on both sides and convinced many Americans that the war in Vietnam was not going as well as the military or the Johnson administration claimed.

[*]*Gulf War of 1990–1991:* The American-led invasion of Kuwait to remove Iraqi troops that had occupied the oil-rich nation after Saddam Hussein decided to invade it in August 1990.

Clarke, who collected it from the various spy agencies." Reflecting a growing administration concern about terrorism, Clinton created the Office of the National Coordinator for Security, Infrastructure Protection, and Counterterrorism in 1998 and named Clarke to be its first head. Clarke was responsible for overseeing programs related to national security and coordinating a response to terrorist attacks. After the East African embassy bombings, Clarke became by his own admission "obsessed" with bin Laden and destroying al Qaeda. He even drew up a plan to destroy any "significant threat to Americans" posed by bin Laden's organization that included military strikes against his bases in Afghanistan, then controlled by the fundamentalist Islamic group, the Taliban.[*] That plan, however, was never implemented, nor were Clarke's proposals for enhanced border security presented in 2000. Near the end of the Clinton administration, a frustrated Clarke passed on to Clinton's national security adviser the conclusions of the Federal Bureau of Investigation, Central Intelligence Agency, and the National Security Council staff: Al Qaeda "sleeper cells" had appeared in the United States and American efforts had "not put much of a dent" in bin Laden's network.

Clarke continued in the same position in the new administration of George W. Bush. The election campaign of 2000 had been marked by a terrorist attack on the USS *Cole*, cruising in waters off the south Arabian peninsula nation of Yemen. The attack left seventeen crew members dead and at least forty more wounded. Terrorism, however, did not surface as an election issue, and Clarke soon began to feel as if he had been demoted in the new administration. Losing direct access to the president, he reported instead to the new national security adviser, Condoleezza Rice. A bitter Clarke grew frustrated in the belief that Rice and other top officials in the Bush administration did not take the threat of terrorism seriously. The dismissive attitude, he concluded, stemmed partly from arrogance and a disdain for the Clinton administration, which had warned the new administration about the threat. He also began to believe that Rice and other top advisers in the Bush administration had a "preconceived agenda." High on it was "to do something about Iraq."

That feeling was reinforced right after the 9/11 attacks. On the evening of September 12, Clarke encountered George Bush in the White House Situation Room. Assembling Clarke and a few other staffers, the president explained that he wanted them to see if Iraq's president Saddam Hussein was linked to the attacks. As Clarke later wrote, he was "incredulous." "But Mr. President," he responded, "al Qaeda did this." Then he went on to tell Bush that prior investigation had revealed no evidence of Iraqi ties to al Qaeda. At that point, according to Clarke, Bush grew testy. "Look into Iraq," he ordered, before leaving the room. Following that order, Clarke later sent a memorandum to the president stating no agencies and departments had found a connection between Saddam Hussein and al Qaeda. Clarke never received any indication, however, that Bush had received it.

The next week, Bush addressed a Joint Session of Congress and declared the nation was engaged in a "war on terror." Shortly after that, Clarke was named a special adviser to the president on national security. Never hesitant to sound off to or about superiors, he would not hold that position long. As the Bush administration proceeded

---

[*]*Taliban:* The extremist Islamic political movement that governed Afghanistan from 1996 until late 2001, when an American-led invasion removed its government. While in power, the Taliban government provided sanctuary to Osama bin Laden and al Qaeda.

to fight this "war" at home and abroad (including in Afghanistan after an American-led attack on the Taliban-led government there and in Iraq after the American invasion of that country in 2003), a dismayed Clarke would find plenty to speak out about. Within a couple of years, he would become one of the administration's harshest critics. And much of that criticism would be aimed squarely at actions that John Yoo had helped to make possible.

"CRUEL, INHUMAN OR DEGRADING TREATMENT"

If the nation's experience in Vietnam helped determine Richard Clarke's future role in government, an earlier war had a similar impact on a much younger John Yoo. Born in 1967 in Seoul, South Korea, Yoo emigrated with his parents when he was three months old. Both of his parents were psychiatrists seeking greater economic opportunity than offered in South Korea, which was still largely agricultural. Although they were not political, Yoo's parents had been refugees during the Korean War, when communist North Korea invaded the South. As a result, as Yoo later put it, they were "very anti-communist."

Growing up in New Jersey and Philadelphia, Yoo imbibed his parents' staunch anticommunism. He was "very conscious" of Ronald Reagan as a teenager because, as he said later, Reagan was staunchly anticommunist and his call for lower taxes and smaller government "made sense" to him. Yoo attended an Episcopalian school in Philadelphia and went off to Harvard in 1985 as a committed conservative. There, he met his future wife, the daughter of a television network correspondent. He also became politically active. He joined the school newspaper staff and wrote from a conservative viewpoint about current events. Coming of age politically in the post-Vietnam period, Yoo arrived at different conclusions about the war than those drawn by Clarke and many others of Clarke's generation. In Yoo's mind, the war was neither a mistake nor a misapplication of military resources. Rather, it was fought for a worthwhile goal—preventing the spread of communist dictatorships. The Korean conflict was a formative influence in his thinking about Vietnam. By not pulling out of South Korea, the United States saved it from communist rule and made it possible for democracy to emerge there by the 1980s. Without that intervention, Yoo concluded, "the whole peninsula would be … living under the most appalling conditions." Interest in American intervention in Korea also influenced Yoo's field of study in college. Impressed by the importance of the American role in the Korean War, he decided to major in history with an emphasis in international relations.

After college, Yoo entered law school at Yale. As an undergraduate, he had been impressed by the importance of constitutional law and the power wielded by the Supreme Court. In law school, he combined his interest in foreign affairs and constitutional law in the study of presidential war powers—the powers that presidents can legally exercise in wartime. Yoo left law school with a very expansive view of presidential war powers, a view shaped as well by the Korean conflict. President Harry Truman had waged war in Korea without Congressional approval. It was a controversial decision, but one that allowed Yoo's family to avoid living under communist rule. Yoo clearly understood the connection between Truman's decision and his family's opportunity to come to the United States and his opportunity to attend Harvard and Yale. When Yoo graduated from law school in 1992, however, defending broad executive war powers did not seem to be a promising career move. The Cold War had ended by then and legal scholars were busy pursuing other topics besides war powers. Moreover, the war in Vietnam had led many Americans to oppose the broad exercise of executive wartime powers. That opposition was reflected in the passage of the War Powers Act[*] by Congress in 1973, which restricted the president's power to deploy American military forces abroad. Yoo had a very different view about the exercise of such powers. As passions surrounding that war subsided, however, Yoo concluded that it would be easier to write favorably about the broad assertion of presidential war powers. As he saw it, the issue had been "so tied up" with views about the Vietnam War that it was difficult to be "objective" about it.

Yoo began to publish extensively on war powers after landing a job teaching in the law school at the University of California Berkeley in 1993. With little patience for international law, he believed that an unrestrained United States needed to assert its power unilaterally and that presidents had broad authority under the Constitution to do so. While these views were not popular among legal scholars, his profile in influential circles rose. Although still only in his twenties, Yoo became active in the Federalist Society, a conservative legal organization that promoted an interpretation of the Constitution based on the Founders' "original intent." In 1994, he took a leave from teaching to clerk for Supreme Court justice Clarence Thomas. A year later, he served as general counsel of the Senate Judiciary Committee, where he worked under Republican senator Orrin Hatch. Returning to Berkeley in 1996, Yoo continued to publish in defense of original intent. He argued, for instance, that the Founders wanted presidents, much like British kings, to be able to wage war almost unilaterally. That view put him squarely at odds with the overwhelming majority of legal scholars, who argue that the Founders were skeptical of executive war-making power precisely because of their experience with British King George III prior to the American Revolution.

Yoo stayed at Berkeley until 2001, when he was asked by the incoming Bush administration to serve as deputy assistant attorney general in the Justice Department's Office of Legal Counsel. Only thirty-four when he joined the office, Yoo had already developed a reputation in legal circles for his controversial views. Handed down from his new position in the government, however, his legal interpretations became the subject of intense public debate. In fact, Yoo would occupy a key position in support of the Bush administration's conduct of a war on terror. Though relatively obscure, the Office of Legal Counsel plays an important role in the executive branch of the federal government because the legal opinions issued by it are legally binding on executive branch employees. When the staff interprets a law in a certain way and the attorney general agrees, the executive branch must adhere to that interpretation. For instance, if the Office of Legal Counsel declares legal a previously outlawed interrogation technique, government officials who use it on prisoners or detainees are virtually immune from prosecution. In short, Yoo's new position, though largely out of sight from the general public, entailed enormous power. As one former head of the Office of Legal Counsel declared, it had the power to hand out "get-out-of-jail-free cards."

---

[*]*War Powers Act:* Passed over President Richard Nixon's veto in 1973, it asserted greater congressional control over military actions abroad. Its main provision prevented presidents from such actions for more than sixty days without congressional approval.

Initially, Yoo had no idea how important his work would be. In fact, by late summer of 2001, he was bored with his job and contemplated leaving the office. The terrorist attacks on September 11 changed all of that. After the attacks, Yoo began to work closely with a small group of lawyers in various posts in the Bush administration, including David Addington, Vice President Cheney's legal counsel, and Alberto Gonzales, then the president's legal counsel. The group, which came to be known as "The War Council," began to transform into law the administration's views regarding the conduct of a war on terror. In coming months, Yoo would begin to issue what one student called "many of the most fateful legal decisions in the post-9/11 era."

Those opinions were rooted in Yoo's belief in presidents' expansive wartime powers. In coming months, Yoo would advance arguments for the administration's right to broaden domestic surveillance, and narrow the constitutional right to a speedy trial and the Fourth Amendment prohibition on unreasonable searches and seizures. His opinions also allowed for the detainment of enemy combatants without applying the Geneva Convention* and narrowing the definition of torture so as to approve interrogation techniques such as waterboarding. This method was used on some captured American soldiers in World War II by the Japanese, who were later prosecuted for doing so. It involves strapping an individual on a bench in an inclined position, placing a wet cloth over his mouth, and applying additional water to the cloth for up to twenty minutes. The result is restricted air flow into the lungs, increased levels of carbon dioxide in the blood, the perception of suffocation and drowning, and panic. Despite warnings from Secretary of State Colin Powell and the State Department's legal counsel not to override international law regarding torture, Yoo provided legal grounds for so-called enhanced interrogation of suspected Taliban captives held at Guantanamo Bay Detention Camp in Cuba and, later, of detainees at the Abu Ghraib Prison in Iraq. In addition to waterboarding, such techniques included the confinement of prisoners in small, dark boxes and slamming them repeatedly into walls. In a memorandum written in 2002 to the president's legal counsel that would later come to be known as the "Torture Memo," Yoo declared that the United States had the right to modify multinational agreements relating to torture. Moreover, interrogators could not be prosecuted as long as their acts were not *specifically intended* to inflict prolonged physical or mental pain. Many of the techniques in question "may amount to cruel, inhuman or degrading treatment," the memo declared, but they do not produce pain or suffering of the "necessary intensity" to constitute torture. **[See Sources 1 and 2.]**

Yoo's analysis of a powerful new eavesdropping program known as the Terrorist Surveillance Program (TSP) was perhaps more directly relevant to American citizens. Outlined by Vice President Cheney and his legal counsel David Addington, the TSP was run by the National Security Agency (NSA)* to intercept private telephone calls and emails coming to and from the United States without first securing a warrant. Such warrantless eavesdropping on Americans was illegal under the Foreign Intelligence Surveillance Act (FISA), passed by Congress in 1978. That law called for the establishment of a secret court made up of people outside the nation's intelligence agencies and appointed by the chief justice of the Supreme Court to review

---

Geneva Convention: The agreements updated or negotiated in 1949 that defined the rights of those captured in a military conflict.

National Security Agency (NSA): The agency created in 1952 to collect and analyze foreign communications.

the NSA's surveillance requests. The intent of the court oversight was to protect the Fourth Amendment prohibition on "unreasonable searches and seizures" while still giving the NSA an effective means to listen to individuals suspected of plotting attacks against the United States. Federal prosecutors and others in and out of the Justice Department who had experience with earlier eavesdropping under FISA overwhelmingly concluded that it in no way impeded the apprehension of suspects. As one Justice Department official put it, "It never hurt our ability to get the bad guys." Yoo's analysis of the new NSA program, however, argued that warrantless surveillance inside the United States was a presidential prerogative during wartime and thus NSA did not need any court to review its monitoring international telephone calls and emails. Furthermore, Yoo asserted, the very absence of such warrantless surveillance had helped make the September 11 attacks possible.

Many other government officials or former officials disagreed with Yoo's assertions. Once they learned of the TSP, they argued that there was no evidence to support his contention that the attacks on September 11 necessitated the elimination of court oversight on domestic spying. "They wanted to go on fishing expeditions," concluded one former federal prosecutor. Other former officials and legal experts were even more direct in their criticisms of Yoo's legal reasoning in support of warrantless eavesdropping. The former solicitor general* in the Clinton administration, for instance, called the TSP a distortion of "the theory of presidential power," while the head of the New York Bar Association's International Law Committee declared that it "made war a matter of dictatorial power."

"THIS IS NOT OVER YET"

From his perch in the Bush administration, Richard Clarke would also come to conclusions directly at odds with Yoo's assertions about the "war on terror." Unlike many of Yoo's other critics who drew on their legal training, however, Clarke relied on years of experience in counterterrorism. As he witnessed actions from inside the administration in the months before and after the September 11 attacks, that experience led him to question its conduct of the "war on terror." In Clarke's view, the failure to prevent those attacks had little to do with a lack of executive power or legal limits on the nation's ability to spy on suspected terrorists. Rather, it stemmed from a failure of officials to heed warnings already loud and clear. The wrong diagnosis of the problem, Clarke came to realize, led the administration to apply the wrong remedies. And far from making the nation safer, those remedies actually put it in greater danger.

In the months before September 11, Clarke had already become alarmed and disillusioned about the Bush administration's apparent lack of concern about the al Qaeda threat. Despite repeated attempts, he was unable to secure a timely cabinet-level briefing with the new administration to review that threat. Removed as national security coordinator from cabinet-level access by National Security Advisor Condoleezza Rice, Clarke asked to be reassigned in the spring of 2001. That fall, he was named to head a new Office of Cyberspace Security. After Clarke's worst fears were borne out on

---

Solicitor General: The individual who is appointed to represent the United States before the Supreme Court.

September 11, his transfer was put on hold. Clarke stayed on as national security coordinator, but his frustration with the Bush administration only mounted. Its focus on Iraq, he concluded, was entirely misguided. He was also convinced that Bush sought "simple solutions" and that the president and those around him had no interest in "complicated analyses." After working so long in counterterrorism, Clarke thought the issues surrounding it were "laced with subtlety and nuance." With little understanding of other cultures, for instance, Clarke believed that the president and his top advisers could not see how a unilateral show of American power in the Middle East would only strengthen the appeal of Islamic radicalism and make the nation less safe.

Clarke lasted in the Bush administration until early 2003, when he retired from government after thirty years of service. He turned much of his energy to writing a book about his experiences in counterterrorism. Published the next year, *Against All Enemies: Inside America's War on Terror* contained a searing attack on the Bush administration, which Clarke accused of ignoring the al Qaeda threat before September 11. The first post-September priority, Clarke declared, was to address the threat of future terrorist attacks at home. Yet he was convinced that the Bush administration did not take the problem seriously enough even after the attacks. First it opposed, then supported, the creation of a separate Department of Homeland Security. The result, Clarke concluded, was at times farcical. The introduction of a Color Code System to indicate the terrorist threat level forced cities and states to spend millions of dollars before it was later abandoned. Meanwhile, lumping various organizations together in the new department created a "disappointing and disorganized mess." Worse, key appointments had been politicized and the entire terror issue was used for political gain. And for all the fanfare, Americans had been left no safer.

Clarke's criticisms created a stir in many quarters. Right after the release of his book, he appeared on the CBS television program *60 Minutes*, where he made the same charges. **[See Source 3.]** The Bush administration reacted to them with strong denials. Some critics argued that Clarke had embellished his account and that his accusations were self-serving and made to gain favor with Democratic presidential candidate John Kerry. Yet Clarke was undeterred. He was also not finished. He appeared on numerous television news programs and spoke to audiences around the country. In March 2004, he also testified before the so-called 9/11 Commission,[*] where he made a personal apology to the victims' families for failing to prevent the attacks. He was the only commission witness to do so.

The commission's report, released later in 2004, did not end the debates about the attacks. As arguments about September 11 and the "war on terror" continued, Clarke remained one of the Bush administration's most vocal critics. In 2008, he published *Your Government Failed You*, which broadened his attacks. In it, for instance, he bristled at the initiatives that John Yoo's legal work supported. Clarke's criticism of the Bush administration's eavesdropping and prisoner detainment and interrogation actions was not the work of a legal scholar. Rather, it reflected his understanding of international law and Americans' constitutional rights. It also reflected his strong belief that torture, prolonged detainment of prisoners without formal charges against them, and domestic spying rode roughshod over both. Such actions, he argued, did nothing to make the nation

---

[*]*9/11 Commission:* The commission established in late 2002 to prepare an account of the circumstances surrounding the September 11 attacks.

safer. In fact, they were actually counterproductive in dealing with the threat posed by al Qaeda. **[See Source 4.]**

Meanwhile, John Yoo had became another prominent public figure in the growing battle over the Bush administration's "war on terror." Yoo left the Office of Legal Counsel in 2003 and returned to Berkeley, but not to a quiet academic life. In 2005, he published *The Powers of War and Peace*, an examination of the powers of presidents and the Congress to wage war and conduct diplomacy. At the same time, Yoo's legal opinions continued to support Bush's policies, including the NSA's electronic surveillance program. Yoo also found himself, however, under increasing public criticism. Unlike many other Bush administration officials, the mild-mannered Yoo did not shrink from the spotlight. Nor did he yield to critics. In 2008, a House judiciary subcommittee held hearings into detainee interrogation under the Bush administration. Called to testify, Yoo sparred with committee members and gave little ground. As journalists made public details of the "enhanced" interrogation techniques and the interception of Americans' private telephone and email messages without court approval, Yoo stepped forward to defend these programs in newspaper columns and public speeches around the country.

After President Barack Obama took office in early 2009, the criticism of Yoo intensified. On his second day in office in 2009, Obama revoked all of Yoo's legal opinions on interrogation. Later that year, the new administration began releasing the Bush administration's Office of Legal Counsel memos justifying enhanced surveillance and interrogation techniques, including Yoo's so-called Torture Memo. The Office of Professional Responsibility in the Department of Justice also launched an investigation of the legal advice given by the Bush administration's Office of Legal Counsel. In the spring of 2009, the administration announced that no legal action would be taken against CIA's interrogators who followed that legal advice. Condemning what he called a "dark and painful chapter in our history," the new president also made clear his opposition to a formal inquiry into the program. Nonetheless, calls for prosecution of Yoo and other Bush administration officials remained.

In the face of this barrage, Yoo continued to defend the Bush administration's conduct of the "war on terror." **[See Source 5.]** Critics charged that his counterattacks were delivered to fend off possible legal action against him. In fact, in early 2009, a Guantanamo detainee named Jose Padilla, who was held for three and a half years without formal charges filed against him, sued John Yoo in federal court for violating his rights to legal counsel, to a speedy trial, to due process, and to other rights guaranteed under the Constitution. That summer a U.S. district court judge refused to dismiss the case. Whatever his motives, Yoo continued his aggressive defense of Bush's policies. In 2010, Yoo published *Crisis and Command: The History of Executive Power from George Washington to George W. Bush*, a broad history of presidential power arguing that national security concerns have frequently boosted presidential power at the expense of the Congress.

At the same time, the retired Richard Clarke also continued to seek an audience for his views about the "war on terror." In addition to running his own consulting firm, he served as a commentator on ABC News. Using his long and varied experience in counterterrorism and status as a best-selling author, Clarke also turned to writing fiction as a vehicle for commentary. In 2005, he published *The Scorpion's Gate*, a futuristic novel about events in the Middle East and arrogant leaders in the United States who seek to change the government of an oil-rich Arab nation. At the opening of Clarke's tale, a bomb explodes in a hotel in the Persian Gulf state of Bahrain. A British intelligence agent, who later proves helpful to the American heroes, wants to assist blast victims, but is dissuaded by his Scottish bodyguard. "Hear all that shootin' out front? This is not over yet," the bodyguard tells him. More than a decade after the attacks on September 11, the battle against Islamic extremists is not over either. And, as the revelations in 2014 of massive NSA surveillance of Americans' electronic communications revealed, neither is the battle over the proper means to wage an ongoing "war on terror." **[See Source 6.]** Today, the questions confronting John Woo and Richard Clarke regarding those means remain questions for us as well.

•PRIMARY SOURCES•

Source 1:　*Memorandum to John Yoo* (2001)

In this memo, William H. Taft, IV, the legal adviser to the secretary of state (and great grandson of the thirty-first president of the United States and tenth chief justice of the Supreme Court), expresses grave doubts about Yoo's conclusions regarding permissible treatment of detainees. What are Taft's concerns? How do his concerns compare to those raised by Richard Clarke?

I attach a draft memorandum commenting on the draft you sent me earlier in the week. While we have not been able in two days to do as thorough a job as I would like in reviewing your draft, I am forwarding these comments to you in draft form now for your consideration. They suggest that both the most important factual assumptions on which your draft is based and its legal analysis are seriously flawed.

Our concerns with your draft are focused on its consideration of the status of detainees who were members of the Taliban Militia as a practical matter. Under the Geneva Conventions, these persons would be entitled to have their status determined individually. We find untenable the draft memorandum's conclusion that this is unnecessary because (1) Afghanistan ceased to be a party to the Conventions, (2) the President may suspend the operation of the Conventions with respect to Afghanistan, and (3) customary international law does not bind the United States. As a matter of international law, the draft comments show, all three premises, are wrong.

The draft memorandum badly confuses the distinction between states and governments in the operation of the law of treaties. Its conclusion that "failed states" cease to be parties to treaties they have joined is without support. Its argument that Afghanistan became a "failed state" and thus was no longer bound by treaties to which it had been a party is contrary to the official position of the United States, the United Nations and all other states that have considered the issue. The memorandum's assertion that the President may suspend the United States' obligations under the Geneva Conventions is legally flawed and procedurally impossible at this stage. The memorandum fails to address the

SOURCE: Accessed via http://www.gwu.edu/~nsarchiv/torturingdemocracy//documents

question of whether customary international law is binding on the United States as a matter of international law. (As John Marshall was fond of saying, to ask the question is to answer it.)

John, I understand you have long been convinced that treaties and customary international law have from time to time been cited inappropriately to circumscribe the President's constitutional authority or pre-empt the Congress's exercise of legislative power. I also understand your desire to identify legal authority establishing the right of the United States to treat the members of the Taliban Militia in the way it thinks best, if such authority exists. I share your feelings in both of these respects. I do not, however, believe that on the basis of your draft memorandum I can advise either the President or the Secretary of State that the obligations of the United States under the Geneva Conventions have lapsed with regard to Afghanistan or that the United States is not bound to carry out its obligations under the Conventions as a matter of international law. That may mean, of course, that we must determine specifically whether individual members of the Taliban Militia in our custody are entitled to POW status, and it may be that some are actually entitled to it. In previous conflicts, the United States has dealt with tens of thousands of detainees without repudiating its obligations under the Conventions. I have no doubt we can do so here, where a relative handful of persons is involved. Only the utmost confidence in our legal arguments could, it seems to me, justify deviating from the United States unbroken record of compliance with the Geneva Conventions in our conduct of military operations over the past fifty years. Your draft acknowledges that several of its conclusions are close questions. The attached draft comments will, I expect, show you that they are actually incorrect as well as incomplete. We should talk.

Source 2:   *Memorandum to Alberto Gonzales* (2002)

This source, written by John Yoo and signed off by Jay Bybee, an assistant attorney general in the Office of Legal Counsel, has come to be known as the "Torture Memo." The following excerpt provides an introductory overview for the lengthy memorandum and a summary of conclusions regarding permissible conduct for interrogation of prisoners held outside the United States. On what grounds do Yoo and the Office of Legal Counsel argue that the interrogation techniques in question do not meet the definition of torture? Given President Barack Obama's denunciation in 2014 of the Bush administration's treatment of prisoners after 9/11, do you think the standard for torture is more influenced by the times or by other factors?

You have asked for our Office's views regarding the standards of conduct under the Convention Against Torture and Other Cruel, Inhuman and Degrading Treatment or Punishment as implemented by Sections 2340–2340A of title 18 of the United States Code. As we understand it, this question has arisen in the context of the conduct of interrogations outside of the United States. We conclude below that Section 2340A proscribes acts inflicting, and that are specifically intended to inflict, severe pain or suffering, whether mental or physical. Those acts must be of an extreme nature to rise to the level of torture within the meaning of Section 2340A and the Convention. We further

SOURCE: Accessed via http://www.gwu.edu/~nsarchiv/torturingdemocracy//documents

conclude that certain acts may be cruel, inhuman, or degrading, but still not produce pain and suffering of the requisite intensity to fall within Section 2340A's proscription against torture. We conclude by examining possible defenses that would negate any claim that certain interrogation methods violate the statute.

In Part I, we examine the criminal statute's text and history. We conclude that for an act to constitute torture as defined in Section 2340, it must inflict pain that is difficult to endure. Physical pain amounting to torture must be equivalent in intensity to the pain accompanying serious physical injury, such as organ failure, impairment of bodily function, or even death. For purely mental pain or suffering to amount to torture under Section 2340, it must result in significant psychological harm of significant duration, e.g., lasting for months or even years. We conclude that the mental harm also must result from one of the predicate acts listed in the statute, namely: threats of imminent death; threats of infliction of the kind of pain that would amount to physical torture; infliction of such physical pain as a means of psychological torture; use of drugs or other procedures designed to deeply disrupt the senses, or fundamentally alter an individual's personality, or threatening to do any of these things to a third party. The legislative history simply reveals that Congress intended for the statute's definition to track the Convention's definition of torture and the reservations, understandings, and declarations that the United States submitted with its ratification. We conclude that the statute, taken as a whole, makes plain that it prohibits only extreme acts.

In Part II, we examine the text, ratification history, and negotiating history of the Torture Convention. We conclude that the treaty's text prohibits only the most extreme acts by reserving criminal penalties solely for torture and declining to require such penalties for "cruel, inhuman, or degrading treatment or punishment." This confirms our view that the criminal statute penalizes only the most egregious conduct. Executive branch interpretations and representations to the Senate at the time of ratification further confirm that the treaty was intended to reach only the most extreme conduct.

In Part III, we analyze the jurisprudence of the Torture Victims Protection Act, 28 U.S.C. § 1350 note (2000), which provides civil remedies for torture victims, to predict the standards that courts might follow in determining what actions reach the threshold of torture in the criminal context. We conclude from these cases that courts are likely to take a totality-of-the-circumstances approach, and will look to an entire course of conduct, to determine whether certain acts will violate Section 2340A. Moreover, these cases demonstrate that most often torture involves cruel and extreme physical pain. In Part IV, we examine international decisions regarding the use of sensory deprivation techniques. These cases make clear that while many of these techniques may amount to cruel, inhuman or degrading treatment, they do not produce pain or suffering of the necessary intensity to meet the definition of torture. From these decisions, we conclude that there is a wide range of such techniques that will not rise to the level of torture.

In Part V, we discuss whether Section 2340A may be unconstitutional if applied to interrogations undertaken of enemy combatants pursuant to the President's Commander-in-Chief powers. We find that in the circumstances of the current war against al Qaeda and its allies, prosecution under Section 2340A may be barred because enforcement of the statute would represent an unconstitutional infringement of the President's authority to conduct war. In Part VI, we discuss defenses to an allegation that an interrogation method might violate the statute. We conclude that, under the current circumstances, necessity or self-defense may justify interrogation methods that might violate Section 23 40 A.

Source 3: *Richard Clarke on George Bush's War on Terror* (2004)

In this excerpt from a CBS News story summarizing Richard Clarke's interview with correspondent Lesley Stahl on the television program 60 Minutes, *Clarke assesses the initial response of the Bush administration to the threat of terrorism. In what ways does he see that response as flawed?*

(CBS) In the aftermath of Sept. 11, President Bush ordered his then top anti-terrorism adviser to look for a link between Iraq and the attacks, despite being told there didn't seem to be one.

The charge comes from the adviser, Richard Clarke, in an exclusive interview on **60 Minutes**.

The administration maintains that it cannot find any evidence that the conversation about an Iraq-9/11 tie-in ever took place.

Clarke also tells **CBS News Correspondent Lesley Stahl** that White House officials were tepid in their response when he urged them months before Sept. 11 to meet to discuss what he saw as a severe threat from al Qaeda.

"Frankly," he said, "I find it outrageous that the president is running for re-election on the grounds that he's done such great things about terrorism. He ignored it. He ignored terrorism for months, when maybe we could have done something to stop 9/11. Maybe. We'll never know."

Clarke went on to say, "I think he's done a terrible job on war against terrorism."

The No. 2 man on the president's National Security Council, Stephen Hadley, vehemently disagrees. He says Mr. Bush has taken the fight to the terrorists, and is making the U.S. homeland safer.

Clarke says that as early as the day after the attacks, Secretary of Defense Donald Rumsfeld was pushing for retaliatory strikes on Iraq, even though al Qaeda was based in Afghanistan.

Clarke suggests the idea took him so aback, he initially thought Rumsfeld was joking....

In the **60 Minutes** interview and the book, Clarke tells what happened behind the scenes at the White House before, during and after Sept. 11.

When the terrorists struck, it was thought the White House would be the next target, so it was evacuated. Clarke was one of only a handful of people who stayed behind. He ran the government's response to the attacks from the Situation Room in the West Wing....

After the president returned to the White House on Sept. 11, he and his top advisers, including Clarke, began holding meetings about how to respond and retaliate. As Clarke writes in his book, he expected the administration to focus its military response on Osama bin Laden and al Qaeda. He says he was surprised that the talk quickly turned to Iraq.

"Rumsfeld was saying that we needed to bomb Iraq," Clarke said to **Stahl**. "And we all said ... no, no. Al-Qaeda is in Afghanistan. We need to bomb Afghanistan."

And Rumsfeld said there aren't any good targets in Afghanistan. And there are lots of good targets in Iraq. I said, "Well, there are lots of good targets in lots of places, but Iraq had nothing to do with it."

"Initially, I thought when he said, 'There aren't enough targets in—in Afghanistan,' I thought he was joking."

"I think they wanted to believe that there was a connection, but the CIA was sitting there, the FBI was sitting there, I was sitting there saying we've looked at this issue for years. For years we've looked and there's just no connection."

Clarke says he and CIA Director George Tenet told that to Rumsfeld, Secretary of the State Colin Powell, and Attorney General John Ashcroft.

Clarke then tells **Stahl** of being pressured by Mr. Bush.

"The president dragged me into a room with a couple of other people, shut the door, and said, 'I want you to find whether Iraq did this.' Now he never said, 'Make it up.' But the entire conversation left me in absolutely no doubt that George Bush wanted me to come back with a report that said Iraq did this."

I said, "Mr. President. We've done this before. We have been looking at this. We looked at it with an open mind. There's no connection."

"He came back at me and said, 'Iraq! Saddam! Find out if there's a connection.' And in a very intimidating way. I mean that we should come back with that answer. We wrote a report."

Clarke continued, "It was a serious look. We got together all the FBI experts, all the CIA experts. We wrote the report. We sent the report out to CIA and found FBI and said, 'Will you sign this report?' They all cleared the report. And we sent it up to the president and it got bounced by the National Security Advisor or Deputy. It got bounced and sent back saying, 'Wrong answer.... Do it again.'"

"I have no idea, to this day, if the president saw it, because after we did it again, it came to the same conclusion. And frankly, I don't think the people around the president show him memos like that. I don't think he sees memos that he doesn't—wouldn't like the answer."

Clarke was the president's chief adviser on terrorism, yet it wasn't until Sept. 11 that he ever got to brief Mr. Bush on the subject. Clarke says that prior to Sept. 11, the administration didn't take the threat seriously.

"We had a terrorist organization that was going after us! Al Qaeda. That should have been the first item on the agenda. And it was pushed back and back and back for months."

"There's lot of blame to go around, and I probably deserve some blame, too." But on January 24th, 2001, I wrote a memo to Condoleezza Rice asking for, urgently— underlined urgently—a Cabinet-level meeting to deal with the impending al Qaeda attack. And that urgent memo—wasn't acted on.

"I blame the entire Bush leadership for continuing to work on Cold War issues when they back in power in 2001. It was as though they were preserved in amber from when they left office eight years earlier. They came back. They wanted to work on the same issues right away: Iraq, Star Wars. Not new issues, the new threats that had developed over the preceding eight years."

Clarke finally got his meeting about al Qaeda in April, three months after his urgent request. But it wasn't with the president or cabinet. It was with the second-in-command in each relevant department.

For the Pentagon, it was Paul Wolfowitz.

Clarke relates, I began saying, 'We have to deal with bin Laden; we have to deal with al Qaeda.' Paul Wolfowitz, the Deputy Secretary of Defense, said, 'No, no, no. We don't have to deal with al Qaeda. Why are we talking about that little guy? We have to talk about Iraqi terrorism against the United States.'

"And I said, 'Paul, there hasn't been any Iraqi terrorism against the United States in eight years!' And I turned to the deputy director of the CIA and said, 'Isn't that right?' And he said, 'Yeah, that's right. There is no Iraqi terrorism against the United States.'"

Clarke went on to add, "There's absolutely no evidence that Iraq was supporting al Qaeda, ever."

When **Stahl** pointed out that some administration officials say it's still an open issue, Clarke responded, "Well, they'll say that until hell freezes over."

By June 2001, there still hadn't been a Cabinet-level meeting on terrorism, even though U.S. intelligence was picking up an unprecedented level of ominous chatter.

The CIA director warned the White House, Clarke points out. "George Tenet was saying to the White House, saying to the president—because he briefed him every morning—a major al Qaeda attack is going to happen against the United States somewhere in the world in the weeks and months ahead. He said that in June, July, August."

Clarke says the last time the CIA has picked up a similar level of chatter was in December, 1999, when Clarke was the terrorism czar in the Clinton White House.

Clarke says Mr. Clinton ordered his Cabinet to go to battle stations—meaning, they went on high alert, holding meetings nearly every day.

That, Clarke says, helped thwart a major attack on Los Angeles International Airport, when an al Qaeda operative was stopped at the border with Canada, driving a car full of explosives.

Clarke harshly criticizes President Bush for not going to battle stations when the CIA warned him of a comparable threat in the months before Sept. 11: "He never thought it was important enough for him to hold a meeting on the subject, or for him to order his National Security Adviser to hold a Cabinet-level meeting on the subject."

Finally, says Clarke, "The cabinet meeting I asked for right after the inauguration took place—one week prior to 9/11."

In that meeting, Clarke proposed a plan to bomb al Qaeda's sanctuary in Afghanistan, and to kill bin Laden.

The president's new campaign ads highlight his handling of Sept. 11—which has become the centerpiece of his bid for re-election.

"You are writing this book in the middle of this campaign," Stahl tells Clarke. "The timing, I'm sure, you will be questioned about and criticized for. Why are you doing it now?"

"Well, I'm sure I'll be criticized for lots of things," says Clarke. "And I'm sure they'll launch their dogs on me."

Does a person who works for the White House owe the president his loyalty?

"Yes ... Up to a point. When the president starts doing things that risk American lives, then loyalty to him has to be put aside," says Clarke. "I think the way he has responded to al Qaeda, both before 9/11 by doing nothing, and by what he's done after 9/11 has made us less safe. Absolutely." ...

Source 4:   Richard A. Clarke, *"Land of Sweet Liberties"* (2008)

In this excerpt from Your Government Failed You, *Richard Clarke blasts the Bush administration for narrowing protections on civil liberties in the name of fighting terrorism. On what grounds does Clarke argue that such an approach is counterproductive in the struggle against this threat?*

The possibility that we have homegrown terrorists causes some to think we need to deal with the current terrorist threat differently than we have other security and law enforcement challenges we have faced. It is the fear of another 9/11 that justifies, in some minds, torturing suspected terrorists in camps in legal no-man's-lands like U.S. military enclaves in Cuba, Afghanistan, and Iraq.

I deeply disagree. Torture and warrantless wiretaps are unnecessary. They also erode the support we need abroad and the unity we need at home to overcome the threat from violent Islamist extremists. Most important, they are steps in the wrong direction, steps a little closer to the horrors that humans can engage in when rights are eroded.

Experts have known for decades that torture draws unreliable information from its victims and that other methods have good track records in producing cooperation and information from suspects and prisoners. We know of specific examples where tortured prisoners have provided false information, such as the erroneous report that Iraq trained al Qaeda terrorists in the use of weapons of mass destruction.

The belief that Americans have used torture in Abu Ghraib and other U.S. military camps in Iraq, Afghanistan, and Cuba has convinced many in the Islamic world that we do disrespect Muslims. It has helped some to justify terrorist tactics and support for al Qaeda and similar groups. It has convinced many that we are hypocrites when we talk about human rights and democracy.

I have long believed that the U.S. Bill of Rights and the U.N. Universal Declaration of Human Rights are among the few membranes, the thin tissues, that separate humanity from another descent into the kind of world that only a few decades ago saw many millions of people degraded and industrially disposed of in the horror camps of Nazi Germany and the Communist Soviet Union. It is in humanity's genes and makeup that people can engage in such atrocities. And many people have done so.

We need to hold the line well this side of the police state, far from the torture chamber. Yet the U.S. Justice Department originated a ruling that the only torture that was out of bounds was that which caused pain equivalent to organ failure. Anything else done by Americans was permissible, as long as it was not done in the United States. The Vice President of the United States drove to the Congress to lobby members to permit what he euphemistically called "alternative interrogation techniques." It is hard to believe. You want to think it's all a bad dream, but it's not. You thought America was a force in the world against this sort of thing, not a nation that would actually engage in it. Thankfully, for a while we had John McCain as our conscience. McCain, who was

SOURCE: "Land of Sweet Liberties," pp. 252–5: 1160 words from YOUR GOVERNMENT FAILED YOU by Richard A. Clarke. Copyright © 2008 by Richard A. Clarke. Copyright © 2008 by Richard Clarke. Reprinted by permission of HarperCollins Publishers.

repeatedly tortured, was there to remind us of what it means to be Americans, what it is that we stand for in this world, and who we are not. Unfortunately, he later voted against a legislated ban on waterboarding by the CIA.

Warrantless wiretaps are far less heinous, but an equally unacceptable step toward a police state. I spent many days struggling to get wiretaps on terrorists. I thought that many of the Justice Department rules about wiretapping terrorists were unfounded impediments to achieving security. The "Chinese wall" that prevented information obtained in intelligence wiretaps from being given to criminal investigators was wrong. The ban on listening to foreigners' communications originating and terminating outside the United States but transiting our switches was foolish. Requiring a different wiretap warrant every time a suspect changed telephones was absurd. The Foreign Intelligence Surveillance Act (FISA), which regulates security-related wiretaps, needed updating. But we should not have ignored it.

Remarkably, the former White House General Counsel and then Attorney General Alberto Gonzalez explained that the reason the administration did not originally try to amend the FISA was a belief that Congress would not have approved the needed changes. So instead, he just violated the law under the specious reasoning that the President had inherent authority to do so in the national interest and that the congressional authorization to fight in Afghanistan somehow implied authority to violate the FISA law. One senator asked that if the President had inherent authority to break that law, what other laws did he have the authority to break? There was no answer.

In my personal experience, the need for getting a FISA warrant never held up surveillance. The FISA judges were willing to hold hearings at any hour of the day or night if they were told that there was an emergency. Moreover, in an extreme emergency the wiretap could be initiated first and the warrant sought after the fact. During the millennium alert period in late 1999, we persuaded the FISA court to process a record number of FISA warrants expeditiously. The need for active judicial oversight of intelligence wiretaps is clear: the FBI abuses its power. The Justice Department and its component, the FBI, admit this. The Justice Department's Inspector General cited hundreds of cases where the FBI acquired records of innocent U.S. citizens without a warrant by, essentially, knowingly misstating facts.

The word *rendition* has become associated with kidnapping people and throwing them into some third-country jail cell, torturing them, and never giving them a trial or any due process. Yet before 9/11, I orchestrated renditions (overseas arrests and subsequent movement out of the country) and extraordinary renditions (those where we acted without the knowledge of the country in which the suspect was captured) without throwing out the U.S. legal system. Terrorist suspects who were subject to these renditions were almost all returned to the United States, read their rights, given defense counsel, prosecuted in criminal courts, and convicted. The United States could have handled cases of rendition after 9/11 as we had done earlier. It would have been burdensome, cumbersome, slow. It would have required an infusion of new resources into the justice system. But it would have been consistent with our principles and laws. We would have been acting in the way Americans used to act, morally, leading the world by example, in a way that differentiates us.

People throughout the world knew at one point that the United States stood for something. Even if they disagreed with us on some things, they respected us for our principles. When we criticized others for violating the Universal Declaration of Human Rights, people knew that we had worked hard to overcome our flaws with regard to slavery and racial discrimination. The world knew that it was the government in Washington that fought against those in our country who still tried to violate human rights on the basis of race. It gave us a strength in the world beyond our military might and economic prowess. What we did in violating human rights in the fight against terrorists showed us to the world as hypocrites, and we lost that strength.

Source 5: *John Yoo Defends Warrantless Wiretaps* (2007)

In an interview on the PBS television program "Frontline," John Yoo discussed decisions made as deputy assistant attorney general in George W. Bush's administration. In this excerpt from that interview, on what grounds does Yoo defend the practice of warrantless wiretaps?

... [L]et me read ... an internal memorandum from you, and a legal opinion, saying that the government ... could use "electronic surveillance techniques and equipment more powerful and sophisticated than those available to law enforcement agencies in order to intercept telephone communication and observe the movements of persons but without obtaining warrants for such uses."...

...[W]hat I would say is this:... One thing our armed forces always do ... is intercept the communication of the other side. It's called signals intelligence. It's something we did, for example, in Word War II, where we intercepted Japanese naval and diplomatic codes that tipped us off to the Midway attacks.

The problem, the difficulty in this war is that the enemy is non-nation, so what they do is they disguise themselves as civilians, and they place their communications through normal channels. The hard thing for our side is to identify where in that stream of civilian, innocent communications Al Qaeda members are disguising their messages to one another, trying to intercept those and find out what they mean....

Could you do that kind of blanket eavesdropping, listening to those calls, under the Foreign Intelligence Surveillance Act [FISA]?

No. This is a good example of where existing laws were not up to the job....

Why couldn't the government operate under the Foreign Intelligence Surveillance Act?

There are two big reasons. One is that you need what's called "reasonable suspicion." You already have to have reason to think a specific individual who you can name is a terrorist, and that's based on things you already know that that person did.... If you're trying to prevent future terrorist attacks, trying to make guesses, trying these probabilities, you may not have a lot of information that says this person for sure is a member of Al Qaeda.

The second difficulty is that it doesn't allow you, for example, to tap streams of communication that might be coming from, say, Afghanistan to the United States to try to

SOURCE: Excerpts from "Spying On The Home Front" from an interview with John Yoo.

search through those for terrorist communications. Even though you don't have a spe-cific name of a terrorist leader, you think there's a high likelihood communications came from a specific city or from a specific mail server or something might involve ter-rorist communications.

The third thing is—and this is another difficulty—OK, you can, and we did in the Patriot Act, get amendments to FISA to make it more effective on terrorism, but one problem is that in order to get those kinds of changes, you have to have a public debate and discussion. One thing we're very conscious of is that Al Qaeda monitors our govern-ment activities; they use the law; they adapt quickly and respond quickly to changes we make or news they hear about what we do. So one thing we've got to be concerned about is if you did have discussions, say, of our ability to tap communications from Afghanistan to the United States, that will cause Al Qaeda to shift, and we will lose a very valuable technological advantage in the war....

Source 6: *Edward Snowden Discusses NSA Spying* (2014)

Edward Snowden, a former employee for the Central Intelligence Agency and the Defense Intelli-gence Agency, leaked thousands of classified documents to media outlets while working for a contrac-tor to the National Security Agency (NSA) in 2013. Those documents included information about NSA global surveillance programs and the cooperation that NSA secured with telecommunications and Internet companies. In this source, Snowden discusses the nature of that surveillance and those companies' cooperation with NSA. What threat does he believe NSA spying poses to individual privacy? What do you think Clark and Yoo would say about Snowden's revelations and his release of classified documents detailing such surveillance?

Life at the NSA

I began to move from merely overseeing these surveillance systems to actively directing their use. Many people don't understand that I was actually an analyst and I designated individuals and groups for targeting.

I was exposed to information about the previous programs like Stellar Wind [used during the presidency of George W Bush] for example. The warrantless wire-tapping of everyone in the United States, including their internet data - which is a violation of the constitution and law in the United States - did cause a scandal and was ended because of that.

When I saw that, that was really the earthquake moment because it showed that the officials who authorised these programs knew it was a problem, they knew they didn't have any statutory authorisation for these programs. But instead the government assumed upon itself, in secret, new executive powers without any public awareness or any public consent and used them against the citizenry of its own country to increase its own power, to increase its own awareness.

Source: "Edward Snowden Interview: The Edited Transcript," THE GUARDIAN (July 18, 2014), pp. 5–8.

We constantly hear the phrase "national security" but when the state begins ... broadly intercepting the communications, seizing the communications by themselves, without any warrant, without any suspicion, without any judicial involvement, without any demonstration of probable cause, are they really protecting national security or are they protecting state security?

What I came to feel – and what I think more and more people have seen at least the potential for – is that a regime that is described as a national security agency has stopped representing the public interest and has instead begun to protect and promote state security interests. And the idea of western democracy as having state security bureaus, just that term, that phrase itself, "state security bureau", is kind of chilling.

So when we think about the nation we think about our country, we think about our home, we think about the people living in it and we think about its values. When we think about the state, we're thinking about an institution.

The distinction there is that we now have an institution that has become so powerful it feels comfortable granting itself new authorities, without the involvement of the country, without the involvement of the public, without the full involvement of all of our elected representatives and without the full involvement of open courts, and that's a terrifying thing – at least for me.

Generally, it's not the people at the working level you need to worry about. It's the senior officials, it's the policymakers who are shielded from accountability, who are shielded from oversight and who are allowed to make decisions that affect all of our lives without any public input, any public debate, or any electoral consequences because their decisions and the consequences of the decisions are never known.

Because of advances in technology, storage becomes cheaper year after year and when our ability to store data outpaces the expense of creating that data, we end up with things that are no longer held for short-term periods, they're held for long-term periods and then they're held for a longer term period. At the NSA for example, we store data for five years on individuals. And that's before getting a waiver to extend that even further.

You have a tremendous population of young military enlisted individuals who, while that's not a discredit to them, ... may not have had the number of life experiences to have felt the sense of being violated. And if we haven't been exposed to the dangers and risks of having our privacy violated, having our liberties violated, how can we expect these individuals to reasonably represent our own interests in exercising those authorities?...

The relationship between the NSA and telecom and internet companies

Unusually hidden even from people who worked for these agencies are the details of the financial arrangements between [the] government and the telecommunication service providers. And we have to ask ourselves, why is that? Why are their details of how they're being paid to collaborate with [the] government protected at a much greater level than for example the names of human agents operating undercover, embedded with terrorist groups?

So the way Prism [the program that deals with the relationship between the NSA and the internet companies] works is agencies are provided with direct access to the contents of the server at these private companies. That doesn't mean the companies can, or the intelligence agencies can, let themselves in. What it means is Facebook is allowing the government to get copies of your Facebook messages, your Skype conversations, your Gmail mailboxes, things like that.

It distinguishes it from where the government is creating its own access – so called upstream operations – where they sort of tap the backbones where these communications cross and they try to take them in transit. Instead they go to the company and they say: "You're going to give us this. You're going to give us that. You're going to give us that." And the company gives them all of this information in a cooperative relationship.

If Facebook is going to hand over all of your messages, all of your wall posts, all of your private photos, all of your private details from their server the government has no need to intercept all of the communications that constitute those private records.

QUESTIONS TO CONSIDER

1. How did the backgrounds of Richard Clarke and John Yoo influence their thinking about the conduct of a war on Islamic extremists? Specifically, what impact did the Vietnam and Korean wars have on each?

2. Citing information from the essay and primary sources in this chapter, what do you conclude were Richard Clarke's primary criticisms of the Bush administration's approach to Islamic extremism and the threat of another terrorist attack? What do the sources reveal about the dangers he sees in that approach?

3. Citing information from the essay and primary sources in this chapter, on what grounds does John Yoo defend the Bush administration's conduct of the "war on terror"? How does that defense relate to his conception of presidential war powers?

4. The authors of the *9/11 Commission Report* on the events surrounding the terrorist attacks on September 11 presented their report as a "foundation for a better understanding of a landmark in the history of our nation." Based on the information and historical sources in this chapter, what important conclusions or lessons do you think can be drawn from a better understanding of that "landmark" and the nation's responses to it?

FOR FURTHER READING

David A. Cole, ed., *The Torture Memos: Rationalizing the Unthinkable* (New York: New Press, 2009), provides the key documents for justifying relaxation of standards regarding torture and an analysis of them by a leading legal scholar.

Glenn Greenwald, *No Place to Hide: Edward Snowden, the NSA, and the U.S. Surveillance State* (New York: Henry Holt, 2014), details the author's investigation of NSA surveillance activities.

Thomas H. Kean, *et al., The 9/11 Commission Report: Final Report of the National Commission on Terrorist Attacks upon the United States* (New York: W.W. Norton & Company, 2004), offers a thorough yet gripping account of the circumstances that allowed terrorists to attack the United States on September 11, 2001.

Jane Mayer, *The Dark Side: The Inside Story of How the War on Terror Turned into a War on American Ideals* (New York: Random House, Inc., 2008), submits a critical examination of the Bush administration's prosecution of the "war on terror."

Bob Woodward, *Plan of Attack* (New York: Simon & Schuster, 2004), provides a "behind-the-scenes" account by an influential journalist of the decisions and planning that led to the American invasion of Iraq in 2003.

Lawrence Wright, *The Looming Tower: Al-Qaeda and the Road to 9/11* (New York: Alfred A. Knopf, 2006), presents an accessible narrative involving the individuals, ideas, and events that led to the September 11 attacks.